T0291539

A Dissimulated Trade

The Atlantic World

EUROPE, AFRICA AND THE AMERICAS, 1500–1830

VOLUME 40

The titles published in this series are listed at *brill.com/aw*

A Dissimulated Trade

*Northern European Timber Merchants
in Seville (1574–1598)*

By

Germán Jiménez-Montes

BRILL

LEIDEN | BOSTON

Cover illustration: Alonso Sánchez Coello (attributed), View of Seville, ca. 1570, oil on canvas, Courtesy Museo de América, Madrid.

The Library of Congress Cataloging-in-Publication Data is available online at https://catalog.loc.gov

Typeface for the Latin, Greek, and Cyrillic scripts: "Brill". See and download: brill.com/brill-typeface.

ISSN 1570-0542
ISBN 978-90-04-46018-8 (hardback)
ISBN 978-90-04-50411-0 (e-book)

Contents

Acknowledgements

This book is the result of the doctoral research I conducted at the University of Groningen. I want to express my gratitude to my supervisors, Raingard Esser and Jan Willem Veluwenkamp, for their confidence, patience and guidance. The support of Ana Crespo Solana was essential, too. As coordinator of ForSeaDiscovery, she gave me the opportunity of participating in an ambitious scientific project with a fantastic group of colleagues. The funding of the Marie-Curie Action: Initial Training Networks (PITN-GA 2013-607545) made this research possible. In 2018, I joined the ANDATLAN II project (HAR2017-85305-P), coordinated by Juan José Iglesias Rodríguez and Jaime García Bernal. I owe a lot to them and to the rest of the members of the chair of Early Modern History in the Universidad de Seville, who inspired me as a student. To complete this PhD project, I received financial support from the Faculty of Arts in Groningen, where I also had the opportunity to teach. I am grateful to my students. Their enthusiasm made me a better historian.

Many people have read earlier versions of the manuscript and have helped significantly improve the final version. In spite of this, the work is far from perfect and I alone am to blame for that. Mike Brown, Nathan Gallagher and Juan Montes Adán proofread different versions of the manuscript. They taught me how to make my ideas sharper in English, although my Mediterranean love for long sentences dies hard. Senior colleagues took time to read my work, improving it with their comments: Oscar Gelderblom, Cátia Antunes, Maarten Duijvendak, Regina Grafe, Manuel Herrero Sánchez, Raymond Fagel, Yolanda Rodríguez Pérez, José Manuel Díaz Blanco, Mercedes Gamero Rojas, Pepijn Brandon and José Luis Gasch Tomás. Their generosity inspires me. I am particularly indebted to Manuel Fernández Chaves and Daniel Gallardo Albarrán for their good counsel.

I also want to thank the staff of the archives I have visited, especially the one working at the *Archivo Histórico Provincial de Sevilla*. My friends Juanma Castillo Rubio, Nacho González Espinosa, Fran García Domínguez, Miguel Royano Cabrera and Sara Jarana Vidal were a great help there. I am especially grateful to Juanma, who also helped me with the illustrations. I would like to thank Brill's editors for their support with the preparation of the manuscript, as well as the anonymous reviewers who contributed to improve it with very valuable comments.

Finally, I want to dedicate this book to my parents and Ana for their care.

Abbreviation of Archives and Digital Sources

AHPSe	Archivo Histórico Provincial de Sevilla
AGI	Archivo General de Indias
AGS	Archivo General de Simancas
AMS	Archivo Municipal de Sevilla
APSC	Archivo de la Parroquia del Sagrario de la Catedral de Sevilla
ARAS	Archivo del Real Alcázar de Sevilla
GAA	Notarial collection of Stadsarchief Amsterdam, as appearing in Cátia Antunes' database.
STRO	Sound Toll Registers Online (http://dietrich.soundtoll.nl)

Illustrations, Figures and Tables

Illustrations

Figures

Tables

Note on Terminology

I have tried to remain as close as possible to the word usage of the Spanish primary sources. Because of this, the word Flemish (*flamencos*) is often used to refer to the community of north European migrants as a whole, regardless of their actual origin. At the end of the sixteenth century, the identification as *flamenco* was still widely used when speaking of an individual coming from any provinces of the Low Countries, including the ones that formed the Dutch Republic. The identification as German (*alemán*) was used for migrants from the Holy Roman Empire, and frequently for those coming from Scandinavian and Baltic coastal towns, too. However, the presence of *alemanes* was very small in comparison to those coming from the Low Countries. Consequently, German migrants were sometimes considered Flemish in notarial deeds. Spanish contemporary sources used the term nation to refer to a community of migrants from a same origin; in this book, the Flemish and German nation corresponds to the community of migrants from northern Europe residing in western Andalusia. The geographical reference "western Andalusia" corresponds to the Kingdom of Seville, a territorial jurisdiction that roughly covered today's provinces of Huelva, Cádiz and Seville. Names of locations have been translated into English. Names of Spaniards and foreigners have been standardised according to their most frequent spelling in the notarial deeds. All translations of Spanish primary sources into English are my own.

Introduction

Sixteenth-century Seville should not differ much from the view attributed to
Alonso Sanchez Coello, probably dating from the 1570s, that illustrates the
cover of this book.[1] Grand but dark, lively and hectic, the view is a realistic
impression of Spain's largest town and economic core at the time. The artist
pictures Seville from the right bank of the Guadalquivir River. He portrays a
darkened urban silhouette crowned by an unusual cloudy sky that contrasts
with a shining *Giralda*, the cathedral's tower. The *Giralda* stands out near the
centre of the composition, revealing the fortune of a city that had been desig-
nated head of the *Carrera de Indias*, the Indies Run, as the Castilian navigation
to the Spanish Americas came to be known. To the left of the cathedral's tower,
the painter highlights *el Malbaratillo*, a mountain of waste that reminds the
viewer of the filth that accompanied such wealth. But neither the splendour of
the *Giralda* nor the decay of the *Malbaratillo* is the main element in the paint-
ing; the Guadalquivir River is. The city comes to life on its water and along its
bank, where the painter depicts ships of all sizes, horses carrying goods, cattle
wandering around, dogs playing, music concerts, sword fights, and individuals
from all estates – merchants, grocers, nobles, slaves, nuns, clergymen.

Those countless scenes mirror the words that Luis de Góngora, a prominent
poet of the Spanish Golden Age, dedicated to Seville:

> The Great Babylon of Spain,
> map of all nations,
> where the Fleming has his Ghent
> and the English finds his London;
> staircase of the New World,
> whose rich steps,
> made out of silver bricks,
> are high-board vessels.[2]

In this Great Babylon of Spain, one of the scenes calling the painter's attention are the piles of trees and planks lying on *El Arenal*, the sandy ground
on the right side of the image. They are in front of the *Atarazanas*, one of
the few non-religious constructions identifiable in the picture, which had

---

1 Alonso Sánchez Coello (attributed), *View of Seville*, ca. 1570, oil on canvas, Museo del Prado,
   Madrid.
2 Luis de Góngora y Argote, *Las firmezas de Isabela* (Málaga: Caja de Ahorros de Ronda, 1991).

originally housed the Castilian royal shipyards in Andalusia. As the ship-building activity ceased, the *Atarazanas* were reconverted into a complex of warehouses; the only ones in the city capable of storing the large amounts of timber that were imported from the Baltic and Scandinavian regions to supplement the meagre capacity of Andalusian forestry resources. Yet, although the painter was not probably aware of it, imported timber is not only present in front of the *Atarazanas*. North European timber is almost everywhere in the picture. This timber formed the imposing oared galleys at the king's service, the overturned vessels being caulked, the anchored ones waiting to be loaded, the smaller boats forming the floating bridge between the two banks and many of the buildings of the city, which was experiencing an extraordinary urban growth.

Timber was, in short, a paramount resource for an expanding commercial city like Seville, and for a maritime power like Habsburg Spain. However evident this fact is, few scholars have explored how access to timber contributed to the rise of European oceanic empires in the Early Modern Period.[3] The close connection between access to timber and maritime empires was the premise of the ForSeaDiscovery project, initiated in 2014 under the coordination of Ana Crespo Solana. Archaeologists, dendrochronoligists and historians collaborated in this multidisciplinary project, which sought to examine how the management and importation of forestry resources shaped the oceanic expansion of Portugal and Spain from the end of the Middle Ages.[4]

---

3   Some important exceptions are Karl R. Appuhn, *A Forest on the Sea: Environmental Expertise in Renaissance Venice* (Baltimore: Johns Hopkins University Press, 2009), and Paul Warde, *Ecology, Economy and State Formation in Early Modern Germany* (Cambridge: Cambridge University Press, 2006). For the Spanish case, an early work on this topic is Gaspar de Aranda y Antón, *Los bosques flotantes: Historia de un roble del siglo XVIII* (Madrid: ICONA, 1990), and a recent one is John T. Wing, *Roots of Empire: Forests and State Power in Early Modern Spain, 1500–1750* (Leiden: Brill, 2015). Félix Labrador Arroyo and Koldo Trápaga Monchet recently coordinated a special issue on the topic "Recursos naturales en la Península Ibérica: los aprovechamientos forestales e hídricos (siglo XV-XIX)," *Tiempos Modernos. Revista electrónica de Historia Moderna* 9, no. 40 (2019).

4   For general information about the project, see Ana Crespo Solana, "Wood Resources, shipbuilding and Social Environment: The Historical context of the ForSEAdiscovery Project," *SKYLLIS. Journal of the German Society for the Promotion of Underwater Archaeology* 15, no. 1 (2015): 52–61. Relevant outcomes of the project are: Marta Domínguez-Delmás, Sara Rich, Mohamed Traoré et al. "Tree-ring chronologies, stable strontium isotopes and biochemical compounds: Towards reference datasets to provenance Iberian shipwreck timbers," *Journal of Archaeological Science: Reports* 34, part A (2020), and Rosa Varela Gomes and Mário Varela Gomes (eds.), *The Management of Iberian Forest Resources in the Early Modern Shipbuilding: History and Archaeology* (Lisbon: Instituto de Arqueologia e Paleociências – UNL, 2015).

Conceived in the framework of the ForSeaDiscovery project, the present book assesses how the importation and distribution of north European timber and other naval provisions, such as rigging or tar, contributed to Seville's apogee as capital of the Spanish seaborne empire during the reign of Philip II. It investigates the socio-economic organisation and commercial strategies of a group of migrants from the Low Countries and northern Germany that, centring on the *Atarazanas* warehouse complex, came to dominate the market of imported timber in western Andalusia. Because their trade entailed contracting with traders and shipmasters from provinces of the Low Countries that had revolted against the Habsburg's rule, the commercial embargoes Philip II ordered against the Dutch in the context of the Eighty Years' War directly targeted them. Yet, at the same time, the strategic goods that these merchants imported were indispensable to maintaining the king's imperial aspirations. Throughout his reign, Philip II stood in a paradoxical situation that required him to find a balance between the extent of the policies that sought to curtail trade with his enemies and the urgency of importing provisions to fight those enemies at sea. The title of this work, *A Dissimulated Trade*, evokes this paradoxical balance, paraphrasing a letter that Philip II sent to his officials in Seville commanding them to turn a blind eye despite the embargo he had called for in 1574: "let them [trade] in a dissimulated manner."[5]

The beginning of this book is 1574, when, in the aftermath of Philip II's first embargo against the Dutch, these *flamencos* commenced to consolidate their dominant position in the trade between Andalusia and northern Europe. The end is set in 1598, the year of the king's death, when many of the foreigners that once controlled the market had passed away, too. Nevertheless, the research broadly covers the last three decades of the sixteenth century (ca. 1570s-1590s), coinciding with the transformation of the Habsburg navy into an Atlantic military force that faced emerging competitors on the North Sea: the Dutch Republic and England. This book, in short, explores the role that the *flamencos* of the *Atarazanas* played in this transformation, which led to the consolidation of Andalusia as a key node in Spain's maritime empire.

---

5 AGS, Estado, 160, f. 69. This and other letters between Philip II and the main commercial cities of Castile were transcribed and analysed by Carlos Gómez-Centurión Jiménez, *Felipe II, la empresa de Inglaterra y el comercio septentrional (1566–1609)* (Madrid: Editorial Naval, 1988).

1   Andalusia in the Transformation of Spain's Naval Power

In the last third of the sixteenth century, long-standing tensions in the Mediterranean Sea abated. The Treaty of Cateau-Cambrésis in 1559 ended a war between Spain and France that Philip II had inherited from his father and predecessor, Charles I. The peace confirmed the Spanish supremacy on the Italian peninsula, and established a durable status quo on the inland borders between France and the Habsburg territories. Similarly, conflicts with the Ottoman Empire and their Islamic allies in northern Africa lessened. Persian pressure on the Ottoman borders, eased the prolonged conflict between the Ottoman and the Spanish empires in the Mediterranean Sea.[6] At the same time, new threats to the Spanish monarchy emerged in the North Sea, with new rising powers contesting its hegemony in the west of Europe.

The Dutch Revolt represented the first serious struggle for the Spanish monarchy there.[7] Starting as a series of popular iconoclastic uprisings in 1566, it developed into an international war when Calvinist rebels, known as Beggars (*gueux* in French, *geuzen* in Dutch), seized several strategic ports in Zeeland.[8] This drastically weakened the Spanish position in a war that was to last eight decades and divided the Low Countries in two. While the southern provinces remained under Habsburg rule, the northern ones formed the Republic of the Seven United Provinces, which very soon after its foundation in 1581 became a thriving maritime empire.[9]

---

6 A vast historiography has analysed this, including two of the most renowned historians in the past century: Fernand Braudel, *La Méditerranée et le monde méditerranéen à l'époque de Philippe II* (Paris: A. Colin, 1982), first edition in 1949, and John H. Elliott, *Europe Divided 1559–1598* (London: Fontana, 1968).

7 For an overview in Spanish, see M. Ángel Echevarría Bacigalupe, *Flandes y la Monarquía Hispánica, 1500–1713*. Madrid: Sílex, 1998. In English Anton van der Lem. *Revolt in the Netherlands: The Eighty Years War, 1568–1648* (London, UK: Reaktion Books, 2018). In the last two decades, the Hispano-Dutch war has been extensively studied by Belgian, Dutch and Spanish scholars. Some collective publications in the topic are Werner Thomas and Robert A. Verdonk, eds., *Encuentros en Flandes: Relaciones e intercambios hispanoflamencos a inicios de la Edad Moderna.* Leuven: Leuven University Press, 2000; Ana Crespo Solana and Manuel Herrero Sánchez, *España y las 17 provincias de los Países Bajos: una revisión historiográfica (XVI-XVIII)* (Córdoba: Universidad de Córdoba, 2002); and Miguel Ángel Echevarría Bacigalupe, "Presentación: Guerra y Economía en Flandes, siglos XVI y XVII," *Studia Historica, Historia moderna* no. 27 (2005): 17–23.

8 A recent overview on the role of the Beggars in the beginning of the war, see Peter Arnade, *Beggars, Iconoclasts, and Civic Patriots: The Political Culture of the Dutch Revolt* (New York: Cornell University Press, 2008).

9 A well-known overview on the emergence of the Dutch Republic is that of Jonathan I. Israel, *The Dutch Republic: Its Rise, Greatness, and Fall, 1477–1806* (Oxford: Clarendon Press, 1998).

England saw the conflict between the Spanish monarchy and the Dutch Republic as a twofold opportunity. By intervening, England could damage the Flemish textile industry, which competed against its national production, while undermining the Habsburgs' hegemony in western Europe.[10] England's support to rebel factions aggravated already existing tensions with Spain, which had originated with the rise of Protestantism on the island. The tension materialised in the opening of a second military front in the North Sea for the Catholic monarchy, whose most famous episode was the attempted invasion of England in 1588 by the *Grande y Felicísima Armada* (Great and Most Fortunate Armada).[11] Despite its failure, the organisation of the Great Armada, in which Spain managed to gather 130 vessels, epitomised the growing importance that Philip II had begun to place on Atlantic affairs.

After the 1588 debacle, the Spanish king expanded the number of ocean-going ships at his disposal. Historians agree that this constituted the first coherent naval policy of a Spanish king.[12] Philip II's shipbuilding program concentrated on the Cantabrian coast, where the monarchy directly financed the construction of new warships and stimulated private shipbuilding with public credit and fiscal exemptions.[13] The two other Iberian regions with a tradition of Atlantic navigation, Andalusia and Portugal – the latter incorporated to the Hispanic monarchy in 1580 – could not contribute to the king's projects for a different reason.[14] While Portuguese shipbuilding remained autonomous from

---

10   On how the Hispano-Dutch war was perceived in Britain, see Hugh Dunthorne, *Britain and the Dutch Revolt, 1560–1700* (Cambridge: Cambridge University Press, 2013).

11   Mía J. Rodríguez-Salgado, and Simon Adams, eds., *England, Spain and the Gran Armada, 1585–1604: Essays from the Anglo-Spanish Conferences, London and Madrid 1988* (Edinburgh: Donald, 1991).

12   Irving A. A. Thompson, *War and Government in Habsburg Spain, 1560–1620* (London: Athlone Press, 1976), Robert A. Stradling, *The Armada of Flanders: Spanish Maritime Policy and European War, 1568–1668* (Cambridge: Cambridge University Press, 2004), or José Luis Casado Soto, "Barcos para la guerra: Soporte de la monarquía hispánica," *Cuadernos de Historia Moderna. Anejos*, no. 5 (2006): 15–53.

13   José Luis Casado Soto, "La construcción naval atlántica española y la Armada de 1588." *Cuadernos monográficos del Instituto de Historia y Cultura Naval* 3, (November 1988): 57.

14   A colleague from ForSeaDiscovery, Koldo Trápaga Monchet, has studied this relation between Portugal and the Spanish monarchy navy. Two interesting outcomes from his research are Trápaga Monchet, "Las armadas en el reino de Portugal en los reinados de los Felipes (1580–1640)," in *Familia, cultura material y formas de poder en la España moderna: III Encuentro de jóvenes investigadores en Historia Moderna, Valladolid 2 y 3 de julio de 2015*, ed. Máximo García Fernández (Madrid, Fundación Española de Historia Moderna, 2016), 843–854 and " 'Traed madera': agentes y vías de provisión de madera para las flotas reales en Portugal (1598–1611)," in *Nuevas perspectivas de investigación en Historia Moderna: economía, sociedad, política y cultura en el mundo hispánico*, eds. María Ángeles

Madrid's influence, Andalusia had not developed a meaningful industry for ocean-going vessels by then.[15]

Several prohibitions banned the use of Andalusian-built ships in the *Carrera*. In principle, these prohibitions were justified by the poor quality of the regional timber used in those ships, but it is fair to suspect that these policies also sought to protect the Cantabrian shipbuilding industry, with a longer tradition of constructing ocean-going vessels.[16] Rodríguez Lorenzo notes that, in fact, the repetitions of the prohibition – the last one in 1593 – suggest the existence of an incipient shipbuilding industry for ocean-going ships in Andalusia, whose relevance is still to be assessed by historians but, in any case, was minor at the end of the century.[17]

Despite the little importance in the production of vessels for the military purposes of the Hispanic monarchy, the western Andalusian region emerged as an important node of Spain's naval organisation during the period. Since the decade of the 1560s, Philip II introduced stricter regulations in the *Carrera de Indias*. This regulation sought a closer supervision over the flourishing route between Seville and the Americas, while at the same time offered protection to those navigating it against foreign privateers.[18] The monarchy defined seasonal convoys, prohibited ships from travelling outside them, and organised a royal navy of galleons that escorted them. This permanent royal navy came to be known the *Armada de la Guarda de la Carrera de Indias*.[19] The English and

Pérez Samper and José Luis Betrán Moya (Madrid, Fundación Española de Historia Moderna, 2016), 106–119.

15   José Luis Casado Soto, *Los barcos españoles del siglo XVI y la Gran Armada de 1588* (Madrid: San Martín, 1988).

16   Michael M. Barkham, *Report on 16th Century Spanish Basque Shipbuilding, c. 1550 to c. 1600* (Ottawa: Parks Canada, 1981).

17   Sergio Rodríguez Lorenzo, "Construcción naval cantábrica y carrera de Indias (circa 1560–1622)," *Altamira: Revista del Centro de Estudios Montañeses*, no. 88 (2017): 37–74.

18   The best-known publication on the navigation between Seville and the Americas is Huguette Chaunu, Pierre Chaunu and Guy Arbellot, *Séville et l'Atlantique, 1504–1650* (Paris: A. Colin, 1955–1959). See also Chaunu and Chaunu, *Séville et l'Amérique aux XVIe et XVIIe Siècles* (Paris: Flammarion, 1977). Some important contributions by Spanish historians were published in the context of the commemoration of the fifth centenary of Colon's arrival in America: Antonio García-Baquero González, *La Carrera de Indias: Suma de la contratación y océano de negocios* (Sevilla: Algaida, 1992), and Antonio Miguel Bernal Rodríguez, *La financiación de la Carrera de Indias (1492–1824): Dinero y crédito en el comercio colonial español con América* (Sevilla: Fundación El Monte, 1992).

19   Carla Rahn Phillips, *Six Galleons for the King of Spain: Imperial Defense in the Early Seventeenth Century* (Baltimore: Johns Hopkins University Press, 1986). Although the book covers a later period, the first chapter provides a brilliant summary of how Philip II's regulations shaped the biannual convoys and the armada that protected them. For a more detailed account on the *Carrera de Indias* and the institution that ruled it, the *Casa de*

Dutch attacks to Iberian ports motivated the creation of the *Armada de la Mar Océano* in 1588. This naval force, whose aim was to defend Castile's Atlantic coast, was under the command of Alonso de Guzmán, the seventh Duke of Medina Sidonia and lord of Sanlúcar de Barrameda, a town in the mouth of the Guadalquivir River.[20] The *Armada de la Mar Océano* complemented the fleet of royal galleys that had traditionally fought Islamic corsairs in the Mediterranean Sea. As tensions with the Ottomans diminished in the 1570s, this Mediterranean fleet of royal galleys, which used to be based in Sicily, began to operate from Andalusia as well.[21] This book aims at explaining the maritime rise of Andalusia in the second half of the sixteenth century, regardless of the absence of a developed industry for the construction of ocean-going vessels.

2 A Revision of the Pessimistic Narrative on Spain's Maritime History

Once powerful, the Spanish mercantile fleet operating the route between the Cantabrian and the Flemish coasts was in decline in the second half of the sixteenth century.[22] This hindered the military potential of the monarchy in Atlantic waters, as Spain still relied on its mercantile fleet for war.[23] Coinciding with the increasing commercial competition and military instability in the

Contratación, see the book edited by Enriqueta Vila Vilar, Antonio Acosta Rodríguez and Adolfo L. González Rodríguez, *La Casa de la Contratación y la navegación entre España y las Indias* (Sevilla: CSIC and Universidad de Sevilla, 2004).

20   Irving A. A. Thompson, "The Appointment of the Duke of Medina Sidonia to the Command of the Spanish Armada." *The Historical Journal* 12, no. 2 (1969); 197–216. Salas Almela has made extensive research into the rise and decline of the House of Medina Sidonia, e.g. Luis Salas Almela, *Colaboración y conflicto: la capitanía general del mar Océano y costas de Andalucía, 1588–1660* (Córdoba: Universidad de Córdoba, 2002), or "Un cargo para el Duque de Medina Sidonia: Portugal, el Estrecho de Gibraltar y el Comercio Indiano (1578–1584)," *Revista de Indias* 69, no. 247 (2009) 11–38.

21   Irving A. A. Thompson, "The Spanish Armada: Naval Warfare between the Mediterranean and the Atlantic," in *England, Spain and the Gran Armada, 1585–1604*, ed. Mía Rodríguez-Salgado and Simon Adams, (Edinburgh: Donald, 1991), 70–94. A more recent approach can be found in José Manuel Díaz Blanco, "Una armada de galeras para la Carrera de Indias: El Mediterráneo y el comercio colonial en tiempos de Felipe II," *Revista de Indias* 74, no. 262 (2014): 661–692.

22   William D. Phillips, "Spain's Northern Shipping Industry in the Sixteenth Century," *Journal of European Economic History* 17, no. 2 (1988): 267–301. Jean-Philippe Priotti, "El comercio de los puertos vascos peninsulares con el noroeste europeo durante el siglo XVI," *Itsas Memoria: Revista de estudios marítimos del País Vasco*, no. 4 (2003): 193–206, and *Bilbao y sus mercaderes en el siglo XVI: génesis de un crecimiento* (Bilbao: Diputación Foral de Bizkaia, 2005).

23   Casado Soto, "Barcos para la guerra." Thompson, *War and government.*

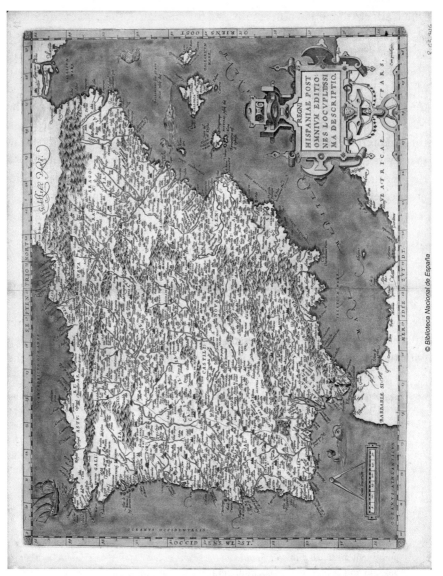

ILLUSTRATION 0.1   Map of the Iberian Peninsula. Abraham Ortelius, *Regni Hispaniae Post Omnium Editiones Locupletissima Descriptio*, 1570, map, Biblioteca Nacional de España, Madrid. http://bdh.bne.es/bnesearch/detalle/bdh0000021069

North Sea, entrepreneurs from Burgos and the Basque region – with a long tradition of exporting wool to the Low Countries – had diverted their investments to safer enterprises like the *Carrera de Indias* or high-sea fisheries.[24] German, English and especially Dutch shippers and traders filled the vacuum they left.[25]

The decline of Spanish shipping in the west coast of Europe became a recurrent concern at Philip II's court, especially as the Hispano-Dutch war progressed. This motivated the monarchy to create a system of loans and fiscal benefits that encouraged entrepreneurs to invest in the construction of commercial vessels on the condition that they could eventually be adapted to warfare to join the king's military enterprises.[26] But the monarchy's plan to incentivise shipbuilding did not go as expected. In fact, by the decade of the 1590s, the production of large-tonnage vessels in Cantabrian shipyards entered a progressive decline that lasted until the middle of the seventeenth century.[27]

---

24   On the increasing importance of migrants from Burgos in Seville, see Rafael M. Pérez García, "La trayectoria histórica de la comunidad mercantil burgalesa en la Sevilla moderna: ascenso social y mutación económica. El caso del mercader Alonso de Nebreda," in *Andalucía en el mundo atlántico moderno. Ciudades y redes*, eds. Juan José Iglesias Rodríguez et al (Madrid. Sílex. 2018), 157–191, and "Mercaderes burgaleses en la Andalucía de los siglos XVI y XVII: procesos de enriquecimiento, ascenso social y ennoblecimiento," in *Monarquías en conflicto. Linajes y noblezas en la articulación de la Monarquía Hispánica*, eds. José Ignacio Fortea Pérez, Juan Eloy Gelabert González, Roberto López Vela and Elena Postigo Castellanos (Madrid: Fundación Española de Historia Moderna, 2018), 617–627. On the activities of Biscaine individuals, see Lutgardo García Fuentes, "Los vascos en la Carrera de Indias en la Edad Moderna: Una minoría predominante," *Temas americanistas*, no. 16 (2003): 29–49.

25   Literature on this topic is extensive. Modesto Ulloa, "Unas notas sobre el comercio y la navegación españoles en el siglo XVI." *Anuario de Historia económica y social*, no. 2 (1969): 191–237; William D. Phillips, and Carla Rahn Phillips, "Spanish Wool and Dutch Rebels: The Middelburg Incident of 1574," *The American Historical Review* 82, no. 2 (1977): 312–330; Hilario Casado Alonso, *El triunfo de Mercurio: la presencia castellana en Europa (siglos XV y XVI)* (Burgos: Cajacírculo, 2003), "El comercio internacional burgalés en los siglos XV y XVI," in *Actas del V Centenario del Consulado de Burgos (1494–1994)*, eds. Floriano Ballesteros Caballero, Hilario Casado Alonso, and Alberto C. Ibáñez Pérez (Burgos: Diputación Provincial de Burgos, 1994): 175–248, "Las colonias de mercaderes castellanos en Europa (siglos XV y XVI)," in Castilla y Europa: comercio y mercaderes en los siglos XIV, XV y XVI, ed. Casado Alonso (Burgos: Diputación de Burgos, 1995): 15–56.

26   José Luis Casado Soto, "Barcos para la guerra," 31–32. Thompson, *War and government*.

27   Álvaro Aragón Ruano, "Transformaciones económicas en el sector costero guipuzcoano central," *Manuscrits: Revista d'història moderna*, no. 26 (2008): 191–236. See also the collective publication Álvaro Aragón Ruano and Alberto Angulo Morales, *Recuperando el Norte: empresas, capitales y proyectos atlánticos en la economía imperial hispánica* (Bilbao: Universidad del País Vasco, 2016).

Intellectuals – known as *arbitristas* – and royal officials struggled to understand the causes of the poor performance of Cantabrian shipyards.[28] They pointed at many and varied reasons to explain why these shipyards could not cope with the naval expansion to which Philip II aspired. According to them, lack of men, lack of capital, lack of technology or lack of forestry resources due to overexploitation hindered the plans of the monarchy for constructing ships suited for Atlantic warfare. Moreover, they usually blamed the decline of shipbuilding production not only for the Spaniards' loss of importance in the trade with northern Europe, but also for the decline of Spain's military hegemony in the region. Such contemporary opinions had a decisive influence on the way historians looked at Spain's naval evolution, and the assumption that, by the end of the century, the Habsburg monarchy became a second-class naval and shipping power. The idea that Spain started a maritime crisis at the end of the sixteenth century, becoming a peripheral European power ever since, permeated Anglo-Saxon historiography.[29] In 1978, Kamen even defined Spain as a "dominated colonial market at whose expense other European nations progressed towards industrial growth."[30]

Nonetheless, the relation between the crisis of Cantabrian shipbuilding and the decline of Spain's shipping, and therefore of its naval force, is not as evident as this pessimistic narrative claims. Firstly, Spaniards' disinterest in trade and navigation through the English Channel, which so much worried Philip II's counsellors, predates the fall in shipbuilding production. Secondly, none of the struggles mentioned above, which hindered the Cantabrian shipbuilding production, were actually endemic to the Spanish case; the lack of men, capital, technology, or natural resources were common circumstances to all early modern maritime powers.[31] Unable to find a distinctive cause that

---

28   A complete and interesting collection of transcribed contemporary reports can be found in José Luis Casado Soto, *Los barcos españoles*.

29   For a critical reflection on this, see Regina Grafe, "The Strange Tale of the Decline of Spanish Shipping," in *Shipping and Economic Growth, 1350–1850*, ed. Richard W. Unger (Leiden: Brill, 2011), 81–116. In there, Grafe names two exception to this approach, Carla Rahn Phillips and William D. Phillips, whose research has been cited earlier.

30   Henry Kamen, "The Decline of Spain: A Historical Myth?" *Past and Present* 81, no. 1 (1978): 46. Kamen's article was contested some years later by Israel, in an article with the same title, Jonathan I. Israel, "The Decline of Spain: A Historical Myth?" *Past & Present* 91, no. 91 (1981): 170–180. Hamilton was one of the initiators of the debate on Spain's decline, arguing economic reasons. Earl J. Hamilton, "Revisions in Economic History: VIII-The Decline of Spain," *The Economic History Review* 8, no. 2 (1938): 168–179.

31   Grafe, "The Strange Tale," 95. Determined to demonstrate such backwardness of the Spanish navy, Goodman even argued a rather odd distinctive cause: a lack of morale

explained the alleged maritime crisis of Spain since the end of the sixteenth century, scholars opted to explain the deterioration of Cantabrian shipbuilding in terms of a failure of the Habsburg political system; absolutism provoked it, contrasting to *more successful* parliamentary states, namely the Netherlands and England, whose maritime empires rose in the seventeenth century. A good example of this view is found in the work of North who, after comparing the English and Dutch regimes with absolutist ones, concluded that centralist bureaucracies stifled "initiatives that would have induced increased productivity, and Spain and Portugal pursued a downward path that would continue for centuries."[32]

The inefficiency of the absolutist state was a main element of Thompson's influential thesis on *War and Government*, published in 1976. In there, he concluded that Spain's military reputation declined because of a process of devolution that began to be noticeable during Philip II's reign. As Spain's centralist policies failed, shipbuilding was increasingly left in the hands of inefficient private contractors (*asentistas*), many of them foreigners.[33] Thompson's book contributed significantly to the reassessment of Spanish maritime history, as he abandoned classic approaches that were mostly concerned with military strategies, which were still largely based on Fernández Duro's gigantic compilation of naval events and figures published in the nineteenth century.[34] Instead, Thompson's interest lay in how warfare and naval affairs shaped the development of the Habsburg state, paving the way for later scholars, most notably

---

among seamen. David C. Goodman, *Spanish Naval Power, 1589–1665: Reconstruction and Defeat* (Cambridge: Cambridge University Press, 2002), 261.

32   Douglass C. North, "Institutions, Transaction Costs, and the Rise of Merchant Empires." in *The Political Economy of Merchant Empires: State Power and World Trade, 1350–1750*, ed. James D. Tracy (Cambridge: Cambridge University Press, 1991), 27.

33   Thompson, *War and government*, 274. The role of foreigners in Spanish finances, especially Portuguese families in the seventeenth century, have attracted great attention in the English and Spanish historiographies. See for instance, James C. Boyajian, *Portuguese Bankers at the Court of Spain, 1626–1650* (New Brunswick: Rutgers University Press, 1983), or Carlos Álvarez Nogal, Carlos, *Los banqueros de Felipe IV y los metales preciosos americanos (1621–1665)* (Madrid: Banco de España, 1997). For a more recent publication, see Álvaro Sánchez Durán, "El crédito portugués en la Monarquía Hispánica de Felipe IV: los asientos de la familia Núñez-Mercado (1640–1652)," *Cuadernos de historia moderna* 42, no. 1 (2017): 57–86.

34   Cesáreo Fernández Duro, *Armada española: Desde la unión de los Reinos de Castilla y de Aragón* (Madrid: Museo Naval, 1973). Originally published between 1895 and 1903, a reedition was made in 1973, available online at "Historia de la Armada Española," accessed June 12, 2020, http://www.armada.mde.es/html/historiaarmada.

Glete, who introduced the Spanish case in a discussion that has attracted major attention in the last decades: the fiscal-military state.[35]

The premise of this debate is that the creation of centralised mechanisms of state administration was driven by states' necessities to obtain and manage financial and material resources for ever-growing military efforts. Discussions about the rise of the fiscal-military state in pre-Modern Europe became especially popular after Tilly's publication in 1991, *Coercion, Capital and European States*.[36] In there, Tilly proposed a linear evolution, covering almost a millennium from 990 to 1990, for the rise of European modern nation-states. According to it, early modern states gradually developed from monarchies and urban republics, which were highly dependent on private entrepreneurs to obtain financial and material resources for war, to nation-states with centralised national economies. Tilly's teleological framework served to underpin the narrative of failure of the Spanish monarchy in the early modern period: when military competition rose in western Europe, Spain soon lagged behind in the international arena because of the incapacity of the absolutist state to assume a direct control over the administration of financial and military resources.

---

35 Most notably, Jan Glete, *War and the State in Early Modern Europe: Spain, the Dutch Republic and Sweden as Fiscal-Military States, 1500–1660* (London: Routledge, 2002). Some years earlier, Glete published *Warfare at Sea, 1500–1650: Maritime Conflicts and the Transformation of Europe* (London: Routledge, 2000). In Spanish, Iván Valdez-Bubnov, *Poder naval y modernización del Estado: política de construcción naval española (siglos XVI-XVIII)* (Frankfurt am Main: Vervuert Verlagsgesellschaft, 2012), and Rafael Torres Sánchez, *El precio de la guerra: el Estado fiscal-militar de Carlos III (1779–1783)* (Madrid: Marcial Pons Historia, 2013). See also the special issue on Studia Historica by Rafael Torres Sánchez, "Presentación. El negocio de la guerra: la movilización de recursos militares y la construcción de la monarquía española, XVII y XVIII," *Studia historica. Historia moderna*, no. 35 (2013): 23–32.

36 Charles Tilly, *Coercion, Capital, and European States, Ad 990–1992* (Cambridge: Blackwell, 1992). The concept "fiscal-military state" was first introduced by John Brewer, *The Sinews of Power: War, Money and the English State, 1688–1783* (London: Hyman, 1989), and has evolved greatly since then. For instance, some authors slightly downplay the importance of warfare Richard Bonney, *The rise of the fiscal state in Europe, c. 1200–1815* (Oxford: Oxford University Press, 1999), while other authors stress the role of the naval affairs e.g. N. A. M. Rodger, "From the 'military revolution' to the 'fiscal-naval state,'" *Journal for Maritime Research* 13, no. 2 (2011): 119–128. The debate is still attracting scholars' attention, see Bartolomé Yun Casalilla and Patrick O'Brien, eds. *The Rise of Fiscal States: A Global History, 1500–1914* (New York: Cambridge University Press, 2012) or Peter Wilson's project at Oxford University on "The European Fiscal-Military System," accessed June 12, 2020, https://fiscalmilitary.history.ox.ac.uk. This debate is closely linked to debates on the "Military Revolution." See the classic works of David Eltis, *The Military Revolution in Sixteenth-Century Europe* (London: Tauris Academic Studies, 1995), or Geoffrey Parker, *The Military*

Spanish historiography did not engage in the previous debate and, for a long time, the former pessimistic narrative was barely contested.[37] Only in the last decades, as English- and Spanish-speaking scholarships began to recognise each other's existence properly, a critical refutation to this long-standing interpretation developed. In "The Strange Tale of the Decline of Spanish Shipping," published in 2011, Grafe brilliantly offered an alternative explanation to the negative narrative on Spanish maritime history. The paper begins with a clear question: "If Spain was so deficient in the naval arts, how did it hold together the largest western empire for three centuries?"[38] In other words, the crisis of Cantabrian shipyards did not lead to Spain's naval backwardness, simply because such naval backwardness did not occur.

With that premise, Grafe revisits the production crisis in the Basque shipyards. She does agree on the fact that a slowdown occurred, which began to be noticeable in the last years of Philip II's reign, but production never came to a complete halt. Her explanation includes two fundamental reconsiderations. Firstly, if the financial, technological or resources capacity of Spain was not very different from that of other European powers, then historians should look somewhere else to explain the production decline. That means, according to her, analysing changes in the demand side, instead of the supply side of the shipbuilding process. Secondly, historians should stop considering Spain as a centralist state. On the contrary, she defines the Spanish monarchy as a composite state or, as she put in a later paper, a polycentric one. This understanding of the monarchy as a polycentric organisation highlights its territorial complexity, emphasising the importance of the interconnection between Iberian peripheral regions, like the Basque or the Andalusian ones, and their different ways of engaging in the Habsburgs' imperial project.[39]

Revolution: Military Innovation and the Rise of the West, 1500–1800 (Cambridge: Cambridge University Press, 1996).

37   For an interesting overview on this, see James S. Amelang, "The Peculiarities of the Spaniards Historical Approaches to the Early Modern State," in *Public power in Europe studies in historical transformations*, ed. James S. Amelang (Pisa: Plus-Pisa University Press, 2006), 39–56.

38   Grafe, "The Strange Tale," 81.

39   Regina Grafe, "Polycentric States: The Spanish Reigns and the 'Failures' of Mercantilism," in *Mercantilism Reimagined: Political Economy in Early Modern Britain and its Empire*, ed. Philip J. Stern and Carl Wennerlind (Oxford: Oxford University Press, 2013), 241–262. Within Spanish scholarship, Manuel Herrero Sánchez is a main advocate of the polycentric model of the Habsburg state, see Manuel Herrero Sánchez, "La Monarquía Hispánica y las repúblicas europeas: el modelo republicano en una monarquía de ciudades," in

The polycentric nature of Spain explains one distinctive characteristic of the monarchy's economy, with a great influence on its naval organisation: Spain lacked an economic integration that permitted the development of a national-scale naval production.[40] Thus, Cantabrian shipbuilding production was heavily dependent on regional- and local-scale economies. Grafe's main argument is that, when Castilian and Cantabrian capitalists turned away from trade with Flanders and invested in safer options such as American trade or fisheries, a domino effect occurred that ultimately debilitated the capacity of Cantabrian shipyards:

> [O]ne blow to demand for northern Spanish shipping followed another [i.e. war in the Low Countries, and a secular decline in whaling]. For a sector that relied on local networks and re-investment of capital and a tight structure of cross-ownership, this protracted decline in demand was disastrous.[41]

Grafe inverts the causation order of the pessimistic view: the disinterest of Basque and Castilian capitalists in trading with northern Europe led to a fall in the demand for mercantile vessels, provoking a crisis in Cantabrian shipyards. After this convincing explanation, Grafe did not further explore the relationship between shipbuilding and shipping in Spain, but her initial question ("[i]f Spain was so deficient in the naval arts, how did it hold together the largest western empire for three centuries?") encapsulates a fundamental conclusion. Cantabrian shipbuilding decline did not necessarily hinder the capacity of Spanish shipping; in fact, nothing indicates a decline of shipping in Andalusia by the end of the sixteenth century.

Republicas y republicanismo en la Europa moderna (siglos XVI-XVIII), eds. Manuel Herrero Sánchez, Giovanni Levi and Thomas Maissen (Madrid: Fondo de Cultura Económica de España, 2017): 273–327. Herrero Sánchez' research group – "Red Columnaria" – published a collective book on the matter in 2012: Pedro Cardim, Tamar Herzog, José J. Ruiz Ibáñez, and Gaetano Sabatini (eds.), *Polycentric Monarchies: How Did Early Modern Spain and Portugal Achieve and Maintain a Global Hegemony?* (Brighton: Sussex Academic Press, 2012). The origins of this polycentric approach was influenced by the concept of composite monarchies that John H. Elliott applied to the Spanish case: "A Europe of Composite Monarchies," *Past & Present*, no. 137 (November, 1992): 48–71.

40   Regina Grafe further elaborates on this in her book, *Distant Tyranny: Markets, Power, and Backwardness in Spain, 1650–1800* (Princeton: Princeton University Press, 2012).

41   Grafe, "The Strange Tale," 106–108. The fragile equilibrium between supply and a changing demand of Cantabrian shipyards is also noted by Rodríguez Lorenzo, "Construcción naval cantábrica."

On the contrary, the number of ships navigating to the Americas experienced a continuous rise, and so did the number of ships connecting Andalusia to other European regions.[42] When the crisis of Cantabrian shipyards began to be noticeable, shippers of the *Carrera de Indias* had already started to use ships built outside Spain, especially in northern Europe and the Americas.[43] In other words, the beginning of the decline of Cantabrian shipyards had limited consequences, if any, in Andalusia by the end of the century, as its shipping capacity developed even without having developed a competitive shipbuilding industry.

The present book revises the pessimistic narrative on Spain's maritime history by asking why shipping flourished in Andalusia in the last third of the sixteenth century, regardless of the structural incapacity of the region's shipbuilding industry and the monarchy's hostility towards trade with northern Europe. The research builds on the premise that, in the framework of a polycentric state, the city of Seville did not simply accept the monarchy's protectionist policies regarding international trade, but influenced them. Inasmuch as urban and regional powers administered the lion share of the monarchy's taxes, they did not limit themselves to accept a growing coercion of central states or revolt against it, engaging in continuous tensions and negotiations with the king.[44] Consequently, a city like Seville, whose fiscal contribution was indispensable for the royal treasury, enjoyed ample political leverage capacity to negotiate with the monarchy in the framework of a polycentric state. This ultimately allowed the local oligarchy to protect the thriving north European population in town, and hence to ensure the supply of imported naval provisions in the region.

The emergence of a notable market of imported naval provisions dominated by *flamencos*, which supplied the fleets sailing every year to the Americas, does not only challenge long-standing narratives of Spain's shipping capacity. The fact that this market developed in a way that permitted royal officials to obtain provisions for the royal navy from there also challenges prevailing interpretations about the supplying mechanisms of the royal navy. Influenced by Thompson's argument on the state's devolution to private hands, researchers

---

42   Gómez-Centurión Jiménez, *Felipe II*, 145.

43   Rodríguez Lorenzo, "Construcción naval cantábrica," and "Sevilla y la Carrera de Indias: las compraventas de naos (1560–1622)," *Anuario de estudios americanos* 73, no. 1 (2016): 65–97.

44   Alejandra Irigoin and Regina Grafe, "Bargaining for Absolutism: A Spanish Path to Nation-State and Empire Building," *Hispanic American Historical Review* 88 no. 2 (2008): 173–209. Bartolomé Yun Casalilla, *Marte contra Minerva: el precio del imperio español, c.1450–1600* (Barcelona: Crítica, 2004).

on Spain's provision strategies have traditionally established a dichotomy between direct administration versus *asientos* – contracts according to which the state outsourced the provision of financial and material resources to private entrepreneurs, *asentitas*, who in exchange received market privileges, such as tax exemptions or monopolies.[45] Yet the *flamencos* of the *Atarazanas* never signed an *asiento* with the monarchy and, in principle, the market remained open to anyone willing to import and supply naval provisions. How, then, did they come to control such a strategic market and why did the monarchy allow them to do so?

3   An Alternative to the Asientos: Foreigners, Seville and the
        Monarchy

A recent approach to the fiscal-military state proposed by Fynn-Paul et al in 2014 helps to reassess the relation between these foreigners and the monarchy.[46] These authors refuse the determinism of Tilly's linear evolution to emphasise different forms in which private entrepreneurs engaged in the supply of capital and provisions for military enterprises to demonstrate the existence of diverse paths to state formation. Covering varied territorial and chronological contexts, the authors identify three major strategies through which early modern states engaged with the market to cope with warfare. States could subvert the market with predatory practices to obtain financial and material resources; they could collaborate with the market by privileging

---

45   Recent research is still very based on this dichotomy, especially in the seventeenth century. See for instance, Rafael Torres Sánchez, "Administración o asiento: la política estatal de suministros militares en la monarquía española del siglo XVIII," *Studia histórica. Historia moderna*, no. 35 (2013): 159–199, Agustín González Enciso, "Asentistas y fabricantes: El abastecimiento de armas y municiones al Estado en los siglos XVII y XVIII," *Studia historica. Historia moderna* no. 35 (2013): 269–303, Ivan Valdez-Bubnov, "Shipbuilding Administration under the Spanish Habsburg and Bourbon Regimes (1590–1834): A Comparative Perspective," *Business History* 60 no. 1 (2018): 105–125. In 1992, Sanz Ayán published an article on Dutch contractors supplying timber in the second half of the seventeenth century: Carmen Sanz Ayán, "Negociadores y capitales holandeses en los sistemas de abastecimientos de pertrechos navales de la monarquía hispánica durante el siglo XVII," *Hispania: Revista española de historia* 52, no. 182 (1992): 915–945. A recent dissertation by Pepijn Brandon on the Dutch case sheds new light on the complex organisation of early modern developing bureaucracies; Brandon, *War, Capital, and the Dutch State (1588–1795)* (Leiden: Brill, 2015).
46   Jeff Fynn-Paul, *War, Entrepreneurs, and the State in Europe and the Mediterranean, 1300–1800*. Leiden: Brill, 2014.

the activity of specific entrepreneurs or outsourcing the administration of specific resources to contractors; or they could absorb a market by assuming total control of it.[47]

Inspired by the threefold model presented above, this book explores why Philip II's monarchy decided to collaborate with foreigners to meet the growing demand of imported naval provisions in the Iberian Peninsula. The analysis of how a group of foreign merchants came to dominate a crucial trade for the monarchy without signing an *asiento* should not be based on the presumption that this solution was detrimental to Spain's military capacity or its international reputation. On the contrary, it should be based on the assumption that this solution demonstrates the resilience of the Hispanic monarchy's maritime organisation, and the influence that coastal powers – like Seville, Lisbon or the Basque towns – had in shaping it, in the framework of a polycentric state.

Furthermore, the *flamencos* trading timber in Seville did not belong to rich, influential families with an already consolidated social position in international trade and in the monarchy's financial and military affairs. Instead, they were young migrants who pursued the opportunity to prosper abroad and, soon after their migration, reached a predominant position in a strategic market. To understand how these migrants managed to dominate this strategic market in such a short time, this research studies how they specialised in the trade in Baltic and Scandinavian timber, and the mechanisms of supply of these strategic commodities for the private-owned mercantile fleet preparing to sail to the Americas, on the one hand, and for the royal navy, on the other.

When analysing the commercial strategies of these merchants, this book engages with a vast scholarly literature on long-distance trade and transnational commercial networks in pre-modern Europe.[48] This is a line of study

---

47   Fynn-Paul, *War, Entrepreneurs, and the State*, 12.

48   See the classic work of Frédéric Mauro, "Merchant communities, 1350–1750," in *The Rise of Merchant Empires: Long Distance Trade in the Early Modern World 1350–1750*, ed. James D. Tracy (Cambridge, Cambridge University Press, 1993): 255–286. A recent critical approach to this topic is Oscar Gelderblom and Regina Grafe, "The Rise and Fall of the Merchant Guilds: Re-thinking the Comparative Study of Commercial Institutions in Premodern Europe," *Journal of Interdisciplinary History* 40, no. 4 (Spring 2010): 477–511. In recent times, most studies on this matter have been influenced by the concepts and debates proposed by the New Institutional Economics (NIE); a line of historical research that reflects on how legal and social norms shaped the institutional solutions that prompted international trade, and ultimately economic growth. Two influential monographs in this regard are Douglass C. North, *Institutions, Institutional Change, and Economic Performance.* (Cambridge: Cambridge University Press, 1990), and Avner Greif, *Institutions and the Path to the Modern Economy: Lessons from Medieval Trade* (Cambridge: Cambridge University Press, 2006).

that has found a fruitful subject in early modern Seville and other Andalusian
towns, due to the important foreign presence; Dutch, English, Flemish, French,
German, Italian or Scottish mercantile communities flourished in the region
in the pre-modern period.[49] In the last two decades, historians focusing on
long-distance trade in Andalusia – most notably Crespo Solana – have introduced the region in debates with a long tradition in the Anglo-Saxon historiography under the umbrella of the Atlantic History.[50] These authors abandoned
previous positivistic approaches to the economic history of Andalusia and the
Spanish empire, mostly concerned with the juridical evolution of foreigners'
legal participation in the *Carrera de Indias*.[51] Instead, they used methodolo-
gies and concepts from sociology and economics to analyse how transnational
networks operated in Andalusia, connecting the region to the main European
and American markets in the Early Modern Period.[52] A similar spirit drives

49   Even though these studies do not engage directly with NIE debates, the list of studies
      on long-distance trade and foreign communities in Andalusia is endless. Some classic
      publications for the case of Seville are Antonio Domínguez Ortiz, *Los extranjeros en la
      vida española durante el siglo XVII y otros artículos* (Seville: Diputación de Sevilla, 1996),
      Enriqueta Vila Vilar, *Los Corzo y los Mañara: tipos y arquetipos del mercader con Indias*
      (Sevilla: Escuela de Estudios Hispano-Americanos, 1991); Albert Girard, *Le commerce
      français à Seville et Cadix au temps des Habsbourg: contribution a l'étude du commerce
      etranger en Espagne aux XVI et XVII siècles* (New York: Burt Franklin, 1967); Michèle
      Moret, *Aspects de la société marchande de Séville: au début du XVIIe siècle* (París: Marcel
      Riviere, 1967); and more recently, Perez, Béatrice. *Les marchands de Séville: Une société
      inquiète (XVe-XVIe siècles)*. París: Presses de l'Université Paris-Sorbonne, 2016.
50   Some of Crespo Solana's main contributions have been cited already. In recent times,
      studies on the position of Andalusia in the Atlantic world are flourishing; the two col-
      lective volumes of the ANDATLAN project are good example of this: Juan José Iglesias
      Rodríguez and Jaime García Bernal, eds., *Andalucía en el mundo Atlántico moderno: agen-
      tes y escenarios* (Madrid: Sílex, 2016) and Juan José Iglesias Rodríguez, Jaime García
      Bernal and José Manuel Díaz Blanco, eds., *Andalucía en el mundo atlántico moderno.
      Ciudades y redes* (Madrid: Sílex, 2018). Recent important contributions to the Iberian
      Atlantic history are Christopher Ebert, *Between Empires: Brazilian Sugar in the Early
      Atlantic Economy, 1550–1630* (Leiden: Brill, 2008); Xabier Lamikiz, *Trade and Trust in
      the Eighteenth-Century Atlantic World: Spanish Merchants and Their Overseas Networks*
      (Woodbridge: Boydell Press, 2010); José Luis Gasch-Tomás, *The Atlantic World and the
      Manila Galleons: Circulation, Market, and Consumption of Asian Goods in the Spanish
      Empire, 1565–1650* (Leiden; Brill, 2018); Cátia Antunes and Amélia Polónia, eds. *Beyond
      Empires: Global, Self-Organizing, Cross-Imperial Networks, 1500–1800* (Leiden: Brill, 2016).
51   See for instance Eufemio Lorenzo Sanz, *Comercio de España con América en la época de
      Felipe II* (Valladolid: Diputación Provincial de Valladolid, 1979), or Antonio Domínguez
      Ortiz, "La concesión de naturalezas para comerciar en Indias durante el siglo XVIII,"
      Revista de Indias 19 no. 76 (1959): 227–239.
52   For a good overview on this historiographical transition, see Regina Grafe, "On the Spatial
      Nature of Institutions and the Institutional Nature of Personal Networks in the Spanish
      Atlantic," *Culture & History Digital Journal* 3, no. 1 (2014): 1–11.

this work, as it explores how the Flemish and German merchants of the *Atarazanas* integrated in Seville and traded with north European markets.

For a long time, the Belgian historian Stols stood as the most relevant authority for the research on the migration from the Low Countries to the Iberian Peninsula in the sixteenth and seventeenth centuries.[53] His influential book published in 1971, *De Spaanse Brabanders*, together with Otte's excellent account on the growth of Seville's foreign population in the sixteenth century, were fundamental for the creation of a widely accepted explanation as to the Flemish rise in early modern Seville.[54] According to it, the presence of north European migrants remained small and relatively irrelevant for a good part of the sixteenth century. Coinciding with the beginning of war in the Low Countries and the expansion of American trade, the number of Flemish and German migrants grew exponentially. Individuals arrived from different territories, southern and northern Low Countries as well as northern Germany. However, since most of them were one way or another connected to the southern provinces and particularly to Antwerp, they were generally known as *flamencos*. Their professional backgrounds were heterogeneous, too; we find artisans, retailers, seamen and even vagabonds among them, although the majority specialized in long-distance trade.[55]

Historians researching the north European presence in Andalusia, including Stols, have mostly paid attention to the seventeenth and eighteenth centuries, when the Flemish and Dutch constituted the largest and most influential foreign community in Andalusia, and were actively engaged in the trade with the Americas.[56] They generally overlooked the origins of the north European presence in Seville, and simply assumed that the number of *flamencos* grew

---

53   Eddy Stols, *De Spaanse Brabanders, of De Handelsbetrekkingen Der Zuidelijke Nederlanden Met De Iberische Wereld, 1598–1648* (Brussel: Palais Der Academiën, 1971). The outcome of this research was disseminated in Spanish through different publications, such as "La colonia flamenca de Sevilla y el comercio de los Países Bajos españoles en la primera mitad del siglo XVII," *Anuario de historia económica y social*, no. 2 (1969): 356–374, or "Experiencias y ganancias flamencas en la Monarquía de Felipe II," in *Las sociedades ibéricas y el mar a finales del siglo XVI*, edited by Luis A. Ribot García, and Ernesto Belenguer Cebrià (Lisbon: Sociedad Estatal Lisboa '98, 1998): 147–169.

54   Enrique Otte, *Sevilla, siglo XVI: Materiales para su historia económica* (Sevilla: Centro de Estudios Andaluces, 2008).

55   Carolina Abadía Flores, "La comunidad flamenca en Sevilla en el siglo XVI," *Archivo hispalense: Revista histórica, literaria y artística* 93, no. 282–284 (2010): 175–178.

56   For Seville, see Eberhard Crailsheim, *The Spanish Connection: French and Flemish Merchant Networks in Seville (1570–1650)* (Cologne: Böhlau Verlag, 2016) or "Behind the Atlantic Expansion: Flemish Trade Connections of Seville in 1620," *Research in Maritime History* 43 (2010), 21–46. For the case of Cádiz in the eighteenth century, see the work

in the second half of the sixteenth century because they were attracted by the opportunities of American trade.[57] As such, Stols' explanation on the rise of the north European community in Andalusia has barely been debated, and the sixteenth century has just been considered as a prelude to a more exciting period, when northerners became central players in the *Carrera de Indias*.

The present book addresses the Flemish and German migration to Seville after the outbreak of the Eighty Years' War on its own terms, not as a prelude to the following century. It does not challenge the chronology of the community's evolution, as explained above, but aims to propose a richer explanation for the rapid growth of the community. The research does not assume the hypothesis that the wave of migration from northern Europe was simply caused by an attraction to the American trade. The opportunities of American trade certainly constituted a main factor for migrants' decision to establish themselves in Seville, but this alone cannot explain the rapid expansion of the north European community in the city. This book proposes that the existence of open-access institutions, as defined by Puttevils in his study on sixteenth-century Antwerp, was a main reason for the growing presence of foreigners in sixteenth-century Seville.[58] These open-access institutions, namely public courts and notaries, offered efficient contract-enforcement solutions to everybody, facilitating the integration of newcomers into the region's socio-economic life. This contrasted to other institutional contexts in which these

of Ana Crespo Solana, e.g. "El comercio holandés y la integración de espacios económicos entre Cádiz y el Báltico en tiempos de guerra (1699–1723)," *Investigaciones de historia económica: revista de la Asociación Española de Historia Económica*, no. 8 (2007): 45–76, or "Merchants and observers: The Dutch republic's commercial interests in Spain and the merchant community in Cádiz in the Eighteenth Century" *Dieciocho: Hispanic enlightenment* 32, no. 2 (2009): 193–224.

57 Besides the works that have been cited already, see Mercedes Gamero Rojas, "Flamencos en la Sevilla del siglo XVII: Actividades económicas entre Europa y América," in *Andalucía en el mundo Atlántico moderno: agentes y escenarios*, Juan José Iglesias Rodríguez, José Jaime García Bernal, eds., (Madrid: Sílex, 2016): 287–310; José Manuel Díaz Blanco and Manuel F. Fernández Chaves, "Una élite en la sombra: Los comerciantes extranjeros en la Sevilla de Felipe III," in *Las élites en la época moderna, la Monarquía española. Volumen 3: Economía y poder*, Enrique Soria Mesa et al, eds. (Córdoba: Universidad de Córdoba, 2009): 35–50.

58 Jeroen Puttevils, *Merchants and Trading in the Sixteenth Century: The Golden Age of Antwerp* (London: Pickering & Chatto, 2015) 12. The use of notarial documents by long-distance merchants has not been thoroughly researched, with some notable exceptions, such as Montserrat Cachero Vinuesa, "Should we trust? Explaining trade expansion in early modern Spain: Seville, 1500–1600" (PhD diss. European University Institute, Florence, 2010).

solutions were provided by guilds, like the Spanish *consulados*, or foreign merchant communities, like the *nationes* in Medieval Low Countries, to its members only.[59]

This research examines how the *flamencos* of the *Atarazanas* relied on one of these open-access institutions, the public notaries, to prompt their integration and participate in long-distance trade, their motivation to notarise certain agreements but not other ones, and how notarial solutions shaped their socio-economic strategies. Notarial deeds permit an exhaustive reconstruction of their socio-economic strategies, and allos us to look at different layers of their business organisation, such as the households and firms they individually ran, their coordination strategies, the partnerships in which they collaborated, and the agency relationships they developed beyond Seville.

Not all of the merchants residing in the *Atarazanas* specialised to the same degree in the trade of Baltic and Scandinavian timber, or reached the same importance in Andalusian society; their paths were different in many respects. But they shared many similarities and grew into a cohesive and interconnected group that managed to have such a strategic market in their hands for at least three decades. A final aim of this book is to analyse how the merchants of the *Atarazanas* generated social capital to ensure their dominant position in a strategic market; that is, it examines their collective strategies to respond to the uncertainties of long-distance trade in a time of war, and to limit competition from outsiders in Seville.

4 A Study Based on Notarial Deeds

The main primary source for this research are the notarial deeds of the Historical Archive of the Province of Seville (*Archivo Histórico Provincial de Sevilla*). Overshadowed by the well-deserved fame of the *Archivo General de Indias* (General Archive of the Indies), which stores the largest collection of documents on the Spanish colonisation of the Americas and the Philippines, Seville's notarial collection has been unfairly disregarded by international scholars, though not by local historians. The protocol section of the Historical Archive of Seville holds the documents formalised by the *escribanos*, public notaries, in the province of Seville before the nineteenth century. The

---

59 For a critical historiographical overview on merchant guilds, see Sheilagh C. Ogilvie, *Institutions and European Trade: Merchant Guilds, 1000–1800* (Cambridge: Cambridge University Press, 2011).

collection is exceptionally well preserved for the early modern period, holding most of the register books from the twenty-four public notarial offices, known as *escribanías de número*.[60]

Escribanos in Castile were public officials with royal authority to notarise, that is, to attest that a document was correctly signed and true according to the parties involved in it. Since the Middle Ages, Castilian kings regulated the activity of *escribanías* and limited their number in each jurisdiction, not only the territorial ones but any public institution, such as royal and local councils.[61] This book is the result of an intensive research on one of the twenty-four public notaries of Seville in the period from 1570 to 1599, although earlier and later years and other *escribanías* were consulted, too, when relevant. The research covered the notarial activity of Francisco Díaz, who worked in the office number XIII from 1570 to the end of 1576, when he moved to the office XV. He remained in charge of this *escribanía* until 1587, when another *escribano*, Juan de Tordesillas, took over the office. De Tordesillas maintained this *escribanía* until at least the first decade of the seventeenth century.[62]

Given the type of activity notarised in the registers of Díaz, and later of De Tordesillas, it is fair to assume that their office was situated close to the *Reales Atarazanas* complex and within the confines of the Santa María parish, the commercial heart of the city.[63] Other notarial offices also contain transactions

---

60   The impressive collection has yielded a vast historiographical production, a great deal of which is published in the journal *Archivo hispalense: Revista histórica, literaria y artística*.

61   Publication on public notaries in pre-Modern Spain are numerous, but mostly devoted to the institutional evolution of the notary. Interesting contributions in this regard are Ramón Cózar Gutiérrez, " 'De lo que yo el infrascripto escribano doy fe:' Los escribanos de la Villa de Albacete durante el siglo XVIII," *Revista de historia moderna: Anales de la Universidad de Alicante*, no. 28 (2010): 269–299. Miguel Angel Extremera Extremera, "Los escribanos de Castilla en la Edad Moderna. Nuevas líneas de investigación," *Chronica nova: Revista de historia moderna de la Universidad de Granada*, no. 28 (2001): 159–184. For the specific case of Seville, see the work of Reyes Rojas García, "La memoria de lo privado en lo público: los escribanos públicos sevillanos" *Historia. Instituciones. Documentos* 31 (2004): 573–584; *La práctica de los escribanos públicos de Sevilla: los manuales (1504–1550)* (Sevilla: Diputacion de Sevilla, 2015); and "De la práctica diaria a la teoría de los formularios notariales: comercio y mercado en la Sevilla del siglo XVI," in *Les formulaires: compilations et circulation des modèles d' actes dans l'Europe médiévale et moderne. Actes du XIIIe Congrès de la Commission Internationale de Diplomatique, Paris, 3–4 septembre 2012*.

62   Office XIII: AHPSe, Sección Protocolos [SP], 7764–7786 (from 1570 1st book to 1576 3rd book). Office XV: 9214–9308 (from 1577, 1st book 1 to 1599, 4th book).

63   The urban distribution of Seville's *escribanías* is a conundrum. They frequently changed location depending on the notary that held them. Other *escribanías* that are rich for studying the Flemish presence in Seville during the period are the offices number V, XII, XVI, and XXIV, as pointed by Crailsheim, *Spanish Connection*, 23–25.

TABLE 0.1   Types of notarial deeds

Type of deed	No.
Powers of attorney	1237
Promissory notes	1044
Receipts	618
Leasing contracts	132
Sale contracts	102
Liquidations (including arbitration)	96
Charter parties	75
Testaments and probate inventories	55
Dowry promises	23
Partnership and labour contracts	15
Other formal statements	283
Total	3680

SOURCE: AHPSE, SP, 7764–7786 AND 9214–9308

of imported timber as well, but not in the same scale. The more than 3500 deeds notarised by Francisco Díaz, and later Juan de Tordesillas, explains the decision to limit the focus on their office alone. This is further justified by the assumption that these *flamencos* of the *Atarazanas* developed a close professional and personal relationship with these *escribanos*, who performed a fundamental intermediation between them and the host society. The types of agreements and contracts these *flamencos* notarised were varied and complex. However, most deeds followed standardised formulas depending on the deed that was notarised, which facilitates the organisation of notarial deeds into different categories, shown in Table 0.1.

The total of 3680 documents allows three different levels of analysis. Firstly, it allows a complete study on the diverse socio-economic activities that were registered by the notaries; from dowry promises to payments. Secondly, it allows an examination of the web of relationships established between the individuals participating in those deeds; from the family ties the group developed to their contacts with the host society, including local and royal authorities, and contacts beyond Seville, along the Andalusian coast and Madrid. Finally, it allows to classify the naval provisions and complementary commodities exchanged between Andalusia and northern Europe, as well as complementary investments in Seville and the city's hinterland.

Other primary sources from Spanish archives complement the research. The collection of the two main Spanish general archives (*Archivo General de Simancas* and *Archivo General de Indias*) offered an interesting qualitative perspective on the relationship of *Atarazanas* merchants with high officials of the Habsburg state and the support of the local oligarchy.[64] Local archives also provided valuable information that complemented that of the notarial sources, and helped to reconstruct the lives of these merchants. The *Archivo de los Reales Alcázares* contained documents issued by the House of the King in Seville, which were important for studying how these merchants came to control the *Reales Atarazanas*. The *Archivo de la Parroquia del Sagrario* holds the registers of the cathedral parish, which were useful to trace their family networks. Unfortunately, the notarial archive of the province of Cádiz (*Archivo Histórico Provincial de Cádiz*), which would have contained sources for sixteenth-century Cádiz and Sanlúcar de Barrameda – the other two main ports of western Andalusia- proved unhelpful for this research due to the damaged state of the collection concerning this period.

Primary sources from north European archives were researched, too. The database developed by Catia Antunes on notarial deeds from the Amsterdam City Archive (*Stadsarchief Amsterdam*) constituted a valuable source for examining trade between Seville, Amsterdam and Norway in the last decade of the sixteenth century.[65] Finally, with the electronic database of the Sound Toll Registers Online (STRO), freely available online, the shipping networks that connected Andalusia with the Baltic region could be traced.[66] With these two collections, in short, this research covered these merchants' activities beyond Seville: in the North Sea and the Baltic and Scandinavian regions.

5   **Outline**

The systematic analysis of one of Seville's twenty-four *escribanías de numero*, complemented with qualitative and quantitative information from a

---

64   Especially the sections of Guerra y Marina [GyM] and Contaduría Mayor de Cuentas [CMC] at Archivo General de Simancas, and the sections of Indiferente General [Indiferente] and Contratacion at Archivo General de Indias.

65   Seventy-one charter parties of Baltic and Scandinavian timber to Andalusia formalised in the period from 1594 to 1599 in the notary of J. Fr. Bruyningh (GAA 63–83). I would like to thank Catia Antunes and Maria Bastiao for letting me use this valuable resource.

66   "Sound Toll Registers Online," accessed June 12, 2020. http://www.soundtoll.nl/index .php/en/.

heterogeneous corpus of primary sources in Spain and northern Europe, has permitted me to write a microhistory of a small group that, from Seville, operated on a global scale, from Danzig to Cartagena de Indias. This microhistory is divided into six chapters, each of them analysing different socio-economic strategies that explain how Flemish and German migrants came to dominate the trade of a strategic resource for the Spanish monarchy.

Chapter 1 begins with the application of the first embargo Philip II called against the rebel provinces of the Low Countries in 1574 in Andalusia. It explores how foreigners reacted to the predatory practices of the monarchy, as well as the converging and diverging interests between the monarchy and Seville's oligarchy. The chapter finally assesses the king's motivations to call these embargoes and eventually tolerate the commercial activity of the *flamencos*, even if it was widely known that their activity involved trading with enemy territories.

Chapter 2 deals with the migration to Seville. It examines the motivation of the city council to attract and protect these foreign merchants and how the group generated social capital to prompt cooperation and avoid external competition. The collaboration between these merchants and the council is examined through two processes, the renting of the *Atarazanas* complex from the 1550s, and the outsourcing of the local tax on timber sales in the 1580s and 1590s, which constituted the basis of the foreigners privileged position in the market.

Chapters 3 and 4 analyse the merchants' business organisation. The third chapter examines how family and commercial strategies intertwined through the analysis of testaments and promises of dowry, and the formation of new households. The chapter depicts the household as the basic commercial unit of the network, the family firm, exploring the composition of the firm and the relation between employers and employees through labour contracts. Furthermore, this chapter considers the extended use of forced-labour servants in the merchants' household.

Chapter 4 analyses strategies of commercial cooperation. It is divided into two parts. The first one establishes a typology of partnership solutions and reflects on why some of these partnerships were formalised in a notarial office while others were not. The second studies how merchants transferred agency through powers of attorney to structure their cooperation networks beyond Seville: on the Andalusian coast, the Low Countries, and the Americas.

Chapter 5 assesses the relation of Andalusia with northern European markets, focusing on the role of timber in the creation of a commercial axis between Seville and Amsterdam. In this chapter, Seville notarial deeds are complemented with Amsterdam notarial deeds and documents from the Sound Toll Registers. The chapter proposes an ambitious interpretation: that the commercial initiative in the trade of Baltic and Scandinavian timber originated in Andalusia.

Finally, Chapter 6 studies the supply of imported timber and other naval provisions to the ships of the *Carrera de Indias* and to the warships of the royal navy. On the one hand, the chapter analyses the contracting practices in the private supply to the ships preparing to sail to the Americas. On the other, the chapter explores the growing logistical importance of Andalusia for the royal navy through a dataset of receipts and promissory notes formalised by Seville's public notaries. This chapter examines how Seville transcended its role as a commercial entrepôt between Europe and the Spanish Americas to become a central node of Spain's naval power.

This comprehensive study of a group of thirty individuals seeks to shed new light on the question of how foreigners contributed to Seville's commercial and maritime apogee at the end of the sixteenth century. By answering this question, the book highlights the complexity of Spain's polycentric organisation, revealing how urban powers tolerated the presence and activity of foreigners, as well as the existence of open-access institutions that prompted participation in long-distance trade. These two factors ultimately reinforced the position of Seville and Andalusia in the Atlantic trade.

CHAPTER 1

War and Trade in Andalusia

In December 1574, Nicolás de Melemburque, a Flemish merchant residing in the *Atarazanas*, appeared before the acting royal deputy (*teniente de asistente*) of Seville, Rodrigo Velázquez. Accompanied by the notary Francisco Díaz, the merchant formalised a statement that described the precarious situation of the stock of quality masts in Seville and the two other main ports of Andalusia, Sanlúcar de Barrameda and Cádiz. If confiscations of north European ships were to continue, he argued, foreign shipmasters would not dare to bring timber, which was essential for the ships sailing to the Americas and the warships of the royal navy anchored in the region. He begged Philip II to put an end to the seizures. This "would be a very convenient thing for the service of His Majesty and the general benefit of these kingdoms," he concluded.[1] Nicolás de Melemburque travelled to Madrid with the notarial deed to address the king's council in person. Days later, the king issued a royal licence that permitted him, and anyone with whom he shared the royal document, to contract with any shipmaster the importation of timber from northern Europe to Andalusia and the exportation of salt in return.[2]

The licence granted to De Melemburque established an exception to the embargo that Philip II had decreed a year earlier, in January 1574, against the territories that had revolted against him in the Low Countries. This embargo marked the beginning of the Habsburg commercial war against the rebel provinces, which sought to prevent their economic rise and put an end to the presence of their allies, the English, in Spain. Despite this being the first of the three embargoes that the king ordered against his former subjects, it has passed almost unnoticed by historians, who at best have treated it as a mere anecdote from the beginning of the Eighty Years' War.[3]

---

1   The petition was notarised by the end of December but the exact day is blurry in the document. AHPSe, SP, 7779, 1365r.

2   We know about the licence through a secondary reference: a company charter De Melemburque signed with Juan Jacart, analysed later in the chapter. AHPSe, SP, 7780P, 281r.

3   Only López Martín studied these embargoes in his unpublished thesis on the Spanish commercial war against the Netherlands. The outcome of this research is disseminated in articles and chapters in collective books, "Embargo and Protectionist Policies: Early Modern Hispano-Dutch Relations in the western Mediterranean," *Mediterranean Studies* 7 (1998) or "Los 'unos' y los 'otros': Comercio, guerra e identidad," in *Banca, crédito y capital: La monarquía hispánica*

Yet, as this chapter argues, the embargo of 1574 had a decisive impact in Andalusia. It paradoxically represented a turning point in the trade with northern Europe, which began to rise precisely when Philip II attempted its prohibition. To understand this paradox, this chapter assumes that the king changed its strategy regarding the trade of imported naval provisions in Andalusia because of the influence of Seville's lobbying. The city's oligarchy and merchants strongly opposed the prohibition, as the commercial connection with northern Europe was key to maintaining Seville's predominant position in international trade.

The present chapter explains the monarchy's change of strategy adopting Fynn-Paul et al's theoretical model. According to it, the monarchy transitioned from a strategy that subverted the market with indiscriminate confiscations to supply the royal navy to another that sought to collaborate with the main actors of the market, the *flamencos* of the *Atarazanas*, to ensure the stock of timber in the region. The first section revisits Philip II's embargoes against the Dutch and, in general, his commercial policies in a war context. The second focuses on the application of the first embargo upon north European trade in Andalusia, analysing how foreign shipmasters and *flamencos* in Seville reacted to the monarchy's predatory practices. The third studies the petition that Nicolás de Melemburque raised to Philip II and the subsequent license to address the monarchy's motivation to permit a commercial activity that, in theory, had been banned. The final section examines the role of Seville's oligarchy intermediating between the king and the *flamencos* residing in the city to consolidate the presence of the north European merchant community in the south of the Iberian Peninsula.

1   Philip II's Embargoes: More than Commercial War

Embargoes were neither a new solution in Castile or exclusively used against the Dutch Republic. The monarchy implemented similar forms of commercial war to fight England, and so did England in return. Philip II, for instance, called for an embargo upon the English in 1563, as a response to Elisabeth I's ban on importations and exportations with the Low Countries.[4] The Dutch

---

y los antiguos países bajos (1505–1700), eds. Carmen Sanz Ayán and Bernardo José García (Madrid: Fundación Carlos de Amberes, 2006), 425–458.

4   Years later, in 1568, the king called another embargo after the English intercepted several Spanish vessels with funds for the supply of an armada in Flanders. Gómez-Centurión Jiménez, *Felipe II*, 51–55.

widely resorted to this form of war, too. William of Orange prohibited trade with the Spaniards for the first time in 1578, even before the formal foundation of the Dutch Republic after the confederation of the rebel provinces in 1581.[5] Nevertheless, none of these provoked a historiographical controversy like the heated, yet short-lived, one initiated by Jonathan Israel on the significance of Spanish embargoes upon the Dutch. He concluded that the underestimation of their relevance to the development of the Eighty Years' War and of the initial steps of the Dutch Republic was "one of the great errors of modern historiography."[6]

Israel's claims did not attract many historians, not even in Spanish or Dutch historiographies, with the notable exception of López Martín and his unpublished dissertation.[7] However, Israel's concern seems still relevant: if embargoes were of no use for the monarchy to fight the Dutch, why did Philip II repeatedly resort to them in 1574–1579, 1585–1590 and 1595–1596? The question, indeed, calls for a reconsideration of the Spanish embargoes upon the Dutch that the present chapter aims to readdress, adopting a different approach to that of Israel. First, it does not assess the consequences of the embargo for the international conflict or for the emergence of the young Republic, but rather for Andalusia, where most confiscations were enforced. Perhaps the consequences of the Spanish embargoes were barely noticed in the Dutch Republic, as the Braudelian view argued, but the prohibition of importing North European commodities surely disrupted trade in Andalusia. Secondly, embargoes did not merely seek to hinder the rebels' economy. With the seizures occurring in the context of the embargoes, the monarchy obtained

---

5   Gómez-Centurión Jiménez, *Felipe II*, 209–210.

6   Jonathan I. Israel, *Empires and Entrepots: The Dutch, the Spanish Monarchy, and the Jews, 1585–1713* (London: Hambledon Press, 1990), 191. Israel published a translated version of this paper in Spanish "España: los embargos españoles y la lucha por el dominio del comercio mundial 1585–1648," *Revista de historia naval* 6, no 23 (1988): 89–106. Besides Braudel, Israel notes a long list of authors belonging to this "Braudelian view," including Henry Kamen, *Spain, 1469–1714: A Society of Conflict* (London: Longman, 1983) and the Spanish authors José Alcalá-Zamora Queipo de Llano, *España, Flandes y el Mar del Norte (1618–1639): La última ofensiva europea de los Austrias madrileños* (Barcelona: Planeta, 1975) and Gómez-Centurión Jiménez, *Felipe II*.

7   See footnote 3. Glete also contributed to the debate, although dealing with a later period, comparing an alleged Spanish failure to the efficiency of the Dutch response – the *handel op den vijand* (trade with the enemy) policy,– in *Warfare at sea*, 166. José Javier Ruiz Ibáñez explored the question in "*Bellum omnium contra omnes*: Las posibilidades y contradicciones de la guerra económica por parte de la Monarquía Hispánica en la década de 1590," *Studia historica. Historia moderna*, no. 27 (2005): 85–109.

naval supplies and ships for the preparation of armadas to fight the rebels in the English Channel.

In essence, an embargo was a prohibition of trade with a specific territory, generally for an indefinite period of time, which often carried along a set of practices that went beyond the commercial prohibition.[8] The complexity of an embargo is finely illustrated in the definition that appears in the dictionary of the Royal Spanish Academy published in 1732:

> Seizure and detention of goods and properties done by order of competent judge. (...) The embargo impedes and hampers the free use of goods and, in some way, detains them and stops them.[9]

In today's Spanish, the noun "embargo" remains a polysemic word: it can mean a prohibition on trade as well as the detention of goods by order of a competent authority.[10] Embargoes became a recurrent measure in sixteenth-century Castile while preparing military enterprises, at a time when military forces were not permanent and the demand of resources for warfare was on the rise. López Martín noted that Castile even *embargoed* its own subjects in the first half of the sixteenth century; the monarchy seized merchant vessels of Andalusian and Biscayne subjects and adapted them for warfare in the Castilian navy, although compensating shipowners.[11] As such, embargoes should be understood as an obligatory service to the ruler rather than a commercial prohibition, and it would be wrong to assume the nature of the embargo only in terms of a protectionist policy.[12]

---

8   According to the Oxford dictionary, the term embargo has evolved from "an order of a state forbidding foreign ships to enter, or any ships to leave, its ports' to 'official ban on trade or other commercial activity with a particular country." "Embargo," Lexico, Oxford University, accessed June 12, 2020. https://www.lexico.com/definition/embargo.

9   "Embargo," *Diccionario de la lengua castellana (1732)*, t. III, p. 382, Nuevo Tesoro Lexicográfico de la Lengua Española, Real Academia Española, accessed January 2, 2020. http://ntlle.rae .es/ A century earlier, in the first monolingual Spanish dictionary, Covarrubias defined the verb *embargar* as "to detain, to impede, especially with an order of a competent judge." "Embargar" Covarrubias, *Tesoro de la lengua castellana o española*, 341. Nuevo Tesoro Lexicográfico de la Lengua Española, Real Academia Española, accessed June 12, 2020 http://ntlle.rae.es/.

10 "Embargo," *Diccionario de la Lengua Española* (2018), Diccionario de la Lengua Española, Real Academia Española, accessed June 12, 2020 https://dle.rae.es/embargo.

11 Lopez Martín "Embargo and Protectionist Policies," 196.

12 The first truly protectionist measure with regards to international trade occurred in the reign of Philip III. The king decreed the *Decreto Gauna* in 1603, which allowed foreign merchants – even the Dutch – to trade in the Iberian Peninsula and the Spanish Low Countries under hard conditions. This included a 30% *ad valorem* tax on exported commodities. Miguel Ángel Echevarría Bacigalupe, "Un episodio en la guerra económica

2   Subversion of the Market

An embargo was a fast way for the armadas to obtain ships suited for Atlantic seas as well as naval provisions to prepare merchant vessels for warfare. Therefore, it is no coincidence that the embargo Philip II called in 1574 coincided with a moment in which the Atlantic naval force of the king was unprepared to face the escalation of war in the Low Countries.[13] In 1572, the coast of the Low Countries became a main scenario of the conflict after the Sea Beggars (*watergeuzen*) took control of important places, namely Den Briel and Vlissingen.[14] The enemy's strong position on the coast was a major preoccupation for Luis de Requesens, the recently appointed governor of the Low Countries, who replaced Fernando Álvarez de Toledo y Pimentel, the Duke of Alva, in November 1573. From Brussels, Requesens arose as the principal advocate of a plan to fight the rebels at sea, a position widely supported by a faction of the Madrid court. His letters encouraged Philip II to take a proactive approach in regaining control of the Channel.

One of Luis de Requesens's first measures as governor of the Low Countries was to send an embassy to the king of Denmark and several Hanseatic towns seeking to forge an alliance against the Dutch. He did not succeed.[15] Later, in January 1574, Requesens had to improvise an attack with poorly prepared ships from Bergen op Zoom and Antwerp to assist Middelburg, the other key to Zeeland, which had been suffering a siege from the Sea Beggars since 1572.[16] Without an adequate naval support from Spain, the enterprise

---

hispano-holandesa: El Decreto Gauna (1603)," *Hispania: Revista española de historia* 46, no. 162 (1986): 57–98; Juan Eloy Gelabert González, "Guerra y coyuntura fiscal: El embargo general de 1598," in *IX Congreso de la Asociación española de Historia Económica, Murcia* (2008); Ángel Alloza Aparicio, "Guerra económica y proteccionismo en la Europa del siglo XVII: El decreto de Gauna a la luz de los documentos contables," *Tiempos modernos: Revista Electrónica de Historia Moderna* 7, no. 24 (2012): 1–34. Roland Baetens, "The Organization and Effects of Flemish Privateering in the Seventeenth Century," *Acta Historiae Neerlandicae* IX (1976), 48–75.

13   Ignacio López Martín, "Entre la guerra económica y la persuasión diplomática: el comercio mediterráneo como moneda de cambio en el conflicto hispano-neerlandés (1574–1609)," *Cahiers de la Méditerranée* 71 (2005): 39.

14   On the reaction in Madrid, Gómez-Centurión Jiménez, *Felipe II*, 54–55. On the economic effects of the beginning of the war in the economic rise of the Netherlands, Jan de Vries and Ad van der Woude. *The First Modern Economy: Success, Failure and Perseverance of the Dutch Economy, 1500–1815* (Cambridge: Cambridge University Press, 1997), 365.

15   Carlos Gómez-Centurión Jiménez elaborated more on the diplomatic relations of the Hanseatic towns with the Habsburg monarchy in the article "Las relaciones hispano-hanseáticas durante el reinado de Felipe II," *Revista de historia naval*, no. 15 (1986): 65–84.

16   Gómez-Centurión Jiménez, *Felipe II*, 113–117.

failed. Impatient for an operational navy in the Low Countries, Requesens urged the king to seize rebel ships in Castilian ports in order to organise an armada to fight in the Low Countries. The plan of Requesens was clear and it is finely described in a letter written by one of his advisors, Philip of Noircarmes:

> Because many properly armed ships have departed from Emden and Enkhuizen to Calis, Sant Lucar, Lisbona, San Vas (sic) and Spain, and among them there are two [ships] from Hamburg, very well prepared, His Majesty could embargo them and put sailors, some artillery and soldiers [in them] to enter in these lands, so that the rebels would grow a great fear and his Majesty would greatly strengthen [his position]. Otherwise, the enemies would strengthen [theirs] with the merchandise that they send to Spain and [they] will be able to easily sustain their wars.[17]

Following his advice, Philip II ordered the organisation of a navy that, to the despair of the governor, never set sail for the Low Countries. The fleet was assembled in Santander under the command of Pedro Menéndez de Avilés, but new problems with the Ottomans required the Habsburg military attention, delaying its departure. The fleet was finally dismissed after an outbreak of pests at the end of 1574.[18]

On January 23 1574, to assemble this fleet, the king had issued a *Cédula Real* (royal decree) of general embargo on any ship anchored in Castilian ports suspected to have stopped in the rebel territories regardless of its actual origin.[19] In a few days, the embargo was put in motion in the main ports of Andalusia. Sanlúcar de Barrameda, the town in the mouth of the Guadalquivir where the House of Medina Sidonia ruled, became the port where seizures were most strongly implemented. Even though the Duke of Medina Sidonia was not an explicit advocate of the commercial war, given that Sanlúcar greatly benefited from the presence of an emerging Flemish community, he cooperated any time Philip II ordered an embargo in the territories under his jurisdiction. Not for nothing, his collaboration went parallel to his ascent in the Spanish military apparatus, which culminated in 1588, when he was appointed captain-general of the Ocean and the Coasts of Andalusia (*Capitán General del Mar Océano y Costas de Andalucía*).[20]

---

17 AGS, Estado, 554, f. 176, transcribed in Gómez-Centurión Jiménez, *Felipe II*, 152.
18 The incapacity to find a viable maritime route during these first years of the war led to the rise of the known as *el Camino español* (the Spanish Road). Geoffrey Parker, *The Army of Flanders and the Spanish Road, 1567–1659: The Logistics of Spanish Victory and Defeat in the Low Countries' Wars* (London: Cambridge University Press, 1972).
19 Gómez-Centurión Jiménez, *Felipe II*, 150–153.
20 Salas Almela, *Colaboración y conflicto*, and "Un cargo para el Duque de Medina Sidonia."

López Martín transcribed the letter that Philip II sent to his deputies (*corregidores*) in the town of Sanlúcar, instructing them on how to undertake the confiscations:

> We order you that, if any ship from the abovementioned parts [rebel ports] come or came with merchandises or other things to the port of that town [Sanlúcar de Barrameda], you shall have it confiscated and detained effectively with the people and the merchandises and the rest that they bring. And you shall do it with convenient dissimulation and secrecy. And you shall not release any of the said people or a thing of theirs until you have informed us about what [ships] has been seized and detained, and the tonnage and the quality of them, and about the merchandises, the people and the rest of things that had come in them.[21]

Sanlúcar's *corregidores* responded to this letter with a detailed explanation of how they proceeded. According to the report, they had embarked in six long boats around midnight ("three hours after night") and detained twenty-eight northern hulks anchored in the mouth of the Guadalquivir.[22] In these first days, 37 vessels were confiscated in Sanlúcar, 15 in Cádiz, and 13 in Seville. The seizures repeated in the following months, although with less intensity; five vessels were detained in Cádiz in May 10, and a total of nine suspected ships were investigated in Sanlúcar between May 22 and June 8. None of the masters affected by the seizures came from a rebel port, nor was there evidence of them stopping in those ports besides the reports sent by Requesens and other officials posted in the Low Countries. When royal officials broke into the properties of influential Flemings in Sanlúcar on February 28 1574, they found fifteen shipmasters, one pilot and seven merchants: eleven were from Emden, 3 from Amsterdam, 2 from Lübeck, 2 from Norden, 1 from Antwerp, 1 from Bremen, 1 from Elsinore, and 1 from Monnickendam. The detained northerners found the support of their compatriots in the region, who often paid bail bonds to release them from jail, although with the obligation of staying within the city limits. By

---

21   This transcription is taken from López Martín, "Entre la guerra económica y la persuasión diplomática," 7, which refers to AGS, Medina Sidonia, 74, f. 63. The reference does not correspond to the nomenclature of the *Archivo General de Simancas*, and the document probably belongs to the *Estado* collection.

22   A detailed account of the event can be found in AGS, Medina Sidonia, 84 (probably AGS, Estado, 84), transcribed by López Martín, "Entre la guerra económica y la persuasión diplomática," 8.

contrast, sailors remained in jail, as royal officials did not believe crew members were trustworthy enough to be freed.[23]

Unfortunately, there is not enough information on how royal officials used the confiscated ships and the commodities they carried. A report made on the ships that had been embargoed to join the navy at Santander stated that only three of the ships were north European hulks; the majority of the armada was formed by ships of Spanish and Portuguese owners who had signed an *asiento* with the monarchy to compensate the seizure of their vessel.[24] Very probably, nonetheless, royal officials did not confiscate the vessels, only the timber and naval provisions they had transported to Andalusia for the preparation of the American fleets. Even if the connection between confiscations in Andalusia and the armada of Santander is imprecise, the correlation between both events is perfectly clear, revealing the real motive behind the embargo of 1574: the appropriation of naval resources to prepare an armada to fight in the Low Countries.

The events of 1574 demonstrate that royal commissaries could rapidly seize dozens of ships in few days. However, detentions and confiscations were applied indiscriminately to any northern ship regardless of the origin of the shipmasters, the crew or the cargo. That indiscriminate application was prompted by the vagueness of the monarchy's plan of action, which even resulted in a comical situation where officials asked Madrid to clarify whether certain towns like Emden or Hamburg were rebel or not.[25] The ambiguity of the plan of action, in the end, favoured the connivance of authorities with the activity of northerners in Andalusia, to the despair of those in Madrid advocating for a stricter application of the embargo. In June 1574, Juan de Isunza, the royal chaplain, complained to the king in the following terms:

> [Shipmasters] said they came from Emden. And they [officials] were contented by that. If they [officials] knew well what Emden is, they would not allow themselves to be fooled.[26]

---

23   López Martín, "Embargo and Protectionist Policies," 202.
24   A complete report can be found in AGS, CMC, 2EP, 576. For the failed organisation of this *armada*, Magdalena Pi Corrales, Magdalena, *'La Otra Invencible' 1574: España y las potencias nórdicas* (Madrid: San Martín, 1983).
25   AGS, GyM, 78, ff. 121, 151 and 167, reported in Gómez-Centurión Jiménez, *Felipe II*, 154.
26   Isunza a Requeséns, 19-VI-1574, AGS, Estado. 558, f.75, in Gómez-Centurión Jiménez, *Felipe II*, 154.

The words of De Isunza show the frustration of part of the king's counsel-lors: the embargoes against the rebel territories benefited adjacent ports in northern Germany, which attracted a great deal of the Flemish and Dutch trade with the Iberian Peninsula. At the same time, the Spanish presence was in a clear decline in the route between the Peninsula and northern Europe, which they used to dominate.[27] The position of the supporters of a hard embargo, like De Isunza, in favour of seizing any northern ship in Spain, directly con-fronted that of the political and commercial elite of Seville. The city depended on the activity of foreigners to consolidate a connection with northern Europe that ensured the importation of naval provisions and other appreciated North European commodities, such as Flemish textiles.[28] Although the embargo of 1574 proved the capacity of the monarchy to effectively stop trade between Castile and the Low Countries, the effects of the commercial war in Andalusia soon became a headache for Philip II.

2.1   Claiming for Compensations

The Flemish and German community in Seville responded quickly to the first set of confications, appointing a legal representation to defend their interests and that of the affected shipmasters. In August 1574, acting as majordomos of "the Flemish nation of the city of Seville," the *Atarazanas* merchants Francisco Bernal and Miguel Arbauts commissioned Guillermo Pérez, a Spanish resident in Seville, to act on behalf of the nation in any lawsuit or business in Seville or at any royal council in Madrid.[29] When confiscations repeated in 1575, Flemish merchants in Seville organised a more ambitious legal defence to support the shipmasters individually.

In the summer of 1575, twenty-three German shipmasters went to the notary office of Francisco Díaz and granted powers of attorney to a number of Flemish residents in Andalusia to claim compensations for the time royal authorities

---

27   Israel, *Empires and Entrepots*. Casado Alonso, "Las colonias de mercaderes castellanos."

28   Ulloa, "Unas notas sobre el comercio." Henri Lapeyre, *El comercio exterior de Castilla a través de las Aduanas de Felipe II* (Valladolid: Universidad de Valladolid, 1981). I analysed the commodities imported by Flemish migrants in Seville in Jiménez Montes, "Sevilla, puerto y puerta de Europa: La actividad de una compañía comercial flamenca en la segunda mitad del siglo XVI," *Studia historica. Historia moderna* 38, no. 2 (2016): 353–386. A recent contribution in English on the Flemish commercial activity in northern Spain is Janna Everaert, "A Trail of Trials. A 'Flemish' Merchant Community in Sixteenth-century Valladolid and Medina del Campo," *TSEG/ Low Countries Journal of Social and Economic History* 14 no. 1 (2017) 5–35.

29   This constitutes the first evidence that we have of the nation, as a collective, delegating political action. AHPSe, SP, 7778, 1013v.

had confiscated their ships.[30] The deeds speak of a total of 28 confiscated ships, although only 23 shipmasters appeared in the notary of Francisco Díaz; this could mean that the other five were still detained or that they notarised the power of attorney in another office in Seville, or perhaps Sanlúcar de Barrameda. On its own, each one of these powers of attorney is scant in information; they do not reveal important aspects of these seizures, such as the specific date when they happened, for how long the ships were confiscated, or the compensation that shipmasters expected to receive. However, when analysed together, they provide an interesting overview about key aspects in the application of royal embargoes and the easy access of foreigners to royal justice in Andalusia.

Once they identify themselves in the contract, declaring their names, nationalities and names of the ships, the 23 shipmasters made an identical statement: That their ship was …

> … [O]ne of the twenty-eight hulks that were seized in Sanlúcar de Barrameda by order and mandate of the illustrious mister *factor* Francisco Duarte, on behalf and commission of His Majesty.[31]

The 23 shipmasters whose ships have been confiscated were granting the merchants in Seville the right to act on their behalf to …

> [A]sk, claim, receive and have and collect in court or outside court, from the illustrious mister *factor* Francisco Duarte, on behalf and commission of His Majesty, or any of his collectors, treasurers or payers (…) the compensation entitled for our hulks, and every of them, because us and every one of us as their masters, must have it as it has been ordered to be given and paid for the time (…) they have been confiscated and detained.[32]

All of them recognised Francisco Duarte as the debtor of the shipmasters. In doing so, they were actually pointing to the king as responsible of the embargo. It was Duarte, acting on behalf of the king, who should pay the compensation for their losses. As *factor* of the *Casa de la Contratación* (House of Trade), Duarte was the top official of the royal institution that ruled over the *Carrera de Indias* and, therefore, one of Philip II's important men in Seville. As this case shows, Duarte's responsibilities were not limited to American affairs and he acted as purveyor of the royal navy until it developed its own administration

---

30   POAs are found in AHPSe, SP, 7781, 637r-991r.
31   AHPSe, SP, 7781, 637r-991r.
32   AHPSe, SP, 7781P, 637r.

in Andalusia in the following decade.[33] In short, by 1575, he was responsible for ensuring the existence of a proper stock of naval supplies for the ships preparing to sail to the Americas, and if necessary, for the king's navy.[34]

Despite his role in the confiscations, Duarte stood as one of the main advocates of the Flemish in Madrid, and an indispensable actor in the ascent of those residing in the *Atarazanas* within the state's naval apparatus. This suggests that, very probably, no one was more concerned about the importance of effectively compensating those confiscations than Duarte himself. In fact, compensations must have been duly paid because these claims left no further trace in notarial sources.

The deeds are also particularly interesting because they give a full description of shipmasters, as well as their attorneys, since it was common practice in any notarial procedure to describe each party with the name, surname, place of origin, profession and – in this case – the name of the ship (generally a hulk), as Table 1.1 illustrates.

All masters in Table 1.1 came from non-rebel ports of the Jutland peninsula (Hamburg, Lübeck, Rostock, Sønderborg, and Stade). The overwhelming presence of Hanseatics on the Andalusian coast by 1575 is not surprising. It accurately reflects the flow of shipmasters and traders out of the rebel ports of the Low Countries to safer and more tranquil places once the war reached the English Channel, and the consequent rise of Hanseatic shipping in the Iberian Peninsula.[35] Since they were not coming from rebel territories, their activity in Andalusia was in theory legal, yet their ships had been seized, proving that the interest of royal officials was not to detain those trading with the enemy but to seize all possible northern hulks to respond to the demands of provisions for the royal navy. Confiscations, in short, did not seem to imply a form of punishment. It was rather a sort of forced service to the monarchy via the

---

33   Chapter 6 contains an overview of his career within the Habsburg's bureaucratic apparatus.

34   Carmen Mena García, "La Casa de la Contratación de Sevilla y el abasto de las flotas de Indias," in *La Casa de la Contratación y la navegación entre España y las Indias*, eds. Enriqueta Vila Vilar et al (Sevilla: CSIC and Universidad de Sevilla, 2004), 250.

35   Oscar Gelderblom, *Cities of Commerce: The Institutional Foundations of International Trade in the Low Countries, 1250–1650* (Princeton: Princeton University Press, 2013), 32–33. Jonathan I. Israel, *Dutch Primacy in World Trade, 1585–1740* (Oxford: Clarendon Press, 1989) 28–29. For a more focused study on Lübeck and Hamburg as destination, see Hermann Kellenbenz, *Unternehmerkräfte Im Hamburger, Portugal- und Spanienhandel, 1590–1625* (Hamburg: Verlag Der Hamburgischen Bücherei, 1954); and Pierre Jeannin, "Le commerce de Lubeck aux environs de 1580," *Annales. Économies, Sociétés, Civilisations* 16, no. 1 (1961): 36–65.

TABLE 1.1   Powers of attorney granted by north European shipmasters to Flemish and German merchants residing in Seville (summer of 1575)

Shipmaster	Name of the hulk	Origin	Attorney	Date
Enrique Estulcman	El Salvaje	Lübeck	Enrirque Aparte	21 Jul
Hans van Minden/ Mynsen	El Ciervo Colorado	Lübeck	Enrirque Aparte	21 Jul
			Gaspar Loscarte	3 Aug
Hans Casten	La Barca de Rustique	Rostock	Enrirque Aparte	21 Jul
Gregorio Tribol	El Grifo	Stade	Enrirque Aparte	21 Jul
			Gaspar Loscarte	11 Aug
Diriq Termuyl	San Miguel	Hamburg	Carlos Malapert	5 Aug
Jorge Matenes	urca El Cisne	Sønderborg	Carlos Malapert	5 Aug
Jochim Elstorp	urca La Fortuna	Hamburg	Carlos Malapert	5 Aug
Hanes Smit	urca El Moruno	Hamburg	Carlos Malapert	5 Aug
Jorge van Bergue	urca El David	Hamburg	Carlos Malapert	5 Aug
Hernan Baquer	urca El Ciervo	Hamburg	Carlos Malapert	5 Aug
Hernan Ditmers	urca El Jonás	Hamburg	Carlos Malapert	5 Aug
Giraldo Ubester Ebola	urca El Muysen	Copenhagen	Carlos Malapert	5 Aug
Joacham Har	urca Ángel	Hamburg	Juan Eberlin	5 Aug
Miguel Siriques	urca El Ángel	Lübeck	Gaspar Loscarte	3 Aug
Hanes Losque	urca El Daniel	Lübeck	Nicolás de la Piedra	4 Aug
Hanes Covre	urca El Pelícano	Lübeck	Nicolás de la Piedra	4 Aug
Gert Simons	El Negro Flamenco	Lübeck	Christobal Osten	4 Aug
Joos Escuneman*	urca San Juan	Hamburg	Gaspar Loscarte	3 Aug
Hans Casten	urca La Barca de Rustique	Rostock	Gaspar Loscarte	3 Aug
Pedro Viles	urca El Falcón/ León Pardo	Hamburg	Gaspar Loscarte	3 Aug
Pedro Leo	urca El Salmón	Sønderborg	Gaspar Loscarte	3 Aug
Enrique Estulcman	urca El Salvaje	Lübeck	Gaspar Loscarte	3 Aug
Joos Escuneman*	urca El Salvaje	Hamburg	Gaspar Loscarte	3 Jul

Note: Asterisk indicates they are different individuals despite their names; different ship names

SOURCE: AHPSE, SP, 7781, 637R-991R

intermediation of the *factor* of the *Casa de la Contratación*, who had taken the ships and would eventually compensate the shipmasters. The poor state of the royal treasury in 1574 was certainly a reason for resorting to predatory practices to obtain strategic resources for the royal navy. In fact, Philip II declared a suspension of payments in September 1575, the second during his reign.[36] The confiscations had been a solution during a specific moment of shortage due to the preparation of an armada in Santander to fight in the Low Countries, but this supply strategy was barely sustainable in the long term.

2.2   *The Seville-Sanlúcar Axis*

It is significant that 23 of the 28 powers of attorney were formalised in a notary of Seville, even though the confiscations had occurred on the coast, in Sanlúcar de Barrameda. The merchants who acted as attorneys of the shipmasters resided in the *Atarazanas*, like Enrique Aparte, or had resided in the *Atarazanas* until very recently, like Gaspar Loscarte and Carlos Malapert, whose move to Sanlúcar coincided with the beginning of the commercial war and the confiscations..[37] The notarial deeds do not explicitly reveal the reasons for their relocation, although the course of events indicate that it coincided with increasing royal hostilities towards the activity of North Europeans on the Andalusian coast. This might have motivated senior merchants residing in Seville, like Francisco Bernal or Enrique Aparte, to establish junior agents as proxies in Sanlúcar de Barrameda, seeking to be close to the headquarters of the Duke of Medina Sidonia, whose influence at Madrid's court was rising, and to organise their activity in a port with a central position for Seville's trade, in the mouth of the Guadalquivir River.

In his first years in the Iberian Peninsula, Carlos Malapert started working as proxy to his uncles Antonio, Nicolás and Luis Malapert, who lived in Antwerp.[38] He married Margarita Bambel, a grand-daughter of Francisco Bernal, in February 1570.[39] Finally, in 1573, he settled down in Sanlúcar, where

---

36   Carlos Álvarez Nogal, "Los bancos públicos de Castilla y el decreto de 1575," *Cuadernos de Historia Moderna* 42, no. 2 (2017): 527–551. In English, Carlos Álvarez Nogal and Christopher Chamley, "Philip II against the Cortes and the Credit Freeze of 1575-1577," *Revista de Historia Económica - Journal of Iberian and Latin American Economic History* 34, no. 3 (2016): 351–382.

37   Carlos Malapert appears as *vecino* of Sevilla in September 1572 (AHPSe, SP, 7773, 88r), and in January 1575 as *vecino* of Sanlúcar (AHPSe, SP, 7780, 230r). Gaspar Loscarte, in February 1573, appeared indistinctly as *vecino* of Sevilla and *vecino* of Sanlúcar (AHPSe, SP, 7774, 319r and 490r).

38   The liquidation of their accounts is found in AHPSe, SP, 7768, 563r (March 1571).

39   APSC, Registros Matrimoniales, años 1565–1598, sin foliar (s.f.).

he became a central actor of the Flemish community in the region, along with Loscarte, Juan Bambel (grandson of Francisco Bernal and his brother-in-law), Martin Búcar (brother-in-law of Enrique Aparte), Juan Yansen and Nicolás de la Piedra. The story of Gaspar Loscarte is more successful. He became the son-in-law of Enrique Aparte, after marrying María Aparte in the cathedral of Seville in December 1565.[40] The young couple lived in the *Atarazanas* until at least 1573, when the notarial deeds begin to identify Loscarte as resident in Sanlúcar. A year later, in the aftermath of the 1574 embargo, he represented the Flemish nation as consul and his political career took off, becoming a close collaborator of the Duke of Medina Sidonia. By 1578 he had been appointed alderman (*regidor*) of the town.[41] The experiences of Malapert and Loscarte are a good example on how the commercial war positively affected the emerging Flemish community in Andalusia, and particularly those that traded in naval provisions, who reinforced their position on the coast, especially in Sanlúcar de Barrameda.

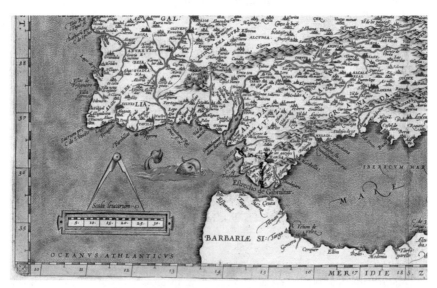

ILLUSTRATION 1.1   Gulf of Cadiz and mouth of Guadalquivir River. Section of the Map of the Iberian Peninsula. Abraham Ortelius, *Regni Hispaniae Post Omnium Editiones Locupletissima Descriptio*, 1570, map, Biblioteca Nacional de España, Madrid. http://bdh.bne.es/bnesearch/detalle/bdh0000021069

40   APSC, Registros Matrimoniales, años 1565–1598, s.f.
41   López Martín, "Entre la guerra económica y la persuasión diplomática," 8. We also learn about his position as alderman from several notarial deeds; the first dating from 1578, AHPSe, SP, 9218, 179v.

3   State's Collaboration with the Market

The application of the embargo against the enemies of the king in 1574 did not follow a clear plan of action. The indiscriminate confiscations were the result of negotiations, pressures and conflicting interests. On the one hand, the king and some of his counsellors in Madrid and Brussels demanded a harder application of the embargo. On the other, royal officials based in Andalusia and Seville's oligarchy demanded the toleration of the trade with northern Europe, essential for the preparation of the fleets of the *Carrera*. Finally, foreign shipmasters saw their activity threatened, and so did the Flemish and German merchants in Seville that traded with them.

If the embargo remained, why would North European shipmasters risk arriving in Andalusia? If they stopped arriving, how could Andalusia ensure the departure of the American fleets? This was the opinion of Nicolás de Melemburque, a Flemish merchant residing in the *Atarazanas*, who in December 1574 notarised a public statement – known as *probanza* – in the presence of Rodrigo Velázquez, representative of the king in Seville. De Melemburque's *probanza* consisted of two parts. The first was a report that denounced the urgent shortage of naval provisions in Andalusia, and reminded the need to import them from outside Castile. The second was an interrogation of seven Spanish ship captains of the *Carrera de Indias*, who corroborated the information presented in the report. The *probanza* began with the following declaration:

> Niculás de Melenburque, Flemish merchant resident in this city of Seville, I say that it is in my interest to make an inquiry by interrogating witnesses about the great need there is in this city [Seville] and in Sanlúcar and in Cádiz and the other ports of this Andalusia, of trees for masts and yards for ocean-going vessels [*navíos de alto bordo*] as well as galleys, and on the necessity of bringing them from Flanders and other parts outside these kingdoms, and why without these trees the vessels and armies of His Majesty and His galleys cannot be equipped nor can they navigate; for presently there are none [trees] in the whole coast and inevitably the Galleys of Spain must come [in] for wintering, and they strongly need trees and spars.[42]

Melemburque's lack of precision when referring to the different fleets of the royal navy, the ships of the *Carrera* or the needed timber supplies is a common

---

42   AHPSe, SP, 7779, 1365r.

practice in notarial documents. Yet Melemburque's words are sufficiently accurate to comprehend the poor state of naval provisions in the region, which had to be imported; indeed, as noted by intellectuals and officials of the time, Andalusia's forestry resources were not good enough to produce large quality pieces of timber, such as masts or bare trees, for ocean-going ships.[43] Similarly, the text is vague when referring to the territories from which timber had to be imported, "Flanders" or "other parts". This should not be understood as an attempt to hide a possible connection with rebel provinces, but the result of the ambiguous rhetoric of notarial documents. This is especially true during this first stage of the war, when Amsterdam – already an important entrepôt for Baltic and Scandinavian commodities – remained loyal to the Habsburgs.[44] Despite the ambivalence, the text clearly reveals the role of the Low Countries as a main market for re-exportation, and the predominant position of Flemish and Dutch commercial networks in the trade of Baltic and Scandinavian goods in Andalusia since the early 1570s. This, as noted before, had become a main concern for the king and his counsellors, frustrated by the decreasing presence of Spaniards in the route between the Iberian Peninsula and the Low Countries.

Nicolás de Melemburque then elaborated on the causes of the shortage of naval resources, for which the seizures of the previous year were to be blamed:

> And the cause of why the said trees are not brought, besides the war of Flanders, is for having seized during this year all the hulks coming to Sanlúcar and Cádiz. And with the fear of not (sic) being seized there is not any ship willing to come to Andalusia with the said trees or any other thing.[45]

Finally, De Melemburque advised that:

> [I]n order to abundantly bring the said trees for ensuring the convenient care of the galleys and armadas of His Majesties and the fleets sailing to the Indies, it would be a very convenient thing for the service of His Majesty and the general benefit of these kingdoms to instruct [the king's commissaries] that the hulks and vessels bringing to the ports of this Andalusia

---

43   Gervasio de Artíñano y Galdácano, *La arquitectura naval española (en madera): Bosquejo de sus condiciones y rasgos de su evolución* (Barcelona: Oliva de Vilanova, 1920), 68.
44   Israel, *Dutch primacy*; De Vries and Van der Woude, *The First Modern Economy*.
45   AHPSe, SP, 7779, 1365r.

the said trees and timber can not be seized, allowing them to ship salt and other things and to return freely and to navigate to their land.[46]

The merchant made no reference to the origin of the shipmasters or their cargo, which were relevant aspects for those in Madrid arguing for the convenience of maintaining the embargo. On the contrary, Nicolás de Melemburque based his argument on a rather practical question: the necessity of ensuring the arrival of northern trees. According to him, permitting hulks to bring in naval provisions and allowing them to ship back salt was in the interest of Philip II to maintain his naval power. With the tone of a servile servant, he shows a great knowledge about the state of the trade with northern Europe, from the lack of stock of imported supplies to the reluctance of northern captains to continue their activity.

Seven ship captains of the *Carrera de Indias* supported his report: Christóbal Belmonte, Bernardo de Andino, Gonzalo Montebernardo, Manuel Díaz, Diego de Luna, Salvador Hernández and a captain named Julio whose surname appears blurred on the document.[47] They were asked seven questions based on Melemburque's previous declaration, addressing aspects such as the state of the stock of quality timber, the necessity of importing extra-peninsular naval stores, and about Melemburque's reputation. The captains' interventions were limited to corroborating the information provided in the questions, demonstrating that Melemburque's commercial activity and opinion was notably valued in the circles of the *Carrera de Indias*.

Questions four and five addressed the importance of Nicolás de Melemburque in the supply to the royal navy. In the fourth question, for instance, he was presented as an assimilated foreigner, with a long tradition of providing the royal navy with north European timber. The captains were asked if they knew that:

> [T]he said Niculás de Melenburque is *vecino* of the city of Seville and is married with a daughter of *naturals* of these kingdoms; and he has been living in this city for many years; and during the time he has lived there, he has always brought the greatest part of the trees spent in the city, because he has people and correspondence with the parts where they [the trees] are cut and transported; and he has provided the armed galleys of the

---

46   Ibid.
47   Ibid.

king and the fleets of the Indies and has sold them [the trees] for a very
moderate price and scarce profit.[48]

The fifth question delved into his decisive intervention that same year of 1574,
when he loaded three hulks with masts and other timber products (*"másteles y
otra madera"*) to Andalusia, which served to supply the ships of the American
convoy and the Mediterranean cities of Oran – a Castilian enclave on the
African coast – and Cartagena; "and if he had not brought the said trees, it
would not have been possible the preparation of the said ships."[49]

These questions promoted him as a major supplier of naval provisions in
the south of the Iberian Peninsula, and a merchant worthy of receiving permission to trade with northern Europe. In fact, in the last question, number
eight, the seven captains are asked if they knew that the activity of Nicolás
de Melemburque was "very convenient for the service of the king and the
common weal of his kingdoms," and therefore the king should "license hulks
and ships so that they are not confiscated nor seized (…) and can return to
their lands."[50] This was precisely what the king did after receiving Nicolás de
Melemburque's report; on January 5 1575, Philip II issued a royal decree (*cédula
real*) that allowed Nicolás de Melemburque to import naval supplies and
export Andalusian salt in return.

3.1   *Royal Licence to Nicolás de Melemburque*
The same day the royal licence was decreed, Nicolás de Melemburque
appeared in a notary public in Madrid, where he obliged himself to only use
the licence with the permission of Juan Jacart.[51] Nicolás de Melemburque, consequently, was not acting on his own. He was certainly speaking on behalf of
other Flemish merchants residing in Seville, who soon profited from the growing toleration of the trade with northern Europe.

On January 25, once he was back in Seville, De Melemburque notarised the
foundation of a company with Juan Jacart. This company charter is particularly interesting, not just because it was the first notarised between merchants

---

48   AHPSe, SP, 7779, 1365v.
49   Ibid.
50   Ibid.
51   The document was formalised in the notary of of Gaspar de Gálvez, on January 5,
      1575. It was attached to the company charter, together with a copy of the royal decree.
      Unfortunately, copies of these two documents were not registered in the protocols and
      therefore we only know about their content through the clauses of the company charter.
      AHPSe, SP, 7780P, 281r.

of the *Atarazanas*, but because the conditions under which the partnership was formed were subject to the content of the the the royal decree. The charter informs that, thanks to the licence granted to De Melemburque ...

> [T]he ships arriving –which I [Nicolás de Melemburque] freight and bring from any ports and parts of Norway and Österland and other parts and kingdoms, to the ports of Cádiz, Sanlúcar and Seville, with masts and yards and other timber- will not be seized nor detained for the service to His Majesty. [They] will be even able to freely freight salt and other merchandise and return to their lands.[52]

The charter then describes the conditions under which the partnership will operate: the expected duration, the labour division, the capital investment and the distribution of returns according to the input of each partner. Nicolás de Melemburque and Juan Jacart established the company for "at least" a year, during which the first committed to travel ...

> [T]o Flanders and, from there, to Norway and Österland and elsewhere that suited me best, to buy, have and bring and send any ship or ships loaded with masts and yards and any other genre of timber and other things.[53]

While De Melemburque obliged himself to travel and contract the transport of timber and other naval supplies in northern Europe, Juan Jacart obliged himself to receive the imported commodities and to sell them in Seville. De Melemburque's initial investment was 600 *ducados*, while Jacart contributed with 200 *ducados*. Accordingly, De Melemburque would receive two-thirds of the profits, while Jacart would gain one third. Nonetheless, a clause stated that before calculating the final returns, the travel costs of De Melemburque (200 *ducados*) had to be deducted from the total profits. The charter finally contained a clause stating that De Melemburque's wife, Francisca Bernal, was in charge of keeping the *cédula real* copy, although Jacart had the right to use it any time. He was even allowed to share it with others, providing that De Melemburque would participate in the profits. This, consequently, opened the

---

52   AHPSe, SP, 7780, 281r.
53   AHPSe, SP, 7780, 281v. Chapter 4 further analyses partnerships and other collaboration strategies.

possibility for other merchants to use this safe-conduct to trade in Baltic and Scandinavian naval provisions.[54]

The journey of Nicolás de Melemburque should be understood as an attempt to gain the confidence of shipmasters. In fact, the licence did not immediately stop the shipmasters' fear of confiscations. We know from another notarial deed that, in September 1575, some months after the licence was issued, Enrique Scot, a shipmaster from Bremen anchored in Lisbon, refused to continue his journey to Andalusia, as he had agreed with Nicolás de Melemburque. He was afraid of having his cargo seized. To convince him to continue the journey, seven Flemish merchants in Seville obliged themselves as debtors of Nicolás de Melemburque, promising to compensate Enrique Scot if the vessel was confiscated.[55]

Northerners gradually recovered trust in the Andalusian market, regardless of the ongoing embargo in Castile, which officially lasted until 1579. The new commercial context of toleration triggered two parallel processes that enhanced the stock of naval supplies in Andalusia: one was the specialisation of the merchants in the *Atarazanas* in the importation of Baltic and Scandinavian commodities; the other was the expansion of the group, with the incorporation of new merchants into the *Atarazanas* circle. Just as the application of the royal embargo in 1574 did not follow a clear plan of action, the monarchy's change of strategy to obtain extra-peninsular naval provisions by collaborating with the main actors involved in the trade did not follow a premeditated policy either.

4   Seville's Opposition to the Embargoes

With the report, Nicolás de Melemburque intervened in a heated discussion occurring at Philip II's Council of War: should the king permit the activity of North European merchants and shipmasters in Spain while the rebels grew stronger in the Low Countries? This matter divided Philip's counsellors and representatives throughout his reign. One faction, in which we find influential actors like the governor of the Low Countries, Luis de Requesens, or the royal chaplain, Juan de Isunza, wanted to prevent any contact with the rebel provinces; for them, it was paramount that Spaniards regained presence in the navigation between the Iberian Peninsula and the Low Countries. Another faction

---

54   Ibid.
55   Christobal Osten, Cornieles van Esper, Juan Altoini, Roberto Corvete, Antonio de Venduilla, Geronimo Andrea and Otto Cornieles. AHPSe, SP, 7782P, 177r.

opposed such drastic measures. Their position is best represented in a report the royal secretary Gabriel de Zayas sent to the king in July 1575, known as the Memorial Zayas, which argued that the commercial prohibition would only damage Spain's naval capacity, as it would negatively affect Andalusian commercial capacity and, consequently, the royal treasury.[56]

The Memorial Zayas summarised very well the position of Seville's local council. The city concentrated the lion share of Castilian international trade and, hence, enjoyed an influential position in the debate. According to Gómez-Centurión Jiménez, Seville's oligarchy succeeded in protecting the region from the destructive effects of war; they managed to keep the American traffic almost untouched and, at the same time, attracted most of the Iberian exchange with Europe.[57] The *factor* of the *Carrera de Indias*, Francisco Duarte, decisively contributed to the lighter application of the prohibition in Andalusia, cooperating actively with the community of *flamencos* in Seville. In 1576, looking for alternatives to the embargo, Duarte met with several of them – those "that presently have in this city most practice in the sailing and trading of Flanders" – to discuss the possibility of establishing a convoy between Seville and the north of Europe, similar to the American one, which would protect the ships operating the route.[58] Duarte's proposal made clear that, by the time, the Flemings residing in Seville were the most important group based in Castile trading with the Low Countries, as many of the Castilian merchants with a tradition in this route had derived their investments to the American trade, a less dangerous enterprise. With Francisco Duarte's solution, foreigners would remain

---

56 The report has been analysed by many authors. Braudel, *La Méditerranée*. Felipe Ruiz Martín, "La etapa marítima de las guerras de religión. Bloqueos y contrabloqueos," *Estudios de Historia Moderna* 3 (1953): 181–214, or Gómez-Centurión Jiménez, *Felipe II*, 158–159. The report can be found in AGS, Estado, 569, f. 84. For a study on Philip II's fiscal policies and the constraints of war, see Mauricio Drelichman and Hans-Joachim Voth, "The Sustainable Debts of Philip II: A Reconstruction of Castile's Fiscal Position, 1566–1596," *The Journal of Economic History* 70, no. 4 (2010): 813–42.

57 Gomez-Centurión Jiménez, *Felipe II*, 272.

58 AGS, GyM, 81, f. 11. Gómez-Centurión Jiménez, *Felipe II*, 162. This attempt must therefore be understood as a precendent of the *Almirantazgo de los comercios de los Países obedientes de Flandes,* a merchant guild for the trade with the loyal provinces of the Low Countries founded in 1624. See Ignacio de la Concha Martínez, "El Almirantazgo de Sevilla. Notas para el estudio de las instituciones mercantiles en la Edad Moderna," *Anuario de Historia del Derecho Español* 19 (1948): 459–525. A more recent analysis of the Almiranzatago is found in José Manuel Díaz Blanco, "La construcción de una institución comercial: El consulado de las naciones flamenca y alemana en la Sevilla moderna," *Revista de historia moderna: Anales de la Universidad de Alicante*, no 33 (2015): 123–145.

in control of the commercial connection, but those foreigners would reside in Seville and, consequently, their activity would be easily monitored by the monarchy.

The *flamencos* addressed by Duarte, probably the ones residing in the *Atarazanas*, refused the proposal. According to the *factor* of the House of Trade, they argued that:

> [I]t is convenient to let them [shipmasters] free (...) to leave and come on their own or in company, as they wished, because it would be very diffi-cult and of a great risk to oblige them to follow an order if it was not that of their kings, especially since they are from different lands and opinions; neither would it be convenient to travel in convoy, since they are used to travel on their own, (...) and they are small, of fifty to one hundred tons, and with very little and poor artillery and men, and when the enemy knew that they went together, they will take care of waiting for them with a stronger force.[59]

Taking the opinion of the *flamencos* into account, Duarte instead advised the king to create an armada of ten or twelve 100-tonne vessels to make the cross-ing of the English Channel safer. Clearly, that plan was not on the king's table by the time, given the difficulties of the royal treasury to meet its financial obli-gations that had culminated in a suspension of payments.[60] As the plan was put on standby, the opinion of those in favour of tolerating north European trade in Andalusia grew stronger. Even though the embargo remained in place, the king ended up accepting the commercial activity of trustworthy members of the Flemish community in Seville, regardless of their connections.

The atmosphere of toleration in Andalusia often infuriated those advocat-ing for a hard implementation of the embargo, who forced the king to repeat the prohibition several times, the last one in 1577.[61] This had little impact in southern Spain, where the activity of northerners, far from being reduced, kept growing. According to a report sent by Duarte to the king, 2300 foreign ships had anchored in Andalusian ports in 1577, 1578 and 1579, the majority of them from northern Europe.[62] This report motivated the king to finally send a letter to his representatives (*corregidores* and *asistentes*) in Andalusia, commanding

---

59   AGS, GyM, 81, f. 11v.

60   Álvarez Nogal and Christopher Chamley, "Philip II against the Cortes."

61   AGS, GyM, 160, f. 71, Gómez-Centurión Jiménez, *Felipe II*, 203.

62   Sanlúcar 673, Cádiz 951, El Puerto de Santa María 384, Puerto Real 120, Málaga 60, Gibraltar 60 and Ayamonte 60. AGS, GyM, 160, f. 41. Gómez-Centurión Jiménez, *Felipe II*, 204.

them to provisionally allow the trade with potential rebels in a dissimulated manner (*"por via de disimulación"*) until he decided on a definitive solution.[63]

The king's provisional solution lasted for several years until he ordered a new embargo in 1585, prohibiting trade with England and the Dutch Republic. By then, the situation for the merchants of the *Atarazanas* and, in general, for the Flemish and German community had changed drastically. Since the embargo of 1574, the community had multiplied and their activity was central for the region's economy and, hence, for Seville's fiscal contribution to the monarchy by means of the two *almojarifazgos*, the *Almojarifazgo Mayor de Indias*, a duty on American trade, and the *Almojarifazgo Mayor de Sevilla*, which taxed foreign importats and exports.[64]

These *almojarifazgos* constituted the greatest source of fiscal income of the monarchy and were, thus, essential for the royal treasury. The monarchy did not directly collect them, but farmed them to the city of Seville. For this, the king and the city negotiated annual lump-sum payments for a period of several years.[65] Between 1583 and 1592, the annual lump-sum payment of the *Almojarifazgo Mayor de Sevilla* always exceeded that of the *Almojarifazgo Mayor de Indias*, which indicate that city obtained greater yearly revenues from European commerce than from the American one. If the trade with northern Europe was curtailed, Seville could always threat the monarchy to reduce its fiscal contribution to the royal treasury.

4.1   *The Embargoes of 1585 and 1595*

Not surprisingly, the embargo called in July 1585 against the English and Dutch coincided with the preparation of an armada to be sent to the Low Countries, which just as in 1574 did not materialise. Nonetheless, the embargo was maintained for five more years, until 1590, and thus coincided with the preparation of the Great Armada against England in 1588. The consequences of this

---

63   AGS, Estado, 160, f. 69. Gómez-Centurión Jiménez, *Felipe II*, 207.

64   Modesto Ulloa, *La hacienda real de Castilla en el reinado de Felipe II* (Roma: Sforzini, 1963). The importance of these taxes for the royal treasury is very well summarised in a letter sent to the Treasury Council in 1607 transcribed by Gelabert in "Guerra y coyuntura," 2. "The *almojarifazgos* of Seville, both *Mayor* and *Indias*, are the greatest revenues that His Majesty has in his monarchy. All Castile relies on them, the principal men, and the most needed people, and all the monasteries." Martín Alvarez de Castro al Consejo; Sevilla, 28 de marzo de 1607, AGS, Consejo y Junta de Hacienda [CJH], 474. On the *almojarifazgos*. See Ildefonso Pulido Bueno, *Almojarifazgos y comercio exterior en Andalucía durante la época mercantilista: 1526–1740: contribución al estudio de la economía en la España Moderna* (Huelva: Artes Gráficas Andaluzas, 1993).

65   Ulloa, *La Hacienda Real de Castilla*, 281–292.

embargo were barely felt by the *Atarazanas* merchants and, in general, by the Flemish in Seville. Philip II even advised his representatives in Andalusia not to be too aggressive with them, fearing that, in response, Seville would seek for a renegotiation of the *almojarifazgos*.[66]

Philip's precaution was not followed by the Duke of Medina Sidonia, who saw the embargo as an opportunity to undermine Seville and Cádiz, favouring Sanlúcar's economic position in the region. In 1587, Seville complained to the king about his abusive practices, arguing that his officials were obliging ships to unload the cargo in Sanlúcar, thus impeding their journey to Seville up the Guadalquivir River. The Duke of Medina Sidonia – the city argued in their letter to the king – did so not out of his zeal to serve the king but greedily seeking to collect the custom duties on the ships entering the Guadalquivir. Once again, fearing the reaction of the city, Philip II ordered that ships sailing up the river to Seville should not be stopped.[67]

In 1585, Philip II even incentivised the activity of the *flamencos* trading in naval provisions with tax exemptions. Prior to the Great Armada of 1588, the king promoted private shipbuilding with an exemption of the *alcabala*, a local tax, in the sales of vessels larger than 200 tons for a period of five years. A clause of this royal decree, ordered in 1585, declared that the sales of timber, hemp and other naval provisions for the building, reparation and preparation of these vessels, were also exempted from *alcabalas*. From several notarial deeds, we know that the tax exemption was extended several times, at least until 1596.[68] Hence, similarly to the experience of the embargo in 1574, the position of the merchants in the *Atarazanas* was reinforced at a moment in which a prohibition of trade with the enemy was in place.

The third embargo upon the Dutch rebels occurred in March of 1595. It was justified by the growing influence of the Dutch and English trade in Spain, and the suspicion that northerners were increasingly sending silver to England and the Dutch Republic. Dozens of north European ships were confiscated and investigated in western Andalusia and Lisbon.[69] The moment for reactivating

66   Gómez-Centurión Jiménez, *Felipe II*, 191.
67   Gómez-Centurión Jiménez, *Felipe II*, 193. AGS, CJH, 242, n. 8 and AGS, GyM, 246, f. 168.
68   This exemption was included as a clause of a royal decree that exempted the sale of vessels larger than 200 tons from the alcabala tax. We know about this royal decree, ordered in October 1588, because *Atarazanas* merchants notarised a copy of its extension for two years. AHPSe, SP, 9290, 646r. And later, AHPSe, SP, 9294, 105v. For more on Philip II's policies after the Great Armada, see Casado Soto, "Barcos para la guerra."
69   López Martín, ""Embargo and Protectionist Policies."

the commercial war, nevertheless, was not an ideal one, since the king was negotiating with Seville the *almojarifazgos* for the next years. Worrying that the city would use the application of the embargo to lower its contribution for the following years, Philip II decided to stop the confiscations in the region. But once an agreement was reached, new confiscations resumed in June 1595. The struggles of the royal treasury were evident, as this time the embargo was directed at the richest foreign merchants in Seville, whose goods and private account-books were seized.[70]

The reaction of Seville, whose council felt betrayed, was immediate: the city will not comply with the promised *almojarifazgos* if the confiscations continued.[71] The Flemish community reacted rapidly as well by sending legal representatives to Madrid. On July 1, twenty-seven Flemish merchants appointed Mateo Doom, Juan Leclerque, Francisco de Conique, Jaques Nicolás, Elías Sirman, Felipe Godin, Pedro le Maire and Jaques Brahusen as representatives of the nation to request the king to put an end to the confiscations.[72] Protests from the Flemish nation and the city council were accompanied by complaints from the Duke of Medina Sidonia, who was assuming an increasing relevance in the maritime affairs of the monarchy after being appointed captain-general of Andalusia and of the *Armada de la Mar Océano* in 1588.. He reported to the king that the embargo was threatening the preparation of the armada of Tierra Firme. Even important *asentistas*, like the Maluenda family, complained to the king about their difficulty in meeting their financial commitments to the monarchy due to the embargo.[73]

Once again, Philip II reconsidered his position and ordered the confiscated goods to be returned without finalising the investigation that had been started against the merchants. Probably compelled by the merchants whose goods had been seized, Diego de Armenteros and Gaitán de Ayala, who had arrived from Madrid to act as royal commissaries for the application of the embargo in Andalusia, notarised the following statement on July 15:

> The gentlemen *licenciado* Diego de Armenteros, from the Royal Council of the Indies, of this city, and Luis Gaitán de Ayala, counsellor of His Majesty and Major Comptroller of his Treasury, said that they lift and have lifted

---

70   For an exhaustive analysis of this negotiation, see Gómez-Centurión Jiménez, *Felipe II*, 283–288.
71   "Sevilla a Felipe II, 11-VII-1595," AGS, Estado, 174, s.f.
72   AHPSe, SP, 9286, 79r.
73   Gómez-Centurión Jiménez, *Felipe II*, 288.

the embargo that, by order of mister *licenciado* Diego de Armenteros, was done to the Flemings and businessmen that treated and dealt with them. And they ordered (...) anyone having their commodities or money or gold or silver or jewellery (...) to return them.[74]

This was indeed a success for the Flemish nation, although it did not mean an end to the royal hostility. Armenteros and De Ayala continued their investigation and the conclusions they obtained were clear: these merchants based their commercial activity on connections with the enemy. In a letter sent to the king on July 16, they reported that the *flamencos* in Seville traded with ports in Zeeland and Holland, with the connivance of local authorities.[75]

But Seville was not an exception in Andalusia. In January 1596, the king sent another commissary to Sanlúcar, Bernardino de Olmedilla, who described a very similar situation: "The Duke of Medina Sidonia is not diligent," he said in a report to the king.[76] Indeed, the Duke had become another active supporter of the Flemish in Andalusia. He even sent a letter to the king, in which Gaspar Loscarte, acting as Flemish consul in Sanlúcar, oddly justified that those fleeing from Flanders to the rebel territories and trading with Spain were actually Catholic:

> [E]veryday they flee from Flanders, (...) because in their lands they cannot live but with great sorrow and unease due to the soldiers, who give them thousand aggravations without considering if they are Catholic or not (...) And, in Holland, it is just the opposite, and they live Catholically without been disturbed.[77]

As odd as this argument may sound, it is true that a good deal of the merchants fleeing to Amsterdam from the southern provinces were, indeed, Catholic.[78] In any case, the king had no other choice than to accept any excuse of the like because the Flemish activity was essential to ensure the monarchy's finances and the supply of the royal navy, and Seville and Sanlúcar were not willing to

---

74   AHPSe, SP, 9286P, 493.

75   "Armenteros a Felipe II, 16-VII-1595," AGS, Estado, 174, sf.

76   AGS, Estado, 177, s.f. and 614, ff. 145–147. Gómez-Centurión Jiménez, *Felipe II*, 289.

77   AGS, Estado, 174, sf, transcription from Gómez-Centurión Jiménez, *Felipe II*, 293.

78   Oscar Gelderblom, *Zuid-Nederlandse Kooplieden en de Opkomst van de Amsterdamse Stapelmarkt (1578–1630)* (Hilversum: Verloren, 2000). For an overview on the migration in the Low Countries during the Eighty Years' War, see Raingard Esser, "From Province to Nation: Immigration in the Dutch Republic in the Late 16th and Early 17th Centuries," in *Imagining Frontiers, Contesting Identities* vol. 2 eds. by Steven G. Ellis and Ludá Klusáková (Pisa: Pisa University Press, 2006), 263–276.

yield. In a letter to the Duke of Medina Sidonia and the royal commissaries of the embargo in Andalusia, Philip II gave rather ambivalent orders: Merchants who, trying to avoid Protestant and English piracy, traded with Holland and Zeeland should not be disturbed. As for the merchants who had received commodities from rebel merchants, officials had to proceed in a soft way to discover the provenance of the commodities and confiscate the Dutch commodities only.[79] Such softness did not apply to those trading with England, who had to be prosecuted by any means, even in the case that "Seville complained in the name of the prosecuted individuals, trying to make a general cause; [the city] must understand that this is nonsense."[80]

The situation of north European migrants in Andalusia was again challenged months later.[81] In response to the Anglo-Dutch attack on Cádiz in June 1596, Philip II ordered to conduct a census of the foreign population in Castilian ports and, in April 1597, he decreed the proscription of any person from "enemy nations" and "rebel territories" 20 leagues from Castilian ports and Madrid.[82] Seville managed to delay the publication of the royal decree in its territory until August 29. In the following days, many *flamencos*, including some *Atarazanas* merchants, notarised powers of attorney to Françisco Ruyz de Cortaçar and Pedro de Echevarria to appear before the *Consejo de Cámara y Justicia* to request that such measure did not apply to them.[83]

The city council also raised a complaint to Philip II that same day, on August 29, arguing that north European residents in town were not enemies; they were citizens of Seville, loyal subjects of the monarchy.

> [M]ost of these persons are men that have been living here more than ten years up until forty-five, and they married in town as Catholic and prove themselves to be good Christians, with houses and real-estate. And they

---

79 The actual phrasing in Spanish is *"procediendo con blandura y suavidad y averiguándolo por buenos medios."* AGS, Estado, 175, f. 236. Gómez-Centurión Jiménez, *Felipe II*, 295.

80 Ibid.

81 The literature on this event is plenty. See for instance Pablo Antón Solé, "El saqueo de Cádiz por los ingleses en 1596, y la Casa de la Contratación de las Indias de Sevilla," *Archivo hispalense: Revista histórica, literaria y artística* 54, no. 166 (1971): 219–232. Manuel Bustos Rodríguez transcribed an interesting contemporary account by fray Pedro de Abreu, *Historia del saqueo de Cádiz por los ingleses en 1596* (Cádiz: Servicio de Publicaciones de la Universidad de Cádiz, 1996).

82 Bethany Aram, "La identificación y ocultación de extranjeros tras el ataque anglo-holandés de 1596." *Tiempos modernos: Revista Electrónica de Historia Moderna*, 8, no. 31 (2015): 3–62.

83 For instance, AHPSe, SP, 9298, 254v.

have forgotten their [foreign] condition and are so concerned with their
deals and profits [in town] that they cannot be considered to be capable
of making any damage to Your Majesty.[84]

That was not the only argument of the city, which not surprisingly threatened
the king in the letter: if the measure continued, the city would not be able to
meet its financial commitments with the monarchy. The monarchy's reaction
to this threat does not surprise either: the royal decree would not be enforced
in Seville until a new investigation on the migrants' connections was conducted;[85] there is no evidence that such investigation was done in the end. The
loyalty of the *flamencos* to the monarchy and their successful integration in
Seville as *vecinos* was rarely contested, not even when the king called for new
confiscations, driven by financial and logistical necessities.

4.2   *Enemies of the Monarchy? Foreigners as Well as Natives*
The narrative in favour of tolerating the *flamencos*' activity was not only based
on their importance for Seville's economy. The city council usually portrayed
the community of Flemish and German migrants as fervent Catholics and
loyal subjects to the Castilian king. Their successful assimilation was a recurrent argument any time city representatives interceded in their favour any
time these foreigners were targeted by the monarchy's hostile policies in the
context of the embargoes.

Their situation contrasted to that of the other largest north European community at the time, the English, which disappeared in the 1580s. After the
embargo of 1585, English migrants were forced out of Andalusia. Most of them
returned to England and, exceptionally, some integrated into the Flemish and
German community.[86] Flemish and German merchants benefited from the
situation, taking over most of the trade with northern Europe, including the
commercial connections with London and other English ports.[87] The English

---

84   Transcribed by Aram, "La identificación y ocultación de extranjeros," 14 from Hispanic
       Society of America, Altamira, 2-IV-49c, Los regidores de Sevilla al consejo real, 29
       agosto 1597.
85   Aram, "La identificación y ocultación de extranjeros," 14–15.
86   Gómez-Centurión Jiménez, *Felipe II*, 189–190. Since the middle of the century and, until
       then, the English had constituted the largest north European community in town. Otte,
       Sevilla, siglo XVI, 276.
87   Otte, *Sevilla, siglo XVI*, 276–84. For a recent research on the English community in
       sixteenth-century Andalusia, see María Grove Gordillo, "El papel de la comunidad mer-
       cantil inglesa en la industria del jabón en el Reino de Sevilla," in *Hacer historia mod-
       erna: Líneas actuales y futuras de investigación*, ed. Juan J. Iglesias Rodríguez and Isabel
       M. Melero Muñoz (Sevilla: Universidad de Sevilla, 2020), 346–361.

disappearance corroborates that the monarchy was indeed capable of implementing the embargoes in an effective way. However, in the Flemish and German case, there was a will of Seville's oligarchy to protect the community of migrants because of the strategic commodities they traded, such as timber. Moreover, whereas English migrants were considered to belong to an enemy nation, Low Countries migrants were still considered Habsburg subjects and Catholic, even if they were originally from rebelled territories, as the lack of Inquisition reports show.[88] In fact, no *flamenco* residing in Seville was ever suspected of being a rebel or an enemy of Spain himself; instead, when the embargoes were ordered, instead they were accused of maintaining commercial ties with enemies and rebels.

By the end of the century, most members of the Flemish and German nation were considered to have completed their assimilation in town, as the reports of the city council suggest. Why, once recognised as full members of the local community, would they keep their identification as Flemish in such a turbulent context for northern Europe migrants? This question is even more striking in the case of the offspring of first-generation migrants who, despite being born in Castile, continued self-identifying as members of the Flemish nation. The answer to this is found in the ground-breaking publication of Tamar Herzog, *Defining Nations*, which discusses the fluidity of the two main categories of belonging in early modern Spain and the Spanish Americas: the *vecindad* and the *naturaleza*.[89]

---

88 On the attention of the Inquisition to Flemish migrants in the Iberian Peninsula, see Werner Thomas, "Los flamencos en la Península Ibérica a través de los documentos inquisitoriales (siglos XVI-XVII)," *Espacio, tiempo y forma. Serie IV, Historia moderna*, no. 3 (1990): 167–196. In English, Werner Thomas, "The Inquisition, trade, and tolerance in early modern Spain," in *Entrepreneurs, Institutions & Government Intervention in Europe [13th - 20th Centuries]: Essays in Honour of Erik Aerts*, eds. Brecht Dewilde and Johan Poukens (Brussels: Academic & Scientific Publishers, 2018), 279–291.

89 Tamar Herzog, *Defining Nations: Immigrants and Citizens in Early Modern Spain and Spanish America* (New Haven: Yale University Press, 2003). A short version of this research was published in Spanish. Herzog, "Naturales y extranjeros: Sobre la construcción de categorías en el mundo hispánico," *Cuadernos de Historia Moderna Anejos* 10 (2011): 21–31. Herzog has also written an interesting paper on merchants, foreigners and citizenship for a later period. Tamar Herzog, "Merchants and Citizens: On the making and Un -making of merchants in early-modern Spain and Spanish America," *Journal of european economic history* 42, no. 1 (2013): 137–164. Relevant to this discussion, although for an earlier period, is Raymond Fagel, "Cornelis Deque, un mercader flamenco en la Castilla del siglo XV: un debate sobre el concepto de 'vecindad' y 'naturaleza' entre mercaderes," in *Castilla y Europa: comercio y mercaderes en los siglos XIV, XV y XVI*, ed. Hilario Casado Alonso (Burgos: Diputación Provincial de Burgos, 1995), 241–264.

The *vecindad* was a category of belonging that recognised the full membership of an individual in a local community, that is local citizenship.[90] Although the word *vecino* literally translates as "neighbour," in pre-Modern Spanish this word should be translated as "citizen," hence *vecindad* should be translated as "citizenship." Herzog notes that the *vecindad* "was constituted on its own, at the moment when people acted as if they felt attached to the community," complying with duties towards the community (e.g. fiscal or military ones), and exercising their rights that citizenship entailed (e.g. use of certain spaces, communal goods or access to local offices).[91] The *vecindad* was constituted at the moment migrants began to behave as members of the local community, which explains why, as soon as the *flamencos* established their household in the *Atarazanas* permanently, they were recognised as *vecinos* in notarial deeds.

The concept of *naturaleza*, translated by Herzog as *nativeness*, "captured the relationship people had with the community of the kingdom."[92] *Nativeness*, however, was not necessarily limited to individuals born in Castile. There were three forms through which individuals could be considered natives (*naturales*) of Castile: by birth (someone born in Castile), by origin (someone whose parents were Castilian) or by royal privilege.[93] Only one *Atarazanas* merchant, Manas Enríquez, applied for *naturaleza* by royal privilege.[94] He did so after an official of the House of Trade refused to allow him to trade with the Americas, which was legally restricted to Castilians. In his petition, submitted in 1588, he reported that he had been living in Andalusia for four decades; he had arrived at the age of eight, when his parents Josefe Enríquez and Francisca Pérez settled in Cádiz. He finally claimed to have houses in Cádiz and Seville and to have been married for twenty years to Gertruds de Angelberto, a daughter of two Flemish migrants who was born in El Puerto de Santa María and hence was native of Castile. Hence, he justified his *naturaleza* by arguing that he was a *vecino*. The king reacted rapidly to his petition, granting him the *carta de naturaleza*; that his, recognising him as a native of Castile.

---

90   A recent relevant contribution to this debate is Maarten R. Prak, *Citizens without Nations: Urban Citizenship in Europe and the World, C.1000–1789* (Cambridge: Cambridge University Press, 2018). Prak's approach to the Spanish case in this book has been recently discussed by Herzog in "Maarten Prak's Citizens without Nations and the Legal History of Spain." *TSEG - The Low Countries Journal of Social and Economic History* 17, no. 3 (2020): 91–100.

91   Herzog *Defining Nations*, 7.

92   Herzog, "Naturales y extranjeros," 23.

93   Lorenzo Sanz, *Comercio de España*, 53–54.

94   AGI, Contratación, 50B, Expediente de Manas Enríquez, s.f.

The rapid reaction of the king and the lack of similar applications suggest that the *flamencos* who integrated well in Andalusia's local communities as *vecinos* were easily recognised as *naturales* by the local community, without needing to apply for *naturaleza* to the king. In other words, *nativeness* became linked to a sustained *citizenship*, implying that the local category of belonging determined the belonging to the kingdom. Manas Enríquez only applied for his *carta* when his commercial rights were violated. A similar case occurred to Francisco Bernal six years before the establishing of the criteria for *naturaleza*. The king granted him a licence to trade with the Americas because "for a while [he] had been trading and trades in those territories of the Yndies" and had recently expressed his fear that "because there is no information in there about his *nativeness*, some official or other person could seize and confiscate his commodities or ships."[95]

The distinction between being a foreigner or a native was therefore blurry and sometimes complementary. The cases of Manas Enríquez and Francisco Bernal evidence that the categories of *natural* (native) and of *extranjero* (foreigner) were not mutually exclusive.[96] Being Seville citizens, Castilian natives, and Flemings or Germans were complementary categories. Such complementarity is particularly clear in the cases of those who were born in Andalusia but kept their self-identification as Flemish, like Juan de Bestoven and Juan Bernal, grandsons of Francisco Bernal, or Diego de Valdovinos, son of Cornieles Valdovinos.[97]

Moreover, the distinction between being a native and a foreigner was irrelevant in juridical terms for merchants, given the fact that migrants were not prevented from using the public notaries or the royal justice, which were open-access institutions. And, while foreigners were not officially allowd to participate in the American trade, migrants who had successfully integrated into Seville's society as citizens barely encountered opposition for doing it.[98] This

---

95 AGI, Indiferente, 425, l.23, ff. 131v-132r.

96 Herzog, "Naturales y extranjeros," 26.

97 The description of Diego de Valdovinos in a notarial deed is very interesting: "[D]e nacion flamenca, vecino y natural de Sevilla," which translates into English as "of the Flemish nation, citizen and native to Seville." AHPSe, SP, 9298, 987v.

98 Only the case of Manas Enríquez was documented in times of Philip II. For the most part, as historians have already noted, authorities showed little opposition to foreigners' participation in the *Carrera de Indias* in times of Philip II. Enriqueta Vila Vilar, "Sevilla, capital de Europa," *Boletín de la Real Academia Sevillana de Buenas Letras: Minervae Baeticae*, no. 37 (2009); Domínguez Ortiz, "La concesión de naturaleza." I analysed the connivance of royal officials with flamencos in sixteenth-century Seville, examining a particular case of corruption, in Jiménez Montes, "Los inicios de una nación: Mercaderes flamencos en Sevilla durante el reinado de Felipe II," in *Andalucía en el mundo Atlántico*

explains the lack of incentive of *Atarazanas* merchants to apply for a formal recognition of *nativeness*. Given the limited legal implications of someone's identification as *flamenco* and the absence of a special fiscal regime for foreigners during this period, which came to existence in the following century,[99] the identification as *flamenco* must have serve to reaffirm an affiliation to the community of Flemish and German migrants, as well as a label that marked their specialisation in the trade between southern and northern Europe.

5   Conclusion

The loss of key ports along the coast of Holland and Zeeland in the early 1570s raised concerns in Brussels and Madrid about the necessity of organising an armada to re-establish the Habsburg authority in the region. The lack of military vessels suited for warfare in the North Sea motivated Philip II to order an embargo on the rebel territories in January 1574, the first of three. This embargo set in motion a series of large-scale confiscations of north European ships anchored in Castilian ports, which were meant to join an armada in Santander that did not set sail in the end. Traditionally, historians understood Philip II's embargoes as failed attempts to curtail the growing commercial influence of northerners in Spain. But the way embargoes were applied in Andalusia suggests that the main motivation for confiscations was rather to obtain military resources rapidly.

   Voices from Andalusia frequently complained about the counterproductive consequences of indiscriminate seizures. Due to the confiscations, north European shipmasters became reluctant to sail to southern Iberia, jeopardising the stock of imported quality timber and threatening the supply of timber to the ships of the *Carrera de Indias* and the royal warships. To avoid the shortage of imported timber, Philip II granted Nicolás de Melemburque a licence to import naval provisions and export salt in return. Unfortunately, primary sources evidencing timber transactions are not consistent enough to analyse how the volume of trade changed throughout the last third of the century, particularly before and after 1574. However, the available sources do offer a qualitative approach to the chronology of this commerce: The *flamencos* of the *Atarazanas* began to specialise in the trade of these provisions after 1574 and, since then, became the main suppliers of imported timber in Castile, as we will

---

moderno: agentes y escenarios, ed. Juan J. Iglesias Rodríguez and J. Jaime García Bernal (Madrid: Sílex, 2016): 215–241.

99   See footnote 12.

see in the next chapters. With their imports, they managed to respond to the increasing demand for naval provisions in the region, driven by the growing participation in the *Carrera de Indias* and by the new military fronts of the monarchy.

The aftermath of the embargo was not only a turning point in the way the royal navy operating in southern Spain obtained imported timber. It also contributed to the consolidation of a commercial axis between Andalusia and the Low Countries. As the next chapter explores, the north European community in Seville grew rapidly in the last third of the century. With the connivance of the king, trade between Andalusia and northern Europe became widely tolerated regardless of the embargo orders, which repeated in 1585 and 1595. The pressure of Seville's oligarchy was essential for this. Confiscations became the exception rather than the rule in Andalusia. And every time confiscations affected the *flamencos* in the region, Seville's council threatened the monarchy with not complying with the city's fiscal commitments. Thanks to the local oligarchy's protection, the north European mercantile community flourished.

Newcomers from northern Europe integrated as citizens (*vecinos*) soon after their arrival, acknowledging their membership of the local community. Besides the support of the oligarchy, this was possible thanks to the existence of impartial open-access institutions, provided by the state, which facilitated their participation in Seville's social and economic life. Despite being recognised as citizens, these migrants continued considering themselves as *flamencos* or *alemanes*; even the second generation of migrants, who were native of Castile. Such identification as *flamencos* and *alemanes* mainly pursued a reputational interest, which manifested their embedment in commercial networks formed by compatriots that connected Andalusia with the main north European markets of the time. For the merchants of the *Atarazanas*, their affiliation to the Flemish and German nation of Seville became a sign of reputation to the eyes of the local community, as good Catholics, loyal vassals of the king, and traders of strategic resources for the Hispanic monarchy.

CHAPTER 2

Atarazanas Merchants

Migration and Social Capital

The monarchy's change of strategy in the supply of timber after the embargo of 1574, which was analysed in the previous chapter, prompted the expansion of the trade of Baltic and Scandinavian commodities in Seville and, consequently, of the number of foreign migrants who specialised in it. In 1574, there were five *flamencos* residing in the *Atarazanas* who occasionally imported timber.[1] By the end of the century, there were at least fifteen Flemish and German merchants that regularly traded in Baltic and Scandinavian timber, with a house in the complex of the *Atarazanas* or the surroundings. This growth went parallel to that of the north European population in Seville during the last third of the sixteenth century. If a local census reported 57 Flemish and German citizens in Seville in 1561, then a later survey on the foreign population revealed that, in 1596, there were at least 173 Flemish and German migrants residing permanently in the city.[2]

A main reason for such a rapid growth is the wave of emigration occurring in the southern provinces of the Low Countries, as a consequence of the turmoil caused by the Eighty Years' War. Migration in the context of the Hispano-Dutch War, especially during the first decades of the conflict, is a well-studied aspect of Dutch and Belgian historiographies.[3] Most research has focused on the migration of merchants and other skilled young individuals from the southern provinces to the northern ones, and its contribution to the rise of the Dutch Republic.[4] But other migration flows from both southern and northern Low Countries

---

1   The report was transcribed and published by María del Carmen Galbis Díez, "Las Atarazanas de Sevilla," *Archivo hispalense: Revista histórica, literaria y artística* 35, no. 109 (1961) 155–184.

2   Aram, "La identificación y ocultación de extranjeros." An analysis of this growth and its urban distribution is Juan Manuel Castillo Rubio and Germán Jiménez Montes, "La construcción de un *entrepôt*: Organización urbana de los mercaderes extranjeros en Sevilla en la segunda mitad del siglo XVI," in *Monarquías en conflicto. Linajes y noblezas en la articulación de la Monarquía Hispánica*, eds. J.I. Fortea Pérez et al (Madrid, Fundación Historia Moderna, 2018): 325–335.

3   For a recent historiographical overview see, Esser, "From Province to Nation,"

4   Wilfrid Brulez, "De diaspora der antwerpse kooplui op het einde van de 16e eeuw," *Bijdragen voor de geschiedenis der Nederlanden* 15 (1960): 461–491. Oscar Gelderblom, "From Antwerp to Amsterdam: The Contribution of Merchants from the Southern Netherlands to the

© KONINKLIJKE BRILL NV, LEIDEN, 2022 | DOI:10.1163/9789004504110_004

have received wide attention, too.[5] In the case of the migration from the Low Countries to the Iberian Peninsula, Stols' book *Spaanse Brabanders* published in 1971 is still the best-known study and has inspired several generations of scholars investigating the Flemish presence in the Iberian Peninsula. It offers an impressive account of *flamencos* residing in Spain and Portugal in the last decades of the sixteenth century and the seventeenth century.[6] However, Stols and later scholars investigating Flemish migration to Castile have generally limited their research to a particular type of Spanish source, the *cartas de naturaleza* (foreigners' application to being recognised as native of Castile, which granted a right to trade with the Americas). Stols even recognised this problem in the introduction of his book, where he laments not having researched more extensively in notarial archives.[7] In the case of the migration to Seville and Andalusia, a consequence of the neglect of local sources, like notarial deeds or council reports, is that historians have overvalued the attraction of the American trade as the main pull factor. This assumption is particularly short-sighted to properly understand the migration flow from northern Europe to Andalusia, given the vulnerable position of the north European population in Spain at the end of the sixteenth century, as Chapter 1 showed.

Until his death in 1598, Philip II saw the toleration of northerners in southern Iberia as a temporary solution. In fact, his policies regarding the commercial war against the Dutch Republic remained unpredictable throughout. The pressure of Seville's council, threatening to reduce the city's contribution to the royal treasury, tamed the monarchy's predatory impulses targeting the *flamencos*. But, as the present chapter analyses, the collaboration between Seville and the Flemish merchantsof the *Atarazanas* went even further, with the city granting them important privileges that ensured their control over the trade of timber in the region.

Commercial Expansion of Amsterdam (C. 1540–1609)," *Review (Fernand Braudel Center)* 26, no. 3 (2003): 247–82.

5 E.g. Wilfrid Brulez, "La navigation flamande vers la Méditerranée à la fin du XVIe siècle," *Revue belge de philologie et d'histoire* 36, no. 4 (1958): 1210–1242; Pierre Chaunu, "Séville et la Belgique (1555–1648)," *Revue du Nord* 42 (1960): 259–292; Marie-Christine Engels, *Merchants, Interlopers, Seamen and Corsairs: The 'flemish' Community in Livorno and Genoa (1615–1635)* (Verloren: Hilversum, 1997); Jan Willem Veluwenkamp, *Archangel: Nederlandse Ondernemers in Rusland, 1550–1785* (Amsterdam: Balans, 2000).

6 Stols, *Spaanse Brabanders*. For other works on the Flemish presence in the Hispanic empire, see note 56 of the Introduction.

7 Stols, *Spaanse Brabanders*, XIV. For a general historiographical overview on the studies of foreigners in early modern Spain, see Óscar Recio Morales, "Los extranjeros y la historiografía modernista," *Cuadernos de Historia Moderna. Anejos*, no. 10 (2011): 33–51.

This chapter is divided into two parts. The first one compares the migration from northern Europe to Seville before and after the outbreak of the Eighty Years' War, through the experiences of the Flemish and German individuals that specialised in the trade of timber. The second one studies the collaboration between the city and the *Atarazanas* merchants, and the creation of social capital among the latter. It explores how the group enhanced its cohesion and limited competition from outsiders, hence consolidating their preeminent position in the trade between northern and southern Europe.

1   Flemish Migration to Seville

American opportunities indeed boosted the foreign population in Seville in the sixteenth century, but the region had attracted Iberian and non-Iberian communities long before the overseas expansion of Castile and the foundation of the House of Trade in 1503.[8] By then, the Genoese constituted the largest foreign group in town, while the presence of north European migrants was insignificant. The Geonese community had flourished since the Christian conquest of the region in the fourteenth century.[9] Until the middle of the sixteenth century, Genoese and Castilian families coming from Burgos and Bilbao carried out most of the trade between Andalusia and the Low Countries, exporting Andalusian wool and importing Flemish textiles in return.[10]

---

8   Mercedes Gamero Rojas and José Jaime García Bernal, "Las corporaciones de nación en la Sevilla moderna," in *Las corporaciones de nación en la Monarquía Hispánica (1580–1750): Identidad, patronazgo y redes de sociabilidad*, eds. Bernardo J. García García and Óscar Recio Morales (Madrid: Fundación Carlos de Amberes, 2014), 349–351.

9   David Igual Luis and Germán Navarro Espinach, "Los genoveses en España en el tránsito del siglo XV al XVI," *Historia. Instituciones. Documentos*, no. 24 (1997): 261–332. Ruth Pike, *Aristocrats and Traders. Sevillian Society in the Sixteenth Century* (Ithaca: Cornell University Press, 1972). On the importance of the Genoese in the Andalusian economy, see Enrique Otte, "Sevilla y las ferias genovesas: Lyon y Besançon, 1503–1560," in *Genova-mediterraneo-atlantico nell'età moderna: Atti del III° Congresso internazionale di studi storici, (Genova 3–5 dicembre 1987)*, 249–276, or more recently, the work of Rafael Girón Pascual, "Los lavaderos de lana de Huéscar (Granada) y el comercio genovés en la edad moderna," in *Génova y la monarquía hispánica (1528–1713)*, eds. Manuel Herrero Sánchez et al (Genova: Società Ligure di Storia Patria, 2011), 191–202 or his published dissertation *Las Indias de Génova: mercaderes genoveses en el Reino de Granada durante la Edad Moderna* (Granada: Universidad de Granada, 2013).

10   Juan Manuel Bello León, "El reino de Sevilla en el comercio exterior castellano (siglos XIV-XV)," in *Castilla y Europa: comercio y mercaderes en los siglos XIV, XV y XVI*, ed. Hilario Casado Alonso (Diputación de Burgos: Burgos, 1995), 74. Gamero Rojas and García Bernal,

The number of Flemish and German migrants in Seville grew slow but steadily since the end of the fifteenth century.[11] Otte could only identify three Flemings before 1500: Miguel Dotre (1475), Miguel de Gra (1475) and Jos Plobier (1472).[12] Six decades later, a fiscal census conducted in 1561, known as *Padrón de las casas y vecinos que hay en la ciudad de Sevilla*, reported 57 northerners -35 Flemish and 22 German- as *vecinos*, that is, owning houses in town and paying local taxes.[13] Fifty-seven citizens still represent a relatively small community in a town that, at the time, probably reached 100,000 inhabitants. Even so, the presence of 57 permanent residents and their families certainly indicates the existence of a stable community at the beginning of the Eighty Years' War.

1.1 *Migration before the War*

The steady growth of the Flemish population in Seville coincided with the commercial expansion of Antwerp and the incipient engagement of Low Countries-based families in international trade.[14] The commercial rise of

---

"Las corporaciones de nación," 357. See also Hilario Casado Alonso, "Los agentes castellanos en los puertos atlánticos: los ejemplos de Burdeos y de los Países Bajos (siglos XV y XVI)," in *Navegación y puertos en época medieval y moderna*, ed. Adela Fábregas García, (Granada: La Nao, 2012), 163–194.

11   Otte identified 43 Flemish and German individuals that contracted in Seville's notaries in the period from 1519 to 1565. Otte, *Sevilla, siglo XVI*, 286–289.

12   Enrique Otte, *Sevilla y sus mercaderes a fines de la Edad Media* (Sevilla: Universidad de Sevilla, 1996), 193–194. Some relevant publications on the early Flemish presence in the Iberian Peninsula are Raymond Fagel, "En busca de fortuna. La presencia de flamencos en España 1480–1560," in *Los extranjeros en la España moderna: actas del I Coloquio Internacional, celebrado en Málaga del 28 al 30 de noviembre de 2002*, eds. María Begoña Villar García and Pilar Pezzi Cristóbal (Madrid: Ministerio de Ciencia e Innovación, 2003), 325–335; Juan Manuel Bello León, "Comerciantes y artesanos de los Países Bajos en Castilla y Portugal (siglos XIII a XVI). Los precedentes de su paso a Canarias," in *Flandes y Canarias. Nuestros orígenes nórdicos*, ed. Manuel de Paz Sánchez (Santa Cruz de Tenerife: Centro de la Cultura Popular Canaria, 2004), 111–152. In the same collective volumen, Ana Crespo Solana, "Flandes y la expansión mercantil europea: Naturaleza de una red atlántica. Siglos XV-XVI," 13–83.

13   The census is known as the *Padrón de las casas y vecinos que hay en la ciudad de Sevilla*, 1561. AGS, Expedientes de Hacienda [EH], 70, ff. 506–692. It has been largely studied from a demographic perspective, e.g. Jean Sentaurens, "Séville dans la seconde moitié du XVIe siècle: population et structures sociales. Le recensement de 1561," *Bulletin Hispanique* 77, no. 3–4 (1975): 321–390. Castillo Rubio and I used the census to study in detail the urban distribution of the Flemish and German population in town by crosschecking it with notarial sources, in "La construcción de un entrepôt."

14   According to Brulez, it became especially noticeable since the 1540s. Wilfrid Brulez, *De firma della Faille en de internationale handel van vlaamse firma's in de 16e eeuw* (Brussels: Paleis Der Academiën, 1959), 445–460. See also, Herman van der Wee, *The Growth of the Antwerp Market and the European Economy (Fourteenth-Sixteenth Centuries)*

Antwerp, after Bruges and before Amsterdam, as main entrepôt of the Low Countries regained historiographical attention in recent times after Gelderblom's publication in 2013, *Cities of Commerce*. In there, he argued that institutional change in the Low Countries' trade was driven by competition of cities that sought to attract international merchants.[15] Gelderblom's book offers a comprehensive analysis of the region's growing importance in international trade and the successive rise and decline of Bruges, Antwerp and Amsterdam from 1250 to 1650. This evolution had an important influence in the north European migration to Seville and, consequently, the city's commercial connection to northern Europe.

Bruges's commercial supremacy in the Low Countries began to decline with the arrival of the Habsburg dynasty. After the death of Mary of Burgundy in 1482, the city opposed the accession of her widower Maximilian of Austria as Count of Flanders. In response, Maximilian of Austria ordered foreign nations in Bruges to move to Antwerp, under the promise that they would maintain the same privileges they had been enjoying so far and would be compensated for any possible loss derived from their relocation.[16]

Antwerp was not the only nearby city that benefited from the Count's punishment. In a recent paper, Fagel identified a group of Andalusian traders that, when moving out of Bruges, became autonomous from the other Spanish groups that had traditionally operated there: the Castilians and the Basques. The Andalusians first settled in Middelburg, where they established a self-proclaimed nation, often called the Seville nation too, and years later moved to the nearby town of Bergen op Zoom.[17] Although information

---

(The Hague: Nijhoff, 1963) and, more recently, Puttevils, *Merchants and Trading*. For a good overview in Spanish, see Werner Thomas and Eddy Stols, "La integración de Flandes en la Monarquía Hispánica," in *Encuentros en Flandes: Relaciones e intercambios hispano-flamencos a inicios de la Edad Moderna*, eds. Werner Thomas and Robert A. Verdonk (Leuven: Leuven University Press, 2000), 1–73.

15 Gelderblom, *Cities of Commerce*. A debate around this thesis was published in a special issue of TSEG. Jessica Dijkman, Jeroen Puttevils, and Wouter Ryckbosch, "Cities of Commerce: an Introduction to the articles," *TSEG/ Low Countries Journal of Social and Economic History* 11, no. 4 (2014), 55–58. In the same issue, Oscar Gelderblom, "Thinking about Cities of Commerce – A Rejoinder," 119–130.

16 Gelderblom, *Cities of Commerce*, 28.

17 Raymond Fagel, "La Nación de Andalucía en Flandes: Separatismo comercial en el siglo XVI," in *Comercio y cultura en la Edad Moderna: Actas de la XIII Reunión Científica de la Fundación Española de Historia Moderna*, ed. Juan José Iglesias Rodríguez et al (Sevilla: Universidad de Sevilla, 2015), 34. Willem S. Unger, "Middelburg als handelsstad, XIIIe-XVIe eeuw)," *Archief, vroegere en latere mededeelingen voornamelijk in betrekking tot Zeeland, Middelburg, Zeeuwsch Genootschap der Wetenschappen* (1935): 1–177.

about this nation is scarce, it is probable that most of the merchants based in Andalusia that traded with the Low Countries by this time must have been linked to this Andalusian group of the Castilian nation in Bruges that eventually moved to Zeeland.

Once peace was restored in 1492, Bruges had lost its momentum and was no longer the dominant entrepôt in the region, despite Bruges's attempts to make foreigners return. Antwerp then began to draw a remarkably international community, more than any other place in the region, especially prompted by the success of the Brabant fairs, which became the only outlet for English cloth on the continent in 1496, after a peace treaty between the Dukes of Burgundy and the king of England. Two years later, the king of Portugal made Antwerp the pepper staple for northern Europe and even appointed a royal representative in the city through the *feitoria de Antuerpia*. Other Iberian communities, like the Aragonese or the Catalan, as well as Italian groups, such as the Genoese, Florentine, and Luccaese, consolidated their presence in Antwerp, too.[18] Even the Basque and Castilian nations, which remained in Bruges because of their staples on the merino wool, reoriented their trade towards Brabant and its fairs, where they could obtain cheaper textiles.[19] Similarly, Hanseatic merchants began to concentrate their activity during the Brabant fairs, although without abandoning their presence in Bruges, where they maintained their *kontor*, a trading post.[20]

The commercial system based on privileged nations, which had seen the commercial rise of Bruges, was in decline. Gelderblom argues that "[o]ne important difference between Bruges and Antwerp was that more and more merchants born and raised in the Low Countries began to participate in international exchange."[21] This conclusion is a cornerstone for Puttevils' thesis, *Merchants and Trading*. There, he claims that the development of open-access institutions, which gradually substituted privileged commercial guilds managed by and for

18   Gelderblom, *Cities of Commerce*, 29. On the internal organisation of foreign nations in Antwerp, see the seminal work by Jan Albert Goris, *Étude sur les colonies marchandes méridionales (portugais, espagnols, italiens) à Anvers de 1488 à 1567: Contribution à l'histoire des débuts du capitalisme moderne* (Nueva York: Burt Franklin, 1971).

19   Ludo Vandamme et al, "Bruges in the Sixteenth Century: A 'Return to Normalcy,'" in *Medieval Bruges: C. 850–1550*, ed. Andrew Brown and Jan Dumolyn (Cambridge: Cambridge University Press, 2018), 460.

20   Gelderblom, *Cities of Commerce*, 29–30. According to Vandewalle, merchants from Navarre and Andalucia remained in Bruges as well. André Vandewalle, "De vreemde naties in Brugge," in *Hanzekooplui en Medicibankiers. Brugge, wisselmarkt van Europese culturen*, ed. André Vandewalle (Oostkamp: Stichting Kunstboek, 2002), 27–42.

21   Gelderblom, *Cities of commerce*, 32.

particular foreign nations, favoured the participation of local families in international trade in Antwerp. Until then, these families, with access to regional industries, had been excluded from long-distance trade due to the privileges and staples that Low Countries cities granted to foreigners.[22] The participation of local families in long-distance trade prompted the incipient expansion of Flemish and Brabant firms across Europe. Brulez's book on the Della Faille family finely shows the spread of Flemish migrants in the main commercial places of Europe by the middle of the sixteenth century; based in Antwerp, the family firm was active in cities like Hamburg, London, Venice and Seville.[23]

Stols argued that most trade between Seville and the Low Countries before the Eighty Years' War was still conducted via Bruges. This is probably true, since the Castilian nation there remained active until then. However, it seems no coincidence that the Flemish population in Seville began to increase as Antwerp emerged as the main northern European commercial hub.[24] In the case of the first *flamencos* that resided in the *Atarazanas* since 1550s, we can see different origins that illustrate the diverse connections that Seville had with the Low Countries at the time, around the provinces of Flanders, Brabant and Zeeland.

No deed reveals the origins of Nicolás de Melemburque and his brother Juan, but an educated guess on their family name suggests that they were originally from Middelburg; Melemburque or Mediaburque was the ancient Spanish translation of this city from Zeeland. This does not come as a surprise since, as seen earlier, Middelburg and later Bergen op Zoom hosted the only Andalusian nation that was ever constituted outside Spain until it disappeared in 1564.[25] Similarly, there is no explicit information about the birthplace of Enrique Aparte, although notarial evidence shows that he maintained extensive connections in Antwerp, where he owned several houses at the time of his death, suggesting that part of his family was based there.[26] Finally, the name and surname of the most influential *flamenco* of the time in Seville, Francisco Bernal, indicate either an early hispanicisation or Spanish roots. The fact that part of his family, including his son Alonso Bernal, resided in Bruges suggests

22   Besides Gelderblom *Cities of commerce,* and Puttevils, *Merchants and Trading*, another relevant contribution to this discussion is the work by Sheilagh C. Ogilvie, *Institutions and European Trade.*
23   See annex XV, in Brulez, *De firma della Faille.*
24   According to Stols, this trade was run by Flemish merchants whose families used to belong to the Castilian nation in Bruges. Stols, "La colonia flamenca de Sevilla," 366. Stols, "Experiencias y ganancias," 167.
25   Fagel, "La nación de Andalucía en Flandes," 37. Unger, "Middelburg als handelsstad," 92.
26   AHPSe, SP, 9227, 893r.

the second. He was probably connected to the Castilian nation there; in fact, there is evidence of migrants that identified as *flamencos* in Seville although they belonged to the Castilian nation in Flanders.[27] Perhaps because the Spanish nation had already lost its previous splendour, Francisco Bernal preferred to identified himself as Flemish merchant once he moved to Seville.[28]

1.2 *Migration During the War*

When, as a response to the Anglo-Dutch attack on Cádiz in June 1596, Philip II ordered a survey on foreigners living in Castile to find individuals with potential links to his enemies, Seville held the largest foreign population by far. Royal officials identified 352 male foreigners there, which was followed at a great distance by Sanlúcar de Barrameda (72), the Cantabrian ports of Fuenterrabía (52) and San Sebastián (39) and other Andalusian coastal towns, like Cádiz (26), El Puerto de Santa María (10) and Ayamonte (10).

Of the 352 foreigners, almost half of them were Flemish (173), evidencing the sudden growth of the community. The report did not register any German resident. By now, the number of migrants from the Holy Roman Empire was minor if compared to those coming from the Low Countries; hence, *alemanes* were often considered as *flamencos*.[29] The presence of individuals from the Upper Rhine area, which had been of importance due to the residence of Fugger's factors decades earlier, do not seem relevant anymore.[30] German

---

27   In Seville's archive, there is a copy of a testament notarised by the clerk of the Spanish nation in Bruges, the one by Juan del Águila AHPSe, Real Audiencia de Sevilla, XV, 1565–2, 1.039, 165. This merchant identified himself as Flemish in Seville. I partially analysed his testament in Jiménez Montes, "La comunidad flamenca en Sevilla durante el reinado de Felipe II y su papel en las redes mercantiles antuerpienses," *Comercio y cultura en la Edad Moderna: Actas de la XIII Reunión Científica de la Fundación Española de Historia Moderna*, vol. 2, ed. Juan J. Iglesias Rodríguez, Rafael M. Pérez García, and Manuel Francisco Fernández Chaves (Sevilla: Universidad de Sevilla, 2015): 43–56.

28   It also appears as Bernaert in Flemish sources. Stols, *De Spaanse Brabanders*, II, 49. According to Stols, this trade was run by Flemish merchants whose families used to belong to the Castilian nation in Bruges. Stols, "La colonia flamenca de Sevilla," 366. Although the nation was already languishing, it remained operative at least until the 1570s.

29   Aram, "La identificación y ocultación de extranjeros," 23. The ambiguity of the report is also shared by notarial deeds.

30   Crailsheim, *Spanish Connection*, 19; Hermann Kellenbenz, *Los Fugger en España y Portugal hasta 1560* (Valladolid: Junta de Castilla y León, 2000). A shorter version of this research is Kellenbenz, "La factoría de los Fugger en Sevilla," in *Sevilla en el Imperio de Carlos V: encrucijada entre dos mundos y dos épocas: actas del Simposio Internacional celebrado en la Facultad de Filosofía y Letras de la Universidad de Colonia (23–25 de junio de 1988)*, eds. Pedro M.Piñero Ramírez and Christian Wentzlaff Eggebert (Sevilla: Universidad de Sevilla, 1991), 59–75.

migrants now came from the Lower Rhine area, around the city of Cologne, and the Baltic basin between Hamburg and Danzig.[31]

After the Flemish, the Italian (141) and the French (38) were the other largest non-Iberian communities.[32] The Italian was a heterogeneous community, formed by individuals coming from different territories of the Italian peninsula, among which the Genoese remained the largest, most influential group. However, by then, the richest Genoese families had fully integrated into the local oligarchy as Castilians, losing their distinctive Italian character, and therefore they were not reported as foreigners.[33] No English was identified; most abandoned Andalusia after the embargo of 1585 and those who stayed probably integrated into the Flemish community. Only 22 English were documented in Castile, all of them in Cantabrian ports, where the smuggling between French and Spanish ports on the Bay of Biscay became a growing preoccupation for Spanish officials.[34] The report did not register migrants from other Iberian territories, because their obedience to Philip II's rule was not questioned. Although the Portuguese and Aragonese presence was remarkable, their participation in long-distance trade was limited, especially insignificant if compared to Castilians groups, such as migrants from the Burgos area and the Basque region.[35]

---

31   Cologne was the origin of Francisco Roelant and Danzig of Esteban Jansen.

32   Aram, "La identificación y ocultación de extranjeros," 6–10. On the French presence, see the classic work by Albert Girard, *Le commerce français à Seville et Cadix au temps des Habsbourg: contribution a l'étude du commerce etranger en Espagne aux XVI et XVII siècles* (New York: Burt Franklin, 1967). On the Italian presence, see footnote 10.

33   Gamero Rojas and García Bernal, "Las corporaciones de nación," 354. Díaz Blanco and Fernández Chaves, "Una élite en la sombra." Eberhard Crailsheim "Extranjeros entre dos mundos: Una aproximación proporcional a las colonias de mercaderes extranjeros en Sevilla, 1570–1650," *Jahrbuch für Geschichte Lateinamerikas* 48 (2011): 179- 202.

34   Gómez-Centurión Jiménez, *Felipe II*, 190.

35   On the Portuguese migration to Seville in the sixteenth century, see Ignacio González Espinosa, "Andalucía como foco receptor de la población portuguesa (1580–1640). Distribución espacial y perfiles socioeconómicos," in *Movilidad, interacciones y espacios de oportunidad entre Castilla y Portugal en la Edad Moderna*, eds. Manuel Francisco Fernández Chaves and Rafael M. Pérez García (Sevilla: Universidad de Sevilla, 2019), 21–40; "Portugueses en Sevilla: sus oficios y profesiones durante el reinado de Felipe II," in *Comercio y cultura en la Edad Moderna: Actas de la XIII Reunión Científica de la Fundación Española de Historia Moderna*, Juan José Iglesias Rodríguez et al (Sevilla, Universidad de Sevilla, 2015), 731–741. On the Aragonese migration, see Miguel Royano Cabrera, "Los mercaderes de la Corona de Aragón y su papel en el tráfico de letras de cambio entre la Baja Andalucía y el Levante peninsular durante el reinado de Carlos V," in *Nuevas perspectivas de investigación en Historia Moderna: economía, sociedad, política y cultura en el mundo hispánico*, eds. María Ángeles Pérez Samper and José Luis Betrán Moya (Madrid: Fundación Española de Historia Moderna, 2018), 130–141; and "La comunidad

The pre-eminence of the Flemish mercantile group in Seville was not only evidenced by its population, but also by their increasing influence in the region's economy. The Flemish control of the trade of imported timber is just one of many examples. By the end of the century, *flamencos* were immersed in American navigation and had spread their tentacles in some of Andalusia's main exports, such as the production of salt along the coast, wool-washing centres in nearby towns and the exploitation of vineyards and olive groves along *El Aljarafe* and the Guadalquvir Valley.[36] Investing opportunities in the American trade and the hinterland, the existence of open-access institutions that facilitated their integration, and the protection granted by the local oligarchy are the main pull factors that motivated the Flemish migration to Seville, yet they alone do not explain the sudden growth of the community. For this, we must look at the extraordinary wave of emigration out of the Low Countries occurring after the outbreak of the Eighty Years' War.

Brulez used the term diaspora to define the unprecedented migration from Brabant and Flanders that led to the international expansion of commercial firms based in the Low Countries in the first decades of the Hispano-Dutch War.[37] Recently, Puttevils questioned the use of this term, because "Low Countries traders did not display a shared sense of community and members of the group could be Catholic or Protestant."[38] While it is true that the concept of a diaspora can make scholars fall into a narrative of religious exile, it finely illustrates the development of transnational commercial networks across Europe that shared a common language and cultural background, and whose activity depended on firms based in the Low Countries.[39] Although this transnational network was already in construction before the war, the conflict and its effect on the economy in the Habsburg Low Countries prompted the emigration of young men in an extraordinary manner.

---

mercantil catalano-valenciana afincada en la Sevilla de la primera mirad del siglo XVI," in *Familia, cultura material y formas de poder en la España moderna: III Encuentro de jóvenes investigadores en Historia Moderna, Valladolid 2 y 3 de julio de 2015*, ed. Máximo García Fernández (Madrid: Fundación Española de Historia Moderna, 2016), 121–130.

36   These industries have been dominated by Genoese families until then. Gamero Rojas and García Bernal, "Las corporaciones de nación," 358.

37   Brulez, "De diaspora."

38   Puttevils, *Merchants and Trading*, 10–11.

39   A similar aspect was noted by Ana Crespo Solana, "El concepto de ciudadanía y la idea de nación según la comunidad flamenca de la Monarquía hispánica," in *Las corporaciones de nación en la Monarquía Hispánica (1580–1750)*, ed. Bernardo J. García García and Óscar Recio Morales (Madrid: Fundación Carlos de Amberes, 2014), 394.

From the beginning of the war, there were three main waves of emigration from the southern Low Countries, which particularly affected Antwerp. The first coincided with the arrival of the Duke of Alva to the Low Countries in 1567 and the prosecution of Protestants involved in the Iconoclastic crisis and noble dissidents. The second occurred ten years later, as a consequence of the violent sackings of cities by mutinous Habsburg armies that were not receiving their pay, which came to be known as the Spanish Fury. The most famous of those sackings was the one of Antwerp in 1576, in which hundreds of residents were murdered, provoking "the largest drain on Antwerp's merchant community," in Gelderblom's words.[40] A third wave took place once Antwerp definitely returned to the Habsburg rule in 1585, after a long siege commanded by the Duke of Parma. The city would remain in Habsburg hands, but the rebels had gained control of the estuary of the Scheldt, making it very difficult for long-distance traders to operate.

The blockade of Antwerp's access to the sea meant a blow for its economy and prepared the ground for the rise of Amsterdam as the region's main entrepôt. Until the war, Antwerp and Amsterdam had formed a complementary economic axis that articulated most trade between the Baltic region and southern Europe. While commercial firms trading with the Iberian Peninsula operated in Antwerp, Amsterdam emerged as a shipping centre for the trade with the Baltic markets, a commercial circuit that came to be known as *moeder negotie* (mother trade) due to its importance.[41] With the war, Amsterdam benefited from Antwerp's drainage of human and economic capital.[42] But the decline of Antwerp did not instantly mean the economic rise of Amsterdam, which was a correlation usually emphasised by Dutch historiography, portraying a canonical image of the Dutch Republic as a tolerant, open society.[43] Esser

40   Gelderblom, *Cities of Commerce*, 33.
41   De Vries and Van der Woude, *The First Modern Economy*, 350–408. Milja van Tielhof, *The 'Mother of All Trades': The Baltic Grain Trade in Amsterdam from the Late 16th to the Early 19th Century* (Leiden: Brill, 2002). Aksel Erhardt Christensen, *Dutch Trade to the Baltic About 1600: Studies in the Sound Toll Register and Dutch Shipping Records* (Copenhagen: Einar Munksgaard, 1941).
42   Israel, *Dutch Primacy*, 28–29. Gelderblom, *Cities of Commerce*, 32–33 and "The Golden Age of the Dutch Republic," in *The Invention of Enterprise: Entrepreneurship from Ancient Mesopotamia to Modern Times*, eds. David S. Landes et alii., (Princeton: Princeton University Press, 2012), 156–181. See also Jan A. van Houtte, *Economische en sociale geschiedenis van de Lage Landen* (Zeist: De Haan, 1964), 137–138, or Clé Lésger, *The Rise of the Amsterdam Market an Information Exchange: Merchants, Commercial Expansion and Change in the Spatial Economy of the Low Countries 1550–1630* (Aldershot: Ashgate, 2006).
43   An interesting reassessment of this can be found in Geert H. Janssen, "The Republic of the Refugees: Early Modern Migrations and the Dutch Experience" *Historical Journal* 60, no. 1 (2017): 233–52.

pointed out that, while this traditional approach depicted a diaspora of "an already successful, rich merchant elite which transferred their money, their networks and their expertise to Amsterdam," recent research showed that "the majority of the southern exiles were young men at the beginning of their careers."[44]

Moreover, those who left the southern provinces did not necessarily move to Holland, especially during the beginning of the conflict, when Amsterdam remained loyal to Philip II and the Catholic faith. During this period, Amsterdam even suffered a blockade by the Sea Beggars, which ended when the city finally joined the rebel cause in 1578. This blockade pushed a great deal of shipmasters and traders specialized in Baltic trade out of Holland to safer ports in East Friesland, most notably Emden, during the first decade of the conflict.[45] In short, once the war started, migrants moved in a larger scale and they did so not only within the Low Countries; they also established in other important economic centres of the time, such as Lübeck and Hamburg in the Baltic area, London and other English cities, Italian towns like Livorno, and the Iberian Peninsula.

Regardless of the final destination, it is possible to establish a general typology of migrants that left the southern provinces during the first decades of the Eighty Years' War. Most migrants were young individuals that had few opportunities to prosper in a territory whose economy was disrupted by war. Nonetheless, Stols' argued that this type of migration was not an exceptional phenomenon in the region. Although to a lesser degree, similar waves had occurred since the late fourteenth century due to growing demographic pressure in Brabant and Flanders, which made the young population particularly susceptible to migrate. Any exogenous factor, like military conflicts, forced out large numbers of youngsters of families involved in long-distance trade, as well as individuals of poorer demographic strata, like seamen.[46]

Despite the complexity of experiences, Stols described a specific typology of those who migrated from the Low Countries to Seville and participated in long-distance trade after the outbreak of the war. Such description is corroborated

---

44   Esser, "From Province to Nation," 267. See also Raingard Esser, "Antwerpens "Altweibersommer." Wirtschaft und Kultur in der Scheldestadt zwischen "Fall" (1585) und "Frieden" (1648)," *Wolfenbuetteler Barock-Nachrichten* 43, no.1 (2016): 65–84.

45   Israel, *Dutch Primacy*, 18, 28, Brulez, "De diáspora," 281–284. The fear of German towns to a commercial rise of Holland stimulated good diplomatic relations between them and the Spanish monarchy. Gómez-Centurión Jiménez, "Las relaciones hispano-hanseáticas."

46   Stols, "Experiencias y ganancias," 165.

by the experience of the merchants residing in the *Atarazanas*. They were young individuals with the motivation to prosper in a city with an expanding economy, which also offered the possibility of moving to America or travelling further to Italian territories if things did not work out as expected. Northerners in Seville were fervent Catholic believers, or at least they successfully pretended to be so, as suggested by the absence of complaints from local and royal authorities in this regard; in fact, most religious prosecutions of *flamencos* in Castile occurred in the period from 1555 and 1565.[47] Moving to the Iberian Peninsula was surely not an option for Calvinist sympathisers, who would have opted for Protestant territories instead. Migrating to Seville implied greater uncertainty than other northern European destinations: a longer journey, a small community of compatriots at the beginning of the war, and a different culture and language; although many, as Stols noted, would have learned Spanish in their childhood.

Migrants' places of origin were heterogeneous, as the case of the merchants in the *Atarazanas* shows. If the first generation of traders in the complex mainly came from Brabant, Flanders and Zeeland, then those who established once the war started came from more diverse territories, mostly from rebel provinces (Jaques Nicolás was from Utrecht, and Guillermo Corinse, Tobías Buc, Juan van Hooren from Holland) and towns outside the Low Countries (Francisco Roelant was from Cologne and Esteban Jansen from Danzig).

The socio-professional backgrounds of the Flemish and German migrants were heterogeneous, too, despite the pre-eminence of the mercantile group. The royal survey of 1596 documented thirteen shopkeepers (*tenderos*), eight tailors (*sastres*), seven coopers (*toneleros*) and two silversmiths (*plateros*); thus, thirty of the Flemish citizens in Seville were artisans or local retailers.[48] To this, we may add an important number of transients who worked as sailors in the *Carrera de Indias* fleets, and even vagabonds who tried their luck in Andalusia.[49] Even within the mercantile community, profiles were diverse: some specialised in the importation of Baltic and Scandinavian provisions, others in the importation of textiles; some were agents of north European firms, others were fully engaged in American trade.[50]

---

47   Stols, "Experiencias y ganancias," 161. Thomas, "Los flamencos en la Península Ibérica"
48   See the annexes in Aram, "La identificación y ocultación de extranjeros." Also Abadía Flores, "La comunidad flamenca."
49   Stols considered that artisans and seamen emigrated in a greater scale than merchants. For them, Seville was not only a market of a growing demand of skilled labour but also a scale for those travelling further to Italy or America. Stols, "Experiencias y ganancias."
50   See the annexes in Aram, "La identificación y ocultación de extranjeros."

2 Collaboration with Seville and Social Capital

As the navigation between Andalusia and America increased in the second half of the sixteenth century, Seville's city council began to favour the activity of those merchants who could ensure the supply of timber, a fundamental resource for a maritime empire. Pine masts and planks imported from the coldest regions of Europe were needed for the preparation of the fleets sailing to the Americas each year. The collaboration between the city and this group of merchants was based on two main privileges granted to the latter, for which the connivance and approval of the king was necessary, too. The first privilege was the control over the main warehouses of Seville, the *Atarazanas*, and the second one was the farming of the *alcabala*, a tax on timber sales.

On the basis of these two privileges, those who specialised in the trade of imported timber generated an intense social capital; which, in the words of Ogilvie, is the "store of value that is generated when a group of people invests in fostering a body of relationships with each other."[51] By generating social capital, *Atarazanas* merchants enhanced trust with each other, improved the information flow among the members of the group while creating information asymmetry with outsiders, and facilitated the coordination of collective actions in the negotiation with local and royal authorities.[52] This, in short, allowed the *flamencos* of the *Atarazanas* to strengthen their position in a strategic trade.

2.1 Control and Conversion of the *Reales Atarazanas*

The Castilian king Alfonso x conceived the construction of the *Atarazanas* in 1252 four years after his father Ferdinand III had captured Seville from the Almohade rulers; hence its official name *Reales Atarazanas* with Arabic etymological roots, which translates into English as "Royal Shipyards."[53] The complex consisted of seventeen naves of 80 to 100 metre-long each and a total width

---

51   Ogilvie, *Institutions and European Trade*, 427.
52   Ibid. For an overview on how historians have adopted the concept of social capital in relation to the Spanish case, see Xabier Lamikiz, "¿Qué tipo de capital social generaron los gremios de comerciantes?: reflexiones a partir del ejemplo del Consulado de Bilbao, 1511–1829," in *Recuperando el Norte: empresas, capitales y proyectos atlánticos en la economía imperial hispánica*, eds. Alberto Angulo Morales and Álvaro Aragón Ruano (Bilbao, Universidad del País Vasco, 2016), 103–12.
53   Pablo E. Pérez-Mallaina Bueno, "Un edificio olvidado de la Sevilla americana: Las Reales Atarazanas," *Cahiers du monde hispanique et luso-brésilien*, no. 95 (2010): 8. A more recent and ambitious publication is Pérez-Mallaina Bueno, *Las Atarazanas de Sevilla. Ocho siglos de historia del arsenal del Guadalquivir* (Sevilla: Universidad de Sevilla, 2019).

of 180 metres, which hosted the construction and repair of the Mediterranean galleys of the Castilian king. However, the size of the complex became insufficient to fit larger vessels required for the oceanic enterprises participated by the king. The shipbuilding production stopped in the fifteenth century and the building languished for decades.[54]

Although in disuse, the *Atarazanas* remained part of the king's estate in Seville, as an eastern annex to the *Real Alcázar* – the royal palace –, which was administered by a member of the local nobility, the *alcaide* or warden of the palace.[55] The *Atarazanas* stood in a privileged position, in an area outside the city walls known as *El Arenal* (the Sandbank) between the Guadalquivir River and the city's economic core, the district of the cathedral and the royal palace.[56] By the end of the century, the monarchy began to grant most of the building for private use, mostly to local artisans, reserving a part for the preparation of the first American voyages and for the necessities of an expanding city.[57] In 1493, the Catholic monarchs permitted the establishment of a new fish market in the nave number 1, in response to the claims of the city council to have it outside the walls. A decade later, the offices of the newly founded House of Trade were established in the nave 17, the one furthest south. The House headquarters eventually moved to the *Real Alcázar*, and the naves 16 and 17 were adapted as royal warehouses for the preparation of American expeditions.[58]

The necessities derived from Seville's monopoly for the Spanish navigation to the Americas motivated the reconversion of the other fourteen naves into warehouses. The transformation of the fourteen naves were offered via public auctions, organised by the warden of the *Real Alcázar* and ultimately sanctioned by the king. Tenants were obliged to maintain, repair and rearrange the facilities; in return, they enjoyed the possession of the spaces for long-term

---

54   Casado Soto, "La construcción naval atlántica española."
55   Pérez-Mallaina Bueno, "Un edificio olvidado."
56   The complex stood between two of Seville's thirteen city-walls gates, *el Postigo del Aceite* (the Oil Gate) and el *Postigo del Carbón* (the Coal Gate). For an archaeological research on the building, see Fernando Amores Carredano and Agustina Quirós Esteban, "Las Atarazanas: El tiempo y los usos," in *Recuperando las Atarazanas: Un monumento para la cultura* (*Exposition: Seville, April 13-May 30 1999*) (Sevilla: Consejería de Cultura, 1999).
57   For a complete study on the urban evolution of the city in times of Philip II, see Antonio José Albardonedo Freire, *El urbanismo de Sevilla durante el reinado de Felipe II* (Sevilla: Guadalquivir Ediciones, 2002).
58   According to Pérez-Mallaina, the expedition of Nicolás de Ovando was the first one that was granted a space in the *Atarazanas* for the preparation of his journey to Isla Española in 1502. Pérez-Mallaina Bueno, "Un edificio olvidado," 10–14.

periods, including the right to sublet them. Pérez-Mallaina estimated that, out of the 10.000 square metres that occupied the fourteen naves (numbers 2–15), almost 65% had come into Flemish hands by 1575.[59] A decade later, the group of northern merchants that specialised in timber trade managed to acquire most of the space available for private use, which had been limited to naves number 2 to number 12 in 1585, once the king granted the naves 13–15 for the construction of the royal custom house, la *Real Aduana*.[60]

The *flamencos* built their houses in the front of the building, facing *El Arenal* and converted the inside into a storage complex, making use of the original arches of the foundations (black squares in illustration 2.1 represent the piers of those arches). Warehouses and cellars (*almacenes* and *bodegas*) occupied the space between two arches, while smaller spaces between arches known as *bajos* or *altos* (literally below and above) were adapted for storage, too. They remained in possession of the houses and the largest spaces, and frequently sublet the smaller ones; the notaries of Francisco Díaz and Juan de Tordesillas contain at least 41 leasing contracts in which Flemish merchants rented a store in the *Atarazanas* to other individuals, usually for a short term, in the period from 1570 to 1600.[61] Although by the end of the century, most north European migrants resided in the area north of the cathedral, in *calle Francos* and *calle Abades*, those specialised in the importation of naval supplies continued living in the *Atarazanas* at least until the early seventeenth century.[62]

Francisco Bernal, Juan Jacart, Juan de Melemburque, Nicolás de Melemburque and Enrique Aparte constituted the first generation of *flamencos* that resided in the *Reales Atarazanas*. The control of the city's main warehouses became a central element in their privileged position in the market of imported timber and, consequently, they made significant efforts to keep their possessions in the building. They transferred their ownership rights to their offspring in testaments and to their future sons-in-law through dowries. They

---

59   For this estimation, he used the report transcribed by María del Carmen Galbis Díez, "Las Atarazanas de Sevilla."

60   Pérez-Mallaina Bueno, "Un edificio olvidado," 17. These naves were taken from Esteban Jansen. AHPSe, SP, 12492, 1153r.

61   Forty-one leasing contracts of cellars and warehouse (1570–1600). E.g. AHPSe, 9230P, 357v-358r.

62   Jiménez Montes, "La comunidad flamenca en Sevilla," 54. The monarchy retook the total control of the complex in 1719. María Amparo López Arandia, "Maderas para el real servicio y el bien común: Aprovechamientos forestales en la provincia marítima de Segura de la Sierra (ss. XVIII-XIX)," in *Árvores, barcos e homens na Península Ibérica (séculos XVI-XVIII)*, ed. Rosa Varela Gomes and Koldo Trápaga Monchet (Zaragoza: Pórtico Librerías, 2017), 25–40.

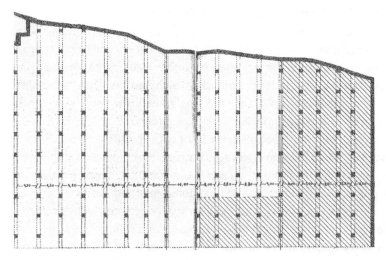

ILLUSTRATION 2.1 Reconstruction of the *Atarazanas* by the 1580s. The complex was
organised into seventeen naves (the one at the top is number 1 and
the one at the bottom, number 17). The merchants' houses are located
between the wall and the first row of piers below. Storing spaces were
located in the spaces between piers (black squares)
SOURCE: LEOPOLDO TORRES BALBÁS, "ATARAZANAS
HISPANOMUSULMANAS." *AL-ANDALUS* 11 (1946): 175–209

even tried to prevent the calling of new public auctions when their contracts
were about to expire, as a dispute between Juan Jacart, who had migrated from
Lille in the late 1560s, and the warden of the *Real Alcázar* reveals in 1571.[63]

After the death of Juan de Melemburque – Nicolás' brother – Juan
Jacart requested Philip II to take over his lease contract of some spaces in
the *Atarazanas*. These included five arches of nave 5, correlative to other

---

63   This is not the only example. After Esteban Jansen died in 1596, Francisco Roelant
      assumed the twenty-five-year contract that Jansen had signed in 1582 with the *Alcázar*,
      which was to expire in 1607. AHPSe, SP, 9293,719v. Justo de Bil, a former employee of
      Jansen, moved into another property left by Jansen for a period of three years, paying 348
      ducados per year to the executors of Jansen's testament. AHPSe, SP, 9296, 1059r. De Bil, by
      the beginning of the 1590s, had moved out of the *Atarazanas* and the house was inhab-
      ited by Simón Enríquez, who had taken over the sublet contract from his relative Jaques
      Enríquez when he died in 1591. AHPSe, SP, 9267, 66r. Years earlier, when the contract that
      Jaques Nicolás had in the *Atarazanas* expired, Jansen commissioned his worker Marcos
      de Abaitua to bid on his behalf the rent for thirty years of the spaces (the ones that Bernal
      had transferred to Nicolás). AHPSe, SP, 9283, 344v.

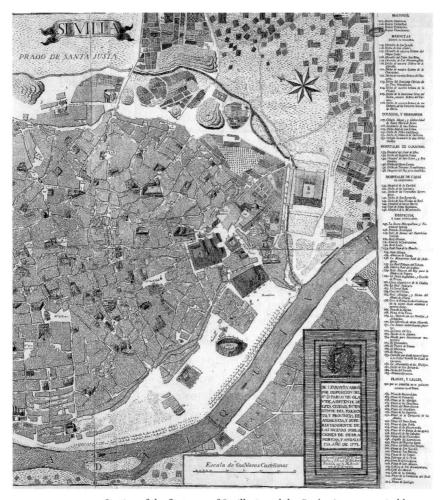

ILLUSTRATION 2.2   Section of the first map of Seville: in red the *Reales Atarazanas*; in blue
the Cathedral; in yellow the *Real Alcázar* (royal palace); and in grew *Casa
Lonja,* whose construction began in 1572
SOURCE: PLANO TOPOGRÁPHICO DE LA M.N. Y M.L. CIUDAD DE
SEVILLA, 1771, MAP, REAL ACADEMIA DE LA HISTORIA, HTTPS://BVPB
.MCU.ES/ES/CONSULTA/REGISTRO.DO?ID=423028

possessions that Jacart already had in nave 6, where he had his house.[64] Juan
Jacart claimed that he needed De Melemburque's possession because his

---

64   Galbis Díez, "Las Atarazanas de Sevilla," 165. About Juan de Melemburque's death: AHPSe,
SP, 7770, 968v.

current space was not enough for importing large masts, which the king very much needed. The king, consequently, initiated an inquiry to consider Jacart's petition, asking the warden of the royal palace – the Count of Olivares – for his opinion. The king wanted to know if the reasons that Jacart had argued were true. These reasons were that …

> [He] and no other person had brought large masts for galleys and *naos* to this city. And, given the current shortage in Cádiz and Sanlúcar, these masts had been very useful and beneficial for our [the king's] service and that of the Republic. And some of the said masts are bigger than 55 cubits, and they must be stored under a roof (…) because they break and crack when they dry and get covered by dust, and with water, when it rains, they get wet to the core so when they are used, they do not serve anymore.[65]

The Count of Olivares did not agree with Jacart's information. According to the report that he sent to the king, Juan Jacart already had enough space to trade in timber, but he had preferred to sublet part of it and now was trying to take over De Melemburque's former possessions by contacting the king directly. The Count, instead, recommended Philip II to call for a public auction, which was the usual procedure, evidencing the will of the local oligarchy to maintain their influence in the administration of the building.[66]

The Count of Olivares finally argued that Juan Jacart was exaggerating his relevance. He was not the only person importing timber; other individuals residing in the *Atarazanas*, namely Francisco Bernal, Juan de Melemburque, Nicolás de Melemburque and Enrique Aparte, had imported timber too. To this list of names, Juan Jacart answered the following:

> Juan de Melemburque died eight years ago, Francisco Bernal has not traded [trees] in twelve years, and Nicolás de Melemburque only brings little masts for ships and boats but not for *naos* or galleys.[67]

While it is impossible to know who was telling the truth – probably neither was – the dispute between the warden of the *Alcázar* and Juan Jacart offers an extraordinary snapshot of the state of the trade in northern timber by the time. By 1571, the demand for imported timber was lower than after the embargo of

---

65   ARAS, caja 138, exp. 8.
66   ARAS, caja 138, exp. 8, ff. 4–6.
67   ARAS, caja 138, exp. 8, ff. 6.

1574, and so was the number of merchants conducting that trade. Moreover, it is clear that the concerns of an endemic shortage of quality masts in Andalusia were already recurrent in the early 1570s, and this concern became the main justification for allowing this group of foreigners to control the strategic building of the *Atarazanas*. In fact, the king finally accepted the petition and Juan Jacart assumed Juan de Melemburque's stores, as shown in the report conducted in 1575 on the state of the building.[68]

That same report evidences that Francisco Bernal was the main investor in the complex. He had obtained the first spaces in 1548, when he rented naves 1 and 2 for a price of 6,000 maravedís per year over 34 years.[69] It is very likely that, by then, timber was the least of his concerns; in fact, he never really specialised in the trade of northern timber, as Jacart accurately argued. Francisco Bernal's economic activity mostly focused on America, for which Philip II granted him a licence in 1555, and on in real estate.[70] He became one of Seville's main constructors during the time, as the conversion of the *Reales Atarazanas* shows He also built houses in San Bernardo, a district outside Seville's city-wall, and in the *Atarazanas de los Caballeros*, a former prison for noblemen next to the *Reales Atarazanas*, where he built a residential complex.[71]

Even though he showed little interest in importing naval provisions, Francisco Bernal is central for understanding how a few Flemish families controlled the trade of imported timber. Through marriage he developed kinship ties with other compatriots residing in the *Atarazanas* and granted access to the building to young migrants. He married his daughter Bárbola to Juan Bambel, a Flemish merchant who used to live in the *Atarazanas* before moving to Sanlúcar. Later, he arranged a marriage between his son Diego Bernal and the daughter of Enrique Aparte, who controlled naves 12, 13, and part of 14.[72] Finally, his granddaughter Bárbola was betrothed to Juan Jacart and, after Jacart died, he arranged another marriage of Bárbola with

---

68   Galbis Díez, "Las Atarazanas de Sevilla,"

69   A substantially cheaper price than that of the previous rents of smaller spaces in the *Atarazanas*. In 1544, Antonio de Cárdenas rented one space to Gonzalo and Gaspar Jorge for two years and a price of 10,000 maravedís per year. Otte, *Sevilla siglo XVI*, 57.

70   AGI, Indiferente, 425, l. 23, f. 131v.

71   On San Bernardo, AHPSe, SP, 7780, 75r-79v. On the *Reales Atarazanas de los Caballeros*, Mercedes Espiau Eizaguirre, *La Casa de la Moneda de Sevilla y su entorno: Historia y morfología* (Sevilla: Universidad de Sevilla, 1991), 43–45. When Valdovinos died, his widow transferred all possesions in the *Atarazanas de los Caballeros* to Francisco Bernal: AHPSe, SP, 9222, 439r. Bernal did so later to his grandson-in-law Jaques Nicolás, AHPSe, SP, 9265,846r.

72   Galbis Díez, "Las Atarazanas de Sevilla," 174–178.

Jaques Nicolás, a former worker of his household. Through family strategies, like the ones of Francisco Bernal, and through direct lobbying to Philip II, like Jacart, Flemish families managed to remain in the building for several generations, and became an essential part of a community of migrants that, by early 1570s, was still far from the size it would reach decades later.

2.2   The *Encabezamiento*

Despite their growing number, merchants that specialised in timber trade remained in, or close to, the *Atarazanas* complex and maintained a significant cohesion.[73] The epitome of such cohesion was their syndication as farmers of the *alcabala de madera*. The *alcabalas* were taxes levied on sales of different types of commodities; e.g. *alcabala del pescado* (fish), *alcabala del jabón* (soap), *alcabala de los esclavos* (slaves) or the *alcabala de la madera* (timber).[74] The *alcabalas* constituted the largest ordinary revenue of the king's treasury together with *almojarifazgos*, custom taxes on imports and exportats as discussed in the previous chapter.[75] The incapacity of the royal administration to collect the *alcabalas* made the king delegate their management to Castilian municipalities, which were better informed about the state of their local markets. Similar to the negotiations of the *almojarifazgos*, explained in the previous chapter, the king agreed with each city a lump-sum payment based on future expectations of the collection of all the different *alcabalas*.

Since large towns like Seville lacked the bureaucratic administration to collect taxes levied on sales, they usually outsourced the collection of each *alcabala* to individuals who were involved in the trade of the specific commodity to be taxed. These individuals negotiated a lump-sum, which was based on annual predictions of the *alcabala* revenues, with the city council, although the council only acted as an intermediary of the king, who ultimately had to sanction the agreement as he was the beneficiary of the tax.

---

73   As Lamikiz noted "living close to one another in the same city made the monitoring of reputations much easier." *Trade and Trust*, 143.

74   Francisco Morales Padrón, *Historia de Sevilla. La ciudad del Quinientos* (Sevilla: Universidad de Sevilla, 1977), 237.

75   A good explanation of the *encabezamiento* mechanism is found in Álvarez Nogal and Christopher Chamley, "Philip II against the Cortes." See also Pilar Zabala Aguirre, *Las alcabalas y la Hacienda Real en Castilla: siglo XVI* (Santander: Universidad de Cantabria, 2000), 87–88 or José Ignacio Fortea Pérez, *Monarquía y Cortes en la Corona de Castilla: las ciudades ante la política fiscal de Felipe II* (Valladolid: Cortes de Castilla y León, 1990). A complete explanation of sixteenth-century tax system is found in the second volume of the classic by Ramón Carande, *Carlos V y sus banqueros* (Barcelona: Crítica, 1977).

This lump-sum was known as *encabezamiento*; hence, those who farmed the *alcabala* were known as *encabezados*. The syndication of the *Atarazanas* merchants as *encabezados de la alcabala de madera* meant the creation of a formal association for the coordination of the group's economic and political strategies, thus reinforcing their control over the market. Although the *encabezamiento* did not grant any commercial monopoly, it intensified the social capital among the merchants residing in the *Atarazanas*. With the *encabezamiento,* the group increased the information asymmetry on the market between them and outsiders, preventing competition from non-members and facilitating the monitoring of each other's activity, which in short translated into a greater cohesion.[76] The *encabezamiento* was an institutional solution that allowed them to share fiscal costs and delegate political action by appointing deputies (*diputados*), who administered the collection of the tax and represented the *encabezados* before local and royal authorities.

The activity of the association left a blurry but revealing trace in the notary. The first document that evidences a Flemish participation in the farming of the *alcabala* dates from 1578, when two Flemish individuals, Juan Leclerque and Felipe Sarens, and two Spaniards, Arias Gonçales de Nabia and Andrés López de Castropol, acting on behalf of the *encabezados,* appointed two proxies to collect the tax in the kingdom of Seville: a Spaniard, Diego del Riego, and a Flemish, Germán Dufelde.[77]

In 1583, the Flemish had taken total control over the *encabezamiento* and the timber market, as we can infer from a document signed in November, in which Felipe Sarens, Guillermo Corinse, Jaques Nicolás and Francisco Roelant, on behalf of "all Flemish traders of timber residing in Seville" appointed a Castilian attorney, Juan Alonso de Carrera, for legal representation.[78] Unfortunately, the power of attorney does not specify what motivated the group to appoint a legal attorney, although it was probably connected to the negotiation of

---

76 An interesting document on how they prevented competition from outsiders is AHPSe, SP, 9290, 730r, in which they punish Pedro de Bil for trading in timber.

77 AHPSe, SP, 6011, 281v. In 1579, this other tax was also controlled by *flamencos*, Diego Bernal and [] Nieto formed a company with that aim. AHPSe, SP, 9220, 574r. The role of Dufelde for the Flemish community as a whole is very interesting; he was not a trader but an attorney who specialised in the representation of *flamencos*. In 1580, he collected 3000 maravedís from Andrés de Arrizabálaga for this tax. AHPSe, SP, 9223, 121r. Already in 1573, we find a POA of Domingo de Ybarra to Germán Dufelde on this (AHPSe, SP, 7774, 350r. Dufelde eventually invested in the farming of timber taxes too, despite not being involved in its trade. (AHPSe, SP, 9233P, 853r).

78 "[P]or nosotros y en nombre y en bos de los demás flamencos mecaderes de madera vecinos e residentes en la dicha çiudad de Sevilla." AHPSe, SP, 9235P,505v.

the exemption from the timber *alcabala* that Philip II decreed in 1585.[79] In January 1585, we can document the existence of *diputados* for the first time. Guillermo Corinse and Francisco Roelant, acting as "deputies of the levy of the *alcabala* of the timber of any kind in this city of Seville," commissioned Andrés Luis, a worker of the German merchant Esteban Jansen, to collect the tax.[80] Unfortunately, the notarial document does not give more information on the deputies' duties, and due to the exemption from the timber *alcabala* ordered in 1585, this is the last deed about the *encabezamiento* until 1597.

The *encabezamiento* resumed that year, and the notarial activity of the group increased, which allows us to know more about the syndication as well as the merchants that participated in it, shown in Table 2.1. In November 1597, ten "Flemish merchants, citizens of Seville" appointed Juan de Bestoven and Guillermo Corinse as deputies of the *encabezados*.[81] The document, which was notarised in the form of a power of attorney, commissioned the deputies to administer and collect the timber *alcabala* on behalf of the *encabezados* and to represent them before Spanish institutions. It is not possible to know how long their term lasted or whether new deputies were appointed every time the *alcabala* was renegotiated, because new ones were elected again in 1598 and 1599 due to the death of one of the deputies. After the death of Guillermo Corinse in 1598, the group notarised a new power of attorney re-electing Juan de Bestoven and electing Simón Enríquez.[82] This time, the number of *encabezados* was higher, twelve Flemish merchants signed the deed. A year later, Juan de Bestoven died and Simón Enríquez became severely ill – he died some months later –, so the *encabezados* elected new representatives. In the office of Juan de Tordesillas, they appointed Juan Bernal and Tobías Buc. Although the number of *encabezados* was the same, twelve, two new *encabezados* were incorporated as signatories instead of De Bestoven and Enríquez.[83]

Days after their appointment in 1599, the deputies Juan Bernal and Tobías Buc commissioned two Castilian attorneys to represent the group before Spanish institutions, Francisco de Sandoval and Gerónimo de Salamanca.[84] It

---

79   AHPSe, 9271P, 726r.

80   "[D]*iputados de la renta del alcavala de la madera de todo género desta dicha çiudad de Sevilla*" AHPSe, 9242, SP, 292r. Adrés Luis was a worker of Esteban Jansen's house since 1581 (AHPSe, SP, 9228, 509v).

81   AHPSe, SP, 9299, 148r.

82   AHPSe, SP, 9301, 369r.

83   "On his own behalf and that of the other Flemish merchants heading the timber alcabala in Seville." Original: "[P]*or sí y en nombre de otros mercaderes flamencos, encabezados de la renta de la alcabala de la madera de Sevilla*" AHPSe, SP, 9303, 788r.

84   AHPSe, SP, 9303, 879v.

TABLE 2.1   Merchants participating in the *encabezamiento* of the timber *alcabala* (1597, 1598, 1599)

Merchant	1597	1598	1599
Cornieles Jansen	x	x	
Cornieles Lamberto	x	x	X
Francisco Roelant	x	x	
Federico Hinquel			x
Guillermo Corinse	(D)		
Jaques Nicolás	x	x	x
Jaques Sesbaut		x	x
Juan Bernal	x		(D)
Juan de Bestoven	(D)	(D)	
Juan Leclerque		x	x
Juan van Hooren	x		x
Juan Sarens		x	x
Justo de Bil		x	
Melchor de los Reyes	x	x	x
Simón Enríquez	x	(D)	
Tobías Buc		x	(D)

Note: (D) indicates the deputies of that year

SOURCE: AHPSE, SP, 9299, 148R; 9301, 369R; 9303, 788R

seems that the transference of the *encabezados'* legal power to local attorneys was a common practice, as this had been done at least in 1583 and 1597.[85] The resort to legal proxies suggests a continual negotiation of the group with local and royal institutions, which also speaks of their increasing economic relevance in the region.

Such relevance eventually led to tensions among them, as shown in the appointment of deputies notarised in 1603. In November, the *encabezados* met in the house of Juan van Hooren, one of that year's deputy, and requested the presence of Juan de Tordesillas to attest the voting. The notary stated that ...

---

85   In 1597, Juan de Bestoven and Guillermo Corinse commissioned a Castilian attorney named Francisco de Sandoval, the same day they had been appointed deputies AHPSe, SP, 9299, 150r.

> [T]hey said that it was their custom to elect deputies that administered
> and collected the said tax on behalf of all the *encabezados* and the other
> traders and contributors that owed the tax. And that they [deputies] paid
> the tax to Seville and shared the contributions. And to that end [depu-
> ties' election], they have gathered in the house of the said Juan Banoren,
> deputy of last year. And due to differences existing among them, they
> have agreed to make the said election casting secret votes in writing (...)
> so that all of them put ten folded written papers on a table (...). And the
> [papers] were seen and read by me, the notary. And it appeared that the
> said Juan Leclerque had eight votes for the deputy's appointment, and
> the said Juan Banoren nine votes, and Tobías Buque three.[86]

De Tordesillas's explanation shed lights on the way the *encabezados* appointed
representatives. This was an annual election and *encabezados* used to cast their
vote in a public way before 1603. However, differences between them obliged
the group to vote secretly. What provoked such disagreements? Was it a failure
in the negotiation of the lump-sum payment? Was it the incapacity of the deputies to gain the trust of the new king, Philip III? And more importantly, does
this document reflect the collapse of the status quo that had led Flemish and
German merchants to control the market of Baltic and Scandinavian provisions? Sadly, with the current state of the research, it is not possible to answer
those questions. One thing is certain: the more merchants involved in the trade
and the richer some of them became, the more difficult it must have been to
find a balance between common interests and individual aspirations.

2.3   *The Nation*

The specialisation of the *Atarazanas* merchants went parallel to the institutional development of the Flemish and German nation in Seville, which served
to create social capital among immigrants from northern Europe and created
mechanisms of support to compatriots.[87] The first Flemish foundation in

---

86   AHPSe, SP, 9325, 471r.
87   In the eighteenth centuries, the community of north European migrants in Cádiz claimed
      to be successor of this nation, calling themselves the "Ancient and Noble Flemish and
      German Nation of Seville and Cádiz." Crespo Solana, "Elementos de transnacionalidad
      en el comercio flamenco-holandés en Europa y la Monarquía Hispánica," *Cuadernos
      de Historia Moderna. Anejos* 10 (2011): 63. The concept of nation here has nothing do
      then with the modern concept one, which is connected to the modern nation-state.
      For an interesting discussion on this, see Bartolomé Yun Casalilla, ""Localism," Global
      History and Transnational History. A Reflection from the Historian of Early Modern
      Europe," *Historisk Tidskrift* 127, no. 4 (2007): 659–678. Applied to the study of the north

Seville was an almshouse known as the *Casa de pobres de la nación flamenca*, located in a peripheral area of town, the Saint Martin parish. This religious institution assisted poor compatriots, especially "honest old men, widows and other honest people of an exemplary life and good fame." It also provided financial support to seamen captured by Muslim corsairs in the Strait of Gibraltar to "return to their lands and not beg around the city," and gave spiritual support to compatriots "troubled in our sacred religion" to reconcile with Catholicism.[88]

The involvement of Flemish citizens in the institution during the early years seems limited, though. In fact, some of the functions that constituted the *raison d'être* of the almshouse were conducted in a private way, outside the religious institution. For instance, Esteban Jansen and Francisco Bernal – probably the richest individuals of the community – took over the payment for the ransoming of two different north European crews attacked by Muslim corsairs and made captive in Tétouan in 1576. Three years later, Bernal and Jansen signed a promise of payment to the Order of Mercy, to rescue the crews and captains, Dirique Fenesen and Juan Oldenburgue. The promise of payment contemplated the ransoming of fourteen sailors for a price that went, depending on the person, from 150 *ducados* to 226. The total of the ransoming could amount up to 2436 *ducados*.[89] Nothing in the document indicates the involvement of

European community in Seville, see Manuel F. Fernández Chaves and Mercedes Gamero Rojas, "Nations? What Nations? Business in the Shaping of International Trade Networks," in *Merchants and trade networks between the Atlantic and the Mediterranean (1550–1800)*, ed. Manuel Herrero Sánchez and Klemens Kaps (New York: Routledge, 2016): 145–168.

88   AHPSe, Audiencia Real de Sevilla [ARS], leg. 29.275, exp. 1. This document is a lawsuit between the Flemish nation and two members that did not want to belong to it anymore, Juan Bautista Sirman and Miguel de Neve; it was analysed in Mercedes Gamero Rojas, "Flamencos en la Sevilla del siglo XVII: La capilla de San Andrés," in *Comercio y cultura en la Edad Moderna: Actas de la XIII Reunión Científica de la Fundación Española de Historia Moderna,* ed. Juan José Iglesias Rodríguez et al. (Sevilla: Universidad de Sevilla, 2015): 715–730. This study sheds some new light on the almshouse. Before, historians knowledge was still largely based on the nineteenth-century work by M. Hye Hoys, *Fondations pieuses et charitables des marchands flamands en Espagne: souvenirs de voyages dans la Péninsule Ibérique en 1844 et 1845,* (Madrid: Fundación Carlos de Amberes, 2000), 25.

89   *"Memoria y relaçión de los flamencos marineros captivos questán en Bervería, en los captiverios de la nao [de ques maestre Dirique Fenesen] / y de la nao de Juan Oldenburgue, el año pasado de mill e quinientos e setenta e seis años"* AHPSe, SP, 9222, 720r We know that Fensen was carrying timber from Amsterdam (set by Jan Persin) to Seville: AHPSe,9214P,947v. Another case from earlier years: AHPSe, SP, 9215P, 784v. On the topic, see Wolfgang Kaiser and Guillaume Calafat, "The Economy of Ransoming in the Early Modern Mediterranean," in *Religion and Trade: Cross-Cultural Exchanges in World History, 1000–1900*, eds. Francesca Trivellato, Leor Halevi, and Cátia Antunes (New York: Oxford University Press, 2014), 108–130.

the almshouse in this. Most likely, the institution was economically unable to cope with this kind of extraordinary expenses, which explains the need to rely on the two richest compatriots.

In any case, the ransoming and the foundation of the almshouse show the interest of well-established migrants in supporting vulnerable compatriots, particularly shipmasters who were fundamental for their commercial connection with northern Europe. In fact, to defend the commercial activity of compatriots on the coast in times of embargoes, the Flemish and German nation of Seville appointed consuls in important Andalusian ports, namely Cádiz, Gibraltar, Málaga, Vélez-Málaga, and Sanlúcar de Barrameda.[90] Likewise, there is notarial evidence that the nation often commissioned attorneys in Madrid to appear before the king to negotiate the application of the embargoes in southern Spain.[91]

The institutional solutions that the nation developed demonstrate that, while integration in the local community was easy, newcomers still depended on other compatriots to enhance their position in the new society. For this, the nation created collective mechanisms of religious and social support, which culminated with Philip III's granting of a licence to the nation to found a fraternity devoted Saint Andrew – *Hermandad* de *San Andrés de los Flamencos* – and to build a chapel to host its meetings and festive activities.[92] In 1624, advised by

90   In Gibraltar AHPSe, SP, 9270, 664r; in Málaga AHPSe, SP, 9282, 473r; AHPSe, in Vélez-Málaga SP, 9285, 438r; and in Cádiz and Sanlúcar in the context of the first embargo AHPSe, SP, 9222, 344r. It is important not to mistake these *ad hoc* consuls with the ones established in the seventeenth century. An overview on the topic of early modern consuls is Manuel Herrero Sánchez, "La red consular europea y la diplomacia mercantil en la Edad Moderna," in *Comercio y cultura en la Edad Moderna: Actas de la XIII Reunión Científica de la Fundación Española de Historia Moderna*, ed. Juan José Iglesias Rodríguez et al (Sevilla: Universidad de Sevilla, 2015): 121–150. The functions of consuls and representatives of foreign nations remained a complex question in the eighteenth century, as Marcella Aglietti discussed in a chapter published in the same collective volume, entitled "El debate sobre la jurisdicción consular en la Monarquía hispánica (1759–1769)," in *Los cónsules de extranjeros en la Edad Moderna y principios de la Edad Contemporánea*, ed. Marcella Aglietti, Manuel Herrero Sánchez, and Francisco Zamora Rodríguez (Madrid: Doce Calles, 2013): 105–118. See also, Crespo Solana, "El juez conservador ¿una alternativa al cónsul de la nación?" In *Los cónsules de extranjeros en la Edad Moderna y principios de la Edad Contemporánea*, edited by Marcella Aglietti, Manuel Herrero Sánchez, and Francisco Zamora Rodríguez, 23–34. Madrid: Doce Calles, 2013.

91   For instance, Valerio Vandala (AHPSe, SP, 9246, 1126r) and Germán Dufelde (AHPSe, SP, 9223, 240r).

92   "AHPSe, SP, 12638, 1008. See also Gamero Rojas "Flamencos en la Sevilla del siglo XVII: La capilla de San Andrés," 718.

his favourite, the Count-Duke of Olivares, Philip IV promoted the foundation of a guild of Flemish merchants in Seville for the trade with the Low Countries, known as *Almirantazgo de los comercios de los Países obedientes de Flandes.* The guild, however, turned out a failure and disappeared in 1630.[93] This commercial institution was the swansong of Seville's commercial predominance in Andalusia, as Cádiz rose as the main entrepôt of the region in the second half of the seventeenth century. At the beginning of the eighteenth century, the largest population of northerners was concentrated in Cádiz, where Dutch migrants played an increasing role.[94]

3   Conclusion

The meetings and appointments made by the *encabezamiento* constitute an excellent source to identify the fifteen merchants that specialised in the trade of Baltic and Scandinavian timber in Seville by the end of the sixteenth century: Cornieles Jansen, Cornieles Lamberto, Francisco Roelant, Federico Hinquel, Guillermo Corinse, Jaques Nicolás, Jaques Sesbaut, Juan Bernal, Juan de Bestoven, Juan Leclerque, Juan van Hooren, Juan Sarens, Justo de Bil, Melchor de los Reyes, Simón Enríquez, and Tobías Buc. These fifteen merchants succeeded the first generation of Flemish traders that originally obtained the long-term leases in the *Atarazanas* to convert the naves of the former shipyards into warehouses: Nicolás de Melemburque, who died in 1578, Juan Jacart

---

93 Ignacio de la Concha Martínez, "El Almirantazgo de Sevilla. Notas para el estudio de las instituciones mercantiles en la Edad Moderna," *Anuario de Historia del Derecho Español* 19 (1948): 459–525. A more recent analysis of the Almiranzatago is found in José Manuel Díaz Blanco, "La construcción de una institución comercial: El consulado de las naciones flamenca y alemana en la Sevilla moderna," *Revista de historia moderna: Anales de la Universidad de Alicante,* no 33 (2015): 123–145.

94 Ana Crespo Solana has done extensive research on this community. See for instance, "El comercio holandés," "Merchants and observers," or the book *Entre Cádiz y los Países Bajos: una comunidad mercantil en la ciudad de la ilustración* (Cádiz: Fundación Municipal de Cultura del Ayuntamiento de Cádiz, 2001). For the community in Seville during this period, see Mercedes Gamero Rojas and Manuel F. Fernández Chaves, "Flamencos en la Sevilla del siglo XVIII: Entre el norte de Europa y América," in *Orbis incognitvs: avisos y legajos del Nuevo Mundo: homenaje al profesor Luis Navarro García,* ed. Fernando Navarro Antolín (Huelva: Universidad de Huelva, 2007), 211–220; and Gamero Rojas and Fernández Chaves, "Flamencos en la Sevilla del siglo XVIII: Las estrategias familiares, redes clientelares y comportamientos económicos," in *Población y grupos sociales en el Antiguo Régimen,* eds. Juan Jesús Bravo Caro and Luis Sanz Sampelayo (Málaga: Universidad de Málaga, 2009), 571–586.

in 1580, Enrique Aparte in 1581, and Francisco Bernal in 1587. There is also a number of merchants that, according to notarial evidences, carried out most of the Baltic and Scandinavian trade in the 1580s and 1590s but died before the deputies' appointment in 1597: Cornieles Valdovinos died in 1579, Felipe Sarens in 1585, Manas Enríquez in 1586, Pedro Gisberto in 1592, Miguel Arbauts in 1593, Juan Sesbaut in 1593, Conrado Ledes in 1593, and Esteban Jansen in 1596. Other individuals, like Juan Gras and Gertruds de Angelberto, ran a commercial firm that traded with imported timber too, but did not join the *encabezamientos* for different reasons. Juan Gras, a former worker of Esteban Jansen, conducted a more local trade and it is unlikely that he ever supplied the royal navy. The case of Gertruds de Angelberto is perhaps the most interesting one, since she took over the firm of her husband, Manas Enríquez, after his death in 1592, and until their son Josefe came of age.[95]

All the thirty individuals mentioned above specialised in the trade of imported timber in Seville between 1570 and 1600. Probably, there were others trading in timber in Seville but certainly this group of merchants dominated the market in the last third of the century. They enjoyed a privileged position, favoured by the intermediation of the local authorities and, ultimately, the connivance of the king, from which these merchants farmed the timber *alcabala* and rented the naves of the *Atarazanas*.

The Flemish increasing dominance of a strategic market coincided with the growing presence of *flamencos* in western Andalusia. While, as discussed in the previous chapter, the king sought to curtail foreigners' activity in order to promote Spanish participation in the trade between the Iberian Peninsula and northern Europe, the city of Seville opted for an alternative solution: to attract and protect the presence of northerners in the city. In a paper published in 1998, Stols called attention to the necessity of rethinking the Low Countries emigration as a *continuum* throughout the fifteenth and sixteenth century, instead of understanding the migration prior to and after the beginning of the Eighty Years' War as two different contexts.[96] This interpretation is certainly relevant in the case of the migration to Seville. Indeed, there are no significant differences between the typology of those who arrived before and after the early 1570s; in both cases, the majority were young single Catholic individuals who sought to improve their socio-economic position. Nonetheless, the Dutch Revolt did mean a turning point in terms of the number of migrants.

---

95   This is further analysed in chapter 3.
96   Stols, "Experiencias y ganancias."

From the 1550s, a small but stable community of northerners is identifiable in Seville, while some Flemish migrants, like Francisco Bernal, began to perform an important role in the town's economic life. In 1548, Bernal obtained the first long-term leases of naves in the *Atarazanas*. At the end of the century, the number of *flamencos* in Seville must have reached a total of two hundred individuals, probably more if including children, women and temporary migrants. By then, Flemish families were in possession of almost all of the *Atarazanas*. For the monarchy, their capacity to trade in Baltic and Scandinavian timber justified their control of Seville's main warehouses. In the last three decades of the century, the merchants residing in the *Atarazanas* developed a remarkable social capital that prompted the cohesion of the group and prevented competition from outsiders, most notably by farming the timber *alcabala*. This explains how a handful of foreign families could maintain their pre-eminent position in the market throughout more than three decades.

CHAPTER 3

Casa y Servicio

> ... [T]hey were loyal vassals, natives of my estates in Flanders in the land
> that remains obedient, as well as citizens and residents with houses, wives
> and children in that city [Seville] for longer than twenty years from now.[1]

With these words, Philip II defended the Flemish merchants from Francisco de
Coloma, who had confiscated their cargoes of grain in 1592. To justify that the
activity of these foreigners was legal, the king argued that they were rightful
vassals of his kingdom and citizens of Seville because they owned houses and
had families for longer than twenty years. If the words of Philip II are of any
worth, then marriage and the owning of a house for a sustained time marked
someone's successful integration into Castilian society. This chapter deals with
how Flemish and German migrants achieved these two milestones: how they
married and how they established a house in the *Atarazanas*.

Notarial sources in Seville often refer to a merchant's household as *casa y
servicio* (house and service), which perfectly illustrates the composition of
the household of most *Atarazanas* merchants, formed by the members of the
nuclear family as well as the workers of the domestic service and the firm.[2]
The Spanish word *casa* itself is a complex concept. It can refer to the physical space in which the family lived, the house, and to the basic unit of early
modern trade, the family firm. The concept of *casa*, thus, encapsulates the
blurred boundaries between family and business in early modern Europe.[3]
In the words of Antunes, "for the conventional wisdom among historians,"
family represented the "cheapest and safest way of doing business before the

---

1 AHPSe, SP, 9278, 384r.
2 Girón Pascual did a similar analysis about the household of Genoese families in Granada in
   a similar period in Rafael M. Girón Pascual, "La corte del mercader: la vivienda y el servicio
   doméstico de los genoveses de Granada (ss. XVI-XVII)," in *Vida cotidiana en la Monarquía
   Hispánica: Tiempos y espacios*, eds. Inmaculada Arias de Saavedra Alías and Miguel Luis
   López Guadalupe Muñoz (Granada: Universidad de Granada, 2015), 293–306. On the family
   firm in sixteenth-century Seville, see Béatrice Perez, *Les marchands de Séville*, 240.
3 The topic has been long discussed by scholars studying long-distance trade, and commercial diasporas in Early Modern Europe. E.g. Avner Greif, "Family Structure, Institutions,
   and Growth: The Origins and Implications of Western Corporations," *The American
   Economic Review* 96, no. 2 (2006): 308–312. See also Francesca Trivellato, *The Familiarity of
   Strangers: The Sephardic Diaspora, Livorno, and Cross-Cultural Trade in the Early Modern
   Period* (New Haven: Yale University Press, 2009).

Industrial Revolution."[4] However evident this interpretation is, Antunes also points at the need to reconsider it; these blurred boundaries between the family and the business does not mean that "an intrinsic inclination to cooperate reigned among members of the same family or religious group," as historians tend to assume.[5]

Following Antunes' critical approach, this chapter departs from the premise that business prompted family, rather than the other way around. It examines how *Atarazanas* merchants built commercial cooperation through marriage and how the organisation of their households overlapped with the organisation of their firms. The first section explores their marriage practices, as well as the role of women in the group. The second one analyses twenty-six promises of dowries to reflect on how fathers- and sons-in-law used marriage as a means for commercial cooperation between them. Finally, the third section examines the *servicio* (service): the domestic servants and slaves of the merchants' households, as well as the interns who worked for their firms.

1   Marriage Practices

As analysed in the previous chapter, there was an unprecedented wave of migration to Seville of single young individuals from the Low Countries in the second half of the sixteenth century. For newcomers, who sought to enhance their socio-economic position in Andalusia, marriage constituted a means for obtaining social and economic capital provided by the in-law family, which was fundamental for their early steps in the new territory. Moreover, marriage represented an essential source of reputation that facilitated foreigners' commercial activity. In his book *Trade and Trust in the Eighteenth-century Atlantic World*, Lamikiz concluded that, for foreigners involved in long-distance trade, marriage went hand in hand with reputation:

> [O]ne would expect a married merchant in Cádiz to be willing to publicise his condition before travelling to America, since in the eyes of potential principals and creditors a wife and children meant a household that depended upon him, a permanent address, a place to which he was likely

---

4 Cátia Antunes, "Cross-Cultural Business Cooperation," in *Religion and Trade: Cross-Cultural Exchanges in World History, 1000–1900*, eds. Francesca Trivellato, Leor Halevi and Cátia Antunes (New York: Oxford University Press, 2014), 150.
5 Antunes, "Cross-Cultural Business Cooperation," 151.

to return (...) Trust and distrust ran parallel to the merchant's marital
status.[6]

Similar mechanisms of reputation certainly applied to sixteenth-century
northerners in Seville, as evidenced by the royal decree quoted at the beginning of the chapter. Unfortunately, notarial sources rarely provide precise
information about foreigners' date of arrival in Seville, and hence it is not possible to assess how long it took them to marry after their migration. However,
it is fair to say that there was an incentive for migrants to marry when they
decided to establish themselves for good in Seville.

Notarial sources are also of little help in the analysis of marriage practices. Marriages were not notarised, and we only know about them through
dowry promises, which were not always formalised before a notary public.
Nonetheless, these merchants' marriages were systematically registered at the
records of *El Sagrario*, the cathedral's chapel where most Flemish merchants
were parishioners according to their testaments. These records offer a rich
insight into the marriage practices of different generations of *Atarazanas* families, from 1565 – when the first marriage was registered – to the end of the
century, as Table 3.1 shows.

Surnames like Bambel, Aparte, Bernal or Arbauts are frequent in the list of
brides. These women, who were natives of Castile, were the daughters of the
first generation of *flamencos* that resided in the *Atarazanas* around the middle
of the century: Juan and Enrique Bambel, Enrique Aparte, Francisco Bernal
or Miguel Arbauts. Other surnames indicate the northern roots of brides, like
Agustina Frisia, Bárbara Broasagan, Catalina Hedebaut, Ana Jacome or María
Belden, although it was not possible to trace who their parents were or when
they migrated to Seville. North European men principally married the daughters of other compatriots, which suggests their limited marriage options at the
time of their arrival and their dependence on already established migrants
during their first years in Seville.

The Spanish-like surnames of other brides indicate that *Atarazanas* merchants married women from Castilian families as well. In those cases, grooms
were either marrying a second time, like Juan de Bestoven Sr. (to Leonor Díaz),
Juan Jacart (Beatriz Núñez) and Esteban Jansen (Isabel de Lorenzana), or were
flamencos of a second generation who were native of Andalusia, like Diego
Bernal (Juana López), Enrique Bambel (María de la Paz), Enrique Aparte
Jr (María For de Montoya), Juan Sarens (Isabel de Lorenzana) and Diego

---

6   Lamikiz, *Trade and Trust*, 148.

TABLE 3.1 Marriages of *Atarazanas* merchants and relatives. Brides belonging to a second-
or third-generation of Flemish families in Andalusia are indicated with an F after
their names. Brides belonging to Flemish families that resided in the *Atarazanas*
are indicated with At

Groom	Bride	Year
Felipe Sarens	Ana Jans de Breda (F)	1565
Gaspar Borman	Margarita Bambel (F, At)	1566
Juan Jacart	Bárbola Bambel (F, At)	1567
Juan de Bestoven Sr.	Leonor Díaz	1568
Gaspar Loscarte	María Aparte (F, At)	1568
Luis Jacart	Agustina Frisia (F)	1569
Carlos Malapert	Magdalena Bambel (F, At)	1570
Bautista Búcar	Margarita Aparte (F, At)	1571
Diego Bernal	Juana López	1572
Felipe Buiter	Margarita Aparte (F, At)	1574
Enrique Aparte	Bárbara Broasagan (F)	1575
Juan Jacart	Beatriz Núñez	1576
Esteban Jansen	Catalina Aparte (F, At)	1575
Cornieles Valdovinos	Catalina Hedebaut (F)	1576
Jaques Nicolás	Ana Jacome (F)	1576
Guillermo Estalengue	Margarita Aparte (F, At)	1577
Pedro Escolín	Francisca Bestoven (F, At)	1577
Jaques Nicolás	Bárbola Bernal (F, At)	1580
Francisco Roelant	Catalina Hedebaut (F, At)	1581
Guillermo Corinse	Margarita Sarens (F, At)	1582
Juan Leclerque	Francisca Seuste (F)	1584
Juan de la Cadena	Ana Aparte (F, At)	1584
Pedro Gisberto	Isabel Arbauts (F, At)	1584
Enrique Bambel	María Belden (F)	1586
Tobías Buc	Ana Martínez	1588
Juan Bermero	Margarita Arbauts (F, At)	1591
Enrique Bambel	María de la Paz	1593
Enrique Aparte Jr.	María For de Montoya	1594
Esteban Jansen	Isabel de Lorenzana	1595
Juan Sarens	Isabel de Lorenzana (F, At)	1597
Juan van Hooren	Isabel Arbauts (F, At)	1597
Miguel Arbauts	Josina Bernal (F, At)	1597
Diego Valdovinos	Ana Reinaldos de la Peña	1598

SOURCE: APSC, REGISTROS MATRIMONIALES, AÑOS 1565–1598

Valdovinos (Ana Reinaldos de la Peña). The case of Tobías Buc, who married Ana Martínez, is somehow different: born in Andalusia, she was the daughter of a Spaniard, Juan Martínez, and Catalina de Angelberto, a woman from an influential Flemish family in El Puerto de Santa María.[7]

In other words, second-generation migrants and those who married a second time often opted for a marriage to a Castilian woman. Their individual reputation – or that of their families – allowed them to take a step forward in their assimilation by marrying Spanish women.[8] In the seventeenth century, successfully integrated Flemish merchants would diversify the marriage strategies of their offspring to promote their socio-economic position by forging alliances with Castilian families as well as other influential Flemish families; for instance, the descendants of Francisco Bernal and Jaques Nicolás maintained an important position in Andalusian trade and were ennobled in the early seventeenth century thanks to these strategies.[9]

To complement the scope of the marriage practices of the group, we must consider those that did not register their union in *El Sagrario* parish records for different reasons. Some migrants married in another Andalusian town, where they first arrived. This is the case of Miguel Arbauts, who married Catalina Enríquez in the early 1560s in Cádiz, and moved to the *Atarazanas* years later.[10] Manas Enríquez, a brother of Catalina, married in Cádiz with Gertruds Angelberto in the 1570s; the married couple settled in Seville in the next decade.[11] And other migrants did not marry at all, like Justo de Bil and Jaques Sesbaut, who jointly ran the same *casa*. De Bil, a migrant from Gorcum who first worked for Esteban Jansen for several years, began an independent commercial career forming a partnership with Jaques Sesbaut, a migrant from Antwerp who first resided in El Puerto de Santa María. They established themselves in a house they rented from Jansen, sited next to the *Atarazanas*, in an area known as *Corral de Jerez*.[12] They lived together for some years, until Jaques Sesabut

---

7   APSC, Registro Matrimoniales, año 1588, s.f.

8   I am taking here a classic definition of assimilation, as a later stage in migrants' integration. As Lucassen and Lucassen put it: "the state in which immigrants or their descendants do not regard themselves primarily as different from the native-born population and are no longer perceived as such." Jan Lucassen and Leo Lucassen. *Migration, Migration History, History: Old Paradigms and New Perspectives* (Bern: Lang, 1997), 23.

9   On the Nicolás family in the seventeenth century, see Crailsheim, *Spanish Connection*, 196–199.

10   Miguel Arbauts' testament, AHPSe, SP, 9276, 165r.

11   See chapter 1, footnote 94.

12   After the death of Juan in 1593, his cousin Jaques Sesbaut, who had been previously representing them in El Puerto de Santa María (AHSe, SP, 9298), moved to Seville. Testament of Juan Sesbaut (AHPSe, SP, 9277, 942r).

moved back to the Low Countries in 1600, leaving De Bil running the household and firm on his own until his death in 1605.[13]

1.1 Flemish Women in the *Atarazanas*

The former analysis presents women as assets of husbands and fathers, considering them as passive players in the socio-economic organisation of *Atarazanas*
families. Unfortunately, notarial sources do not permit an examination of
women's agency in depth. Women only appear as principals in a notarial deed
when their husband was leaving the city temporarily and, for that, he had to
grant her a licence in advance. For instance, Juan de la Cadena authorised
his wife, Ana Aparte, to act on his behalf during his travel to the Americas.[14]
Another Flemish merchant travelling to the Americas, Gaspar Borman, granted
a similar licence to his wife Margarita Bambel in 1576.[15] But these are exceptional cases. For the most part, women barely participated in notarial deeds
and, when they did, they were juridically dependent on a male figure: their
husbands, their fathers, their brothers or even their brothers-in-law.

Nonetheless, the previous analysis of marriage practices offers interesting
hints about women's role within the group of Flemish families specialised in
timber trade. The most evident one is that women were essential for migrants'
integration into the receiving society; many were natives of Castile and could
be sociocultural intermediators between husbands and the local community.
When merchants lacked the incentive of strengthening their socio-economic
integration into the local community, either because they were second-generation migrants or had lived long enough in Andalusia, they often married a
woman from a Castilian family, which sped up their assimilation into the local
community.

The marriage of widows illustrates women's economic relevance for the
group, as well. Table 3.1 shows several cases of women who, after being widowed, married other *Atarazanas* merchants: Catalina Hedebaut married first to
Cornieles Valdovinos and later to Francisco Roelant, Isabel de Lorenzana married first to Esteban Jansen and later to Juan Sarens, and Isabel Arbauts married first to Pedro Gisberto and later to Juan van Hooren.[16] Widows inherited

---

13 AHPSe, SP, 9310,163r-164r.
14 A document that she used at least in eight notarial contracts in which she acted as principal and on behalf of De la Cadena. AHPSe, SP, 9242, 1176v; 9245P, 161r; 9259, 823v; 9275,
777v; 9255, 695r; 9257, 930r; 9260, 44r; 9290, 911v.This happened before they finally established in Cádiz in 1589 AHPSe, SP, 9241, 1006r-1009r.
15 AHPSe, SP, 7784, 457r.
16 Notarial deeds reveal similar cases. For instance, Margarita Sarens who, after the death of
Guillermo Corinse, married to Federico Hinquel; and Ana Aparte, widow of Diego Bernal,

the stock of products and the accounts of the late merchant and remarried an individual that belonged or was close to the group of *Atarazanas* merchants.[17] For many of the deceased migrants, in-laws were the only kin that they had in Andalusia and, normally, a relative of the widow – either brother or father – took over their unfinished business, acting as testamentary executors, until the widow married again.

Only on exceptional occasions did widows become risk takers, administering the estate and remaining stock that they and their offspring had inherited from late husbands.[18] When Pedro Gisberto died in 1592, the father of his wife Isabel, Miguel Arbauts, became tutor of Pedro and Isabel's children.[19] However, Miguel Arbauts died in 1594, at a time in which Isabel's brother was in America, so she began to administer the household and the firm for at least two years until she finally married another Flemish merchant, Juan van Hooren, in 1597, to whom she granted a generous dowry of almost 6000 *ducados*.[20] During that time, Isabel even contracted a freight of timber from Hamburg to Seville for which she paid 7022 *reales* to the German ship captain Giles Simone.[21]

Isabel Arbauts's case is similar to the one of Gertruds de Angelberto, widow of Manas Enríquez. De Angelberto administered the firm for at least six years after his husband's death in 1592, without delegating to any relative until her son Josephe came of age. A notarial deed dated in January 1598 shows her active involvement in timber trade: she claimed (and received) 26 *ducados* from Juan Gras, after he had sold by mistake two trees that were lying by the front door of his *casa*, which actually belonged to Gertruds de Angelberto.[22]

---

who remarried to Juan de la Cadena. Moreover, the table includes the case of Margarita Aparte (Bautista Búcar, Felipe Buiter, Guillermo Estalengue), although she is not included in the analysis because her husbands did not specialise in timber trade.

17   The practice was not exceptional to the group of the *Atarazanas*. Crailsheim identified several cases among the Flemish migrants of Seville in which a "widow remarried a compatriot and possible business partner of the deceased husband." Crailsheim, *Spanish Connection*, 118. The Jews even had an institution that obliged widows to marry a relative of their husbands, the levirate marriage Trivellato, *The Familiarity of Strangers*, 135–136.

18   Peter Mathias, "Strategies for Reducing Risk by Entrepreneurs in the early modern period," in *Entrepreneurs and Entrepreneurship in Early Modern Times: Merchants and Industrialists within the Orbit of the Dutch Staple Market*, eds. Clé Lesger and Leo Noordegraaf (Den Haag: Stichting Hollandse Historische Reeks, 1995), 7.

19   AHPSe, SP, 9274, 31v. She commissioned his younger brother to collect Gisberto's remaining debts AHPSe, SP; 9285, 848.

20   AHPSe, SP, 9298, 590r. Her activity is documented in at least ten timber sales. AHPSe, SP, 9280, 896; 9280, 983; 9280, 984; 9281, 196; 9281, 237; 9283, 519r; 9284, 634r; 9284, 399r; 9285, 124; 9285, 807.

21   For a total price of 1950 *Carolusgulden*. AHPSe, SP, 9284, 297r.

22   AHPSe, SP, 9299, 689r-690r. More on the role of Josephe helping his mother: AHPSe, SP, 9296, 696.

She even worked on commission for other merchants; in November 1597, she notarised an agreement to sell 2323 pieces of timber, of different sorts and qualities, which she had received from Van Hooren, for a commission of six percent on the sale price.[23]

2   Cooperation between In-laws

For older well-established migrants, marrying a daughter to a recently arrived compatriot represented an opportunity to seek the continuity of their business by strengthening their commercial ties in northern Europe. The repetition of surnames, especially Aparte or Bernal, in Table 3.1 gives a good account of that. Since their arrival in the middle of the century, Enrique Aparte and Francisco Bernal built a network of kinship ties with which they extended their business beyond Seville and through different economic sectors.

Enrique Aparte married four times (Virginia Sarens, Ana van Aca, Elvira Jacome, and Bárbola Brabisaguen), although he only had children with Virginia and Elvira. The marriages of his oldest daughters in Seville were rather modest. He married his daughters Josina and Catalina to Flemish coopers, Gerónimo Cantú and Melchor de Haçe, who resided in the district of Triana, just across the Guadalquivir River.[24] The marriages of his youngest daughters show greater ambition and a better economic situation. Two of them married merchants that became influential members of the Flemish community in Sanlúcar de Barrameda: Maria Aparte to Gaspar Loscarte, whose history was discussed in previous chapters, and Margarita Aparte to Baptista Búcar. After Margarita became widowed, she married Guillermo Estalengue, an English merchant with whom she left Andalusia after the proscription of the English in Spain. A third daughter, also named Catalina, married Esteban Jansen, the greatest timber merchant in Castile, while a fourth one, Ana, married Diego Bernal, the son of Francisco Bernal. When Diego died, Ana married Juan de la Cadena, a Flemish merchant who moved to Cádiz. His only surviving son, Enrique Aparte Jr., was too young to marry at the time of his father's death in 1581. He eventually married a Castilian woman in 1594.

Francisco Bernal implemented a similar strategy with the offspring he had with his wife Bárbola Gomar, as well as his orphaned grandchildren. He

---

23   Ninety-six dozen pine planks and five more planks, one thousand *tripitrapes*, thirty oak trees, one hundred small beams, thirty-six long beams. AHPSe, SP, 9299, 266r.

24   They were frequently involved in the trade of Baltic timber as well, e.g. AHPSe, SP, 9227, 891v.

married his oldest daughters to merchants that were established in Sanlúcar. His daughter Bárbola married the Flemish Juan Bambel, with whom she moved to Sanlúcar in the 1570s.[25] His daughter Catalina married Juan de Bestoven Sr. They lived in Sanlúcar, where Catalina gave birth to Juan and Francisca. When Juan de Bestoven Sr. and Catalina Bernal died, Francisco Bernal took care of the future of his grandchildren. He made Juan de Bestoven Jr. work in several *casas* of the *Atarazanas* in the early 1580s, until he finally owned one of his own by the end of the decade. Francisca de Bestoven married Nicolás de Melemburque at an early age. After De Melemburque's death, she entered the convent of the *Espíritu Santo*.[26] Francisco Bernal also took care of the marriages of the orphaned offspring of his son Alonso Bernal, who was living in Bruges with his wife Dorotea Jacome. He married Bárbola Bernal to a former worker of his house, Jaques Nicolás, who soon assumed an influential position in the Flemish and German nation.[27]

The lives of Enrique Aparte and Francisco Bernal demonstrate that daughters were a valuable asset for the socio-economic ambitions of merchants. As Wijnroks noted in his study of Dutch families trading with Russia in the second half of the sixteenth century, given the notable age gap with their sons, fathers sought to marry their daughters to older merchants to ensure the continuity of the family firm until their sons came of age.[28] The dowries that older merchants promised for marrying their daughters illustrate their desire to seal a commercial cooperation tie with their prospective sons-in-law.

2.1   Dowry Promises

A typical dowry promise consisted of a statement made by the father-in-law to the groom promising a cash payment "to sustain the burdens of marriage," as well as an estimation of the bride's trousseau, a number of belongings that she contributed to the future household that were often listed in detail.[29] According to Mathias, dowries reflected a "carefully estimated reciprocity" between father- and son-in-law, based on the "presumptions about the prospective earning of power of the groom."[30] Trivellato goes a step further,

---

25   AHPSe, SP, 7772, 1482r.
26   AHPSe, SP, 9251, 78r-v.
27   Stols, *Spaanse Brabanders*, II, 49.
28   Wijnroks, *Handel tussen Rusland*, 181. Something that Puttevils corroborates for Antwerp merchants participating in long-distance trade. *Merchants and Trading*, 81.
29   One example of dowry is AHPSE, SP, 9216, 851r. A dowry often included some extraordinary clauses, such as the donation of slaves, like in the one granted by Francisco Bernal to Jaques Nicolás AHPSe, SP, 9224, 1143r.
30   Mathias, "Strategies for Reducing Risk," 12. Puttevils, *Merchants and Trading*, 89. For a complete study on marriage practices in the Low Countries, see Martha Howell, *The*

arguing that, for the Jewish families she studied, dowries constituted implicit contracts of commercial partnerships between in-laws, and were the largest one-off capital input that individuals received.[31] Dowries certainly meant the largest capital input that many *Atarazanas* merchants received on one-off occasions, and implied the creation of a sustained cooperation tie between the older merchant and his younger son-in-law.[32] However, as the following chapter analyses, only on a few occasions did marriage lead to the creation of general partnerships between in-laws, with a joint stock of commodities and a clear estimation of capital and labour inputs.

We could find sixteen promises of dowries participated by *flamencos* in the notaries of Francisco Díaz and Juan de Tordesillas, although testaments frequently contain references to non-notarised dowries, which allows us to form a total sample of twenty-six dowries. The high levels of trust between parties probably made such notarisation unnecessary; many grooms had worked for their future fathers-in-law before the marriage and they would live in the same building complex. Table 3.2 offers an overview of the value of the dowries participated by *Atarazanas* merchants during four decades, either giving or receiving them. In the column at the far right, DP indicates whether dowry promises were notarised, while those identified through testaments are indicated with TS. Notarised promises are richer in detail and often distinguish between capital (Cap. in the table) in *reales* and the estimation of the trousseau's value (Trous.) in *reales*. For dowries identified from testaments, this distinction is not possible and consequently only the total (Total) in *reales* is indicated. The column Year provides a precise date of the wedding – not the dowry promise – when this is certain, according to the parish records of *El Sagrario*. For the cases in which this is not possible, the field indicates an estimation of the decade in which the wedding took place.

Table 3.2 shows that, with some exceptions, most dowries were valued in a range that went from 11,000 to 22,000 *reales* (1000 and 2000 *ducados*). Many of the more modest dowries were granted by grandfathers and brothers-in-law who arranged marriage of orphaned female relatives. For instance, Francisco Bernal granted a dowry of 3300 *reales* to Pedro Escolin, a Flemish tailor, to marry his granddaughter. A bit more exceptional is the dowry that Miguel Arbauts granted another tailor from Antwerp residing in Seville, Silvestre

---

  Marriage Exchange: Property, Social Place, and Gender in Cities of the Low Countries, 1300–
  1550 (Chicago: University of Chicago Press, 1998). Howell, *The Marriage Exchange*.

31 Trivellato, *The Familiarity of Strangers*, 139–140.
32 Trivellato, *The Familiarity of Strangers*, 136.

TABLE 3.2   Dowries participated in by *Atarazanas* merchants and relatives

Bride	In-law (granter)	Groom (granted)	Cap.	Trous.	Total	Year	NC.
Catalina Enríquez	Francisca Pérez*	Miguel Arbauts Sr.			13200	1560	TS
Josina Aparte	Enrique Aparte	Gerónimo Cantú			11000	1560s	TS
Catalina Aparte	Enrique Aparte	Melchor de Haçe			11000	1560s	TS
Felipe Sarens		Ana Janse			5500	1565	TS
Nicolás de Melemburque		Francisca Bernal			33000*	1565	TS
Agustina de Frisia	Germán de Frisia	Luis Jacart	5500	5500	11000	1570	DP
Adriana Enríquez	Jaques Enríquez (Cádiz)	Jaques Brahusen			18700	1570s	TS
Magdalena Bambel	Bárbola Bernal*	Carlos Malapert	14250	5000	19250	1571	DP
Margarita Aparte	Enrique Aparte	Bautista Búcar	13200	8800	22000	1571	DP
María Enríquez	Francisca Pérez* (Cádiz)	Luis Cloet	11000		11000	1573	TS
Catalina Aparte	Enrique Aparte	Esteban Jansen	16500	5500	22000*	1575	DP
Margarita Aparte		Guillermo Estalengue	22000		22000	1577	DP
Francisca Bestoven	Francisco Bernal*	Pedro Escolín	2500	800	3300	1577	DP
Bárbola Bernal	Francisco Bernal*	Jaqués Nicolás	16500	1650	18150	1580	DP
Isabel Arbauts	Miguel Arbauts	Pedro Monel	11000	2640	13640	1581	DP
Margarita Sarens	Felipe Sarens	Guillermo Corinse			16500	1582	TS
Isabel Arbauts	Miguel Arbauts	Pedro Gisberto	19556	4644	24200	1584	DP

TABLE 3.2   Dowries participated in by *Atarazanas* merchants and relatives (*cont.*)

Bride	In-law (granter)	Groom (granted)	Cap.	Trous.	Total	Year	N.C.
María de Oliver	Guillermo de Lunia	Juan de Bestoven	6600	1100	7700	1586	DP
Bárbola de Vanoys	Miguel Arbauts*	Silvestre de Gamarra	700	987	1687	1588	DP
Margarita Arbauts	Miguel Arbauts	Juan Bermero	11000	4400	15400	1591	DP
Juana Isac	Elías Sirman*	Juan van den Brug	22000		22000	1594	DP
Isabel de Lorenzana		Esteban Jansen	55000	33000	88000	1595	TS
Josina Bernal	Jaques Nicolás*	Miguel Arbauts Jr.	8414	2586	11000	1597	DP
Isabel Arbauts		Juan van Hooren	64935		64935	1597	DP
Margarita Sarens		Federico Hinquel			115500	1599	DP
María Nicolás	Jaques Nicolás	Nicolás Antonio	29627	36373	66000*	1602	DP

Note: The asterisk indicates those who were not the father of the bride but granted the dowry
SOURCE: SEE ANNEX D

de Gamarra, to marry Bárbola de Vanoys, an orphan from Antwerp that had been serving in his *casa*. The promised dowry was valued at only 1700 *reales*.[33] Widows who married again often administered their own dowry. In these cases, the amounts are notably high. Isabel Arbauts promised 64,935 *reales* to Juan van Hooren, while Margarita Sarens promised 115,500 *reales* to Federico Hinquel. The reason for such high amounts is that, by means of dowries, they were promising what they had inherited from their deceased husbands; this was the "*mitad del multiplicado*," that is half of the wealth that the late husband had gained since the marriage.

33   AHPSe, SP, 9252, 622r.

Dowries represent a good proxy to estimate the evolution of these merchants' wealth.[34] The available dowries permit us to identify the economic progression of the two most influential merchants of the group in the 1580s and
1590s, Esteban Jansen and Jaques Nicolás. While the first dowry Esteban Jansen
received from his first marriage in 1575 to Catalina Aparte was set at 22,000
reales (2000 *ducados*), the Castilian family Lorenzana promised him 88,000
reales (8000 *ducados*) to marry Isabel in 1595; the value of dowries quadrupled
twenty years later.[35] The case of Jaques Nicolás is similar; in 1580, he received
18,150 *reales* for his marriage to Bárbola Bernal and, twenty years later, in 1600,
he promised 66,000 *reales* – which tripled the dowry he received – to Nicolás
Antonio Jr. to marry his daughter María Nicolás.[36]

Some well-established merchants used the prospect of a house and
warehouses in the *Atarazanas* to attract young entrepreneurs to marry their
daughters. For these young entrepreneurs, a space in the *Atarazanas* meant
a logistical advantage in the early steps of their career and introduced them
into the social capital of other compatriots specialised in timber trade.[37]
Cases marked with an asterisk in the column Total indicate that the dowry
promise included an estimation of the value of a rent in the complex. Enrique
Aparte granted Esteban Jansen a promise of dowry in September 1575 to marry
Catalina. Aparte promised Jansen 2000 *ducados*: 1000 *ducados* to be paid in
cash in six months, 500 *ducados* from the value of his daughter's trousseau,
and 500 *ducados* from the estimation that Enrique Aparte did on how much
his subsistence during a year could cost. He made this estimation because,
as agreed in the dowry, Jansen would take over Aparte's possessions in the
Atarazanas under the condition that the father-in-law would live with the
newlyweds until his death.[38] In a following notarial deed, Aparte declared that
he transferred to Jansen the contract that he had signed with the king for the

---

34   Trivellato, *The Familiarity of Strangers*, 138. For an overview of wealth in Seville in the
       seventeenth century through the analysis of testaments, see Jesús Aguado de los Reyes,
       Fortuna y miseria en la Sevilla del siglo XVII (Sevilla: Ayuntamiento de Sevilla, 1996).

35   This was not paid according to the testament. AHPSe, SP, 9292, 302r.

36   AHPSe, SP, 9224, 1143r. AHPSe, SP, 9312, 520r.

37   Ogilvie defines social capital as "promotion of mutual and reciprocal links within a group
       that aspires to become close and cohesive." Ogilvie, *Institutions and European Trade*, 427.
       According to Lamikiz, "living close to one another in the same city made the monitoring
       of reputations much easier." *Trade and Trust*, 143.

38   Aparte also transferred the domestic service of the house to Esteban Jansen and his
       daughter Catalina. AHPSe, SP, 7781, 947r.

rent of his possessions in the *Atarazanas*, which expired in three years.[39] This way, Enrique Aparte was stepping down in his commercial activity, ensuring the future of his daughter Catalina, who by this time was fourteen, and that of his son, Enrique Aparte Jr., who was nine.[40]

Francisco Bernal followed a similar, although more ambitious, strategy. In 1565, for the dowry of his daughter Francisca, he transferred to Nicolás de Melemburque a great deal of the third nave of the *Atarazanas* for a period of twenty years, which they estimated at 3000 *ducados*.[41] Fifteen years later, in 1580, Francisco Bernal transferred his house and business to a younger in-law, just like Enrique Aparte had done some years earlier. Bernal rented the house where he was living at that moment (*"que yo, al presente, vivo y resido"*) to his former employee, Jaques Nicolás, who was marrying his granddaughter Bárbola.[42] Jaques Nicolás was taking over the contract Bernal had signed with the king in 1575, which expired in 1595, for which he committed to pay 22,000 maravedís (58.8 *ducados*) per year to Francisco Bernal, in addition to the 38,000 maravedís (101.6 *ducados*) that they had to pay every year to the royal palace.

Finally, Francisco Bernal transferred another long-term lease in the *Atarazanas* to one of his daughters, also named Bárbola and widow of Juan Bambel, in 1582. Bárbola was taking over the contract that Francisco had signed in 1581 with the royal palace for a period of twenty years, at a price of 45,000 maravedís (ca. 120 *ducados*) per year. With this, Francisco Bernal was privileging a daughter who, as a widow, was in a more precarious condition, although a clause in the contract stated that this property had to be discounted from her future share in the heritage. According to the contract, Francisco Bernal was moving out from Jaques Nicolás's house to his daughter's Bárbola, with whom he lived until his death in 1587.[43]

---

39   The value of this rent would cover Aparte's subsistence from the second year on, AHPSe, SP, 7781, 948r.

40   AHPSe, SP, 7781, 562r.

41   From Francisco Bernal's testament AHPSe, SP, 9251, 79v-80r.

42   This time the transference was independent to the dowry promise, although the leasing contract was notarised the same day, estimated at 1650 *ducados* (AHPSe, SP, 9224, 1140r and 9224, 1143r.). The house was in the *atarazana* next to the hospital of Saint George, facing the bank of the river ("arenal del río").

43   "[E] me constituyo por vuestro tenedor e poseedor ynquilino." The lease included houses and stores at the main gate of the *Atarazanas*, between the house of Felipe Sarens and the hospital of Saint George. The contract between Bernal and Alcázares had been signed in in 1581. AHPSe, SP, 9231, 557r-v.

3   *Servicio*

The distinction between the two complementary spheres of the *casa,* the domestic and the business ones, becomes clearer when examining those who worked for the merchant and resided in his house, known as the *servicio* (staff). The *servicio* was formed by servants and slaves that mostly took care of the domestic chores, on the one hand, and young interns that worked for the firm, on the other. Merchants' testaments offer a snapshot of the composition of the *servicio*, which varied greatly from merchant to merchant, representing a good proxy of their importance within the group. The most modest household was the one run jointly between Jaques Sesbaut and Justo de Bil, who had no one working for the firm and only one person taking care of their house, Jertruite van Santelanda, a cousin of Justo de Bil.[44] At the other extreme, Esteban Jansen and his second wife Isabel de Lorenzana lived with five slaves (Pedro, Juan, Cecilia, María and a daughter of Maria), as well as a Spanish housekeeper named Juana Sánchez and her daughter María. At the time of his death, he also employed two nephews in his firm, Juan Cornieles, who lived in Jansen's house, and Juan van Çelar, who was representing him in Germany.[45]

3.1   *Domestic Workers*

All of those who served the householder and family, undertaking domestic chores and errands of the *casa*, constituted an unpaid labour force, although not all of them had the same status. The domestic service was formed by free workers, mostly housekeepers ("*amas,*" or "*doncellas*" if they were young), and slaves ("*esclavos*") from Africa or captured in the Moriscos' wars in Granada.[46] Some housekeepers were poor Spanish women, like Catalina de Valles who served Juan Sesbaut, or Juana Sánchez who worked for Esteban Jansen. Some came from the Low Countries, like Jertruite van Santelanda, Justo de Bil's cousin and worker of his house. A more interesting case is the one of Bárbola de Vanoys, a Flemish girl born in Antwerp who migrated to Seville with his father. When he died, she notarised her entry into the household of Miguel Arbauts, declaring her commitment to serve for a period of four years to Arbauts's "wife, house and family," and to "accompany your [Arbauts'] wife when she goes to church."[47]

---

44   AHPSe, 9301, 332r-334r.
45   AHPSe, SP, 9289, 564r.
46   In the sale contract they would normally specify that the slave had been captured in war, and not in time of peace. "[V]os vendo por de buena guerra e no de paz" (for instance, AHPSe, SP, 9257, 321r.).
47   AHPSe, SP, 9233, 1017r.

The absence of more contracts of the like limits the analysis of free domestic workers; their presence mostly come to light through the bequests that some of them received from the merchants or their wives. Simón Enríquez left 30 *ducados* to Ana, a worker in his house.[48] So did Esteban Jansen, who bequeathed 200 *reales* (almost 20 *ducados*) to his housekeeper, Juana Sánchez, for her service, and other 200 *reales* for her daughter Maria.[49] Some even paid for the dowries of their younger maids. For instance, the wife of Miguel Arbauts, Catalina Enríquez, ordered in her last will to pay 20 *ducados* to Francisca Cara, the daughter of a servant, for her future dowry.[50] This was not the only dowry the Arbauts family paid to servants; as analysed above, Miguel Arbauts had paid 1700 *ducados* for the dowry of Bárbola de Vanoys to marry Silvestre de Gamarra, a tailor from Antwerp that had migrated to Seville.[51] Dowries and bequests may have been the only meaningful economic contribution these women received from their employers, since nothing indicates that they received a salary, besides the accommodation, food and clothing that householders must have provided.

Free domestic workers were outnumbered by slaves, who were treated as the merchants' property and, as such, they were often traded.[52] There is a surprisingly high number of notarised slave sales, which speaks of a dynamic local market for slaves in Seville.[53] *Atarazanas* merchants were involved in at least 29 notarised transactions of slaves either as sellers or buyers. These contracts generally followed a standardised model, with brief information about slaves based on age, sex, any physical defect, and their origin. Furthermore, each deed contained a risk declaration, in which the seller stated that the slave concerned was not drunkard, thieve, demonic or blind, had never run away before, and had been captured in a fair way (in "a good war and not in

---

48 AHPSe, SP, 9312, 517r.

49 AHPSe, SP, 9289, 722r.

50 AHPSe, SP, 9266, 523r.

51 AHPSe, SP, 9252, 622r.

52 Despite the high number, they did not specialise in the Atlantic slave trade. Only two of them, Francisco Bernal and Enrique Aparte Jr, participated in this trade. On Francisco Bernal: Abadía Flores, "La comunidad flamenca," 181. On Enrique Aparte: AHPSe, SP, 9280, 246 and 9281, 886.

53 We owe a great part of this historiographical contribution to recent research conducted by Manuel Fernández Chaves and Rafael Pérez García. See Rafael M. Pérez García, Manuel F. Fernández Chaves and José Luis Belmonte Postigo, eds., *Los negocios de la esclavitud: Tratantes y mercados de esclavos en el Atlántico Ibérico, siglos XV-XVIII* (Sevilla: Editorial Universidad de Sevilla, 2018).

peace time.")[54] Finally, the contract informed about the price and the mode of payment. Table 3.3 contains those transactions, with information about sellers and buyers, the name and basic description of slaves, their age, price in *ducados* (Dcs), and the year in which the deed was notarised.

Table 3.3 shows a diversity of origins for the slaves, although there is a clear preponderance of black slaves from sub-Saharan Africa, twenty in total, four of which were described as *boçal*, which means that they did not speak Spanish at the time of the sale.[55] There were three slaves described as mulatto, one of them was a young girl with the colour of a "quince", and another one was an old morisco. Six slaves were captured after the Moriscos' rebellions in Granada; some are described as white.[56] Surprisingly, there is one woman identified as Portuguese, who was sold for a price of 90.9 *ducados* in 1573.[57]

There is no clear preference between men (16) and women (17), although prices did vary depending on sex: women were usually sold for a higher price than men of a similar age. Nevertheless, the highest price was paid for a black man, Antón, who at the time was 20 years old. Miguel Arbauts paid 150 *ducados* to Jaques Nicolás for him in 1588.[58] Melchor de los Reyes paid a slightly lower price (140) for Juana, a 22-year-old black slave.[59] A bit more exceptional seems the sale of Pedro de Lasove and Felipa de Maricongo, a married couple probably from the Congo region according to Felipa's surname. Francisco Bernal sold them to Alexandre de Niza in 1577 for 162 *ducados*.[60] There are

---

54   "[E] vos la aseguro que no es boracha, ladrona, ni huidora, otica ni endemoniada, ni tiene gota, coral ni los ojos claros sin ver." AHPSe, SP, 9257, 321r. Jansen bought a slave from Hans Veltrus (AHPSe, SP, 9526, 165r) but turned to be a drunkard and was sent away from the house (AHPSe, SP, 9291, 811r).

55   "[E]l negro que no sabe otra lengua que la suya." "Boçal" Covarrubias, *Tesoro de la lengua castellana o española*, I, 285. Nuevo tesoro lexicográfico de la lengua española, Real Academia española, accessed January 2, 2020 http://ntlle.rae.es/ On the slavery circuits between Seville, Africa and the Americas, see Manuel F. Fernández Chaves and Rafael F. Pérez García, "Sevilla y la trata negrera atlántica: Envíos de esclavos desde Cabo Verde a la América Española, 1569–1579," in *Estudios de Historia Moderna en homenaje al Profesor Antonio García-Baquero*, ed. León Carlos Alvarez Santaló (Sevilla: Universidad de Sevilla, 2009), 597–622.

56   AHPSe, SP, 7772, 868r; 9219,563r; 9232, 563r; 9284,669r; 9248, 925r; 9286, 486r. On the Moriscos wars, see the recent work by Rafael M. Pérez García and Manuel F. Fernández Chaves, *Las élites moriscas entre Granada y el Reino de Sevilla. Rebelión, castigo y supervivencias* (Sevilla: Universidad de Sevilla, 2015).

57   AHPSe, 7776, 743r.

58   AHPSe, SP, 9256, 778r.

59   AHPSe, SP, 9293, 453r.

60   AHPSe, SP, 9215, 870r.

TABLE 3.3   Sales of slaves participated in by *Atarazanas* merchants

Seller	Buyer	Slave	Sex	Description	Age	Dcs	Year
Sebastián Sánchez	Gaspar Loscarte	Juan	M	Black	14	75	1570
Enrique Aparte & Elvira Jacome	Juan Antonio Corso	Francisco	M	Black	30		1571
Gaspar Borman	Francisco Núñez	Luisa	F	Black	30	55	1571
Luis de la Peña	Enrique Aparte	Catalina	F	Morisca from Granada	24	90	1572
Benito del Alcáçar	Miguel Arbauts	Ynés	F	Portuguese, white	24	90,9	1573
Manuel Hernández	Gaspar Borman	Miguel	M	Black	20	90	1574
Francisco Bernal	Alexandre de Niza	Pedro de Lasove & Felipa de Maricongo	F & M	Black, married	32 & 25	162	1577
Francisco Bernal	Diego de Vera	Juan (with a little donkey)	M	Black	50	40	1578
Diego Vázquez	Felipe Sarens	Pedro	M	White morisco from Granada	6	35	1578
Enrique Aparte	Jaques Nicolás	Juan	M	Black	24	Gift	1581
Luis Esteban	Guillermo Corinse	Catalina and her white daughter, Sebastiana	F & F	White morisca from Granada	30 & 5	80	1582
Pedro Mendes	Manas Enríquez	Isabel	F	Black *boçal*	18	80	1585
Andrés de Quintarnaya	Guillermo Corinse	Blanca	F	*Morisca*	12	100	1586

TABLE 3.3   Sales of slaves participated in by *Atarazanas* merchants (*cont.*)

Seller	Buyer	Slave	Sex	Description	Age	Dcs	Year
Jaques Nicolás	Melchor de Haçe	Francisco	M	Black *boçal*	16	80	1588
Jaques Nicolás	Miguel Arbauts	Antón	M	Black *boçal*	20	150	1588
Pedro Gisberto	Francisco González	María and her baby, Francisco	F & M	Black	26	25	1588
Pedro Gisberto	Bartolomé García	Esperança	F	Black	20		1589
Jacome Angelberto	Tobías Buc	Antona	F	Mulatto, *color de membrillo*	30	18	1589
Hans Veltrus	Esteban Jansen	Juan (in Sanlúcar)	M	Black	40	40	1591
Jaques Nicolás	Pedro de Madariaga	Ysabel	F	Black	20	120	1592
Manuel de Acosta	Juan Gras	Juan	M	Black	21	70	1594
Ana de Guzmán	Jaques Nicolás	Francisco	M	Mulatto morisco	12	60	1595
Antón Gómez	Esteban Jansen	María	F	Morisca	11	54	1595
Juan Bernal	Antón del Castillo	Ana	F	Black	21	125	1595
Pedro Osten	Melchor de los Reyes	Ysabel	F	Black	40	80	1595
Gerónimo Ramírez	Melchor de los Reyes	Juana	F	Black	22	140	1596
Executors Esteban Jansen	Diego de Vargas	Juan	M	Black, drunkard and thief	40	50	1596
Pedro Ustarte	Jaques Nicolás	Juan	M	Mulatto	26	100	1597
Antonio de Rivero	Miguel Arbauts Jr.	María Brama	F	Black *boçal*	18	116	1598

also two cases in which a woman is sold together with an infant: Catalina, a *morisca*, and her daughter Sebastiana aged 5, and María, a black slave, and her four-month-old son Francisco.[61]

Sales contracts do not state the duties they performed in the house but, according to the different profiles of slaves, these must have varied greatly. As with housekeepers, householders provided them with accommodation, food and clothing, but not with a salary. Contrary to housekeepers, slaves rarely received a bequest, although merchants sometimes developed a certain bond of affection with them, as various cases of emancipation show. For instance, Jaques Nicolás freed Cristóbal de la Peña, a thirty-year old, tall, bearded man, with two scars on his forehead and another one on his lips, who had been born in Jaques Nicolás's house. Nicolás freed him for his good service, out of the "much love" that he had for him, evidencing how slaves formed an integral part of the *casa* too.[62]

3.2 *Workers of the Firm*

Employees who assisted merchants to run the family firm were usually young migrants who hoped to begin their own career as merchants. Their role resembled that of apprentices working for an artisan. They were inexperienced workers that performed a wide range of activities for the firm in return for food, accommodation and, often, a modest salary. A similar thing was noted by Stols, who argued that it was a common practice for Flanders-based merchants to send younger relatives to cities like Lisbon and Seville to complete their education, while also representing the firm in important southern European ports.[63] Interestingly enough, there is evidence of merchants in Seville sending younger relatives to northern Europe for the same purpose. Guillermo Corinse, for instance, sent his two orphaned brothers-in-law, Lucas and Andrés Sarens, to work for his brother Talem Corinse in Amsterdam.[64]

---

61   AHPSe, SP, 9232, 563r and AHPSe, SP, 9256, 780r.
62   AHPSe, SP, 9306, 859r. Other examples: AHPSe, SP, 9289, 853; 9300, 860r; 9227, 502r.
63   Stols, "La colonia flamenca de Sevilla," 365. A good example of this is the employment of Guillermo Cornieles by Juan Gras in October 1598. Cornieles "did not understand the Spanish language" and, consequently, Gras would not pay any salary in the first year. He would only provide him with food and accommodation. He is described as *boçal* in the document. In the second year, Cornieles would receive 1 *ducado* (11 *reales*) per month and in the third and last two *ducados* (22 *reales*) per month. AHPSe, SP, 9304, 92r.
64   In his testament, Guillermo Corinse states that he had sent his brothers-in-law to Flanders with his brother. AHPSe, SP, 9977, 739r.

Atarazanas merchants employed at least thirty-seven young workers in the period from 1570 to 1600. Table 3.4 indicates the name and nationality of these workers, the name of the employer and the date in which the relation employer-employee was documented in a notarial deed. The asterisk beside the year indicates that a labour contract was signed, which was an exceptional practice; in fact, most employees were identified through secondary references in testaments and powers of attorney.

Except for three Spaniards, all young interns were northern European migrants, some of whom were relatives of their employers. For instance, Guillermo Corinse employed his younger brother Buchart, who had arrived from Amsterdam.[65] The majority of workers listed on the table, nonetheless, did not seem to have a kinship tie with their employees. According to Stols, Flemish-based merchants paid traders in Seville an allowance for supporting the expenses of their relatives, which could go up to 1000 *ducados* in the seventeenth century. He argued that, by 1630–1640, there was a glut of young interns in Seville and young migrants had to stay in guesthouses before moving to a *casa*.[66] Stols does not support this explanation with any bibliographical or archival references, so it must be taken cautiously, but this is in line Mathias' description of a market for apprenticeships in early modern Europe, which was based on apprenticeship fees that interns paid.[67] No notarial evidence indicates that such fees were in use by then; and had they existed, they would not have been as high as the sums that they reached decades later, according to Stols' findings.

The supply of this form of labour was high, as a result of the continuous arrival of north European young migrants. The demand for this labour was high as well, as suggested by the salaries that principals paid, besides food and accommodation. The employment of young migrants represented a commercial opportunity for establishing cooperation ties with firms based in the Low Countries, and a form of investing in the education of prospective collaborators and, in more exceptional cases, future sons-in-law.[68] In fact, seven of the workers

---

65 We learn about the death of his brother Buchart (Bigar) Corinse in a very interesting document. In there, another brother of Guillermo Corinse, Francisco Talen, accused important nobles of Spain, Don Pedro Tellez Girón and Don Alonso Melgarejo de Guzmán, of murdering his brother. AHPSe, SP, 9277, 291r.

66 Stols, "La colonia flamenca de Sevilla," 365.

67 Mathias noted that these fees imposed a barrier for newcomers. Mathias, "Strategies for Reducing Risk," 11.

68 Lamikiz, *Trade and Trust*, 123. Luuc Kooijmans, "Risk and Reputation. On the Mentality of Merchants in the Early Modern Period," in *Entrepreneurs and Entrepreneurship in Early Modern Times: Merchants and Industrialists within the Orbit of the Dutch Staple Market*, eds. Clé Lesger and Leo Noordegraaf (Den Haag: Stichting Hollandse Historische Reeks, 1995), 32.

TABLE 3.4   Employees of *Atarazanas* merchants

Employer	Name	Nat	Year
Juan Jacart	Galtier Herder	Bremen	1575*
Esteban Jansen	Joaquin Blanco	GER	1575
Juan Jacart	Riqartten Bruq	FLE	1576
Francisco Bernal	Juan de Bestoven	FLE	1577
Nicolás de Melemburque	Alberto Pinsesnos	Hamburg	1578*
Francisco Bernal	Guileyn van Unimelbeque	Bruges	1579*
Enrique Aparte	Jaques Nicolás	FLE	1581
Esteban Jansen	Juan de Bestoven	FLE	1581*
Esteban Jansen	Tobías Buc	Amsterdam	1581*
Esteban Jansen	Cornieles Boyque	FLE	1583
Guillermo Corinse	Buchart Corinse	FLE	1585
Esteban Jansen	Juan Bernal	FLE	1586*
Manas Enríquez	Bernal Pérez		1586
Esteban Jansen	Diego de Apontes	FLE	1587
Esteban Jansen	Antonio Desaudrenguen	GER	1587
Jaques Nicolás	Enrique Giraldo	FLE	1587
Esteban Jansen	Juan Vanoy	FLE	1588
Esteban Jansen	Justo de Bil	FLE	1589
Esteban Jansen	Juan Giraldo	FLE	1589
Esteban Jansen	Gonzalo Balvin	FLE	1589*
Esteban Jansen	Bartolomé Sánchez	SPA	1589
Jaques Enríquez	Christóbal Enríquez	SPA	1590
Esteban Jansen	Peres Valentín	GER	1590*
Juan Sesbaut	Ortega Verchinan	FLE	1591
Simón Enríquez	Cornieles Jansen	FLE	1593
Juan Sesbaut	Rodrigo Opemar	FLE	1593
Esteban Jansen	Mateo de Bus	FLE	1593*
Juan Florido	Andrés Buvarte	FLE	1593
Jaques Nicolás	Juan de Sagre	FLE	1594
Esteban Jansen	Marcos de Abaitua	FLE	1594
Lamberto Beruben	Juan Paris	FLE	1596
Esteban Jansen	Juan Cornieles		1596
Executors Jansen	Bartolomé Sánchez	SPA	1596*
Cornieles Lamberto	Pedro de Macra		1598

TABLE 3.4   Employees of *Atarazanas* merchants (*cont.*)

Employer	Name	Nat	Year
Juan Gras	Jiles Jilessen	FLE	1598*
Juan Gras	Guillermo Cornieles	FLE	1598*
Simón Enríquez	Godar	FLE	1600

Note: The table indicates nationality or, when possible, place of origin of the worker
SOURCE: SEE ANNEXES C, E AND F

appearing in Table 3.4 eventually settled for good in Seville and specialised in timber trade: Juan de Bestoven, Jaques Nicolás, Tobías Buc, Juan Bernal, Justo de Bil, Juan Giraldo, and Cornieles Jansen.

The working conditions of many of these young employees are described in twelve notarised labour contracts held in the registers of Francisco Díaz and Juan de Tordesillas. Although representing a small share of the total, the twelve contracts give a good account of the variety of duties interns could perform, and consequently about the organisation of Flemish firms in sixteenth-century Seville. The first documented contract is the one through which Juan Jacart hired Galtier Herde, a boy from Bremen, to assist him in the company he had founded with Nicolás de Melemburque in 1575.[69] Herde committed "to do anything that you commanded me, in your house or outside it, during the day or night" for a period of three years and a total salary of 20 *ducados* (220 *reales*). Jacart would not pay that salary in cash but in two sets of new clothes: one at the beginning of the contract and another at the end. Galtier Herde would live in Jacart's house and be provided with "food and drink,"no matter if he was "healthy or sick."[70] This formula is common to all contracts, ensuring the sustenance of employees – who usually did not have any other support in Seville – if they fell ill.

Once Nicolás de Melemburque returned to Seville, after travelling through northern Europe to supply timber to the company, he employed a boy from Hamburg, Alberto Pinsesnos. The contract, signed in January 1578, stated that Alberto Pinsesnos would work for two years for a salary of eight *reales* per

69   AHPSe, SP, 7782P, 813r.
70   AHPSe, SP, 7782, 813r.

month, plus accommodation and food. A year later, Francisco Bernal hired a man from Bruges called Guileyn van Unimelbeque in October 1579, who was to live in his house for 18 months in return for accommodation, food and drink as well as a salary of 1 *ducados* (11 *reales*) per month in the first six months, 1.5 *ducados* (16.5 *reales*) per month in the following six months, and 2 *ducados* (22 *reales*) per month in the last six months. This time, the main duty of the employee is stated, although in a vague way; Van Unimelbeque declared that he would work "as carpenter and in any other thing that you told me and ordered me to do in your house or outside it."[71]

In January 1581, Esteban Jansen employed two young interns who, years later, established a household of their own, Juan de Bestoven and Tobías Buc.[72] These contracts are richer in detail, giving the working conditions and the duties the employees would assume. While Tobías Buc came from Amsterdam, De Bestoven came from Sanlúcar and already had some experience working for his grandfather Francisco Bernal. Juan de Bestoven would receive 80 *ducados* (880 *reales*) the first year, 100 *ducados* (1100 *reales*) the second and 115 *ducados* (1265 *reales*) the last and third year, as well as accommodation and food. De Bestoven committed to work as cashier, taking care of the account books of Esteban Jansen.[73] Tobías Buc was firstly hired for two years only, although his contract was later extended for two more years.[74] His salary was 50 *ducados* (550 *reales*) the first year and 100 *ducados* (1100 *reales*) the second. His function in the firm differed from that of Juan de Bestoven. His contract stated that he would work in Seville and "in other parts, kingdoms, provinces, at sea and on land." When, in 1584, Buc signed a new contract with Jansen, he explicitly committed to go to Flanders and Norway to buy and send timber to Seville. For this, he would receive a salary of 100 *ducados* (1100 *reales*) during his travels, and 15 *ducados* (165 *reales*) for new clothing, as well as the costs for accommodation and food in Seville and during his travels.

Esteban Jansen's business became so notable that, as the case above shows, he had several employees working for his firm simultaneously, including individuals that were not accommodated in his house. That was the case of Juan Bernal, grandson of Francisco Bernal. Born in Bruges, he was employed in the firm of Esteban Jansen for three years in November 1586 for a rather high salary

71   AHPSe, SP, 9222, 696r.

72   Juan de Bestoven (AHPSe, SP, 9226, 132v) and Tobías Buc (AHPSe, SP, 9226, 265r).

73   "[T]heniendo a mi cargo todos los libros tocantes a la dicha vuestra hazienda." AHPSe, SP, 9226, 132v.

74   AHPSe, SP, 9236, 113v.

of 4.5 *reales* per day ("not only working days but also holidays and Sundays.")[75] In July 1589, Jansen employed Gonzalo Balvin for four years and an annual salary of 150 *ducados* (1650 *reales*). He would not reside in Jansen's house, and would travel abroad on Jansen's behalf if necessary, at the principal's expenses.[76] In the same period, Esteban Jansen contracted Peres Valentin, a German apprentice, for a salary of 400 *reales* per year, plus accommodation and food expenses. The last such contract that Jansen made was in 1593, when he hired Mateo de Bus to work for his firm in Seville and Sanlúcar for three years.[77]

The sample of contracts analysed above evidences that a variety of labour relations coexisted between *Atarazanas* merchants and the employees of their firms. However, notarised labour contracts were the exception rather than the rule. A plain oral agreement between employer and employee was enough, as evidenced in the testament of Diego de Apontes, a Flemish migrant who worked in Esteban Jansen's house until his death in 1587.[78] In his testament, De Apontes declared to have worked ten years for Jansen's *casa y servicio*, although he had only been paid for the first two years. He was not claiming any compensation for this, though, because they had not agreed upon a salary at the time he entered Jansen's *casa*. To estimate the sum that Jansen owed him for his service, De Apontes named four arbiters, Jaques Nicolás, Guillermo Corinse, Miguel Arbauts and Francisco Roelant, all of them *Atarazanas* merchants, to reach a "friendly" agreement, avoiding any litigation and taking into consideration that Jansen had provided him with accommodation and other living expenses except for clothing.[79] Diego de Apontes's testament, in conclusion, shows the nature of most of these employments: a reciprocal relation between well-established merchants and young migrants starting their trading career abroad and probably seeking to marry and establish a *casa y servicio* of their own in southern Europe; something that De Apontes did not achieve in the end. For young migrants, this early experience was a crucial step for completing their education and eventually marrying the daughter of a compatriot in Seville, as several of them did in the last third of the century.

---

75   AHPSe, SP, 9226, 132v.
76   AHPSe, SP, 9259, 897r. Gonzalo Balvin later worked for other Flemish merchants, like Jaques Sesbaut, on behalf of whom he did several errands in 1596. AHPSe, SP, 9290, 739r.
77   AHPSe, SP, 9276, 744r.
78   AHPSe, SP, 9250, 395v.
79   The agreement was easily reached between the arbiters and Jansen, who duly paid to De Apontes's executors, Miguel Arbauts and Manas Enríquez. In the following days, these executors paid the bequests that De Apontes had promised in his testament. i.e. AHPSe, SP, 9250, 398v, 402v, 412r, 428r, 447r, 450v, 558r, 597r, 646r, 1053r.

4   Conclusion

Family and commercial strategies went hand in hand, and in the marriage of *Atarazanas* merchants, family interests and commercial ambitions merged. Marriage was the result of the intention of young migrants and older ones to cooperate. The support given by an in-law family permitted the young grooms to start a household and a firm of their own, which meant a definitive boost for their settling in the new territory. For fathers-in-law, the marriage of their daughters represented a commercial opportunity for establishing new alliances or strengthening existing ones with other compatriots. The economic terms in which this cooperation was established was generally assessed and formalised through dowry promises, which left a trace in the notaries on a few occasions.

Historiography has traditionally neglected the agency of women in long-distance trade. This research is not an exception to this and, for the most part, it presents women's socio-economic activities in relation to a male relative to whom they were usually dependent juridically: a husband, a father, a son, a brother and sometimes an in-law. However, they sometimes became risk takers, assuming the administration of their husbands' estate once they were widowed and participating in long-distance trade. As such, widows were fundamental for keeping their family afloat and, in general, for preserving the stability of the group of traders, who depended on each other to maintain their control over the market. Another good example of this is their efforts to keep the warehouses of the *Atarazanas* in the hands of Flemish families, whether through dowries or donations. In the end, enjoying a space there granted access to the trade of imported timber, and this became an important element for older merchants' strategies that sought to attract migrants to marry their female relatives.

The *casa* remained the basic unit in the organisation of the group. The family household was the basic unit of their social organisation, and the family firm was the basic unit of their business organisation. The *casa* was also formed by individuals that were not members of the family: *el servicio*. On the one hand, housekeepers and slaves –mostly *moriscos* from Granada and black slaves from sub-Saharan Africa – who assumed the domestic chores of the household, and constituted an unpaid labour force. On the other, merchants employed young interns that helped them run the firm, for a low salary, accommodation and food. Many of those beginning their commercial career as interns of a firm in Seville, eventually married the daughter of a compatriot and settled for good in Andalusia.

Cooperation in Long-Distance Trade

While, as the last chapter showed, family firms (*casas*) remained the basic unit of the business organisation of *Atarazanas* merchants, the intense social capital generated by the group – based on reciprocal ties and common commercial aspirations – created a fruitful environment for collaboration. In the notarial registers, we can identify fifteen partnerships formed between *Atarazanas* merchants . If we include those that they established with outsiders of the group, we count at least twenty-eight partnerships specialised in the trade of timber operating in Seville in the last third of the sixteenth century. Most partnerships were temporary, in which partners' liability was limited to their investment, allowing merchants to embark on larger operations that they could not otherwise have undertaken on their own.Unfortunately, collaboration ties are not always evident in notarial sources. Not all partnerships were notarised. Many only come to light once they were stopped, through the settlement of the remaining debts between partners or the testaments of a deceased partner.

The scarce number of notarised partnership contrasts with the more than 1200 powers of attorney (henceforth POA) these merchants registered, delegating a wide range of socioceconomic activities.Many of these deeds reveal the existence of a commercial cooperation bond between individuals involved in long-distance trade. In 1976, Lopez complained about this lack of attention, for which he blamed the very nature of POAs, which were "depressingly vague and discouragingly alike (...) none of which really tells what is the business at hand," making historians prefer "more complex and specific contracts."[1] Four decades later, few historians have focused on the implications of this notarial tool in the organisation of transnational business, with the exception of a specific line of research: women's socio-economic agency in the absence of their husbands who were residing or travelling abroad.[2] At best, POAs receive anecdotal

---

1   Robert S. Lopez, "Proxy in Medieval Trade," in *Order and Innovation in the Middle Ages: Essays in Honor of Joseph R. Strayer*, eds. William Chester Jordan, Bruce McNab and Teofilo F. Ruiz (Princeton: Princeton University Press, 1976), 189.

2   Some examples of literature on the transference of agency to wives are Linda L. Sturtz, " 'As Though I My Self Was Pr[e]sent.' Virginia Women with Power of Attorney," in *The Many Legalities of Early America*, eds. Christopher L. Tomlins and Bruce H. Mann (Chapel Hill: University of North Carolina Press, 2001), 250–271; and Nicole Dufournaud and Bernard

mentions in publications on long-distance trade, failing to comprehend its contribution to the development of anonymous markets in the pre-modern period, as Eloire, Lemercier and Santarosa questioned in a recent article.[3]

This chapter studies *Atarazanas* merchants' cooperation strategies in long-distance trade, and reflects on to what extent notarised agency in the form of POAS was an alternative solution to partnerships when establishing cooperation ties. The chapter is divided into two parts. The first one examines how they adapted different solutions to share risks, capital and labour to their collaboration strategies, based on a systematic analysis of their partnerships. Moreover, this part assesses to what extent the limited liability offered by partnerships prompted collaboration with individuals who did not share ties of familiarity (kinship, residence in the same area of town or nationality), thus allowing outsiders from the *Atarazanas* circle to invest in timber trade. The second part analyses the POAS participated by *Atarazanas* merchants in order to examine how the notarisation of agency shaped their commercial expansion beyond Seville. This section shows the variety of socio-economic solutions that this notarial instrument offered, but focused on those that facilitated long-distance trade. Finally, similarly to the first section of the chapter, this second part addresses to what extent agency was transferred to workers and familiar individuals or, alternatively, to proxies that principals did not necessarily know well.

1   Partnerships

Originating in Medieval Italy, hence the frequent reference to their Italian names, the commission partnership (*commenda*) and the equity partnership (*accomandita*) were the two most frequent solutions for collaboration in early modern Europe. While the commission partnership consisted of one merchant providing another with commodities to be sold for a percentage, the equity partnership was an association formed by two or three partners in which the initial input in either capital, labour or both was shared, and the returns were calculated accordingly. By limiting partners' liability and thus curbing risks in

---

Michon, "Les femmes et le commerce maritime a Nantes (1660–1740): un role largement meconnu," *Clio. Femmes, Genre, Histoire*, no. 23 (2006): 311–330.

3   Their work is an exception to the general neglect on the use of POAS. Fabien Eloire, Claire Lemercier and Veronica A. Santarosa, "Beyond the Personal-Anonymous Divide: Agency Relations in Powers of Attorney in France in the Eighteenth and Nineteenth Centuries," *Economic History Review* 72, no. 4 (November 2019): 1229–1250.

long-distance operations, the commission and the equity partnerships played a key role in the expansion of international trade during the early modern period.[4]

These types of associations were widely used in sixteenth-century Seville. In his famous book on *La Carrera de Indias*, García-Baquero classified three main types of partnership that merchants used for trading with the Americas: commission partnerships (*comisión* or *encomienda*), equity partnerships (*compañía*), and one-venture equity partnerships limited to one shipment to America (*compañía de cargazón*).[5] In his recent dissertation, Crailsheim noted the difficulty of distinguishing between different partnership solutions, and broadly assumed that a *compañía* was any collaboration in which "either, the term *compañía* was applied in the records, or the outcome of a joint business took several months or even years (not just the payback of an obligation), or merchants were selling or buying jointly on several occasions."[6] Both García-Baquero and Crailsheim concluded that improvisation determined the way merchants collaborated, and that merchants generally opted for non-formalised temporary solutions.

The impression that merchants improvised stems from the fact that partnerships were temporary solutions and were barely registered in the notary. Moreover, as noted by Crailsheim, the ambiguous use of the terms *compañía* (partnership or company) and *compañeros* (partners) in sixteenth-century Spain complicates the categorisation of partnerships. The term *compañía* was indistinctly used in notarial deeds to refer to any type of partnership. In fact, Covarrubias, the author of the first monolingual Spanish dictionary, defined *compañía* in very general terms as "the common dealing of two or more merchants."[7] It is, therefore, true that notarial evidence evidences the existence of

---

4   Casado Alonso even claimed that they *democratised* early modern European trade. "Las colonias de mercaderes castellanos," 54. Puttevils summarisez that "[p]artnerships offered merchants a solution to several problems at once: attracting capital, arranging liabilities, incentivising partners (through a share of the profit) not to cheat, streamlining the organization's workings and acquiring partners' useful commercial knowledge and skills for the firm." *Merchants and Trading in the Sixteenth Century*, 9.

5   García-Baquero González, *La Carrera de Indias*, 239–245.

6   Crailsheim, *Spanish Connection*, 113–114.

7   "Compañía" Covarrubias, *Tesoro de la lengua castellana o española*, II, 455. Nuevo tesoro lexicográfico de la lengua española, Real Academia española, accessed June 12, 2020 http:// ntlle.rae.es/ This term includes family enterprises, too, as analysed in the previous chapter. *Compañía* can also refer to the Italian word *compagnia*, which Trivellato described as "a network of interconnected branches (some directed by salaried employees and others by junior partners, with varying degrees of independence) under the main house's control." Trivellato, *The Familiarity of Strangers*, 143. Nonetheless, *Atarazanas* merchants did not develop this form of organisation, which in the sixteenth century was only adopted by the most influential families involved in European trade and finance, like the Fugger, the Ruiz or the Della

a diversity of solutions for temporary collaboration, but this diversity should not be mistaken as mere improvisation. It was the result of adapting different forms of sharing risk, capital and labour to two definable types of commercial associations: the equity and the commission partnerships.

1.1   *Equity Partnerships*

Although in contemporary sources the word *compañía* usually referred to any form of partnership, the *compañía* was a very concrete type of association with a specific notarial deed: the company charter (*contrato de compañía*). With this contract, two or three merchants publicly stated the establishment of a partnership for a particular purpose – in the case of *Atarazanas* merchants, the trade of Baltic and Scandinavian timber – and declared how the initial input of the company was shared, how the returns were expected to be calculated according to each partner's input, and the expected duration of the partnership. Sometimes the partnership could be limited to one venture. The initial investment was divided into equal parts, commonly two-halves or three-thirds regardless of the number of partners; in a *compañía* of two, one partner usually invested two-thirds and the other one-third. This investment could be done in capital, labour or in both.

Table 4.1 contains the equity partnerships participated in by *Atarazanas* merchants. Those partnerships for which a company charter was notarised are indicated with a cc (Company charter) at the far-right column, which informs about the type of notarial deed (Not) in which the association was identified. The other partnerships were identified *ex post* once they were liquidated, either through testaments (Tst), in which merchants often expressed their will to end unfinished businesses including partnerships, or through *finiquitos* (Fin), which constituted a specific notarial deed for declaring the cancelation of a debt or the liquidation of a shared account between partners. The table also indicates the nationality of partners (Nat), the existence of kinship ties (Kin), and if partners resided in the *Atarazanas* (Atr), as well as the duration (Dur) of the company and its initial capital in *ducados* (Cap.) when the information is available.

The most evident conclusion from this overview is that equity partnerships were mostly formed by individuals that shared ties of familiarity. Nine of the twelve *compañías* were established between *Atarazanas* merchants; that is,

---

Faille. Kellenbenz, *Los Fugger en España*; Brulez, *De firma della Faille*; Henri Lapeyre, *Une famille de marchands: les Ruiz: Contributions à l'étude du commerce entre la France et l'Espagne au temps de Philippe II* (Paris: A. Colin, 1955).

TABLE 4.1   Equity partnerships of *Atarazanas* merchants

Partners	Nat	Kin	Atr	Dur	Cap	Not
Geronimo Andrea	Flemish		Yes	1573	750	CC
& Cornieles Valdovinos	Flemish		Yes	for 1 year		
Nicolás de	Flemish	In-law	Yes	1575	1100	CC
Melemburque & Juan Jacart	Flemish		Yes	for 1 year		
Felipe Sarens	Flemish	In-law	Yes	?-1586	5000	Tst
& Guillermo Corinse	Flemish		Yes			
Jaques Nicolás	Flemish	In-law	Yes	1586–1591	3000	Fin
& Juan de Bestoven	Flemish		Yes			
Simón Enríquez	Flemish		Yes	1592	4500	CC
& Cornieles Jansen	Flemish		Yes	for 3 years		Fin
Jaques Nicolás	Flemish	In-law*	Yes	?-1593	4000	Fin
Elias Sirman	Flemish		No			
& Conrado Ledes	Flemish		No			
Jaques Nicolás	Flemish	In-law*	Yes	1594	5500	CC
Elias Sirman	Flemish		No	for 3 years		
& Juan Gras	Flemish		No			
Juan Sesbaut	Flemish		Yes	1588–1596		Tst
& Antonio Anselmo	Flemish		No			
Jaques Nicolás	Flemish		Yes	1596 (one venture)		Tst
& Juan Sesbaut	Flemish		Yes			
Simón Enríquez	Flemish		Yes	1599 (one venture)		Tst
& Juan van Hooren	Flemish		Yes			
Tobías Buc	Flemish		Yes	1590–1598		Tst
& Guillermo Corinse	Flemish		Yes			
Jaques Sesbaut	Flemish		Yes	?-1600		Fin.
& Justo de Bil	Flemish		Yes			

Note: The asterisk indicates that only Jaques Nicolás and Elias Sirman were in-law
SOURCE: SEE ANNEXES C, E AND F

between traders who resided in the same building complex and specialised in the same commodity. The table also evidences the economic progression of the group: if the earliest two, established in 1573 and 1575, had an initial investment of 750 *ducados* and 1100 *ducados* respectively, the last partnership notarised *ex ante*, formalised in 1594, had an initial capital of 5500 *ducados*. In twenty years, equity partnerships of the group multiplied their initial value by 3.5, if we take inflation into account.[8] Finally, the duration of the companies varied greatly. Although *ex ante* notarised partnerships in principle had a limited duration of one to three years, the duration of non-notarised *compañías* varied: from one venture to those established for an indefinite period.

All partnerships established for an indefinite period were formed by relatives, like the one by Jaques Nicolás and his nephew Juan de Bestoven, liquidated in 1591.[9] The *finiquito* they notarised is exceptionally detailed and offers an interesting perspective on how non-notarised equity partnerships could work. Nicolás and De Bestoven declared to have had a company since 1586 for "the trade of the timber that is brought from Flanders and other parts" but that they did not "make any company charter" back then. Each had invested 1500 *ducados* in "labour and capital." Very probably, a large part of Juan de Bestoven' initial investment had been estimated according to his labour, because he had been working as "president" of the *compañía*, in charge of its daily administration, managing the store and sales. After five years of activity, they had obtained a return of 6000 *ducados*, which was to be split into two equal parts.[10]

Equity partnerships facilitated intergenerational cooperation between experienced and young traders like the one above, since the second could contribute to the company with his work instead of capital. When such intergenerational collaboration occurred between relatives, there was little incentive for formalising it in a company charter. That was also the case in the partnership between Felipe Sarens and his son-in-law Guillermo Corinse, which comes to light in the testament Sarens notarised in 1586, a few days before his death. In the testament, Sarens declared to have had a *compañía* with Corinse for the

---

8   Prices in Seville experienced an increase of 42% in the period from 1573 to 1594 according to Manuel González Mariscal, "Inflación y niveles de vida en Sevilla durante la revolución de los precios," *Revista de Historia Económica / Journal of Iberian and Latin American Economic History* 33 n. 3 (2015): 353–386; see "Cuadro A."

9   AHPSe, SP, 9269, 360v.

10 The company's final returns – once the initial investment had been deducted – were 3000 *ducados* which was to be split in two. Thus, De Bestoven, as administrator, obliged to pay 3000 *ducados* to Nicolás (1500 *ducados* of the initial investment and 1500 of his share in the profits). AHPSe, SP, 9269, 360v.

trade of "timber, rigging, tar and other merchandise," in which each had invested 2500 *ducados*.[11] By the time the testament was notarised, they were waiting for shipments that had to arrive from "other kingdoms," and because of this, Sarens allowed Corinse to keep the partnership going for at least a year before liquidating it. There is no reference to the foundation of this commercial association, which was probably sealed around the time Corinse married Sarens' daughter Margarita in 1582, for which he received a 500- *ducados* dowry.[12]

This was not the only company Guillermo Corinse had. In his testament, formalised in 1598, Corinse mentions that he had a partnership with Tobías Buc in a very vague way: "I declare that, between I and Tovias Buque, there were and we had various accounts (...) for timber and rigging and other things."[13] Nothing else is known about the partnership activity from the testament or earlier notarial deeds, but the lack of public notarial deeds was not an impediment for Tobías Buc to claim his part in their shared business.

Months later, after Guillermo Corinse's death, Tobías Buc notarised a protest against the executors of Corinse's testament, Juan de Bestoven and Juan Leclerque, which reveals more information about their collaboration. The partnership was founded in 1590 to trade with imported timber from Norway and to export ginger, and Guillermo Corinse was its main administrator. According to Buc, the executors owed him the returns that Corinse had not paid back, because they had "maliciously hidden the papers and books and deeds about the trees that [Corinse] had sold from the importations and had hidden the other debts from the said ginger."[14] Later in the document, Buc complained that he still had to receive 2000 *ducados*, according to his account books; this estimation included the timbers that Corinse had not yet sold before his death, which were likely to "rot or to be carried away by the river in case of flooding" if they were not given to him.[15] To solve this problem, Buc offered to make his account books available to the executor and any arbitrator.

Tobías Buc's protest illustrates that partners' private documents could serve to enforce their agreements, as it implied a threat to Juan de Bestoven and Juan Leclerque, who could be taken to royal court. More interestingly, his protest indicates that, despite the strong reciprocal ties built between *Atarazanas* merchants, relationships began to erode in an increasingly larger group at the end of the

---

11   "[M]adera e jarçias, alquitrán e otras mercaderías" AHPSe, SP, 19976, 501v.

12   AHPSe, 19976P, 501v.

13   In his testament, Corinse regreted that, due to his illness, he couldn't liquidate the account of the partnership. AHPSe, SP, 9977, 741r-v.

14   AHPSe, SP, 9301, 422r.

15   AHPSe, SP, 9301, 422r.

century. This is a good example to see how the death of one of them challenged the group's status quo. This was evidenced as well in the creation of a partnership by Jaques Nicolás, Elias Sirman and Juan Gras, which came to succeed a previous one formed by Jaques Nicolás, Elias Sirman and Conrado Ledes.[16]

Despite not living in the *Atarazanas*, Elias Sirman's was Jaques Nicolás's brother-in-law. For Sirman, partnering up with Nicolás was a good way of diversifying his investments. The participation of Conrado Ledes and Juan Gras is more interesting, though. They were modest Flemish merchants who resided in Triana, a suburb (*arrabal*) on the west bank of the Guadalquivir River with an active harbour life. It was here, with this partnership, that Jaques Nicolás established a branch of his trade in imported timber. Conrado Ledes knew Elias Sirman well. Both Sirman and Ledes were married to daughters of Juan Ysaac, an important Flemish merchant in Seville who passed away in 1582; this may explain why the partnership was not registered *ex ante*.[17] When Ledes died in 1593, Jaques Nicolás and Elias Sirman decided to maintain the partnership in Triana by collaborating with another Flemish merchant, Juan Gras, who had been appointed legal custodian of Ledes's orphans and curator of his remaining capital and goods.[18] This time, they notarised the foundation of the partnership, which was initially established for three years with an initial capital of 5500 *ducados*. Nicolás and Elias put 4000 *ducados* in cash and the timber that had not been sold by Ledes. Gras contributed a lesser amount, 1500 *ducados*, and his labour as main administrator.[19]

All equity partnerships had one partner working as main administrator, which was usually regarded as part of his input. In company charters, the division of labour is always described in detail, as with the charter notarised by Geronimo Andrea and Cornieles Valdovinos in May 1573.[20] The *compañía* was founded for trading in timber for at least a year, with an initial capital

---

16 AHPSe, SP, 9282, 477 Another example of reorganisation of partnerships after someone's death is the company founded by Justo de Bil and Jaques Sesbaut after Juan Sesbaut's death, explained in the previous chapter. AHPSe, 9310,63r-64v.

17 Jiménez Montes, "Sevilla, puerto y puerta de Europa," 359.

18 AHPSe, SP, 9282, 477.

19 AHPSe, SP, 9282, 477.

20 AHPSe, SP, 7775, 203r. The story of Andrea is very interesting: in several occasions, he appears in notarial deeds as *vecino*, with a house in the *Atarazanas* (AHPSe, SP, 9223, 84r). However, he lived in different countries during his life. When establishing the company, the notary described him as a resident in Seville. Less than a year before the foundation of the company, a notarial deed describes him as a resident in Lille. (AHPSe, SP, 7772, 1480r). He is identified as visitor in Rouen in Karel Degryse, *Pieter Seghers: Een Koopmansleven in Troebele Tijden* (Antwerp: Hadewijch, 1990), and established in Antwerp in Brulez, *De firma della Faille*, 543.

of 750 *ducados*. Andrea deposited his share, 500 *ducados*, in the bank of Pedro de Morga and Juan de Arregui, from where Valdovinos could retrieve it. Valdovinos invested 250 *ducados* and was appointed administrator, although he had to allow Andrea's "council and consent." Cornieles Valdovinos's labour was estimated at 250 *ducados*, which equalled Andrea's initial investment, so that they would share profits or, "God forbid," losses equally.[21]

The contract continued with a series of very specific clauses limiting Valdovinos's agency. He promised exclusivity to the partnership, that is not allowing participation in any other ventures outside it. If he failed in this commitment, he would share his profits with Andrea. Valdovinos could use the company capital to rent a house and a warehouse in the *Atarazanas,* but he could not use it to reimburse personal expenses, such as food or clothing. Finally, he would have a special "box" (*caja*) for administering the capital of the partnership, with two keys, one for each partner, so that Andrea had to be present any time money was withdrawn or collected; in principle, the box should be opened every month.[22]

Clauses of administrators' exclusivity are frequent in other contracts, as in the company created by Nicolás de Melemburque and Juan Jacart, already introduced in Chapter 1.[23] Despite the bonds of familiarity between Jacart and Melemburque – they were both married to daughters of Francisco Bernal and lived in the *Atarazanas* – they notarised the foundation of their partnership in 1575. Certainly, a lack of trust did not drive the notarisation, so the motivation should be found elsewhere. Probably they needed the notarial deed, to which it was attached a copy of the royal licence to import timber and export salt in return, to raise the confidence of north European shipmasters in a period of growing uncertainty of their activity in Andalusia. Very likely, a similar motivation drove Simón Enríquez and Cornieles Jansen to notarise the foundation of their partnership in May 1592, whose purpose was the trade in "timber, rigging, tar, pitch, trees and (...) other things related to the preparation and restoring of *naos* and ships and other vessels in the trading and sailing to the Indies."[24] They originally established the company for three years, during which Simón Enríquez committed to travel to "Germany and Flanders and other parts" in

---

21   AHPSe, SP, 7775, 203r.

22   AHPSE, SP, 7775, 203r.

23   Inmediately, the clause says "and if you do so, you have to share the profits." (AHPSe, SP, 7775, 203v).

24   To store those products, they included into their agreement the leasing of a "cellar and a corral" that Simón Enríquez owned next to San Telmo, by the southern façade of the *Atarazanas*. AHPSe, SP, 9270, 722r.

order to ship naval products to Andalusia. Enríquez was probably looking for new market opportunities in a changing scene, in which Amsterdam's trade with Spain was raising after Philip II had lifted the second embargo. In fact, Enríquez appears contracting a shipment of naval stores to Andalusia in the notary of J. F. Bruyningh in Amsterdam, in March 1594.[25]

The function of Cornieles Jansen was to receive the imports and redistribute them in Andalusia. Several clauses restricted Jansen's participation in other partnerships, each time in a different manner. One clause prohibited him from working for others. Immediately later, another clause provided that, in case he did so, it had to be in the form of *encomienda* (*commenda*, commission), and the profits to be shared with Enríquez. Another clause highlighted that he was "even less allowed" to trade outside the partnership with illegal products ("*ni menos en mercaderías prohibidas y vedadas*"), probably indicating a growing pressure from Spanish authorities.[26] Finally, Jansen could not marry without the consent of Simón Enríquez. If he failed to meet those commitments, Enríquez had the right to receive all the returns of the partnership. Despite Enríquez's strict control, Cornieles Jansen had enough agency to run the daily operations of the *compañía*, being responsible for the sales, administration and accounting during Enríquez's absence. He could hire a young assistant and, if needed, rent more warehouses, charging those expenses to the partnership. Simón Enríquez's share in the partnership was two-thirds, for which he would contribute 1500 *ducados* per year, to be spent in the preparation and contracting of shipments to Seville. The share of Cornieles Jansen, one-third, proceeded exclusively from his work. The company was liquidated half a year earlier than stipulated in the contract, according to a *finiquito* contract signed in December 1594.[27]

Thanks to labour division, equity partnerships facilitated merchants' access to international trade by having one partner abroad and the other running the company in Seville. However, these partnerships should not be regarded as a stable form of transregional cooperation, since the travels of one partner across northern Europe were temporary. In the end, as shown in Table 4.1, all partnerships were formed by residents in Seville, regardless of the international scope of their operations. There is one exception to that rule: the equity partnership between Antonio Anselmo, a merchant from Antwerp, and Juan Sesbaut. This came to light through the activity of the executors of Sesbaut's testament, Jaques Sesbaut and Justo de Bil, who in a deed mention the existence of an

---

25 J. F. Bruyningh in March 1594 (GAA, 65/4).
26 AHPSe, SP, 9270, 722r.
27 AHPSe, SP, 9283P, 470r.

agreement (*concierto*) notarised in Hamburg on May 1588 for the foundation of a *compañía*.[28] Unfortunately, there is no more information about this partnership and the lack of further examples suggests that this one was rather extraordinary: a truly transnational equity partnership, signed in Hamburg between a merchant residing in Antwerp and another one in Seville.

Finally, there are two cases of one-venture partnerships that resemble the *compañía de cargazón* described by García-Baquero in his work about Seville's trade with the Americas.[29] These are revealed *ex post*, after the death of one of the partners. In his testament, Simón Enríquez declared to have had a shared account with Juan van Hooren for a shipment of oak boards, beams and rigging that they jointly ("*en compañía*") had imported from Flanders.[30] Likewise, Jaques Nicolás claimed a compensation of 110 *ducados* from the executors of Juan Sesbaut's testament, from the returns of a shipment of trees and staves that they had imported jointly ("*en compañía*").[31] These one-venture partnerships are very rare in notarial sources and, because of their short duration, they are rarely mentioned in testaments. However, the reference to "*en compañía*" indicate that they were done in equity. Moreover, the small risk that one-venture partnerships implied suggest that these operations could be a recurring collaboration strategy for individuals that trusted each other, like the merchants of the *Atarazanas*.

1.2   *Silent Equity Partnerships*

The principle of equity allowed for a form of collaboration other than the company, in which individuals received capital from outsiders who were not necessarily involved in the administration of the business. As such, they constituted a strategy to finance business without resorting to external borrowing. Silent partnerships worked fine for both the active partner and the external investor; while the first raised extra capital for their *casa*, the second diversified investments for a very limited liability restricted to the capital they transferred. Although there is no information on legislation about silent partnerships in Seville, conditions related to liability must have resembled that of Antwerp, where silent partners could only be sued for debt less than their total investment.[32]

---

28   AHPSe, 9290P, 312v.
29   García-Baquero González, *La Carrera de Indias*, 239–245.
30   At the time of the testament, he still owed Van Hooren 402 *ducados*. AHPSe, SP, 9312, 517r.
31   AHPSe, SP, 9295, 1042r.
32   For a discussion on silent partnerships in Antwerp, see Puttevils, *Merchants and Trading*, 99.

This type of association left little trace in notarial deeds. Except for one notarised contract, silent partnerships only come to light when two merchants liquidated their shared account through *finiquitos* or after the death of a partner with testaments. Unfortunately, besides some exceptions already explained before, *finiquitos* tend to be scarce in detail when it comes to describing the nature of a collaboration tie. In the cases of the silent partnerships identified in Table 4.2, *finiqiuitos* only refer to the existence of shared accounts between partners for an indefinite period and no commodities are mentioned, which suggests that investors and debtors did not have a commission partnership. Moreover, from *finiquitos* it is not always possible to discern if the existence of a shared account was the result of a one-direction payment, in which only one merchant transferred capital to the other, or the result of a reciprocal collaboration, in which both merchants invested in each other's firms. Nonetheless, it is fair to assume that both forms of equity collaboration coexisted.

Table 4.2 contains the seven silent partnerships identified in the notaries of Francisco Díaz and Juan de Tordesillas. As in the previous table, this one indicates the nationality of partners (investors and debtors) and the existence of kinship or proximity ties. Additionally, the table includes information about the type of notarial deed (Not) where the partnership was identified – *finiquito* (Fin), testament (Tst) or a notarised transfer (*Ex ante*), as well as the year in which that document was notarised.

TABLE 4.2   Silent partnerships of *Atarazanas* merchants

Investor	Debtor	Nat.	Kin	Atr.	Not	Year
Francisco Bernal	Juan Jacart	FLE / FLE	In-law	Yes	Fin	1576
Nicolás de Melemburque	Francisco Bernal	FLE / FLE	In-law	Yes	Fin	1578
Juan Jacart	Miguel Arbauts	FLE / FLE		Yes	Fin	1578
Esteban Jansen	Sibol Wonderer	GER / GER			Fin	1584
Conrado Hinquel	Francisco Roelant	GER / GER			Fin	1596
Bernal Pérez	Juan de Bestoven	FLE / SPA			Ex ante	1597
Guillermo Corinsen	Juan Sarens	FLE / FLE	In-law		Tst	1598

SOURCE: SEE ANNEX C, E AND F

Similarly to *compañías*, most collaboration occurred among familiar individuals; in four out of seven cases, partners shared kinship ties or lived in the *Atarazanas*. In at least two other cases (Conrado Hinquel-Francisco Roelant and Bernal Pérez-Juan de Bestoven), there is ample evidence that the partners knew each other well, even though they did not live in the same building or shared a kinship tie. This resembles the strategies followed by merchants in sixteenth-century Antwerp, where "[t]he available bits of evidence of private equity transfers show that partnership shares were mostly transferred to family members, not to strangers," according to Puttevils.[33]

The only Spaniard appearing in the table, Bernal Pérez, was not alien to the trade of timber, since he had been working in Manas Enríquez's house for ten years, until Enríquez died in 1592.[34] Bernal Pérez's partnership with Juan de Bestoven was the only one notarised *ex ante*. In November 1597, Pérez paid 1300 *ducados* to Juan de Bestoven so he could use it in the trade with "timber and other goods."[35] The contract does not state how they would calculate the returns, but the testament Juan de Bestoven signed a year later does inform us about this. In it, De Bestoven declared to have received those 1300 *ducados* from Bernal Pérez to trade in timber in gain and loss (*"a gançia e perdida"*), and required his executors to return the said amount plus a very modest sum, 1000 *reales* (ca. 90 *ducados*), which the investment had yielded until then.[36]

Familiarity bonds might explain why partners did not feel the need to notarise their agreement. Another reason for that might have been that most transfers yielded only small returns, as evidenced in the amounts that debtors declared to transfer to investors in the *finiquitos*: Juan Jacart paid 381 *ducados* to Francisco Bernal, Miguel Arbauts paid 150 *reales* to Juan Jacart, and Francisco Roelant paid 407 *reales* to Conrado Hinquel.[37] Two other *finiquitos* did not state a payment of the debtor to the investor. The investor just stated that he was happy, satisfied and paid (*"contento y satisfecho y pagado"*) and partners declared the cancellation of their shared accounts and the absence of remaining debts.[38] The *finiquito* notarised by Esteban Jansen and Sibol Wonderer in 1584 is more exceptional, since there is no clear explanation as to who was the

---

33   Puttevils, *Merchants and Trading*, 100.
34   Four years later, in 1596, the executors of Enríquez' testament paid him for his service. AHPSe, SP, 9290, 944v.
35   AHPSe, SP, 9298, 764v.
36   Testament of Juan de Bestoven. August 30 1598. AHPSe, SP, 9303, 122r.
37   AHPSe, SP, 7784, 1185v; AHPSe, SP, 9217, 919v; AHPSe, SP, 9293, 885r.
38   AHPSe, SP, 9217, 249r.

principal in the operation, which perhaps suggests that this was a reciprocal collaboration.[39]

With the available notarial information, it is not possible to address the duration of these collaborations, although the lack of references in *finiquitos* to its beginning or duration indicates that most silent partnerships were indefinite. Yet if those were sustained collaborations, merchants should have declared them in testaments more frequently. Because of this, silent partnerships were probably the result of short-term investments of little capital between familiar individuals.

Only one silent partnership is known from merchants' testaments, and this was the result of a very exceptional collaboration. In his testament, Guillermo Corinse explained that he had a shared account with his brother-in-law Juan Sarens, for which Corinse was in debt. Sarens had given him a total of 14,000 *reales* in three different payments (9000, 4000 and 1000 *reales*), for which they had not yet settled their account. What is interesting about this case is that this equity transfer was one of the two means of commercial collaboration that they had, because Sarens had also provided Corinse with 100 dozen planks, 100 oak trees and 200 small oak trees to sell in commission, for which Guillermo Corinse had already returned 17,125 *reales*.[40] This example, in short, illustrates the complementarity and fluid forms of collaboration, especially when it came to individuals that shared kinship ties.

Familiarity, in short, might have been an essential element in silent partnerships, which explains the absence of notarial evidence. In this regard, a final consideration about this form of collaboration is to what extent dowries could fall under the category of equity transfers. Trivellato noted that, in the Jewish community of Livorno, dowries served to found general partnerships between in-laws with no expiry date, based on mutual agency and full liability.[41] This extreme case, perhaps, occurred in the company established between Guillermo Corinse and his father-in-law Felipe Sarens, analysed before. This may be the exception that proves the rule and, in any case, the liability of partners was clearly stated. Dowries did not seem to represent an equity transfer, since fathers-in-law did not acquire any right to their sons-in-law's enterprises through this transference. However, it is true that they could be claimed back if fathers-in-law understood that their sons-in-law were not meeting their commitments towards the wife and the family; or if the wife died. In the *finiquito* between Juan Jacart and Francisco Bernal,

---

39   AHPSe, SP, 9237, 864r.
40   AHPSe, SP, 9977, 740r-740v.
41   Trivellato, *The Familiarity of Strangers*, Chapter 5.

Jacart declared that, in the estimation for the liquidation of their shared accounts, he was including the 300 *ducados* he had received as dowry, which he had to return due to the death of his wife, Bárbola Bernal.[42] So dowries did set up an economic bond between in-laws, although this was not necessarily a commercial collaboration.

1.3   *Commission Partnerships*

In commission partnerships, known in Spanish as *encomienda* or *comisión*, a merchant provided goods to another to be sold for a percentage commission. The liability of principals was limited to the products they supplied, whereas the profits of the agent strictly depended on their performance.[43] Commission partnerships, thus, established a clear division of labour between partners as well as their liability. *Atarazanas* merchants were involved in at least ten commission partnerships, four of them notarised *ex ante* in a contract that explicitly stated the labour division, the range of products provided and, sometimes, the commission that agents received for the sales. The other six came to light through *finiquitos*, in which there is information about commodities being transferred between the two parties. Table 4.3 contains the ten partnerships, indicating the principal partner (investor) and the agent, the existence of familiarity ties between them (nation, kinship ties and whether they lived in the *Atarazanas*), the type of notarial deed (Not) in which the collaboration was identified, and the year in which the collaboration was formalised *ex ante* or liquidated in a notarial deed.

Table 4.3 reveals one main difference of commission associations in comparison to equity partnership: most of them occurred between individuals that did not share kinship ties or lived close to each other. This certainly speaks of a collaboration that required less liability from principals than the other two, and this lower risk favoured seeking cooperation opportunities with non-familiar individuals. This explains why Flemish citizens of Seville who did not reside in the complex or were specialised in other commodities embarked in the trade of timber sporadically as principals, which in turn allowed *Atarazanas* merchants to raise the scale of their commercial operations.

---

42   AHPSe, SP, 7784, 1185v.

43   On the role of commission partnerships in the commercial emergence of the Low Countries, see Roland Baetens, "El desarrollo social y económico de Flandes durante los siglos XV, XVI y principios del XVII," in *Encuentros en Flandes: Relaciones e intercambios hispanoflamencos a inicios de la Edad Moderna*, eds. Werner Thomas and Robert A. Verdonk (Leuven: Leuven University Press, 2000), 84–85.

TABLE 4.3 Commission partnerships of *Atarazanas* merchants

Investor	Agent	Nat.	Kin	Atr	Not	Year
Cornieles Valdovinos	Juan de Bos	FLE / FLE		Yes	Fin	1574
Jaques Enríquez	Simón Enríquez	FLE / FLE	Uncle/ Nephew		Fin	1591
Jaques Enríquez	Simón Enríquez	FLE / FLE	Uncle/ Nephew		*Ex ante*	1591
Jaques Giraldo	Simón Enríquez	FLE / FLE			Fin	1592
Francisco Ustarte	Miguel Arbauts	FLE / FLE			*Ex ante*	1594
Conrado Hinquel	Juan de Bestoven	GER / FLE			Fin	1596
Nicolás Estal	Justo de Bil	FLE / FLE			Fin	1596
Rodrigo Groenenberg	Justo de Bil	FLE / FLE			Fin	1596
Juan van Hooren	Gertruds de Angelberto	FLE / FLE		Yes	*Ex ante*	1597

SOURCE: SEE ANNEXES C, E AND F

Justo de Bil, for instance, received the commission of two outsiders of the *Atarazanas* group, Nicolás Estal and Rodrigo Groenenberg, with whom he signed *finiquitos* in 1596 to liquidate the shared account he had with each of them for the timber, rigging and tar he had sold on their behalf.[44] That same year, Conrado Hinquel and Juan de Bestoven notarised a *finiquito*, in which Conrado Hinquel stated that De Bestoven had paid him the returns from the rigging, timber and other merchandise that De Bestoven's company had sold on his behalf.[45] The fact that the three partnerships were liquidated in 1596 could have to do with the growing difficulties for those in Seville trading in north European commodities, as they were signed two months after the Anglo-Dutch

---

44   Nicolás Estal: AHPSe, SP, 9293, 364r. Rodrigo Groenenberg: AHPSe, SP, 9290, 311r.
45   AHPSe, SP, 9293, 404r.

attack on Cádiz, which reduced the interest of outsiders in investing in a trade that they did not know that well.[46] The vagueness of the *finiquitos* clauses suggests that these three commission partnerships constituted collaborations sustained in time.

Indeed, commission partnerships allowed for a multiplicity of solutions, including a reciprocal sustained collaboration, like the commission between Juan de Bos, who resided in the *Atarazanas* in the early 1570s, and the timber merchant Cornieles Valdovinos. The first supplied timber to the second, and the second supplied leather in return, which each would sell. This way the two participated in each other's firm as a means to diversify their investments in town.[47] The flexibility of this solution explains why there was no specific type of charter for notarising commission partnerships. Of the four *encomiendas* formalised *ex ante*, two were notarised in the form of a power of attorney in which the principal commissioned an agent to sell on his behalf the provided commodities, and two in the form of a bill of receipt in which agents declared to have received a set of commodities from the other party.[48] In contrast to non-notarised commission partnerships that appeared to be sustained in time, three of the four cases were limited to one venture: the set of commodities that principal gave to agents.

One of the commission partnerships notarised *ex ante* in the form of a bill of receiptwas that of Gertruds de Angelberto, widow of Manas Enríquez, who received from Juan van Hooren a varied set of timber products – 102 dozen pine planks, 1000 *tripitrapes*, 30 oak trees, 100 small beams, and 36 beams – which she committed to sell for a 6% commission in 1597.[49] This was not the only commission partnerships notarised *ex ante* with a bill of receipt. In this case, the commodity involved was not timber but grain, which is not strange, since grain was the other main north European product that *Atarazanas* traders imported. In 1591, Esteban Jansen reached an agreement with the owners of an inn (*Mesón de los Carros*) in Seville's outskirts, Juan Esteban and Catalina Ruiz. The married couple received 569.5 *fanegas* of barley harvested in 1590, which they committed to sell at their inn. They did not set a commission percentage but promised to pay back Jansen 7 *reales* per *fanega* they sold.[50]

---

46 Aram, "La identificación y ocultación de extranjeros."

47 AHPSe, SP, 9219, 727r.

48 POA granted by Jaques Enríquez to Simón Enríquez AHPSe, SP, 9266P, 910r; POA granted by Francisco Ustarte to Miguel Arbauts 9279P, 88. Bill of receipt granted to Esteban Jansen by Juan Esteban and his wife Catalina Ruiz (AHPSe, SP, 9267, 225r); and another one by Juan van Hooren to Gertruds de Angelberto (AHPSe, SP, 9299, 266r).

49 AHPSe, SP, 9299, 266r.

50 The reason to notarise this agreement was that the previous owners, Alonso González and his wife, had sold the inn to Juan Esteban and Catalina Ruiz, and they were taking

The other two commission partnerships *ex ante* notarised for the trade of timber followed similar conditions, although they were formalised with a power of attorney. In the first, signed in 1594, Francisco Ustarte commissioned Miguel Arbauts the sale of 11,000 pine-boards.[51] The other power of attorney was granted by Jaques Enríquez to Simón Enríquez for the sale of 144 dozen Flemish pine-boards, 221 Prussian boards, 26 dozen large and medium-sized oak trees, 200 dozen barrel-staves of 7 palms each, 93 dozen barrel-staves of 8 palms each, 88 dozen small barrel-staves of 4 palms each, 138 dozen trees, 300 small pine beams, 11 dozen small pines, and 580 *botijas* of tar.[52] The commission contract gave Simón Enríquez ample room to manoeuvre; he had to store the products in his *Atarazanas*, and could sell them for the price and according to the payment method he found more convenient. For this, he would receive a commission of three percent.[53]

The same day and before signing this contract, they liquidated a former shared account they had for all the commodities and payments that Jaques had done on behalf of Simón in Cádiz.[54] This illustrates a reciprocal collaboration between two relatives in interrelated ports, Cádiz and Seville, in the form of a commission. In a similar way, Simón maintained a commission partnership with Jaques Giraldo, a resident in Sanlúcar, although they did not share any kinship tie in this case. Giraldo had provided Simón Enríquez with commodities that Enríquez sold on his behalf in Seville. To liquidate their shared account, Enríquez paid Jaques Giraldo 5507 *reales*.[55]

In short, Simón Enríquez's ties in Cádiz and in Sanlúcar reveal the fluid connections between the inland city and the main ports of the coast, already analysed in previous chapters. The number of commission partnerships to structure such regional ties may have been greater than what Table 4.3 shows, as the many powers of attorney suggest. Most powers of attorney, which are analysed in the following chapter, do not give explicit information about the commission; hence, they have not been included in this analysis. *Encomiendas* must have represented a common form of collaboration, despite the scarce evidence in notarial registers. Commission on sales brought the interest of

---

over the agreement González and his wife had reached with Esteban Jansen. AHPSe, SP, 9267, 225r.

51 AHPSe, SP, 9279, 88r.
52 AHPSe, SP, 9266, 910r.
53 AHPSe, SP, 9266, 910r. Until then, Jaques lived in Cádiz. Months later he signed a testament (AHPSe, SP, 9265, 526r) and, in the following months, he delegated part of his operations in Simón Enríquez (AHPSe, SP, 9267, 64r).
54 Simón promised Jaques a payment of 19,276 *reales* for that AHPSe, SP, 9266, 908r.
55 AHPSe, SP, 9272, 338v.

partners in different towns closer, making this a very attractive solution not only for structuring regional trade but especially for long-distance connections. Stols saw this as the main form of partnership merchants used in the context of Antwerp-Seville trade.[56] If we assume that international collaboration at the time, like the one described by Stols, was mostly based on kinship ties, then we should also assume that trust between partners was high enough to need the notarisation of *encomiendas*.

1.4   *Notarisation of Partnerships*

The small number of equity and commission partnership notarised *ex ante* in relation to the total number of partnerships identified through *finiquitos* or testaments is not unusual. In his study on early modern Antwerp, Van Hofstraeten noted a similar practice: "registers contain numerous documents by means of which earlier established private partnerships were liquidated officially. As regards their initial establishment, however, no notarial deeds could be retrieved."[57] Law and customs across Europe recognised the validity of verbal agreements as long as they could be corroborated by private documents shown in court.[58] Consequently, for merchants who trusted each other, there was little incentive for formalising a partnership in public institutions to prevent partners' opportunistic behaviours. This has led historians to conclude that, given the lack of publicly formalised partnerships, early modern merchants mostly collaborated with familiar contacts – relatives or individual they knew well. This reasonable argument, nonetheless, gets complicated when is taken one step forward, assuming that merchants notarised a partnership *ex ante* when they did not know each other sufficiently. Puttevils's analysis of partnerships in sixteenth-century Antwerp illustrates this interpretation well. He identified twenty-seven partnerships, which he defined as "anomalous" because they were "likely to pertain to contracts between strangers who, not knowing each other, felt that registration was prudent."[59]

---

56   Stols, "La colonia flamenca de Sevilla," 364.

57   Bram van Hofstraeten, "The Organization of Mercantile Capitalism in the Low Countries: Private Partnerships in Early Modern Antwerp (1480–1620)," *TSEG/ Low Countries Journal of Social and Economic History* 13, no. 2 (2016), 9. See also Gelderblom, *Cities of Commerce*, 94.

58   Trivellato, *The Familiarity of Strangers*, 139. Bram van Hofstraeten, "Private Partnerships in Seventeenth-Century Maastricht," in *Companies and Company Law in Late Medieval and Early Modern Europe*, ed. Bram van Hofstraeten and Wim Decock (Leuven: Peeters, 2016), 125.

59   Puttevils, *Merchants and Trading*, 83. Van Hofstraeten noted that "during the second half of the sixteenth century, notarised partnership gained importance among related partners

TABLE 4.4   Partnerships of *Atarazanas* merchants formalised *ex ante*

Partnership type	Agents	Year	Nat.	Kin	Atr.
Equity	Geronimo Andrea & Cornieles Valdovinos	1573	Yes		Yes
Equity	Nicolás de Melemburque & Juan Jacart	1575	Yes	Yes	Yes
Commission	Jaques Enríquez & Simón Enríquez	1591	Yes	Yes	Yes
Commission	Esteban Jansen & Juan Esteban, Catalina Ruiz	1591			
Equity	Simón Enríquez & Cornieles Jansen	1592	Yes		Yes
Equity	Jaques Nicolás & Elias Sirman & Juan Gras	1594	Yes	Yes	
Commission	Miguel Arbauts & Francisco Ustarte	1594	Yes		
Silent	Juan de Bestoven & Bernal Pérez	1597			

SOURCE: SEE ANNEXES C, E AND F

Nonetheless, Table 4.4, which assesses on familiarity ties (nationality, kin and the residence of both partners in the *Atarazanas*) between partners who notarised their collaboration, shows a rather different reality:

Ties of familiarity were present in almost all partnership that were notarised before beginning to operate. All partnerships except two were established between members of the Flemish nation; and even in one of these two cases, Bernal Pérez was close to the circle of *Atarazanas* merchants, having worked for Manas Enríquez for ten years. This challenges the idea that the main objective of notarial contracting was to encourage trust between parties, which may hold true for one-off transactions but it was certainly not the case of the establishment of commercial associations. If notarisation did not merely serve to curb a lack of trust between partners, what other implications could this practice have? The notarised partnerships analysed throughout this chapter

as well. By 1600, more than one third of all notarised partnerships had been concluded between family members." Van Hofstraeten, "The Organization of Mercantile Capitalism," 18. These two publications are very interesting because they evidence remarkable similarities between notarial and collaboration practices in Seville and Antwerp.

suggests that the main motivation was reputation; especially when travelling abroad, a partnership contract could have been used to build the confidence of prospective third parties.

2   Agency

The first Spanish dictionary, published in 1611 by Sebastián de Covarrubias, defined *poder* as "the authority that one grants to another to do something on his behalf."[60] Although the word most commonly translates into English as "power," this particular meaning of *poder* fits into the juridical definition of agency in English:

> The relationship that exists when one person or party (the principal) engages another (the agent) to act for him (…). The law of agency thus governs the legal relationship in which the agent deals with a third party on behalf of the principal.[61]

A POA deed was, in short, the formalisation of agency. A glimpse at Seville's notarial records shows that the notarisation of agency was not a practice exclusive to *Atarazanas* merchants; POAs seem to be the most registered deed at the time. It was the flexibility of the deed, which could transfer different forms of legal and economic agency through the different formulae and clauses, that made POAs so popular.

Like most notarial deeds, POAs began with a description of the two parties: the principal or principals on the one hand, and the agent or agents on the other. Notaries stated their name and surname, their nation and place of residence in case of coming from abroad, and their status in town (*vecino, residente* or *estante*; citizen, resident or sojourner in English). This description was especially relevant in this kind of deed because it provided third parties with information about the principals on behalf of whom agents were operating. After the description, notaries stated the extent of the agency that principals

---

60   "[L]a facultad que uno da a otro para que en lugar de su persona haga alguna cosa." "Poder" Covarrubias, *Tesoro de la lengua castellana o española*, 1182. Nuevo tesoro lexicográfico de la lengua española, Real Academia española, accessed June 12, 2020 http://ntlle.rae.es/.
61   "Agency" *Encyclopaedia Britannica*, accessed June 12, 2020 https://www.britannica.com/topic/agency-law.

were transferring, explaining the operations that agents could perform through fixed formulae.

In contrast to partnership contracts, POAs do not usually elaborate on the conditions in which a cooperation was established, they only inform about the type of agency that was being delegated. Yet they provide a rich overview of the diversity of socioeconomic ties that merchants could develop, with familiar individuals in which trust was presupposed and with individuals whom they did not necessarily know. Based on the formulae delimiting agency, we can establish the following typology:

TABLE 4.5   Typology of POAs according to the agency principals transferred to agents

Type of agency	Definition	No.
Commercial	A granter commissions a proxy to perform one or more commercial operations, such as collecting commodities (41), shipping commodities (26), buying commodities (24), selling commodities (12), and leasing real-estate (10).	113
Legal	A granter commissions a proxy to represent them before judicial institutions, such as state courts as well as royal and local authorities.	156
Financial	A granter commissions a proxy to collect debts on their behalf (720) or to oblige a payment on their behalf (2). Sometimes the rights over a debt were transferred as well to the agent (137), with the principal renouncing to them.	859
General	Known as *poder general*, a granter provided a proxy full agency to act on their behalf, including the right to collect debts and, if necessary, take the initiative to prosecute debtors.	22
Substitution	A proxy, who had previously received a commission from a principal, transfers the rights and duties of that commission to a third party.	76

SOURCE: AHPSE, SP, 7764–7786 AND 9214–9308

At least 113 POAs transferred commercial agency.[62] The example of husbands transferring agency to wives, shown in Chapter 3, illustrates how important it was for individuals to delegate part of their operations when they were abroad or participating in increasingly larger-scale activities.[63] Moreover, as seen in the previous section, through POAs partners also notarised the terms of a commission partnership between individuals that knew each other well.[64] By explicitly delimiting the extent of the agency to specific commercial operations, merchants curbed the risks of principal-agent relations in long-distance trade. Therefore merchants frequently used it to cooperate with non-partners or even individuals with whom they did not share familiarity bonds.

In fact, many POAs signed by *Atarazanas* merchants did not imply a familiarity tie, but a professional one. This was especially the case with legal POAs, in which principals granted proxies agency to participate in judicial institutions, namely state's courts and royal and local councils on their behalf. As analysed in previous chapters, *flamencos* usually transferred legal agency to proxies when negotiating with local and royal authorities. But they also resorted to legal proxies to defend their individual commercial rights. They signed 156 legal POAs, in which 43 different professional attorneys – known as *procuradores* or *solicitadores de causas* – were appointed. While many of the 43 attorneys were appointed only once, some played an essential role for the group of the *Atarazanas* and the Flemish and German nation, in general. Germán Dufelde and Valerio Vandala (probably van Dale), two Flemish migrants, specialised in the legal representation of compatriots; they represented one or several timber traders 39 and 34 times respectively.[65] *Atarazanas* merchants developed a close relationship with Castilian attorneys too; Pedro Núñez de San Juan acted as attorney for one or several of them at least on 21 occasions, Juan de Urive did so on 16, and Gerónimo de Salamanca on 13.

The high number of POAs granted by foreigners to professional attorneys speaks of their reliance on public justice for managing their conflicts with other individuals or with local and state authorities. Unfortunately, the vague nature of legal POAs, which did not usually mention the cases that they involved,

---

62 I analysed many of them in a recent article. Jiménez Montes, "Sepan quantos esta carta vieren: poderes notariales y comercio transnacional en Sevilla, 1570–1600," *Studia Historica, Historia Moderna* 42, no. 1 (2020): 39–64.

63 See footnote 14 of Chapter 3.

64 Francisco Ustarte commissioned Miguel Arbauts the sale of 11,000 pine-boards. AHPSe, SP, 9279, 88r. The other power of attorney was granted by Jaques Enríquez to Simón Enríquez AHPSe, SP, 9266, 910r.

65 I.e. AHPSe, SP, 9246, 1126r (Valerio Vandala) and AHPSe, SP, 9223, 240r (Germán Dufelde).

hinders a systematic analysis on foreigners use of justice. Nonetheless, the 156 legal POAs notarised by this group makes it safe to conclude that the transference of legal agency became an ordinary strategy to defend their economic and political rights in Seville.

Sometimes the main purpose of a POA is not clear, because principals could delegate more than one activity. For instance, most financial and commercial POAs had a clause that allowed proxies to prosecute debtors in order to enforce a contract, which implies a transference of legal agency, too. In a similar way, since legal cases were often driven by unpaid debts, most legal POAs notarised for prosecuting a debtor before Spanish courts contained a clause that allowed agents to collect debts on behalf of principals. Many times, principals just granted a *poder general*, providing agents with full agency to act on their behalf, normally to collect debts and appear before royal or local institutions on the principals' behalf for an indefinite period. General POAs were infrequent; only twenty-two are documented in the sample.

Individuals usually preferred more specific forms of agency, in order to limit the liability of principals regarding the performance of agents. In fact, when agents did not act according to the expectations of principals, their agency could be revoked. There are at least eight cases of notarised revocations, in which *Atarazanas* merchants publicly stated the annulment of a POA. One occurred when Esteban Jansen dealt with the misconduct of Juan Banoy, his cashier, who was temporarily in Galicia selling Andalusian olive oil on his behalf. After receiving reports on Banoy's malpractice, Jansen granted Gonzalo Balvin, another of his workers, and Juan Giraldo, his agent in Sanlúcar, a POA that revoked the previous one with Banoy and authorised Balvin and Giraldo to take over his business in Galicia.[66] Principals could also take agency back on good terms; for instance, Esteban Jansen revoked a POA he had previously granted to Juan Bernal, declaring that he left Juan Bernal "in his honour and good fame."[67]

POAs, hence, were not exclusively a solution for individuals that trusted each other. Agency could be transferred to individuals that principals did not know at all. Sometimes agents retransferred agency to new agents in a deed known as *substituciones de poder*, agency-substitution deeds. Notarial sources document at least 76 of these deeds, in which an agent who had previously been commissioned by a principal transferred the agency to a third party who

---

66 "[A] mi noticia es venido que el dicho Juan Banoy no acude al benefiçio, venta y despacho de los dichos mis bienes con el cuidado que[s razón] y que abido e ay desbarate de su persona." AHPSe, SP, 9260, 562r.

67 AHPSe, SP, 9250, 806v.

may have not been necessarily related to the principal. For instance, in February 1578, Dirique Bovver, a citizen of Amsterdam, retransferred the legal agency that he had received from his father in a POA signed by the notary Pedro Cort van Shoon (*sic*) in Amsterdam on September 11, 1577. He transferredhis agency to three north European citizens of Seville, Esteban Jansen, Germán Dufelde and the Spanish attorney Juan de Criales. The previous example, again, speak of the flexibility of the notarial tool, which merchants used to transfer agency to familiar individuals and to strangers, delegating a wide range of legal and economic operations, to be represented in Seville or abroad, for a single operation or for an indefinite period.

2.1   *A Financial Tool*

POAs that transferred financial rights became a very useful solution for those participating in long-distance operations.[68] *Atarazanas* merchants participated in at least 859 of them in three decades. Many financial POAs were used to formalise an economic tie between individuals that resided in different territories. With these deeds, agents who lived abroad were allowed to collect money on behalf of principals based in Seville.[69] Similarly, temporary migrants granted POAs to *Atarazanas* merchants to collect debts in Spain once they travelled back to their homeland. Many of them were north European seamen who had either been working in ships of the *Carrera de Indias* and expected to receive their salary in the future, or were shipmasters who expected to receive the payment for their shipments.[70]

Most financial POAs were used as a debt cancelling instrument, on local and regional scales but also on an international one, in a way that resembles the use of bills of exchange. The extensive use of debt-collection POAs indicates the necessity to resort to tools that allowed for transferring capital without

---

68   Cachero Vinuesa explored this notarial tool in her thesis: Cachero Vinuesa, "Should we trust?"

69   For instance, Esteban Jansen commissioned his worker Justo de Bil to go to Flanders in 1590 to collect payments on his behalf there, and to urge Cornieles Yesque, a shipmaster, to deliver the cargo of timber he had committed to carry to Andalusia. AHPSe, SP, 9266, 8r.

70   The first was the case of the brothers Cosme Adrian and Juan Adrian, who worked as gunners in one of the royal warships escorting the *Carrera* fleet, and appointed Germán Dufelde their attorney to collect their salaries before returning to Flanders.AHPSe, SP, 9226, 372r and AHPSe, SP, 9226, 373r. The second was the case of Rodolfo Adriansen, from Danzig, who commissioned Melchor de los Reyes and Conrado Hinquel before returing to his country. AHPSe, SP, 9285, 1043r.

having cash move, as the scale of commercial operations grew larger. Braudel beautifully described the importance of credit instruments for early modern trade in his second volume of *Civilization and Capitalism*:

> Closing the circuit, rarely a simple matter, could not always be effected with goods for goods, or even with goods for coin; so merchants were regularly obliged to resort to bills of exchange. Initially a form of compensation, they also became, in Christian countries where interest on loans was forbidden by the Church, the most frequent form of credit.[71]

In the quotation above, Braudel pointed to bills of exchange as the main tool for transnational payments, which Lapeyre defined as the business tool *par excellence*.[72] For De Vries and Van der Woude, who studied the rise of what they called *The First Modern Economy* in the Netherlands, the bill of exchange became the backbone of the emergence of Amsterdam's entrepôt.[73] They provided with a brief and precise explanation on how bills of exchange worked:

> [A] product of fourteenth-century Italian communes, the bill of exchange became the principal and most flexible vehicle for creating credit, effecting exchanges between currencies, and transferring payment internationally. The bill of exchange was drawn by a creditor on his debtor – typically, by the seller of goods on his customer. It required the debtor to pay a stated amount (in another currency than that in which the debt is reckoned), at a stated time (usually, some months after the date of the transaction) and at a stated location (usually that of the creditor).[74]

The fact that bills of exchange allowed currency exchange boosted transnational operations. However, what made this financial instrument so essential for trade was its transferability; in other words, creditors' capacity to transfer a debt to new creditors through a bill of exchange and, consequently, creditors' capacity to cancel their own debt by transferring it to a third party to whom they owed money. As De Vries and Van der Woude noted:

---

71   Fernand Braudel, *Civilization and Capitalism, 15th-18th Century, Vol. II: The Wheels of Commerce* (London: W. Collins, 1982), 142.

72   Lapeyre, *Une famille de marchands*, 275. A classic work on this is Raymond de Roover, *L'évolution de la lettre de change: XIVe-XVIIIe siècles. Affaires et gens d'affaires* (Paris: Armand Colin, 1953).

73   De Vries and Van der Woude, *The First Modern Economy*, 134.

74   De Vries and Van der Woude, *The First Modern Economy*, 130.

In contrast to a simple promissory note, the drawer did not ordinarily hold the bill of exchange to maturity but rather sold it or placed it with a correspondent. (…) In this way two debts might be cancelled out with a minimal use of actual cash and avoidance of the danger and expense of transporting cash over long distance.[75]

A similar, although more modest, mechanisms of credit and debt transference is documented in Seville notaries, in the form of financial POAs in which a principal granted an agent the capacity to claim a debt from a third party, renouncing any right he held over that debt.[76] This way, the principal, who was creditor of the third party and debtor of the agent, cancelled a debt or a part of it, converting the transference of agency into the transference of capital. Consequently, POAs served as a discounting method similar to the bill of exchange. Together with a description of principal and agent, this type of deed always contained a description of the third party, which became the agent's debtor, and an explanation of the business that had originated the debt, normally a promissory note. The deed concluded with the principal's declaration renouncing any right over the transferred debt, which normally followed this structure: "[you can] receive and collect the said quantity in your name and for you, as if it was your very thing, because I renounce, give and transfer it to you."[77] There are 96 POAs of this kind, which moved up to 416,163 *reales* in the period from 1570 to 1599, as Figure 4.1 indicates.

Except for 1581, an exceptional year in term of *reales* transferred, Figure 4.1 suggests that financial POAs moved rather modest quantities, while the number of such POAs per year rarely exceeded five. The peak of 1581 deserves an explanation. That year, Guillermo Estalengue, an English merchant who had

---

75   Ibid.
76   In fact, in the notarial registers of Francisco Díaz and Juan de Tordesillas, the number of this type of POA outnumbered the number of bills of exchange, which rarely appear. They only left a trace when a creditor declared to collect the payment issued from somewhere else (66 bills of receipt involved the collection of a bill of exchange) or, on more exceptional occasions, when a merchant claimed the collection of one with a notarised protest. For instance, Jaques Nicolás appeared before Juan de Tordesillas on November 26 1594, to formalise a protest against Miguel Martínez de Jauregui, who owed him the payment of a 1000-*ducados* bill of exchange issued in Antwerp a month earlier, on September 7 (AHPSe, SP, 9283, 476r). On the POA as a financial tool between Seville and America, see Cachero Vinuesa, "Should we trust?" On banking and international finances in Seville, see Enrique Otte, "Sevilla, plaza bancaria europea en el siglo XVI." In *Actas del I Coloquio Internacional de Historia Económica. Dinero y Crédito (siglos XVI al XIX)* (Madrid, 1978), 89–112.
77   AHPSe, SP, 7772, 622r.

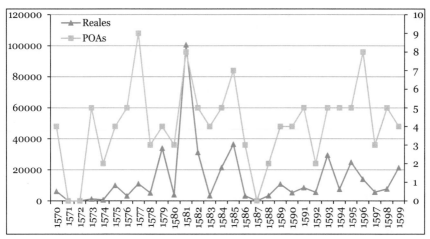

FIGURE 4.1   Financial POAs participated in by *Atarazanas* merchants
Note: The darker line shows the total amount of *reales* transferred each year (left
vertical axis). The lighter line shows the number of contracts granted each year
(right vertical axis)
SOURCE: AHPSE, SP, 7764–7786 AND 9214–9308

married Enrique Aparte's daughter, left Seville probably due to the increasing
hostility against English migrants. Before leaving, he granted several POAs to
Esteban Jansen, his brother-in-law, in which he transferred the right of several debts that Jansen had previously advanced to him "to please me and make
good to me."[78] The debt transferred included payments that he was to receive
from six different individuals from Tierra Firme (so Jansen had to wait until the
arrival of the American fleet),[79] and four bills of exchange that Estalengue had
not claimed yet: two granted in San Sebastián in the summer of 1581 and two
issued in Antwerp.[80]

This type of POA was also used between individuals that, in principle, did
not share bonds of familiarity, which may explain that only modest amounts
were transferred. In fact, it seems that this tool was mostly used for cancelling debts between residents in the same city, contrasting to the bill of
exchange –international in essence, as it implied a promise of payment in a
different currency. There is only one exception to this; the POA that Christobal
Osten granted to Guillermo Persin, who was travelling back to Amsterdam,

78   AHPSe, SP, 9227, 1110r.
79   AHPSe, SP, 9228, 26r.
80   AHPSe, SP, 9227, 1007r; 9227, 1110r; 9228, 831r.

claiming from Oto Cornelis, a merchant residing in Amsterdam, 1846 *reales*. Guillermo Corinse had paid Osten such a sum, on behalf of Persin, because the two had a shared account for the trade between Amsterdam and Seville; in this way, Corinse cancelled his debt with Osten, while Osten cancelled his with Persin. Very probable, Persin and Corinse would compensate this with further business between the two.[81]

2.2 A Global Tool

In the deeds, principals usually described the geographical scope in which agents could represent them, seeking once again to delimit the extent of the delegated agency. Although the clauses that delimit the agency's geographical scope tended to be vague, frequently ending with the formula "or in any other part" (*o otras cualesquier partes*), geographical references offer a good account of the global scale of these merchants' operations and the importance of POAs to organise them.

More than half of the POAs were expected to be used in Seville (762). Almost half of them (344) were used for debt-collection purposes in which *Atarazanas* merchants acted either as principals or proxies. POAs were widely used as a regional tool. Besides Seville, other Andalusian ports – especially Sanlúcar (139), Cádiz (68), El Puerto de Santa María (31) or Málaga (13) – take the lion's share of geographical references. This demonstrates the fluid communication between Seville and the coast. Towns in the hinterland, from Jerez to the Sierra Norte – a mountain range north of Seville – are present in the sample, too, with 56 POAs, which is a good illustration of how these merchants' commercial activities extended in the region. The political centrality of Madrid is also evident in the sample, with 62 POAs; they were mostly meant to deal with royal institutions.

Also, Portugal appears several times. In this case, the reason is the importance of Portuguese ports for the Baltic trade with southern Europe, which made towns like Lisbon (19) a base for shipmasters connecting Andalusia with the Baltic markets.[82] For a similar reason, ports along the Cantabrian region, especially Ribadeo (4), often appear in these merchants' POAs; many ships travelling between Andalusia and northern Europe stopped by ports on the Cantabrian coast.[83] Besides the Iberian Peninsula, references to American

---

81   AHPSe, SP, 9232, 850r.
82   For instance, Juan Vogalar – a German merchant – commissioned Esteban Jansen to sell timber that he would ship from Lisbon. AHPSe, SP, 9242, 536r.
83   I.e. AHPSe, SP, 9297, 437v.

ports are common, which indicates the growing interest and involvement of these merchants there, despite protectionists policies that sought to curtail foreigners' activities there.[84] POAs meant to be used in America generally contained more than one geographical reference, although the most repeated towns were main ports of the *Carrera de Indias* at the time: Cartagena de Indias, Veracruz and Nombre de Dios. The expansion of these foreigners' networks into the Americas is further analysed in the next chapter.

Finally, there are 93 references to European territories outside the Iberian Peninsula, among which the southern provinces of the Low Countries stand out with 36 references. From these, at least 25 POAs contain the vague reference of *Flandes* (Flanders) alluding to any parts of the Low Countries, even the northern provinces. Some cities are specifically mentioned, such as Antwerp (8 times), Bruges (2), and Lille (1). Despite the commercial prohibitions, Amsterdam is mentioned 9 times, while vague references to Holland and Zeeland appear sporadically, 2 and 1 times respectively. As the case of Flanders showed before, POAs generally speak of lands in a broad sense, Norway is mentioned 4 times, and Sweden 2. Mentions of Germany (7), *Alemania* in the original sources, refer vaguely to the Baltic ports of the German Empire; sometimes POAs explicitly indicate specific ports there: Danzig, Hamburg and Lübeck are mentioned twice each, and Rostock once.

Thanks to POAs, these merchants structured their business beyond Seville, on a regional and an international scale. The ambiguity when describing the territories suggests that the main aim of the geographical description was not the delimitation of agency merely. Instead, this seems a mechanism for providing information in order to help agents deal with third parties on behalf of principals. The numerous and varied geographical references in these deeds also indicate that POAs were popular throughout Europe, and widely acknowledged for those involved in long-distance trade. This is in line with a majority of historians who sees a convergence of commercial practices emerging from the regular exchange between different European territories.[85] In this early phase of European Atlantic trade, it seems more accurate to speak of a market of solutions across Europe, instead of a standardisation of contracting practices. As Fusaro recently argued, "the existence of a landscape of different legal systems offered myriad opportunities in which

---

84   Jiménez Montes, "Sepan quantos esta carta vieren."
85   Gelderblom, *Cities of Commerce*, 8. See also Paul R. Milgrom, Douglass C. North and Barry R. Weingast, "The Role of Institutions in the Revival of Trade: The Law Merchant, Private Judges and the Champagne Fairs," *Economics and Politics* 2 no. 1 (1990).

the entrepreneurial activities of many actors could flourish."[86] Foreigners' extensive use of POAs, which permitted them to participate in international markets delegating agency to relatives, workers, professional attorneys and even shipmasters, is a good example of this.

3   Conclusion

Not all *Atarazanas* merchants followed the same cooperation strategies. The most powerful trader of the group, Esteban Jansen, only appears in one partnership, a shared account with Sibol Wonderer. His position in the market must have been important enough to depend on equity investors or partners to raise capital and enlarge the scale of his business. Alternatively, as the previous chapter showed, he had several individuals working for his firm in Seville and abroad, to whom Jansen frequently delegated his economic activities through the transference of agency. His lack of participation in partnerships contrasts with another central player in the timber trade, Jaques Nicolás, who established many and varied commercial associations. Other merchants of the *Atarazanas*, especially Guillermo Corinse, Justo de Bil, Simón Enríquez and Juan de Bestoven, relied widely on partnerships to organise their business, too.

The partnerships these merchants formed were varied. Merchants adopted equity and commission in a flexible way, adapting them to their needs. Despite the heterogeneity of solutions, all partnerships analysed shared a common aim: to limit partners' liability. In these partnerships, merchants only responded for their investments, which facilitated them to maximise the scale of their operations by joining forces with others or accepting the investment of others, while diversifying their operations by investing in several partnerships at the same time or other merchants' firms. Hence, partnerships improved their individual businesses capacity, contributing to consolidate the group's pre-eminence in the trade in timber between southern and northern Europe.

Atarazanas merchants only diversified their investment within the scope of timber trade, a sector they knew well, and they mostly partnered with

---

86   Maria Fusaro et al, "Entrepreneurs at Sea: Trading Practices, Legal Opportunities and Early Modern Globalization," *The International Journal of Maritime History* 28, no. 4 (2016): 775. Grafe made a similar question in one of her publications. Grafe, "Was There a Market for Institutions in Early Modern European Trade?" in *Union in Separation: Diasporic Groups and Identities in the Eastern Mediterranean (1100–1800)*, ed. Georg Christ et al (Rome: Viella, 2015) 593–609.

merchants very close to them. The lack of systematic evidence hinders the analysis of the preferences of long-distance traders between equity or commission partnerships. Nonetheless, the available evidence shows a clear preference for equity from partners sharing familiarity ties, while collaboration with individuals from outside their familiar circle or residing outside Seville often took the form of commission, in which investors only risked the products they had sent to an agent.

Most partnerships (especially the non-notarised ones) reveal sustained and stable collaborations between familiar partners, while notarised partnerships often established temporary associations. Since family and commercial interests bonded most merchants residing in the *Atarazanas*, it is fair to assume that they collaborated beyond the evidence available in notarial registers. In the end, collaboration primarily was a matter of familiarity. If most notarised partnerships occurred between individuals that shared a bond of familiarity, we should assume that notarisation did not seek to curb a lack of trust. Instead, these deeds sought to enhance partners' reputation to facilitate their cooperation with third parties. Reputation was the *raison d'être* of power of attorneys too, facilitating principals to trade with third parties with the help of agents.

Merchants found in POAs a fundamental tool for the implementation of their commercial strategies due to its flexibility. With the same deed, principals could transfer different forms of agency, allowing for a varied range of socio-economic solutions beyond a local scale. As this chapter discussed, POAs even substituted more specific forms of contracting, like commission partnerships contract, company charters or bills of exchange. As such, POAs were not necessarily an instrument used between individuals about whom a relationship of trust can be presupposed. The main reason for that was the possibility of delimiting agency through the clauses of the notarial deed, which curbed possible risks associated to the activity of agents. POAs allowed for the creation of less durable cooperation ties than commission and equity partnerships, favouring cooperation with less familiar individuals.

Timber Trade and Andalusian Exports

> To those who may read this letter: Be aware that I, Esteban Jansen, German merchant citizenship of Seville in the parish of Santa Maria, grant and know that I give and grant all my fulfilled power and enough faculty, as I have it and the law rules it, and with whole, free and general administration, to Bastian Amensen, a Flemish individual temporary residing in the city of Seville, who is departing with the good fortune to Flanders and Norway ...

∵

This was the beginning of the power of attorney that, on February 4 1580, Esteban Jansen granted Bastian Amensen to transport different sorts of north European timber to Seville on his behalf.[1] As discussed in the previous chapter, POAs like this one give a good account on how merchants organised their business on an international scale. Thanks to the clauses of POAs, we obtain rich information about their proxies abroad, the regions in which they operated, the activities that proxies were allowed to perform on their behalf or the most traded commodities.

The document presented above shows how, as a result of the 1574 embargo, Esteban Jansen and other northerners began to specialise in the importation of naval provisions, on which the city of Seville and the Hispanic monarchy relied, and how they expanded internationally.Due to the unstable international arena and Philip II's changing policies regarding trade and war with northern Europe, the group's preeminent position heavily depended on their ability to sustain a steady supply of Baltic and Scandinavian timber for the *Carrera de Indias* and the royal navy. Since the end of the 1570s, *Atarazanas* merchants began to build a commercial network that extended beyond Seville, from the Andalusian coast to Baltic and Scandinavian ports, ensuring their access to the main supply markets of timber of the time.

---

1 AHPSe, SP, 9223, 524r.

This chapter addresses the extent of this network and the strategies in the trade between northern and southern Europe through the analysis of commercial POAs and charter parties notarised in Seville. This analysis is complemented with the study of primary sources from northern Europe: a collection of charter parties notarised in Amsterdam in the period from 1591 to 1599, and passages registered in the Sound Toll in the last three decades of the century. These primary sources evidence how, in the last third of the sixteenth century, Amsterdam emerged as a main entrepôt for European trade. However, contrary to what historians have long assumed, the commercial rise of Amsterdamwas not only the result of the expansion of firms based there. As this chapter aims to show, the initiative in the construction of a commercial connection between Spain and the Dutch Republic was taken by Flemish and German merchants operating from Andalusia, in close cooperation with north European shipmasters, whose relevance in long-distance trade is more often than not neglected by historians.[2]

The first part of this chapter builds a chronology on how *Atarazanas* merchants gained access to the main markets for the supply of naval provisions, especially Amsterdam, since the 1570s. A second part looks at the emergence of a hierarchical port system in Andalusia and how the region participated in the shipping circuits that connected southern and northern Europe, which were operated by Dutch and Hanseatic shipmasters. A third section finally looks at how *Atarazanas* reinvested their profits in Andalusian exports, with which they financed the importation of timber to southern Spain.

1   Access to Supply Markets

The first POA a merchant of the *Atarazanas* granted for the importation of naval supplies from northern Europe dates from 1578. On April 19, Francisco Bernal commissioned Arnaut Baven, a citizen from Amsterdam, to charter a 400 or 500-ton ship with any captain, master or owner. The shipshould receive a cargo of timber in Langesund (Norway) and carry it to Las Horcadas, a port between the mouth of the Guadalquivir River and Seville.[3] Although Bernal dominated

---

2 Only in recent times, historians are reinterpreting their roles as entrepreneurs and go-between actors in long-distance trade in Europe. Fusaro et al, "Entrepreneurs at Sea."

3 AHPSe, SP, 9217, 925r. This was not the first POA about timber trade. On July 20, 1575, Francisca Bernal, on behalf of her husband, Nicolás de Melemburque, granted Jaques Levasur a POA to go to Sanlúcar to compel Miguel Xirez, German master of *El Angel*, the issue of a receipt for 4500 *reales* (409 *ducados*). AHPSe, SP, 7781, 621r.

a great deal of the *Atarazanas*, he rarely engaged in the trade of timber. The death of his son-in-law Juan Jacart left Bernal as guardian of the under-aged orphans, probably pushing him to take on Jacart's unfinished business, such as this timber cargo in Norway.[4]

That same year, Esteban Jansen granted a POA to Claes Hem Aliasvocht, Flemish master of the ship *Santiago,* to import up to 400 *ducados* in masts, planks, and other timber from London, which Jansen would pay at his return to Andalusia.[5] The fact that the cargo would be obtained in London indicates the wide extent of these merchants' networks, which not only covered Scandinavian or Baltic ports but also important European entrepôts, like London, Amsterdam and Lisbon.[6] As discussed in Chapter 1, trade between Andalusia and England eventually fell into decline after the second embargo that Philip II placed upon England and the Dutch Republic in 1585.

Esteban Jansen did not grant this POA to one of his workers or a merchant residing abroad but to a shipmaster, to whom he delegated commercial agency to buy up to 400 *ducados* in timber.[7] Unfortunately, the notarial deed does not give information about the gains that Claes Hem Aliasvocht expected from this operation, although it does illustrate that shipmasters did not only act as carriers of commodities; they often acted as commercial intermediaries. Some shipmasters even played a more active role in the trade between Andalusia and northern Europe, commissioning *Atarazanas* merchants to sell the products they had imported. In 1581, the Flemish master of *El Jonas*, Adrian Jance, granted a POA to Felipe Sarens for the sale of 1400 oak beams and more than thirty dozen pine planks, which he had stored in Sarens's house.[8]

---

4   Bernal's administration of Jacart's estate left more traces in the notary registers. For instance, he commissioned Miguel Arbauts for collecting commodities that Juan Jacart was to receive from Joergen Haer, a shipmaster from Cambuur. (AHPSe, SP, 9223, 424r). Similarly, Gerónimo Andrea claimed his part of the same cargo, commisioning Guillermo Dupont as his proxy in 1580 (AHPSe, SP, 9223P, 456r). In fact, Jacart's death led to a conflict between Andrea and Jacart's heirs. (AHPSe, SP, 9222, 128r).

5   AHPSe, SP, 9217, 513r.

6   For instance, the POA granted by Juan Vogalar, German resident in Lisbon, to Esteban Jansen to sell 1000 bornes and other German products that he had left in Jansen's warehouses in 1584. AHPSe, SP, 9242, 536r.

7   Later on, he had many problems collecting the money, which led to a lawsuit that left trace on the notary's registers: AHPSe, SP, 9217, 346v and AHPSe, SP, 9217, 538r.

8   AHPSe, SP, 9228, 1213r. Likewise, Herman Aquerman, a German shipmaster, commissioned Pedro Gisberto to sell the timber that he had imported in 1588. (AHPSe, SP, 9254, 758v). Another example is the one of Bernardo Escuder, a Lubecker shipmaster that arrived in Seville from Sweden in 1583, who granted a POA to Esteban Jansen to sell his cargo of staves and beams (AHPSe, SP, 9234, 1138r).

From the early 1580s, Esteban Jansen gained a foothold in the main north European markets by commissioning agents there.[9] On February 2, 1580, he granted a POA to Bastian Amensen – the deed cited at the beginning of this chapter. On behalf of Jansen, Amensen would travel to Flanders and Norway to contract the shipment of timber to Seville. That same day, they notarised a labour contract that established a salary for Bastian Amensen of 300 florins per year with no expiry date, suggesting that he would represent Jansen abroad for an indefinite period.[10] A year later, Jansen formalised a labour contract with Tobías Buc and, on the same day – January 30, 1581 – he granted him and his brother Hendrik, a resident in Amsterdam, a POA to run his businesses abroad.[11] The formalisation of a POA and a labour contract the same day highlights the different purposes of the two types of deeds; POAs served to inform third parties about the relation between principals and agents, which resulted from a labour contract. The POA Jansen granted to the Buc brothers explicitly limited their agency to a particular commercial operation: "to contract in Amsterdam, or wherever they found more suitable, one, two or three hulks to load my timber, which is masts, planks, oaks, *tripitrapes* [low-value timber for making barrels] and other things."[12]

The case of the Buc brothers shows the growing importance of Amsterdam as an entrepôt between Scandinavia-Baltic area and the Iberian Peninsula by 1580, with the deed's explicit mention to the Dutch city. Yet Esteban Jansen's commercial contacts went beyond Amsterdam and extended through the Sound Strait, especially in Danzig, where he was born. In 1588, a merchant from Danzig, Simon Hilcont, granted him a POA to receive and sell a shipment he had sent in the ship *San Adolfo*.[13] In this case, Jansen was not acting as principal but as agent, which evidences the complexity – and probably reciprocity – of the international networks participated in by *Atarazanas* merchants.

POAs transferring commercial agency, like the ones above, became more infrequent after 1583. The causes for this probably had to do with the fact that many of the merchants had already consolidated their position in the main

---

9   Esteban Jansen sent several agents to northern Europe: Bastian Amensen in 1580, and
     Tobías Buc and his brother Hendrik in 1581. AHPSe, SP, 9223, 524r and AHPSe, SP, 9226, 266r.
10   No expiry date was mentioned. AHPSe, SP 9223, 529r.
11   AHPSe, SP, 9226, 265r.
12   AHPSe, 9226P, 266r-266v.
13   AHPSe, SP, 9256, 831r. This also worked the other way around: Esteban Jansen commissioned Paulo Giraldo, a resident in Amsterdam, to claim unpaid debts for a cargo of oil he had sent to Holland. AHPSe,9263P,280r, AHPSe,9263P,280v.

north European markets, especially in the Low Countries and Norway. It is important to remind here that Nicolás de Melemburque had travelled himself to different parts in northern Europe ("Flanders and, from there, to Norway and Österland") for several years in the 1570s, surely creating cooperation ties there with shipmasters and other merchants.[14]

Another reason is that, by then, the activity of north European shipmasters was tolerated, as a consequence of the protests against the 1574 embargo, and therefore their presence on the Andalusian coast grew. Consequently, many shipments of timber to southern Spain must have been contracted in Andalusia already by 1580s. Unfortunately, the damaged state of the notarial collection of the Historical Archive of the Province of Cádiz concerning this period does not allow to research their shipping activity in Cádiz and Sanlúcar de Barrameda in a systematic way.

The second embargo, ordered in 1585, did not impact the commercial expansion of the group much. Plenty of notarial deeds indicate that it did not put a stop to their activity. One of them was a POA notarised in February 1589 by Guillermo Corinse, commissioning his father and his brother, who resided in Amsterdam, to claim a compensation for a timber cargo that had not been delivered due to the death of the shipmaster carrying it, for which Corinse had initiated a legal case in Seville.[15] The fact that, by the 1590s, their network of contacts was well established is evidenced by the more ambitious strategies these merchants undertook, for instance, by investing in the ownership of hulks to transport timber. In November 1593, Guillermo Corinse, Tobías Buc, Juan Leclerq and Juan Gerbrausen granted a POA to Reinaldo Cornielesen to buy "in Emden or anywhere in Germany" a ship from 160 to 200 tons, which they will name *San Diego*.[16] Some years earlier, in 1590, Manas Enríquez had granted a similar POA to a resident in Hamburg to contract in "any part and port in Germany" the building of a ship up to 450 tons.[17]

The notarisation of agency for the trade in timber was resumed in 1594, when Francisco Roelant commissioned Jan Molenar, a merchant from Wismar in Germany, to contract a shipment of timber from Denmark, Sweden and Poland to Sanlúcar or Las Horcadas, to be paid upon the ship's arrival.[18]

---

14   AHPSe, SP, 7780, 281v.
15   AHPSe, SP, 9258, 97r.
16   AHPSe, SP, 9278, 150r.
17   AHPSe, SP, 9263, 778r.
18   AHPSe, SP, 9279, 975. Francisco Roelant notarised a similar POA to Pedro Adriansent Heust, a master from Langesund in 1598. This time Adriansent would send timber from Norway and Germany. AHPSe, SP, 9303, 401r.

Roelant's interest in those Baltic regions, different to the Norwegian and the Low Countries markets, may corroborate the hypothesis posed earlier: that by the middle of 1580s, Seville-based merchants already had a network of contacts in the Low Countries and Norway that made the appointment of new agents unnecessary. This is confirmed by the POA Justo de Bil granted to Antonio van der Bequen for contracting the transport of timber with a particular shipmaster, Cornieles Antonio, who was anchored in Sanlúcar waiting to set sail for Flanders. On behalf of Justo de Bil, Antonio van der Bequen would contract with Cornieles Antonio a continuation of this journey; once in Flanders, the shipmaster would go on to Norway, where a contact of Justo de Bil would deliver a cargo of timber to be imported to Las Horcadas.[19]

In 1595, we find the first charter parties of timber signed in Seville. In January 18, Esteban Jansen formalised the agreement with Yami Lessen, a German master of the ship *La Caridad*, who would go to "Coperbique" (Koperbik, Norway) to receive 16 masts of different sizes detailed in the document, and as many "planks from Denmark" as possible.[20] For the shipment, Jansen would pay Yami Lessen, once he returned to Andalusia, all the salt that fitted in his ship, plus an amount of cash to be determined by four external arbitrators, two proposed by Jansen and two by Lessen.[21] That same year, in November, Jansen contracted a second charter with Juan Pitersen, a German master of the ship *El Cuervo Negro*, to import the maximum possible cargo of timber of different sorts from Konigsberg in Prussia.[22] An agent working for Jansen in the region would deliver the cargo to Pitersen within three weeks of his arrival. For the transport, Pitersen would receive as much salt as he could fit in his ship on his return to Andalusia plus 300 *ducados*.

Juan de Bestoven and Melchor de los Reyes contracted three charter parties with three different shipmasters in the same week of January 1598: with Juan Pitersen of the ship *El Cuervo Negro*, the same shipmaster that years earlier had contracted with Esteban Jansen; Giraldo Juan of the ship *San Jorge*; and Adrian Gerche Bras of the ship *El Jonas*. The three shipmasters committed to go to Langesund, where, they would receive a cargo from a contact of De Bestoven and De los Reyes within a period of 30 days.[23] While the three contracts had a similar purpose, they were negotiated separately. The first and

---

19   AHPSe, SP, 9295, 16r.
20   AHPSe, SP, 9284, 119r.
21   AHPSe, SP, 9284, 119r.
22   "[T]oda la carga de madera, bornes y tripitrapes y bornetes y maderas de pipas" (November 2 1595). AHPSe, SP, 9288, 343r.
23   AHPSe, SP, 9299, 509v, AHPSe, SP, 9300, 14r and AHPSe, SP, 9300, 12r.

the second deeds do not mention the quantity of timber that the agent in Langesund would provide, but set the price of the freight at 875 *ducados* plus a primage of 25 *ducados* for master's coat and the piloting of the ships on the river from Sanlúcar to Seville.[24] The third contract, by contrast, was arranged for 1000 *ducados* and, in this case, Adrian Gerche Bras was obliged to load all possible timber beneath the ship's deck. The master's coat and the piloting of the ship from Sanlúcar to Seville were established at 30 *ducados*.[25]

As the clause of the contracts signed by Juan de Bestoven and Melchor de los Reyes indicate, most north European shipmasters did not travel up the Guadalquivir River to Seville, but stayed on the coast instead, especially in Sanlúcar and Cádiz. As such, charter parties notarised in Seville represent an exception, since most shipping agreements between merchants – or their proxies – and shipmasters should have occurred in Sanlúcar and Cádiz. Nonetheless, these exceptional charter parties notarised in Seville illustrate the culmination of *Atarazanas* merchants' search for stable supply lines of extra-peninsular timber. If in the 1575 they began this search travelling themselves, as the case of Nicolás de Melemburque showed, since 1578 they delegated on others. Based in Seville, they transported timber to Andalusia, transferring agency to travelling workers from their firm, foreign shipmasters who enjoyed commercial leeway, or other merchants with whom they developed reciprocal relationships. By the decade of 1590s, *Atarazanas* merchants enjoyed a network of contacts that covered the most important supply and intermediary markets of timber in Europe.

1.1   *The Amsterdam-Seville Connection*

A key process in the business expansion of *Atarazanas* merchants was the consolidation of a commercial connection with Amsterdam, regardless of Philip II's hostility towards the trade between the Iberian Peninsula and the rebel provinces. The notarial registers of Jan Fr. Bruyningh and Jac. Gijsbertsz in Amsterdam contain at least 110 charter parties for the transport of Baltic and Scandinavian timber from 1591 to 1599.[26] The majority, 70 contracts, had Andalusia as the final destination, which indicates the relevance that the southern European region had for Amsterdam's entrepôt at the end of the century.

---

24   AHPSe, SP, 9299, 509v, AHPSe, SP, 9300, 14r.
25   AHPSe, SP, 9300, 12r.
26   I have had access to these deeds thanks to the database created by Cátia Antunes and Maria Bastiao, in the framework of the ForSeaDiscovery project, with 1953 contracts that related to shipbuilding in Amsterdam from the end of the sixteenth to the end of the eighteenth centuries.

TABLE 5.1   Merchants contracting a shipment of timber to Andalusia in Amsterdam (1594–1599)

No.	Merchants (*bevrachters*)
8	**Gerrit Claess Leijenaer**
5	**Elbert Pieterss Can, Jan Mollenar, Jan Persijn,** Isaacq Ouwerock
4	**Cornelis Jansen,** Jacob Andriess
3	**Frans Taelingh, Jacques Bernart, Marten Jansen Aep,** Isaacq le Maire, Dirck Dircksz Pelser, Sijmen Fransen
2	Hendrick Jansen Aep, Hendrick Mieuss Rotgans, Joos van Peenen, Pieter Luijtss
1	**Hendrik Buijck, Jacob Bouwens, Jacop van der Burch, Pieter Pietersz, Symen Hendricxsen,** Agge Jaricxss, Barnart Barrewijns, Claes Andriess, Dirck Lock, Gerrit Jacopsen Hulft, Herman van Santbeeck, Jacob Jacobss Brasser, Jacob Jacobss Lantss, Jan de Nijs, Jan Hillebrants Futs, Joost Dirckss ter Velde, Pauwels van Lutselen, Pouwels van Lutselen de Jonge, Roelant Willemss, Rombout Jacobss.

Note: The highlighted names had a documented direct connection with *Atarazanas* merchants
SOURCE: ANTUNES' DATABASE

Thirty-eight different merchants participated in the 70 charter parties and only fourteen of the contracts were participated by two, which suggest that this was a rather accessible investment. This impression is in line with Jou's unpublished thesis, defended in 1992, which studied the trade of timber between Amsterdam and Königsberg. In there, he concluded that merchants in Amsterdam did not specialise in the trade of timber; instead, this was one of the many commodities that merchants in the Dutch entrepôt dealt with by the end of the century.[27] Table 5.1 shows the individuals appearing as charteres in the 70 shipping contracts that had an Andalusian port as final destination.

While the many names in Table 5.1 confirms that Jou's conclusion about the accessibility of this trade is accurate, this does not necessarily mean that the shipping of timber to Andalusia was dominated by local merchants. At least twelve out of the thirty names in the list were directly connected to *Atarazanas*

---

27   Kyung-Chul Jou, "Le Commerce des Bois entre Königsberg et Amsterdam, 1550–1650," (PhD diss. École des hautes études en sciences sociales, Paris, 1992), 40. He based this conclusion on Schreiner's work, Johan Schreiner, *Nederland Og Norge, 1625–1650: Trelastutførsel Og Handelspolitikk* (Oslo: Dybwad, 1933).

merchants, evidencing the importance that Seville-based traders had in the construction of a commercial axis between Holland and Andalusia. At least two *Atarazanas* merchants, Cornieles Jansen and Simón Enríquez, contracted in Amsterdam notaries the transport of timber to Andalusia. On March 24, 1594 Simón Enríquez contracted with Cornelis Opper, shipmaster of *De Wilster* of 100 *lasten* (Dutch unit of tonnage), a shipment of timber from Zeeland to Cádiz, for a freight price of 275 Spanish *ducados*; Opper was allowed to load in Zeeland other commodities but only under the condition that the returns should be shared with Enríquez.[28] The activity of Simón Enríquez in Amsterdam is not surprising. This was part of the travels about which he informed in the partnership he notarised with Cornieles Jansen in May 1592, analysed in the previous chapter, where he committed to travel to "Germany and Flanders and other parts" to transport timber over the course of three years.

Cornieles Jansen signed four contracts once his partnership with Simón Enríquez had expired. On June 18, 1596, he agreed with Cornelis Teunissen, master of the ship *Sint Pieter* of 150 *lasten*, to carry timber from Amsterdam to Cádiz via Ribadeo, in northern Spain, for a freight price of 675 *ducados*.[29] He contracted the other three shipments of timber jointly with other partners. On August 4, 1597, he contracted together with Pieter Pietersz a shipment of timber from Amsterdam to Sanlúcar in the ship of Jan Schellinger, called *De Swarte Os* of 70 *lasten*, for 650 *Carolusgulden*.[30] With Marten Jansen, he chartered two different ships in November 1597: one with Govert Corneliss, shipmaster of the *Sint Jacob* of 80 *lasten*, from Amsterdam to Seville for 1000 *Carolusgulden*,[31] and the other with Outger Janss, master of the *Sint Andries* of 90 *lasten*, from Amsterdam to Sanlúcar for 340 *ducados*.[32]

In fifteen charter parties, the merchant explicitly identified himself as an agent of a Seville-based merchant, which demonstrates that POAs notarised in Seville were often used when contracting with third parties abroad.[33] Jan Mollenar (also Juan Jansen Molenar) represented Francisco Roelant in five charter

---

28　GAA 65/4.

29　GAA, 74/160.

30　GAA, 32/485. Some months earlier, in July 1597, Marten Jansen had sent Cornieles Jansen timber (77/111), a ship of 100 tons, shipmaster Sibble Sijbrants, for a price of 400 *ducados*. The shipmaster agrees that if he is to buy salt in Andalusia, before his journey back to the Netherlands, he had to buy from Cornieles Jansen.

31　GAA, 78/141.

32　GAA, 82/171.

33　The other two were: Adolff Dirckssen from Cádiz (GAA 67/3v) and Adriaen Jansen Verdonck from Rotterdam (GAA 73/49). Only once a contract was agreed with the owner of the ship (in this case Fernando de Monde, a resident in Seville, GAA 74/160).

parties between June and July 1594, making use of the POA that Roelant had granted him seven months before.[34] The five contracts followed a similar structure: the shipmaster committed to go to Langesund, where he would buy the timber he would carry to Andalusia. To buy this timber, shipmasters could borrow money in advance, which was to be deducted from the final freight price or refunded on their arrival in Andalusia, in which case the freight price increased. The shipmasters were always paid in southern Spain, normally with a full load of salt plus a freight price that varied depending if the shipmaster had borrowed capital or not, from 282 *ducados* to 670.[35] These charter parties confirm a crucial aspect in this trade, already mentioned in the previous section: agency was transferred to shipmasters who not only took care of the cargo's transport but also bought this cargo at the supply market; in this case, Norway. Here, moreover, the principal's agency, which Molenar had received from Roelant, was being retransferred to the shipmasters.

Elbert Pieterss Can (probably Pedro Can in Seville sources) represented Roelant in three charter parties, one of them together with Jacob Bouwens (probably Jaques Brahusen in Seville sources).[36] On July 1595, Elbert Pieterss Can contracted with Gerrit Feijkisen, shipmaster of *Die Swarte Ruijter* of 80 *lasten*, a shipment of timber from Amsterdam to Sanlúcar for 500 *Carolusgulden*.[37] In the other two charter parties, signed in April 1596 and June 1598, the shipmasters Cornelis Janss and Cornelis Tonis committed to go to Langesund to buy timber and carry it to Sanlúcar with their ships of 240 and 150 *lasten* respectively. The shipmasters borrowed 500 *rijksdaalders* for buying timber, and once they arrived in Andalusia, Roelant would pay the freight price: 1150 *Carolusgulden* for Cornelis Janss, and 950 *ducados* for Cornelis Tonis.[38]

Jaques Nicolás appears six times as principal of a charter party represented by an agent in Amsterdam. Gerrit Claess Leijenaer represented him five times,

---

34   AHPSe, SP, 9279, 975.
35   Shipmaster Cornelis Symenssen, *Het Paradijs*, 100 tons, freight price of 282 *ducados* plus salt (GAA 65/33v). Shipmaster Albert Dirckss Backer, *Die Kerseboom*, 150 tons, freight price of 580 *ducados* plus salt (66/166v). Shipmaster Merten Jansen, *Suurwoude*, 100 tons, freight price of 282 *ducados* plus salt (65/35v). Shipmaster Bouwen Heinjesz, *De Neerman*, 165 tons, freight price of 490 *ducados* plus salt (66/7). Shipmaster Jan Jacopssen Melcknap, *Die Bruijnvis*, 190 tons, freight price of 670 *ducados* plus salt (66/175v).
36   They are described in the document residents of Seville. Pedro Can visited Andalusia at least twice, once in 1577 and again between 1594 and 1596. (AHPSe, SP, 9283, 610r and AHPSe, SP, 9289, 922). Not being himself a trader specialised in timber, Jaques Brahusen had a very close connection with *Atarazanas* merchants. His first document in Seville dates from 1579 (AHPSe, SP, 9222, 698v).
37   GAA 72/9v (1595-07-26).
38   GAA 32/474v (1596-04-18) and 81/32v (1598-06-11).

between May 1596 and October 1598; in two of them Cornieles Lamberto was acting as principal together with Jaques Nicolás. In two of the charter parties formalised by Gerrit Claess Leijenaer on behalf of Nicolás, the shipmaster committed to buy timber in Langesund to be transported to Sanlúcar.[39] In the other three, the shipmaster departed directly from Zeeland or Amsterdam to Andalusia.[40] Nothing is known about Gerrit Claess Leijenaer, but he could be a relative of Jaques Nicolás, whose Dutch surname would have been Claes. This, in short, would indicate the existence of family networks in the commercial axis between Seville and Amsterdam.

The fact that a brother of Guillermo Corinse, Frans Taelingh (Francisco Talmis in Spanish sources), represented Jaques Nicolás, at least once, points to that conclusion. He signed a contract with Gerrit Evertdz, master of 't Fortuijn of 180 *lasten*, for a charter from Amsterdam to Langesund and, from there, to Sanlúcar or Las Horcadas for a freight price of 900 *ducados*.[41] Some months later, in March 1596, Francisco Talmis contracted on behalf of Juan de Bestoven (Jan de Westhoven in the Dutch source), a charter party with Claes Heijn under similar conditions for a price of 825 *ducados* in a 160-*last* ship.[42] Francisco Talmis also contracted on behalf of Juan van Hooren (Jan van Hoorn in the Dutch contract) a shipment of timber from Amsterdam to Sanlúcar for 376 *ducados*.[43]

Interestingly enough, there is no evidence of Francisco Talmis sending timber to his brother, Guillermo Corinse. However, Corinse does appear as principal in a charter party that Hendrik Buijck (Hendrik Buc in Spanish sources) notarised in September 1594 on behalf of Corinse and Hendrik's brother, Tobías Buc. In the charter party, Hendrik Buc agreed with Hermen Ellertsen, shipmaster of *De Drije Coningen* of 150 *lasten*, a journey from Amsterdam to Langesund, where Ellertsen would spend up to 600 *rijksdaalders* in timber to be sent to Sanlúcar. In return, the shipmaster would receive a full load of salt and 450 *ducados*.[44]

---

39   GAA 74/219v (1596-05-28): Cornelis Jacobss, *Den Jongen Tobias*, 150 tons, 725 *ducados*. GAA
     80/1 (1597-08-11): Adriaen Gerritss, *Jonas*, 200 tons, 1050 *ducados*. GAA 82/74 (1598-10-
     02): Jelle Rutgers, *'t Huijs de Muijden*, 130 tons, 1100 *ducados*.
40   GAA 78/119v (1597-09-17): Tomas Evertss, *Die Blauwe Leeuw*, 115 tons, journey via Ribadeo,
     505 *ducados*. GAA 78/70 (1597-09-25): Adriaen Gerritss, *Die Jonas*, 200 tons, for 600 *duca-
     dos*. 78/118 (1597-10-17): Willem Claessen, *Raijboijer*, 80 tons, journey via Ribadeo or
     Luarca, 400 *ducados*.
41   GAA 72/41v. On Francisco Taelingh (Talmis in Seville sources): AHPSe, SP, 9258, 97r.
42   GAA 73/54.
43   GAA 77/109 (1597-07-08). Wijbrant Ijsbrantsen, *Die Boer*, 80 tons.
44   GAA n.b. (1594-09-06).

Other individuals sending commodities to Andalusia do not make an explicit reference to their principal there, but their connections to *Atarazanas* merchants come to light from Seville notarial records. This is the case of Jacques Bernart, Francisco Bernal's grandson and resident in Amsterdam, who signed a contract with Cornelis Dircxss Blancker, shipmaster of *Die Nachtegael*, to send timber from Amsterdam to Cádiz and import wine, fruits and salt in return.[45] Another example is that of Jacob van de Burg, brother of Juan Sesbaut and resident in Delft, who contracted with Jacop Corneliss, shipmaster of *Die Gulden* of 200 *lasten*, a shipment from Langesund to Sanlúcar in return of a full cargo of salt and 590 *ducados*.[46]

The case of Jan Persijn (Juan Persin in Spanish sources) is more unusual. In the charter parties, there is no explicit mention to him representing a principal based in Andalusia. On the contrary, notarial sources in Seville evidence that he was probably one of the few Amsterdam-based merchants who developed agency ties in Andalusia at the time, together with Isaac le Maire.[47] Juan Persin notarised five charter parties to Andalusia, none of which passed by Langesund. They all consisted of a single voyage from Amsterdam to Andalusia.[48] In one of the deeds, signed in 1595, he agreed with the shipmaster, Jacop Cornelissen, that if his agents in the region, Marten and Cornieles Jansen, did not pay him in eight days while he was on the coast, he should travel the river up to Seville to find them and claim the price of the freight.[49] Before this contract, there is plenty of evidence of different merchants that worked on his behalf in Seville. Esteban Jansen was his agent for a short period of time in 1577.[50] Later, Guillermo Corinse represented him until 1586. A misunderstanding between the two provoked Persin to send another proxy to Seville, Nicolas Rumar, to revise Corinse's accounts. Corinse avoided a lawsuit by agreeing with Rumar a payment of 50 *ducados* to Persin.[51] This is the only trace of Rumar in Seville

---

45   For a freight price of 36 *Carolusgulden* per last of the imported cargo. GAA 80/226v (1598-08-18).

46   GAA 64/167v (1591-03-24).

47   A relative of Isaac le Maire, Pedro, was active for a while in Seville. In May 1595, he signed a charter party with Corin Juan, a Flemish owner of a fluyt, on his name and on behalf of Francisco de Conique, to transport wine to Emden. AHPSe, SP, 9285, 158.

48   One of them from Texel to Sanlúcar, GAA 65/132v (1594-11-15). The other ones: 69/118 (1595-04-11), 72/209v (1595-11-10), 72/212v (1595-11-10).

49   GAA 72/207v.

50   This occurred after Juan Persin's brother, who resided in Lisbon, passed the commission he held from Juan Persin on Jansen with a substitution POA. AHPSe, SP, 9214, 947v.

51   AHPSe, SP, 9248, 63r.

notarial registers, as he probably left the city after the agreement, being substituted by Juan Sesbaut as his agent.[52]

Persin and his new agent had some troubles as well. To solve this, Persin commissioned Juan Lucas as his legal proxy in town but soon revoked this POA in favour of Simón Enríquez in the notary of Giles van den Bosche in Antwerp (December 9, 1589).[53] With this POA, Enríquez took over Persin's operations in the region and claimed Sesbaut a debt on masts and other timber that he had received from Persin.[54] It is, thus, logical that Cornieles Jansen appeared as factor of Persin in Seville in 1595, since Jansen was the partner of Simón Enríquez by then, as explained in Chapter 4.

The creation of agency ties between merchants in Andalusia and Holland occurred in the context of Amsterdam's commercial rise. The axis built between Seville and the Dutch city benefited from the development of powerful shipping industries in Holland and Friesland.[55] Indeed, the majority of shipmasters contracting the charter parties to Andalusia declared to be from Holland (49) or Friesland (11), out of 70. The relevance of Dutch shipmasters in the construction of this commercial axis went beyond their role as carriers of commodities. As the Seville's POAs and Amsterdam's charter parties showed, they were fundamental for contracting in supply markets; this is why merchants often transferred agency to shipmasters, commissioning them to buy the cargo of timber that was to be transported to Andalusia. This commercial delegation was possible thanks to the precision of notarial contracts like charter parties, which delineated the liability of both parties, such as the capital that shipmasters were expected to borrow from principals or to spend abroad. In many cases, shipmasters even pledged to bear the liability of the cargo during the transport through a clause of bottomry, according to which shipmasters used the ship as a means of insurance until the timber was successfully delivered.[56]

---

52   AHPSe, SP, 9267, 414r.

53   AHPSe, SP, 9262, 382v.

54   The POA was granted to Enríquez and two more merchants in town, Juan van Herps and Luis Cloet, for collecting any debt in Andalusia. AHPSe, SP, 9267, 414r. They finally resorted to arbiters: Sesbaut named Francisco Roelant and Enrique Fuent, while Enríquez, on behalf of Persin, named Mateo Doom and Elias Sirman. AHPSe, SP, 9526, 713r. The arbitration process sheds light on the labour relation between Sesbaut-Persin. For instance, Sesbaut had been working exclusively for Persin for several years for a salary of 250 *ducados* per year.

55   De Vries and Van der Woude, *The First Modern Economy*, 350–408. Werner Scheltjens, *Dutch Deltas: Emergence, Functions and Structure of the Low Countries' Maritime Transport System, Ca. 1300–1850* (Leiden: Brill, 2015).

56   George F. Steckley, "Bottomry Bonds in the Seventeenth-Century Admiralty Court," *The American Journal of Legal History* 45, no. 3 (2001): 256–77.

TABLE 5.2   Routes of the shipments of timber contracted in Amsterdam to Andalusia
            (1594–1599)

No.	Freight routes
28	The Netherlands –Andalusia
24	The Netherlands – Norway – Andalusia
5	The Netherlands – North Spain – Andalusia
4	The Netherlands – Andalusia – The Netherlands
3	The Netherlands – Norway – Andalusia – The Netherlands
2	The Netherlands – Denmark – Andalusia
2	The Netherlands – Poland – Andalusia
1	The Netherlands – Andalusia – London/ The Netherlands
1	The Netherlands – Denmark – Ibiza
1	The Netherlands – Poland – Andalusia – London/ The Netherlands

SOURCE: ANTUNES' DATABASE

Charter parties were also explicit when defining the routes and ports of
the transport. This complete information allows for a reconstruction of the
main routes and ports involved in the trade of timber between Seville and
Amsterdam, which Tables 5.2 and 5.3 illustrate.

As Table 5.2 shows, the most frequent route (28 times) consisted in a direct
voyage from Amsterdam to Andalusia. Additionally, five of the contracts
planned a stop in northern Spain (Ribadeo) before resuming the voyage to
Andalusia, which surely had to do with the construction of royal warships
in Cantabrian shipyards.[57] The fact that the majority of shipments did not
imply a stop in Scandinavian or Baltic ports highlights Amsterdam's role as
entrepôt, with a large stock able to re-export Baltic and Scandinavian timber

---

[57]   On the shipyards in Ribadeo, see José Luis Gasch-Tomás, Koldo Trápaga Monchet,
        and Ana Rita Trindade, "Shipbuilding in Times of War: Contracts for the Construction
        of Ships and Provision of Supplies in the Spanish Empire in the Early Seventeenth
        Century," *International Journal of Maritime History* 29 no. 1 (2017): 187–192. Seville notarial
        sources give account of the increasing activity of these Cantabrian shipyards, with char-
        ter parties contracted to transport timber there with the following shipmasters: Herman
        Eles, Flemish (AHPSe, SP, 9284, 513r); Rodrigo Cornieles, Flemish (AHPSe, SP, 9292,
        208r); Enríquez Tape from Emden (AHPSe, SP, 9296, 682); Juan Alebrense, German from
        Tosbergue (AHPSe, SP, 9296, 1052v); and Juan Jansen, German (AHPSe, SP, 9300, 95v).

TABLE 5.3   Ports from where timber was obtained for the shipments
             to Andalusia contracted in Amsterdam (1594–1599)

No.	Ports
34	Amsterdam
22	Langesund
3	Norway, Zeeland
2	Danzig, Marstrand, Drammen
1	Bergen, Danzig, Königsberg, Riga, Texel

SOURCE: ANTUNES' DATABASE

to southern Europe.[58] Norway (26 times), and especially the port of Langesund near the south of the Scandinavian Peninsula (22 times), was the main source of the timber carried by Dutch shipmasters to Andalusia in the 1590s. Much of the time, the shipmaster would receive a cargo of salt in Andalusia as a means of payment together with the freight price, which was commonly paid in *ducados* once in Andalusia, not in Amsterdam; this occurred 42 out of the 70 cases.

1.2   *Two Shipping Networks*

Mentions of Baltic ports, like Danzig or Königsberg, are almost anecdotal in the charter parties, contradicting a received wisdom that Dutch networks had dominated the Baltic trade since the end of the sixteenth century.[59] This suggests that Hanseatic shipmasters still played an important role in the transport between Andalusia and Baltic ports, as previous chapters have highlighted, especially in times of embargo against the Dutch Republic.Nothing indicates that the presence in Andalusia of shipmasters from Lübeck and the Danzig-Königsberg area declined by the 1590s. In fact, a search in the Sound Toll Registers Online database shows that the majority of the shipmasters departing from the Iberian Peninsula and crossing the Sound Strait were indeed from the Baltic basin.[60] Of a total of 445 passages, 178 of the shipmasters

---

58   Jou also noted the increasing importance of Norwegian timber in Amsterdam by the end
      of the sixteenth century. Jou, *Le commerce des bois,* 38–39.
59   Jou, *Le Commerce des Bois,* 43–44. The concern of Spanish contemporaries about this is
      thoroughly discussed by Gómez-Centurión Jiménez, *Felipe II.*
60   The registers only inform about the port of departure of the ship crossing the Sound
      Strait. Because of this, we can only work with voyages that departed from Andalusia. On

came from the Dutch Republic (30 of them from Amsterdam), while 217 came from Baltic ports (96 of them from Lübeck).[61] In short, the growing importance of Amsterdam for Andalusia's trade with northern Europe did not occur at the expense of the Hanseatic shipping, which were still important players in the trade between the Baltic markets and southern Europe in the last third of the sixteenth century.

If one looks at the Sound Toll registers in this period to compare the passages departing from Portugal and those from Spain, the picture of the routes of trade between the Iberian Peninsula and northern Europe becomes even more interesting. While no charter party was contracted to go to Portugal in Amsterdam's notarial registers, the majority of the ships crossing the Sound Strait from the Iberian Peninsula departed from Portugal, as Figure 5.1 shows.

Figure 5.1 does not reveal anything new about the trade between the Iberian Peninsula and northern Europe. Portugal's relevance in this commerce is well known by historiography.[62] There were some voyages from Andalusia, generally from Sanlúcar de Barrameda, but they are unimportant if compared to the shipments departing from Portugal. Since the Middle Ages, Lisbon had been in the orbit of the Hanseatic League, which was very interested in Setubal's salt ponds.[63] By the end of the century, the Dutch came to dominate this commercial route despite the frequent embargoes imposed by the Habsburg monarchy upon the trade with the Republic.[64]

Taking into account the transcription of IJzerman on shipments to Spain and Portugal between 1593 and 1603, Israel concluded that most of the trade between the Peninsula and northern Europe occurred via Lisbon.[65] Therefore, Lisbon must have worked as an intermediary node for many of

---

the use of the Sound Toll Registers for historical analysis, see the recent collective publication by Jan Willem Veluwenkamp and Werner Scheltjens, eds. *Early Modern Shipping and Trade: Novel Approaches Using Sound Toll Registers Online* (Leiden: Brill, 2018). A good methodological explanation on the use the Sound Toll Registers for researching Spain's trade with the Baltic region is Nathan Gallagher, "A methodology for estimating the volume of Baltic timber to Spain using the Sound Toll Registers: 1670–1806," *The International Journal of Maritime History* 28, no. 4 (2016): 752–773.

61   From the Sound Toll Registers Online (STRO) Database, accessed June 12, 2020 http://dietrich.soundtoll.nl/public/.

62   See for instance Christopher Ebert, "Dutch Trade with Brazil before the Dutch West India Company, 1587–1621," in *Riches from Atlantic Commerce: Dutch Transatlantic Trade and Shipping, 1585–1817*, eds. Johannes Postma and Victor Enthoven (Leiden: Brill, 2003), 49–75.

63   For the activity of Hanseatic shipmasters in Portugal, see the classic work: António Henrique R. De Oliveira Marques, *Hansa e Portugal na Idade Média* (Lisbon: Presença, 1993).

64   Ebert, *Between Empires,* 53.

65   Israel, *Empires and Entrepots,* 138. He based his analysis on IJzerman, J.W. *Amsterdamsche Bevrachtingscontracten 1591–1602* (The Hague: Martinus Nijhoff, 1931).

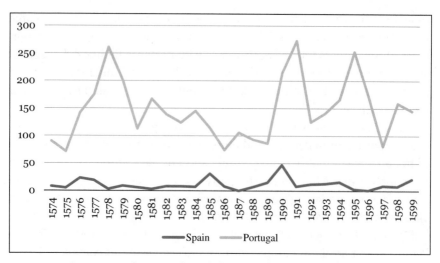

FIGURE 5.1   Comparison of passages through the Sound Strait from Spanish and Portuguese
ports (1574–1599)
SOURCE: NINA E. BANG, *TABELLER OVER SKIBSFART OG VARETRANSPORT
GENNEM ØRESUND, 1497–1660: UDARBEJDEDE EFTER DE BEVAREDE
REGNSKABER OVER ØRESUNDSTOLDEN* (COPENHAGEN: GYLDENDAL,
1906), 62–165

the commodities that reached Andalusia via the Low Countries. However, if
we consider Figure 5.1 and Table 5.2, we notice that Seville did not depend on
Lisbon for the importation of naval stores. This, consequently, suggests the
existence of two main transport circuits that connected Andalusia with north
European markets by the end of the century. One dominated by Hanseatic networks and later by the Dutch that connected Portugal with the Baltic markets,
and to which Andalusian ports were subordinated, and another one dominated
by Dutch shipmasters that connected Andalusia with Norway via Amsterdam.

2   The Andalusian Port System and the North-European Shipping Networks

One aspect that explains the attraction of north European shipmasters to
Andalusia was the regional production of salt, which was in high demand in
northern Europe.[66] As seen in the deeds notarised in Amsterdam, part of the

---

66   See the classic collective volume Michel Mollat, *Le rôle du sel dans l'histoire* (Paris: Presses
universitaires de France, 1968), especially the work by Pierre Jeannin, "Le marché du sel

freight price was usually paid in salt and many charter parties even stipulated exclusivity clauses through which shipmasters committed to obtain salt from the specific contacts in Andalusia. Similarly, almost all ships coming from Spain registered in the Sound Toll were carrying salt.[67] However, it was the access to silver what made southern Spain especially attractive for foreign shipmasters. Most shipping operations were paid in silver *ducados* in Andalusia. Furthermore, their easy access to silver, through the supply to ships travelling to and from the Americas, implied that *Atarazanas* merchants usually enjoyed enough liquidity to reinvest in new shipments of timber , which consequently explains their initiative in the trade between northern and southern Europe. Next chapter will address how theymerchants obtained American silver by supplying the ships of the *Carrera de Indias*.

Andalusia was by far the preferred region for the shipments of timber to Spain contracted in Amsterdam, and Andalusian ports were the most repeated origins of the voyages crossing the Sound Strait from Spain. Remarkably, Seville had a marginal role in these shipping circuits, as Figures 5.2 and 5.3 illustrate. Lying on the mouth of the Guadalquivir River and ruled by the Duke of Medina Sidonia, Sanlúcar de Barrameda concentrated most of the shipping activities in Andalusia, followed at great distance by Cádiz, which was the largest port directly ruled by the monarchy on the western Andalusian coast.

References to Seville or Las Horcadas, a harbour on the Guadalquivir about 40 kilometres south of from the city, are infrequent.[68] At first sight, this is striking: if shipping occurred along the Andalusian coast, why did timber merchants reside in Seville? The answer is found in the well-known history of Seville's commercial rise and downfall, as the only port allowed for the navigation with the Americas.[69] Being the only inland port of the Iberian Peninsula, Castilian kings found this a better alternative than coastal towns to protect American fleets from sea attacks, and to oversee American navigation and trade, the arrival of silver and the collection of royal taxes. However, as the tonnage of ships grew and the deposition process of the river continued, sailing the Guadalquivir became increasingly risky, making shipmasters reluctant to call at Seville. In this regard, Otte noted that ships larger than 250 tons

---

marin dans l'Europe du Nord du XIVe au XVIIIe siècle."

67   STRO database, accessed June 12, 2020 http://dietrich.soundtoll.nl/public/.

68   On Las Horcadas, Jiménez Montes, "Sepan quantos esta carta vieren."

69   Antonio Domínguez Ortiz, *Orto y ocaso de Sevilla* (Sevilla: Universidad de Sevilla, 1991); García-Baquero González, *La Carrera de Indias*. For an overview on the evolution of the western Andalusian port system, see Pablo E. Pérez-Mallaina Bueno, "Auge y decadencia del puerto de Sevilla como cabecera de las rutas indianas," *Cahiers du monde hispanique et luso-brésilien*, no. 69 (1997): 15–39.

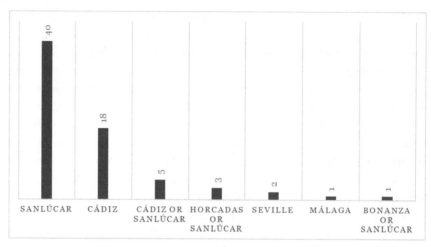

FIGURE 5.2 Ports of destination of shipments of timber contracted in Amsterdam to Spain
(1594–1599)
SOURCE: ANTUNES' DATABASE

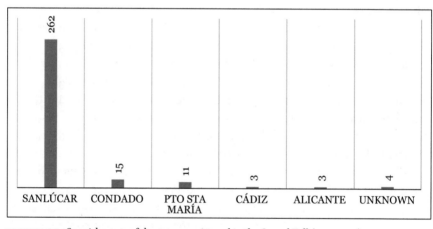

FIGURE 5.3 Spanish ports of departure registered in the Sound Toll (1574–1599)
SOURCE: BANG, *TABELLER OVER SKIBSFART*

could not travel up the river to Seville full loaded and it is estimated that 8%
of shipwrecks in the *Carrera de Indias* between 1504 and 1650 occurred in the
Guadalquivir River.[70] The situation of the river, in short, equally affected the

---

70   Otte, *Sevilla y sus mercaderes*, 106. Pérez-Mallaina, "Auge y decadencia," 34.

ships of the *Carrera de Indias*, which began to operate *de facto* on the coast, and north European ships that, as Figures 5.2 and 5.3 showed, rarely made it to Seville.

Most shipping activities occurred on the line of coast between Cádiz and Sanlúcar, which was especially favoured by the interest of the Duke of Medina Sidonia in attracting foreigners.[71] Yet Seville continued housing the institutions regulating trade and navigation with the Americas and, thus, attracted most human and economic capital involved in international trade until the middle of the seventeenth century; in the meantime, commodities were probably transported across the river to Seville by local ships better suited to its shallow waters, and exceptionally transported in the same hulks guided by local pilots, as evidenced in the charter party agreed by Juan de Bestoven and Melchor de los Reyes with Adrian Gerche Bras analysed earlier.[72] By the end of the sixteenth century, Seville still remained the principal centre of information in Andalusia and, thus, the place to be for new commercial opportunities, especially if they involved the *Carrera de Indias* and the supply to the monarchy, as in the case of *Atarazanas* merchants.

The western Andalusian coast developed into a hierarchical port system, in which Seville was the commercial capital while the shipping activities occurred in Cádiz and Sanlúcar.[73] The structure of this port system explains why Flemish and German merchants remained in the *Atarazanas*, which kept them close to royal institutions and allowed them to store abundant stock of timber. However, to fully engage in north European trade, they needed to extend their network of agents to the coast, where they could contract transport to export and import commodities directly with Dutch and German shipmasters. This is why *Atarazanas* merchants notarised 254 POAs for use on the western Andalusian coast over barely thirty years: 139 were meant to be used in Sanlúcar, 68 in Cádiz, 31 in El Puerto de Santa Maria, 5 in Puerto Real

---

71   This was already discussed in Chapter 1. For more information about the role of the Duke of Medina Sidonia in Andalusia's trade, see Luis Salas Almela, "Poder señorial, comercio y guerra: Sanlúcar de Barrameda y la política de embargos de la Monarquía Hispánica, 1585–1641," *Cuadernos de historia moderna*, no. 33, (2008): 35–59, and "Los antepuertos de Sevilla: señorío, comercio y fiscalidad en la Carrera de Indias (s.XVI)," in *Mirando las dos orillas: intercambios mercantiles, sociales y culturales entre Andalucía y América*, eds. Enriqueta Vila Vilar and Jaime J. Lacueva Muñoz (Sevilla: Fundación Buenas Letras, 2012), 105–127.

72   AHPSe, SP, 9300, 12r. Seville's notarial registers contain rich information about the activity of a guild of river pilots (*compañía de cargadores*), which has not been studied yet.

73   Otte, *Sevilla, siglo XVI*, 129–134.

and 1 in Rota. In those places, they commissioned agents for a variety of operations, including the collection of cargoes imported by shipmasters,[74] the sale of part of the cargo on the coast,[75] or the contracting of new charters parties.[76]

3 Andalusian Salt, Other Exports and Imported Grain

Another factor that explains that Dutch and Hanseatic shipmasters concentrated their operations along the coast between Cádiz and Sanlúcar was the presence of salt ponds.[77] The high demand of this product in northern Europe led many *Atarazanas* merchants to invest in salt by accumulating a large stock or directly engaging in its production. In fact, as explained earlier, in many charter parties notarised in Amsterdam, merchants obliged shipmasters to get salt from their contacts in Andalusia, using the cargo of salt as a complement to the freight price. Unfortunately, their investment in salt left little trace in Seville's notarial sources, given that it mostly occurred outside the city. Information about this activity is sketchy, but it is enough to conclude that some of them invested in the importation of salt as a complementary trade to the exportation of timber.

In 1577, Esteban Jansen commissioned Jaques Enríquez, a Flemish citizen of Cádiz, to buy salt to be exported to northern Europe.[78] In Sanlúcar, Jansen collaborated frequently with Gaspar Loscarte, who owned several salt ponds.[79] Jaques Nicolás appears buying salt to be loaded on the ship *La Maria,* which had arrived in Sanlúcar with a cargo of timber from Norway in July 1584.[80] In

---

74   AHPSe, SP, 9223, 424r.

75   AHPSe, SP, 9230, 1081r. As well as to collect the payments from this: AHPSe, SP, 9271, 435v.

76   For instance, the POA that Esteban Jansen granted to his proxy in Cádiz, Jaques Enríquez, in 1579. In there, Jansen delegated ample agency and permitted Enríquez to contract with *any* captain, master or owner the charter of a wide variety of commodities ("timber, planks, masts, clothes, merchandises and other things") from *any* part or port of Flanders, Germany and Norway to Seville or Sanlúcar de Barrameda. AHPSe, SP, 9220, 287r. Other examples, AHPSe, SP, 9223, 424r; 9230, 1081r; 9271, 435v.

77   For a recent study on Andalusian salt ponds, see David González Cruz, "La red de salinas y el comercio de la sal en el estuario del Tinto durante la Edad Moderna: Huelva, San Juan del Puerto, Palos de la Frontera y Moguer," *Studia Historica. Historia Moderna* 42, no. 1 (2020).

78   AHPSe, SP, 9217, 13r.

79   In August 1586, Esteban Jansen bought 2000 *cahizes* of salt from Gaspar Loscarte: *1000 cahizes* from the salt ponds of Loscarte himself (AHPSe, SP, 9248, 28r) and other 1000 *cahizes* from the salt pond of doña Leonor de Velasco, which Loscarte bought on behalf of Jansen (AHPSe, SP, 9248, 26r).

80   AHPSe, SP, 9239, 1285r.

December 1594, Francisco Roelant and Juan Leclerque sent an agent to the coast to buy salt. Curiously enough, this salt would not be shipped to northern markets but was to be carried to Seville instead, probably to be stored in Roelant's warehouse.[81]

There is also evidence about the purchase of salt ponds by at least two *Atarazanas* merchants. Manas Enríquez, who lived in Cádiz before moving to Seville, owned salt ponds in Puerto Real, which his widow sold after his death.[82] Esteban Jansen was the other merchant investing in the production of salt. Thanks to his close relationship with Gaspar Loscarte, who by then was a close collaborator of the Duke of Medina Sidonia, he acquired two salt ponds near Sanlúcar in 1588.[83] From that moment on, there are several notarial deeds informing about him selling salt to Juan Sesbaut in February 1594 (a total of 8050 *reales* for 1100 *cahíces*, meaning 7.5 reales per *cahíz*)[84] and 650 *cahíces* for the same price (7.5 reales per *cahiz*) to Marten Jansen, Juan Persin's agent in Andalusia.[85] Some months before his death, Esteban Jansen became responsible for the "administration of the salt ponds of Andalusia." This epitomised the culmination of the group's predominant position in the trade with northern Europe, which by 1595 was in control of the taxation on the sales of timber and salt in western southern Spain.[86]

Finally, it is interesting to note that these merchants' investment in salt ponds contrasts with other commercial groups within the Flemish and German community in Seville. For instance, those specialised in the importation of northern textiles and the exportation of wool bought washing centers for wool in towns near Seville, like Écija or Huéscar.[87]

---

81   AHPSe, SP, 9283, 686r.

82   AHPSe, SP, 9291, 656r and AHPSe, SP, 9246, 715v.

83   AHPSe, SP, 9255, 412r, AHPSe, SP, 9256, 931r. For the maintenance of the salt ponds, a man had to be full-time employed in the task (AHPSe, SP, 9290, 667r and AHPSe, SP, 9302P, 86r). Seasonal and more specific work for which locals were hired, as well: AHPSe, SP, 9265, 736r, AHPSe, SP, 9298, 873v, AHPSe, SP, 9298, 874r, and AHPSe, SP, 9290,1009v.

84   AHPSe, SP, 9279, 632.

85   AHPSe, SP, 9291, 785r.

86   AHPSe, SP, 9287, 578r.

87   This industry – and trade –had been dominated by Genoese families until then. See Gamero Rojas and Garcia Bernal, "Las corporaciones de nación," 358.See also Carla R. Phillips, "Spanish Merchants and the Wool Trade in the Sixteenth Century," *The Sixteenth Century Journal* 14, no. 3 (1983): 259–282; and Rafael Girón Pascual, "Redes mercantiles en la Castilla del siglo XVI a través de las 'licencias de saca de lana con destino a Italia,'" in *De la tierra al cielo. Líneas recientes de investigacion en historia moderna.* ed. Eliseo Serrano Martín (Zaragoza: Fundación Española de Historia Moderna, 2013), 757–771.

3.1   *Other Exports*

Most *flamencos* participating in long-distance trade, regardless of their specialisation, traded in agriculture products, especially olive oil and wine.[88] In Seville's notaries, there is plenty of evidence of *flamencos* exporting them by contracting charter parties with German and Dutch shipmasters.[89] For obtaining these commodities, they extended their operations across Seville's hinterland, buying the seasonal production from regional suppliers. For instance, Jaques Nicolás together with Jaques Brahusen commissioned Adan Becquer, a Flemish merchant, to buy in the town of Écija 6,000 *arrobas* of olive oil from that year's crop.[90] As for the wine, they mostly invested in the trade of sherry (*vino de Jerez*) produced in the area of Jerez.[91]

At least three *Atarazanas* merchants went a step further and bought lands in Seville's hinterland for the exploitation of olive-tree lands and vineyards.[92] The first of them was Francisco Bernal who bought a piece of land with vineyards and orange trees, in the outskirts of Seville, by the Guadaíra River, in 1571.[93] Esteban Jansen inherited from his father-in-law, Enrique Aparte, some lands by the Guadalquivir River, in the area of Tablada, which was used for the cultivation of orange trees.[94] In the 1590s, Esteban Jansen rented this land to a family of *moriscos* who paid 210 *ducados* per year for it.[95] In 1598, his nephew Cornieles Jansen also bought some lands in the town of Aznalcázar, located in the Guadalquivir Valley.[96] In this case, it was a pine grove although nothing indicates that this piece of land was used for the production of naval provisions.

Notarial deeds reveal as well that this group of merchants traded in colonial commodities, like leather, ginger, clove, pepper or sugar.[97] They often obtained these commodities as part of the payment that shipmasters of the

---

88   Jiménez Montes, "Sevilla, puerto y puerta."
89   Esteban Jansen sending wine to Danzig: AHPSe,9284P,118r and AHPSe,9284P,229r. We also document him exporting olive oil to Holland AHPSe, SP, 9263, 280r. However, the man that is almost every time when it comes to charter parties in Seville is Francisco Conique, who did not belong to the group of the *Atarazanas*. For instance, with Pedro le Maire. AHPSe,SP, 9285, 158.
90   AHPSe, SP, 9283, 534v.
91   AHPSe, SP, 9277, 69r.
92   AHPSe, SP, 9245, 511r.
93   AHPSe, SP, 7768, 119r.
94   AHPSe, SP, 9227, 893r.
95   AHPSe, SP, 9265, 214r.
96   AHPSe, SP, 9302, 814v.
97   Cow leather from the Indies ("cueros bacunos a el pelo de Indias") AHPSe, SP, 9297, 353r, ginger (AHPSe, SP, 9250,1003r), sugar (AHPSe, SP, 9290, 140r), and pepper and clove (AHPSe, SP, 9262, 465v).

Carrera de Indias promised to them for the supplied masts and rigging.[98] Unfortunately, notarial deeds do not offer information on how they re-exported them to northern Europe. The little evidence about their trade in these commodities suggests that they did not invest large sums in them.

3.2   *Wheat from the Sea*

Grain was, together with naval provisions and salt, the great driver of the trade between southern and northern Europe; after timber and salt, it was the commodity that *Atarazanas* merchants traded the most. Although, in contrast to timber, Andalusia was rich in grain, crops were usually subject to uncertainty and the region suffered several crises in the sixteenth century.[99] The crises required the importation of grain from outside the Iberian Peninsula, which came to be known under the generic name of "wheat from the sea" (*trigo de la mar*). Traditionally, grain was imported from other Mediterranean areas, especially Sicily. But as the presence of Flemish and German merchants grew, grain began to be increasingly imported from the Baltic region, too.[100]

The activity of *Atarazanas* merchants distributing Baltic grain, mostly wheat, is documented by 370 promissory notes, in which buyers obliged themselves to pay for the sold product in the near future.[101] Most of these deeds, as seen in Figure 5.4, concentrate in three periods (1583–1584, 1588–1589 and 1592–1594), coinciding with crop failures in the hinterland.[102] Through these deeds we can trace these merchants' introduction into Seville's hinterland. Most promissory notes were granted by individuals from rural towns of the

---

98   AHPSe, SP, 9297, 353r.

99   The state even had officials operating in these towns to obtain a regular supply of grain. The most famous of them was Miguel de Cervantes, who at the end of the 1580s, worked as commissary of the royal purveyor in the area for the provision of the royal armada. On the administration and supply of grain in Seville in times of crisis, see Rafael M. Pérez García, "El gobierno de Castilla y la gestión de las crisis de subsistencia de mediados de siglo XVI en la ciudad y el reino de Sevilla," in *Do silêncio a ribalta: os resgatados das margens da História (sêculos XVI-XIX)*, eds. Maria Marta Lobo de Araújo and María José Pérez Álvarez, (Braga: Lab2PT - Laboratorio de Paisagens, Património e Território, 2015), 205–226.

100   On the increasingly important role of Dutch traders supplying grain, see Maartje van Gelder, "Supplying the Serenissima: The Role of Flemish Merchants in the Venetian Grain Trade during the First Phase of the Straatvaart," *International Journal of Maritime History* 16, no. 2 (2004): 39–60.

101   The promissory notes can be found in AHPSe, SP, 9240–9244 and 9257–9260.

102   These failures are evidenced in the discussions held at the city council: in 1584, AMS, III, t19, n23; in 1589 AMS, III, 19, 24; and in 1595, AMS, III, tomo 19, n. 26. This sometimes led to confiscations: AMS, III, tomo 19, n 27.

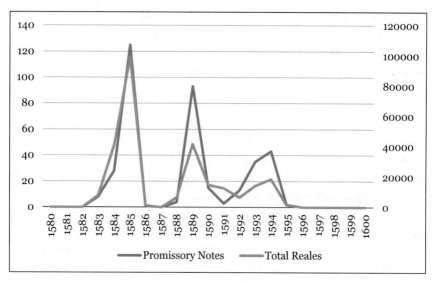

FIGURE 5.4   Sales of grain according to promissory notes granted to *Atarazanas* merchants
SOURCE: AHPSE, SP, 7764–7786 AND 9214–9308

hinterland, especially from a sub-region known as *Campiña* that was a main supplier of wheat for the city and the monarchy: Alcalá de Guadaíra, Alcalá del Río, Arahal, Carmona, El Viso del Alcor, Gelves, La Algaba, Mairena del Alcor, Morón and Utrera.

These deeds followed a similar structure. The granter party – generally a council member or influential resident of one of the rural town – promised to pay a certain amount of *reales* to one of the foreign merchants for the imported wheat, for a price of 20–25 *reales* per *fanega*. Sometimes they bought barley, too, whose price was cheaper – around 15 *reales* per *fanega*.[103] With time, these promissory deeds began to include a collateral clause, according to which the granter responded with his house or lands in case of not meeting the promise.[104] No notarial evidence suggests that this clause was ever activated, but it certainly shows these *flamencos* increasing interest in investment in the hinterland.

Atarazanas merchants were also capable of creating a large stock of imported grain, mostly wheat, for the victualling of the royal navy when the

---

103   I.e. AHPSe, SP, 9256, 1185v.
104   I.e. AHPSe, SP, 9243, 441r.

Andalusian crop was not enough.[105] But this supply did not always occur in the terms that they wanted. In March 1592, several shipments of grain addressed to them and other *flamencos* were seized in Sanlúcar by Francisco de Coloma, *adelantado mayor* of Castile and general captain of the *Guardia de Indias*, that is, the person responsible of organising the military defense of Castile and the armed convoy protecting the fleets of the *Carrera*.[106] Coloma's confiscations repeated in the summer of 1593 in the Portuguese port of Lagos.[107] The affected merchants then began a tedious process that followed two different strategies: a legal one and a political one. On the one hand, they individually appointed attorneys in the ports of Lagos and Sanlúcar to claim the compensations directly from Coloma's commissaries in those ports.[108] On the other hand, the group of affected merchants commissioned a Fleming and a Spaniard to represent them before royal institutions in Madrid.[109] The Flemish attorney was Valerio Vandala, who specialised in the legal and the political representation of the Flemish individuals first in Seville and then in Madrid.[110] The Spanish attorney was nothing less than a member of the city council, the *veinticuatro* don Pedro de los Céspedes, showing the council's concerns on the monarchy's confiscations, which was jeopardising the city's stock of grain.

On March 30, 1592, the eleven Flemish signatories of the power of attorney stated that:

> According to a privilege, ordered in a royal decree, for the provision and remedy of these kingdoms, due to the great shortage that there was and

---

105 See for instance the eleven payments received that royal officials made to *Atarazanas* merchants for the supply of grain in 1598. AHPSe, SP, 9301, 454r, 458r, 477r, 528r, 549r, 554r, 589r, 597r, 619r, 807r, and 822v.

106 AHPSe, SP, 9270, 413v.

107 AHPSe, SP, 9276, 414r.

108 Pedro Gisberto to Juan van Hooren (AHPSe, SP, 9270, 389v) Juan Enríquez and Alberto Felipe to Juan y Enrique Bambel (AHPSe, 9270P, 413v). Pedro Gisberto had to appeared before Juan de Tordesillas to present a statement before Coloma. In this document, Gisberto stated to be a reliable citizen, with a state of more than 6000 *ducados*, able to act as guarantor of Van Hooren. The document was supported with the declaration of witnesses: Elias Sirman, Miguel Arbauts and Francisco Bernal. AHPSe, SP, 9270, 549r.

109 AHPSe, SP, 9270P, 510r.

110 Valerio Vandala used to live in Seville as *vecino* by 1579 before moving to Madrid: AHPSe, SP, 9222, 128r. His role within the community was similar to the one that German Dufelde had a decade earlier, as seen in the previous chapter.

is of wheat, many of us have been encouraged to receive and warn in the estates of Flanders and Germany to send us and ship us wheat to be sold and traded in this town.[111]

Not only was their trade legal, as they argued, but it had even been encouraged to alleviate the shortage of grain in Castile. On November 29, 1593, Philip II issued a royal decree compelling Coloma to pay for the commodities he had seized; as soon as the document reached Seville, the nation made Juan de Tordesillas notarise a copy.[112] Through the notarised copy, the royal decree reveals the influence some Flemish merchants, including those residing in the *Atarazanas*, had gained in few decades. In it, the king acknowledged that they had been treated unfairly because they were …

> … [L]oyal vassals, natives of my estates in Flanders in the land that remain obedient, as well as citizens and residents with houses, wives and children in that city [Seville] for longer than twenty years from now. And with their trades and dealings, imports and exports and *alcabalas* they pay me every year more than three hundred thousand *ducados* and the commodities that came in those ships were theirs, produced in the lands of the said estates that remain obedient.[113]

This process did not come to an end easily. The situation that had originally motivated the confiscations did not change: royal officials had no means to pay for the provisions. Italian merchants, who had suffered similar seizures, joined the complaint. Gerónimo Escorza and Baltasar de Espínola demanded the compensation of their partners abroad: Gerónimo Lomelin in Antwerp, Francisco Gondi in Amsterdam, and Juan Batista Baliano in Genoa. They had also assisted the city with grain and were equally affected by Coloma's confiscations.[114] Urged by the situation, the king resorted to an exceptional and drastic measure. He gave this group of Flemish and Italian merchants the right to collect 320,806 *reales* from the *alcabalas*, local taxes, of the Castilian cities of Merida, Badajoz, Jerez de la Frontera, Ronda, Almuñécar, Llerena, Cáceres, Motril and Salobreña.[115]

---

111 AHPSe, SP, 9270, 510r.

112 AHPSe, SP, 9278, 384r.

113 AHPSe, SP, 9278, 384r.

114 AHPSe, SP, 9282, 5r.

115 AHPSe, SP, 9282, 284 and AHPSe, SP, 9282, 286. The difficult situation continued until 1597: AHPSe, SP, 9295, 998 and AHPSe, SP, 9297, 585r.

The monarchy's inability to meet its financial commitments was not extraordinary and, as the last chapter shows, *Atarazanas* merchants got used to getting paid late, if at all, for the timber they supplied. However, this was a price they were certainly willing to pay for ensuring their privilege position in the region's economy and in the trade between Andalusia and northern Europe.

4   Conclusion

By cross-checking deeds notarised in Seville with charter parties from Amsterdam as well as voyages registered in the Sound Toll, this chapter has shed new light on the trade between Andalusia and northern Europe by the end of the sixteenth century. It has drawn attention to the central role that Dutch and German shipmasters had for connecting merchants based in Seville to foreign markets. Shipmasters were not mere carriers of commodities; many were commissioned by *Atarazanas* merchants to buy timber on their behalf, especially in Norway, the main region of provenance of the timber imported to Andalusia. For their activity, shipmasters normally received a payment for their freight in silver as well as a full load of salt. Together with timber trade, *Atarazanas* merchants invested in the importation of grain and the production and exportation of salt, buying salt ponds along the western Andalusian coast. To a lesser extent, they also traded in American commodities and agricultural products cultivated in Seville's hinterland. They did not depend on the activity of firms based abroad. On the contrary, they contracted directly with foreign shipmasters in Andalusia or in northern Europe, where they developed a network of agents. Access to American silver and, therefore, to liquidity allowed them to take this initiative. Next chapter analyses how these foreigners obtained access to silver by supplying naval provisions to the ships preparing to sail to the Americas.

Another important aspect of their business organisation revealed in this chapter is the growing importance of a commercial connection between Seville and Amsterdam. The Dutch city played an increasing role as an intermediate market for Norwegian timber, as it emerged as an entrepôt for the trade between northern and southern Europe. The increasing activity of shipmasters from Holland and Friesland in Andalusia is a good proof of such importance and constitutes an early precedent of a process that culminated in the following century: the Mediterranean expansion of Dutch shipping through the Strait of Gibraltar, a route that came to be known as the *straatvaart*.[116] Nevertheless, this did not hinder the presence of Hanseatic shipmasters, who operated in Andalusia although most of their activity concentrated in Portugal. Interestingly enough, Antwerp played an irrelevant role for the connection of Seville with the Baltic and Scandinavian markets by the end of the century, despite the common wisdom that most trade of Seville with northern Europe occurred via Antwerp. The city of the Scheldt, in any case, remained a central node for the importation of other commodities, especially Flemish textiles.[117]

Even though most of the imported timber was stored in the *Atarazanas* of Seville, foreign shipmasters rarely sailed up the Guadalquivir River. As the navigation of the river became increasingly difficult, a hierarchical port system developed in western Andalusia. Shipping activities concentrated on the coast between Sanlúcar and Cádiz, while Seville continued as the main commercial centre, as most royal institutions – including the American ones – remained there. So did most foreign communities, like our group of Flemish and German merchants, who, though based in Seville, managed to extend their commercial operations on a regional and a global scale.

---

116   Israel, *Empires and Entrepots,* 133–162 and Israel, "Spanish Wool Exports and the European Economy 1610–40," *The Economic History Review* vol. 33, no. 2 (May, 1980): 202. Van Gelder, "Supplying the Serenissima."

117   Stols, *De Spaanse Brabanders.*

Supply to the *Carrera de Indias* and to the Royal Navy

The historiography on early modern Seville has always gone hand in hand with that on the *Carrera de Indias*. A brilliantly well-conserved source material consisting of more than 80 million pages preserved at the *Archivo General de Indias* has stimulated a prolific scholarly production of Seville and the Spanish colonisation of the Americas. The most celebrated work of all is *Séville et l'Atlantique*, in which the *Annales*-school authors Huguette and Pierre Chaunu analysed the structures and trends of the navigation between the Andalusian city and the Americas for more than two centuries.[1] Their titanic study soon became a source of inspiration and information for later researchers, contributing to making the *Carrera de Indias* one of the most researched topics in Spanish historiography.[2]

The well-researched history of the *Carrera de Indias* has often prompted grandiloquent histories about the importance of Seville for Spain's colonial past. Influenced by a nationalist narrative, traditional approaches long disregarded the role of foreigners in the development of the *Carrera*. This narrative frequently abused the term "American monopoly" to speak of the privileged position of Seville as the only port allowed for the navigation with the Americas, leading to the assumption that there existed a commercial monopoly in which only Spaniards could participate and, consequently, the activity of foreigners was an anomaly.[3] Recent research, nonetheless,

---

1   Chaunu and Chaunu, *Séville et l'Atlantique*.

2   E.g. Lorenzo Sanz, *Comercio de España;* Bernal Rodríguez, *La Financiación de la Carrera de Indias*; García-Baquero González, *La Carrera de Indias*.

3   In this regard, Grafe notes: "The loose use of the term "monopoly" in this context is at least imprecise, at worst misleading." Grafe, "On the Spatial Nature," 4. The misleading vision is present in most seminal works on the *Carrera de Indias* mentioned in the previous note and in many works on the participation of foreigners in the *Carrera*. See for instance, Antonio García-Baquero González, "Los extranjeros en el tráfico con indias: entre el rechazo legal y la tolerancia funcional," in *Los extranjeros en la España moderna*, eds. M. B. Villar García and P. Pezzi Cristóbal (Madrid: Ministerio de Ciencia e Innovación, 2003) 73–99 or Manuel Bustos Rodríguez, "La problemática acerca de los comerciantes de la Carrera de Indias," in *Comunicaciones transnacionales. Colonias de Mercaderes extranjeros en el Mundo Atlántico (1500–1830)*, ed. Ana Crespo Solana (Madrid: Doce Calles, 2010), 29–45.

emphasises the private nature of the colonial enterprise, as well as the importance that foreigners had in it.[4] *Atarazanas* merchants offer an interesting case study to examine this because, thanks to their supply, they began to participate in the commercial circuits of the *Carrera* without joining the guild of merchants trading with the Americas, the *Consulado de Cargadores a Indias*.

By the end of the century, their activity became essential for meeting the growing demand for timber and other naval provisions for the maintenance of the ships sailing to the Americas. These *flamencos* did not supply timber for the construction of new ships in Andalusia, simply because at the time the region did not develop a meaningful industry able to build ocean-going ships of large tonnage due to the poor quality of its forestry resources.[5] Given the inadequate capacity of its shipyards, Andalusia barely contributed to the expansion of the Spain's royal navy, which Philip II promoted during his reign, seeking to compete against rising Atlantic powers, namely England and the Dutch Republic. The construction of ocean-going vessels was mainly incentivised in the shipyards along the Cantabrian coast, which had a long tradition of Atlantic seafaring and was close to the resources of north Iberian forests.[6] The monarchy drew ambitious plans for constructing new royal warships and stimulating private shipbuilding through public loans and tax benefits, on the condition that the ships could eventually be used by the royal navy.[7] Yet, while rich in oak for the framework of vessels, these forests lacked suitable pines for the masts of large tonnage ships, which had to be imported from northern Europe.[8] Strikingly, royal officials usually purchased that timber from the warehouses of the Seville's *Atarazanas*. This challenges the classical interpretation on the way the Habsburg navy was organised that assumes that Spain's naval administration increasingly relied on entrepreneurs who, through *asiento* contracts, undertook the construction of new warships or the supply of strategic resources, such as imported timber, to the royal navy.[9]

---

4 Grafe, "On the Spatial Nature." Antunes and Polónia, *Beyond Empires*. Although we still lack monographical studies on the topic.
5 Casado Soto, *Los barcos españoles,* Rodríguez Lorenzo, "Construcción naval cantábrica." This ocurred until the eighteenth century. López Arandia, "Maderas para el real servicio."
6 Casado Soto, "La construcción naval atlántica española."
7 Casado Soto, "Barcos para la guerra," 31. Thompson, "The Spanish Armada" 88. Stradling also speaks of a turning point in this period, Stradling, *The Armada of Flanders*, 5–6.
8 Casado Soto, "Barcos para la guerra," 47.
9 Thompson, *War and Government*.

The activity of *Atarazanas* merchants suggests the existence of more complex ways of supply in the sixteenth century, based on a sustained relationship developed by royal officials and foreign entrepreneurs. This way of supply calls for a reconsideration of the role the city and Andalusia played in Spain's maritime organisation. The city, which housed the bureaucratic apparatus of the *Carrera de Indias,* and the region, which enjoyed a powerful shipping infrastructure thanks to American navigation, became fundamental in the organisation of Philip II's navy, despite having an inadequate shipbuilding industry.

This chapter examines the contribution of *Atarazanas* merchants to the consolidation of Seville as a main node of the Spanish maritime empire in the time of Philip II. It does so by comparing their supply to the ships sailing to the Americas, on the one hand, and for the warships of the royal armada, on the other, focusing on the agents that participated in this activity, the contracting mechanisms and the commodities that were demanded.

1   Regulation of the *Carrera de Indias*

In 1503, a decade after Christopher Columbus set foot in the Americas, Isabella I established *la Casa de la Contratación de Indias* (also House of Trade or House of the Indies) in Seville to organise the colonisation of the continent, from the taxation of trade to the education of pilots navigating the new routes. It even served as a court of justice until the foundation of the *Consulado de Cargadores a Indias*, in 1543.[10] In essence, the House of Trade was a supervisory apparatus that controlled compliance with the state's regulation over American navigation and trade, which intensified throughout the sixteenth century due to the rising piracy in Atlantic waters. Rahn-Phillips defined early attempts to regulate American navigation as a "hit-and-miss affair," while Mira Caballos concluded that they were defined by spontaneity and improvisation.[11] Both authors agree that the phase of spontaneity and improvisation ended in the 1560s, when two *cédulas reales* (royal decrees) in 1561 and 1564 set up a biannual system of fleets with a military escort, forbidding ships to travel outside the seasonal convoys.[12]

---

10   Enriqueta Vila Vilar et al, *La Casa de la Contratación.*
11   Phillips, *Six Galleons,* 9. Esteban Mira Caballos, "Pedro Menéndez de Avilés diseñó el modelo de flotas de la Carrera de Indias," *Revista de Historia Naval,* no. 94 (2006), 8.
12   Mira Caballos, "Pedro Menéndez de Avilés," 9.

Although the navigation calendar was usually affected by weather and market conditions, especially to shortage of money or commodities, the system of two escorted convoys remained with minor variations for two centuries.[13] Each year, the New Spain fleet (*Flota de Nueva España*) departed in April for Central America, and the other, the Tierra Firme fleet (*Flota de Tierra Firme*), departed in August for the northern coast of South America. The two fleets usually returned before August of the following year, ideally together after gathering in Havana, although the two made their journey together only fourteen times during Philip II's reign, as the fleet of New Spain usually departed earlier.

The formation of an armed fleet to protect the American route was first attempted in 1522, when Charles I assembled an armada (*Armada de la Guarda de las Indias*) to patrol the waters between Andalusia, the Canary Islands and the Azores.[14] This armada did not last long. Military protection of the route only became a permanent reality during Philip II's reign. Every fleet had to go with at least two military-equipped ships, the *nao capitana* (flagship) and the *nao almiranta* (rear-flagship), which were led by a general-captain and an admiral of the fleet respectively, and for which specific regulations on manning, arming and size applied.[15] Eventually, the number of royal warships, mostly galleons, grew and formed a permanent force, the *Armada de la Guardia de Indias* which was assigned exclusively to accompany the Tierra Firme fleet to protect the silver shipments from Peru.[16] The armed defence of the New Spain fleet, on the other hand, remained under the protection of the two military ships, the *capitana* and the *almiranta*.[17]

---

13   This routine is slightly different from the original plan established in the 1564 ordinances. Chaunu and Chaunu, *Séville et l'Amérique*, 232–233. Phillips, *Six Galleons*, 10–12.

14   Díaz Blanco suggests that this first attempt to protect the Atlantic fleets navigating to America was not necessarily a response to growing activity of European corsairs in the Atlantic but a consequence as well of rising hostilities with the Ottomans and north African corsairs. Díaz Blanco, "Una armada de galeras" 663–664.

15   Stradling notices the confusion between Spanish and English terms. The flagship was not the nao almiranta but the nao capitana. Stradling, *The Armada of Flanders*, "Glossary," XIII. As for the different requirements, the *capitana* and *almiranta* ships were required to load 100 *toneladas* less than their recommendable tonnage, and the first had to be a galleon that weighed at least 300 *toneladas* before the cargo was loaded. Clarence H. Haring, *Trade and Navigation between Spain and the Indies in the Time of the Hapsburgs* (Cambridge: Harvard University Press, 1918), 209.

16   Casado Soto, "Barcos para la guerra," 32–33.

17   Haring, *Trade and navigation,* 10. Phillips, *Six Galleons,* 14.

A decisive turning point for the *Carrera de Indias* occurred in 1591, when the members of the *Consulado* assumed the funding of the military escort through the payment of the *avería*, a tax paid *ad valorem* on the commodities imported from and exported to America.[18] The *Consulado de Cargadores de Indias* originally emulated the *Consulado de Burgos* – the Medieval Castilian guild for the trade with Flanders – as a court of justice for its members. In the second half of the century, the *Consulado* became an effective instrument for Seville's mercantile elite to lobby the royal institutions.[19] The imposition of the *averia* tax paradoxically marks the rising influence of the *Consulado de Cargadores de Indias* on the navigation and trade with the *Carrera*.

The central importance of the *Consulado* in the second part of the sixteenth century highlights the private nature of the *Carrera de Indias*. It was basically organised as a private enterprise, supervised by the House of Trade. Ships sailing to the Americas were usually owned by one, two or three investors.[20] Most of the vessels had been constructed in Cantabrian shipyards, especially in the areas of Cuatro Villas (today's Cantabria) and the Basque coast.[21] Ships built in the Mediterranean and north European shipyards still played a small role in the *Carrera*, because for the most part they did not comply with the regulations on tonnage established by the monarchy for participating in the American convoys. In a similar way, the monarchy did not allow ships built in Andalusia to join the fleets, because of the poor quality of the region's timbers.[22] It was not until the eighteenth century, when the pines from the Sierra de Segura (Jaén) began to be exploited for naval purposes, that the shipyards of Cádiz became key for Spanish shipbuilding.[23]

1.1   Preparation of the American fleets

Regardless of the monarchy's lack of trust in Andalusia's shipbuilding, the region did develop a potent industry for the repair and preparation of vessels sailing to the Americas, including the caulking – known as *carena*. This

---

18 According to Díaz Blanco, this was a way of compensating the establishment of the *Almojarifazgo de Indias*. José Manuel Díaz Blanco, *Así trocaste tu gloria: Guerra y comercio colonial en la España del siglo XVII* (Madrid: Marcial Pons, 2012), 42.

19 Díaz Blanco, *Así trocaste tu gloria*, 45–47; Thompson, *War and government*, 194–195.

20 Sergio Rodríguez Lorenzo, "Sevilla y la Carrera de Indias."

21 Chaunu, Chaunu and Arbellot, *Séville et l'Atlantique*, VIII, 255–256. Casado Soto, *Los barcos españoles*, 119. Casado Soto, "La construcción naval," 64.

22 It was still green when cut and was not dry enough to hold nails properly. De Artíñano y Galdácano, *La arquitectura naval española*, 67–68.

23 Ana Crespo Solana, "La acción de José Patiño en Cádiz y los proyectos navales de la Corona del siglo XVIII," *Trocadero: Revista de historia moderna y contemporanea* no. 6–7 (1994-1995): 35–50.

industry has never received close attention by historians, which is especially odd considering the seminal study of Artíñano in 1914, where he documented that Cantabrian ships sometimes arrived in Seville unfinished; once there, the *obra muerta* (freeboard) was completed with timber imported from northern Europe.[24] The fact that buyers might have found it cheaper to complete the freeboard in Seville, rather than in the Cantabrian shipyards, illustrates the remarkable dimension of the market of imported naval provisions that emerged in southern Spain to meet the growing demand of the *Carrera de Indias*.

A dataset of 158 promissory notes that ship captains and masters granted *Atarazanas* merchants after the purchase of naval provisions for the repair and preparation of their vessels gives good account of that market.[25] By definition, a promissory note implied a payment in credit. Because of that, the clauses of these deeds tended to be rich to specify how buyers and sellers shared the risk of the transaction.[26] The deeds began with a description of the two parties, which was particularly exhaustive in the case of the granter party, the debtor. When the reason of payment was the purchase of commodities, very often these were described in detail. The main part of the document was the statement of promise, through which debtors committed to pay before a specific date in a specific place, recognizing the authority of royal and other jurisdictions to prosecute them in case of failing to comply with this, with a collateral clause or stating who bore the liability over a transaction until the fulfilment of the payment.The sample provides a deep insight into a key stage in the *Carrera* about which very little is known: the private arrangements for the preparation of ships departing for the Americas.[27] These documents reveal the range of imported naval provisions that were supplied, as well as the mechanisms involved in the purchase and payment of these provisions.

Given the private nature of the *Carrera de Indias*, the maintenance of the ships joining the fleets depended on the owners. This task was frequently

---

24   De Artíñano y Galdácano, *La arquitectura naval española*, 68, 273.

25   The use of this type of deed seems to be widespread in early modern Seville; *Atarazanas* merchants, for instance, appear in at least 1044 promissory notes in the period from 1570 to 1600. A total of 455 promissory notes are related to timber transactions of any type, not only to ship owners and masters.

26   For further explanation on the use of this tool in Seville, see Jiménez Montes, "Sepan quantos esta carta vieren." For an analysis on its use in Antwerp, see Puttevils, *Merchants and Trading*, 11.

27   Carmen Mena García, "Nuevos datos sobre bastimentos y envases en armadas y flotas de la Carrera," *Revista de Indias* 64 no. 231 (2004): 447–484.

TABLE 6.1   Profiles of granter parties in promissory notes of naval provisions

No.	Rank
41	Owner
36	Owner and master
27	Master
26	Owner and captain
23	Captain
17	Owner, captain and master
7	Captain and pilot
1	Owner and pilot

SOURCE: AHPSE, SP, 7764–7786 AND 9214–9308

undertaken by the two most important members of the crew, the captain and the master; while the captain was the highest authority on the ship, masters were responsible for its maintenance and finances. Thanks to the sample of 158 promissory notes, we can assess the involvement of owners, captains and masters in the process of preparation of the vessels sailing to the Americas. Table 6.1 illustrates the profiles of those who purchased naval supplies and granted a promissory note for its payment in the 1590s, when most of the deeds were notarised. Sometimes, those promissory notes were granted by more than one person and, consequently, the total of individuals grating those deeds is 178 instead of 158.[28] The table is complemented with Figure 6.1, which shows the total number of times owners or specific ranks and professionals took care of the supply of timber for the repair and preparation of the ship before sailing.

According to Table 6.1, owners (*señor* or *dueño* in the original sources) granted most of the promissory notes, participating in 121 of them. The debtor of the deed appears only as an owner in 41 deeds, and in 80 deeds the owner held a rank on his ship, too: in 38 deeds, the owner was described as master of the ship (*dueño y maestre*), in 26 the owner was described as captain (*dueño y capitán*), and in 17 the owner was described as captain and master of the vessel (*dueño, capitán y maestre*). Exceptionally, in one case the owner was described as the pilot, whose role was in theory limited to the steering of the

---

28   The table does not consider those who participated as guarantor (*fiadores*) of the debtors, who assumed the payment in case the promise was not fulfilled. Their participation was exceptional in these deeds.

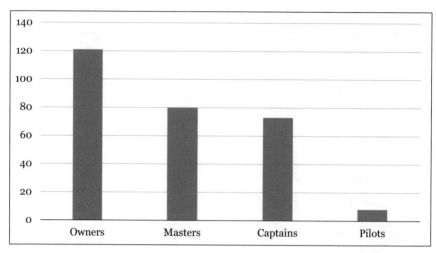

FIGURE 6.1   Owners and officials paying naval provisions for the preparation of ships
SOURCE: AHPSE, SP, 7764–7786 AND 9214–9308

ship. Probably because of their professional activity, pilots were hardly
involved in the repair process. They only appear purchasing naval provisions
in 7 promissory notes; in six of them, they were also the captain of the ship and
in one, as mentioned before, the owner. The fact that many captains and masters owned ships is in line with recent research by Rodríguez Lorenzo, in which
he concluded that the ownership of American vessels was a relatively accessible investment in the sixteenth century; in fact, ownership was mostly individual and rarely shared between two or three partners.[29] Moreover, although
the majority of owners were merchants, brokers (*corredores de lonja*) or were
officers of the ships, Rodríguez Lorenzo noted that their socio-professional
profiles were more heterogeneous, including tailors or clerics, who in theory
had little connection with the Atlantic navigation.[30]

There is a number of captains and masters who did not own any share of the
ship but were involved in the purchase of naval provisions: captains granted
23 of the promissory notes, and masters 27 of them. Given the role they performed on the ship, it seems only natural that they would participate in the
preparation of the ship before sailing. What is not so evident is that, by granting the promissory notes, they financed the purchase of the provisions. The

29   Rodríguez Lorenzo, "Sevilla y la Carrera de Indias," 72. In those cases, the form of both the
      initial investment and the calculation of the returns must have been similar to limited-
      liability partnerships, as explained in Chapter 4.
30   Rodríguez Lorenzo, "Sevilla y la Carrera de Indias," 69.

most probable explanation for this is that this was the result of an arrangement between them and the owners, through which they committed themselves to finance its preparation and maintenance until the ship returned to Seville, when they would liquidate accounts with the owners.

Finally, it is important to remember that notarised deeds represented the exception rather than the rule. Owners, captains and masters of *Carrera de Indias* ships must have developed close and sustained economic relationships with the merchants that provided them with timber. Those ties are evident in the 49 promissory notes that only offered vague reference to the supply of naval provisions, like the one granted by the captain Diego de Narea to Juan de Bestoven for "the accounts that you and I had since a long time ago until today, from the planks and yards and tar and other things that you have given me."[31] These promissory notes, through which debtors promised a payment to liquidate an account that they had with supplier of naval provisions, suggest a generalised familiarity and trust between many ship owners, captains and masters travelling to the Americas and the *flamencos* that supply them.

1.2   *Access to American Silver*

Although one might be tempted to assume that the absence of promissory notes implies a lack of activity before the 1590s, the familiarity of *Atarazanas* merchants with owners, captains and masters probably indicates a lack of incentive to notarise these deeds. In fact, other types of notarial deeds analysed throughout this book speak of the continuous activity of the market in the 1570s and 1580s. Consequently, the notarisation of promissory after 1590s had little to do with the state of the market of imported naval supplies or the commercial activity of *Atarazanas* merchants. Instead, the lack of notarised deeds suggests a change of contracting strategies by these foreigners who sought a more active participation in the *Carrera de Indias*.

The change of contracting strategies becomes evident when looking systematically at one particular clause of promissory notes: the place of payment. Figure 6.2 illustrates the different places from which owners, captains and masters promised to fulfil the payment of their purchases, evidencing that they increasingly committed to do it in the Americas, which implied that creditors – the Flemish suppliers – would receive the payment in American silver (*plata quintada*).

Figure 6.2 shows that, as the notarisation of promissory notes became more frequent in the decade of the 1590s, so became frequent for debtors to promise

31   AHPSe, sp, 9279, 72or.

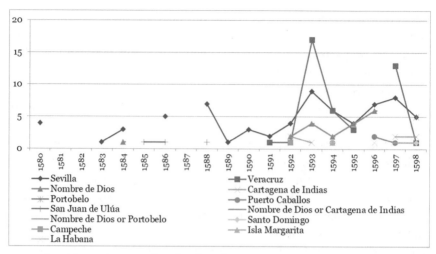

FIGURE 6.2 Places of payment for sales of naval provisions (1580–1598)
        SOURCE: AHPSE, SP, 7764–7786 AND 9214–9308

to remit their payments directly from the Americas. The ports of Veracruz (42) and Nombre de Dios (19), which were the main destination of the New Spain fleet and Tierra Firme fleet respectively, appear as the most common payment places. In fact, in two years (1593 and 1597), Veracruz surpassed Seville as the place where more payments were promised. Veracruz and Nombre de Dios are followed by other eight destinations: Cartagena de Indias (7), Portobelo (5), Puerto Caballos (4), San Juan de Ulúa (3), Santo Domingo (2), Campeche (1), Isla Margarita (1) and Havana (1). Two deeds specify the payment place to be either Nombre de Dios or Cartagena de Indias, and two other deeds do the same with Nombre de Dios and Portobelo. Such variety evidences the growing extension of *Atarazanas* merchants' involvement in American businesses.

Promissory notes normally included a clause in which the debtor committed to pay "in a period of thirty days after the arrival of the ship to the said port."[32] This means that debtors would not wait until their ship completed the voyage to America and its return to Seville, known as *tornaviaje*. They would remit the payment in the first possible fleet; this way the creditor would

---

32   Juan Martínez de Echaue to Guillermo Corinse in January 1593. AHPSe, SP, 9274, 120r. Rodríguez Lorenzo noted something similar for the payment of American charters in Sergio Rodríguez Lorenzo, "El fletamento de mercancías en la carrera de indias (1560–1622): introducción a su estudio," *Procesos de mercado: revista europea de economía política* 8, no. 1 (2011): 183.

receive the payment approximately a year before the ship returned. Since the journey could be delayed and not meet the fleet from the previous year departing from America to Seville, parties often agreed that debtors could ultimately fulfil the payment upon the ship's return to Spain.[33] The Andalusian city remained indisputably the principal place of payment, with a total of 69 cases, yet these payments were in American silver too and, thus, depended on the arrival of the fleet, as well. In the payments promised in Seville, debtors normally committed to comply in a period of a year and a half, which corresponded to a complete duration of a voyage to America and the *tornaviaje*.[34]

Through the promissory notes, these *flamencos* made an important concession to their debtors, assuming the risk in the transaction until the ship arrived in the Americas. Many promissory notes included a clause according to which the sellers pledged to bear the liability of the naval provisions until 24 hours after the arrival of the ship to the port of destination. If the ship was lost, due to "sea and wind (*sic*), fire, bad people, friends and enemies, and any other danger," debtors did not have to pay for the masts or the naval provisions that they had bought; this risk clause, of course, did not include malpractice by the crew.[35] Such an agreement between *Atarazanas* merchants and ship owners, captains and masters made the sale of naval provisions similar to the shipment of other types of merchandise in the *Carrera*, in which the shipper bought the merchandise to the seller in Seville, who bore the risk of the transaction until the ship arrived in the Americas.[36] The difference is that, in this case, the commodity was not meant to be resold, as the naval provisions was used in the ship.

The fact that, one way or the other, all payments were subjected to the arrival of the American fleets indicates a clear practice: *Atarazanas* wanted to receive their payment in silver. With these promissory notes, either fulfilled at the return of the fleet or with a payment remitted from an American port, these foreigners gained access to silver and, consequently, liquidity; a key for

---

33 I.e. AHPSe, SP, 9274, 120r.

34 Or before if the fleet arrived earlier; "*o antes si antes biniere de tornabiaje a esta ciudad de Seuilla la dicha flota o la plata de resulta dello.*" AHPSe, SP, 9297, 621r.

35 AHPSe, SP, 9241, 977r. Simón Enríquez even formalised such a declaration of risk *ex post*, after having been granted a promissory note, in the next notarial deed. AHPSe, SP, 9273, 206r.

36 This was known as "préstamo de seguro a riesgo." García-Baquero González, *La Carrera de Indias,* 252. We still lack research on the topic, as Rodríguez Lorenzo argues. Sergio Rodríguez Lorenzo, "La financiación a riesgo marítimo en la carrera de Indias (c. 1560–1622)," paper presented at the conference Iberians in the First Atlantic Economy, 1500–1650), University of Évora, February 7–8 2019.

their predominant position in the trade with northern Europe. The payment on credit at the return of the American fleets was, according to Everaert, the main strategy that foreigners had in the seventeenth century to overcome the Spanish "monopoly" on the trade with the Americas in a "semi-legal" way.[37] However, as mentioned in the introduction of this chapter, such monopoly did not actually exist in times of Philip II; as analysed in previous chapters, foreigners who were *vecinos* of Seville found little obstacles when trading with the Americas. Thus, the growing number of promissory notes registered in the decade of 1590s does not seem to be a consequence of increasing xenophobic practices by the House of Trade. Instead, it seems to be a consequence of the group's own dynamics.

By the end of the century, most *Atarazanas* merchants had completed their integration into the local community and they probably encountered little resistance when collecting payments in silver at the House of Trade. This probably motivated them to demand the payment of naval provisions in silver at the arrival of the first possible American fleet in Seville, instead of waiting for the payment to be fulfilled once the debtor returned. As an alternative, they sometimes asked to receive American commodities. For instance, we know that, in November 1592, the owner and master of the ship *Santo Domingo*, Hernando Guerra, promised to pay Jaques Nicolás 3792 *reales* within a period of thirty days after Guerra's arrival in Campeche, New Spain.[38] They agreed that if Guerra did not find an agent of Nicolás in the said port to collect the payment, Guerra would send to Seville the required amount in *palo campeche*, a dyestuff that was highly valued in the Flemish textile industry.[39]

This notarial deed also evidences that, by the last decade of the century, these *flamencos* had established a network of commissioned agents in the Americas. Figure 6.3 shows a correlation between a growing number of promissory notes granted to *Atarazanas* merchants to be fulfilled in the Americas (dark grey) and the number of POAs that these merchants commissioned there (light grey).

While it is not possible to establish a causal relationship between the growing notarisation of each type of deed, the high number of POAs and

37   John G. Everaert, "Infraction au monopole?: Cargadores-navegantes flamands sur la Carrera de Indias (XVIIe siècle)," in *La Casa de la Contratación y la navegación entre España y las Indias*, eds. Enriqueta Vila Vilar et al (Sevilla: CSIC and Universidad de Sevilla, 2004), 761–777 762.

38   AHPSe, SP, 9273, 636.

39   García-Baquero González, *La Carrera de Indias*, 214–215.

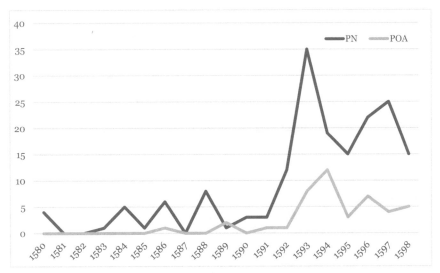

FIGURE 6.3   Evolution of POAs granted to agents in the Americas, in comparison to
promissory notes (1580–1598)
SOURCE: AHPSE, SP, 7764–7786 AND 9214–9308

promissory notes that were meant to be used from the Americas certainly
indicate that *Atarazanas* merchants had extended their operations there.
For this, they resorted to relatives of a second and third generation. Notarial
deeds document that the grandsons of Enrique Aparte, Lorenzo and Melchor
de Haçe Jr. , the son of Felipe Sarens, Felipe Sarens Jr., and the son of Jaques
Nicolás, Francisco, lived in the Americas for a short period in the 1590s, and
represented their relatives there.[40] *Atarazanas* merchants also granted POAs
to ship captains and masters travelling to the Americas, which highlights the
familiarity that some of these foreigners developed with some captains and
masters.[41]

For agents commissioned in the Americas, having copies of notarised promissory notes must have been very useful tool to claim debts on behalf of their
principal. In a similar way, copies of notarised promissory notes could be a
safeguard for merchants in case they found any problem when claiming a silver
payment at the House of Trade, because although the activity of the Flemish
suppliers was not illegal, there could be difficulty claiming a shipment of silver

40   More on this can be found in Jiménez Montes, "Sepan quantos esta carta vieren."
41   Lamikiz noted a similar aspect. Merchants from Bilbao relied on ship captains to oversee
      people abroad. Lamikiz, *Trade and trust.*

due to their foreign origin.[42] Such uncertainty in a credit payment that, in the best-case scenario, took half a year, must have pushed *Atarazanas* traders to make their debtors formalise the promises of payment.

1.3   *Demand of Imported Naval Provisions*

In the report sent to Philip II in December 1574, and analysed in Chapter 1, Nicolás de Melemburque described a shortage in Andalusia "of trees for masts and yards (...) for the convenience of the galleys and armadas of His Majesty and the fleets that navigate to the Indies."[43] He continued explaining how, due to the lack of imports, the masts of high-board vessels had to be fixed by assembling multiple pieces of timber.[44] The report states that long trunks for masts were the products most in demand by the ships of the *Carrera*, as well as by the warships of the king. However, the dataset of promissory notes suggests a more complex picture of the demand from the vessels preparing to sail to America, and therefore of the varied stock of naval supplies available in the *Atarazanas* warehouses.

Most promissory notes specified the products that were being sold, except for 49 cases in which the deeds made only vague references to "timber and other things." Many times, promissory notes even offered a nuanced description of those products, including the price per unit or set of products, the function within the ship (e.g. "a tree for foremast"),[45] size (e.g. "large trees"),[46] quantity (e.g. "two cables of hemp that weighted fourty-nine quintals"),[47] quality (e.g. rigging of the good sort"),[48] or provenance (e.g. "pine planks from Flanders").[49] Such detailed descriptions allow for a categorisation of the supplied products into four different groups, depending on the type of commodity and its function in the vessel. In the first category are the long pieces of timber that were used to form what contemporary sources called *arboladura,* that is the set of masts and yards that supported the ship's rigging and sails. A second category is formed by sawn-timber products that belonged to a part of the ship other than the *arboladura*; these pieces, normally planks, arrived in Andalusia as already semi-manufactured products. The third

---

42   Jiménez Montes, "Los inicios de una nación," 206–207.

43   AHPSe, SP, 7779, 1365r.

44   "[Y] *las que están en ellas tienen muy mal recaudo de másteles y entenas y se an de remediar con hazellos de peças y con [jimielgas].*" AHPSe, 7779, 1365v.

45   "[*Á*]*rbol para trinquete*" AHPSe, SP, 9274, 120r.

46   "[*Á*]*rboles grandes*" AHPSe, SP, 9275, 927r.

47   "[*D*]*os cables de cáñamo que pesaron quarenta e nueve quintales*" AHPSe, SP, 9239, 1231r.

48   "[*J*]*arcia de la buena en un cable*" AHPSe, SP, 9281, 230.

49   "[*T*]*ablas de pino de Flandes*" AHPSe, SP, 9275, 927r.

category lists non-timber resources that formed the rigging, normally cables and cords, used to stabilise the masts and manipulate the sails. Finally, a fourth category contains non-timber forestry resources used for the caulking and insulation of the hull and for the coating of the rigging, namely tar and pitch.

Table 6.2 uses the categorisation proposed above to illustrate the diversity of products that *Atarazanas* merchants supplied to the ships of the *Carrera*, indicating plausible market prices in the decade of the 1590s. Unfortunately, the sample is not enough to conduct a conclusive analysis on the evolution of prices or of the demand, because these contracts do not always provide the same type of information and are concentrated in a very specific period, the decade of the 1590s, when the notarisation of promissory notes became frequent. Table 6.2 does show some basic information about the quantities and prices for which a given product could be traded, according to the sample of 113 promissory notes – as mentioned earlier, 49 of the deeds offered vague references only. The column Product keeps the Spanish name of commodities in the form in which they usually appeared in notarial sources, although they are later translated in the text. The third column (N) reflects the number of times a set of the same product appears in a contract, and the fourth (Unit) indicates the most frequent unit of measure used when trading such product. The columns Qmin and Qmax respectively gives the minimum and maximum number of items of a given commodity appearing in a single transaction according to the unit of measure. The last three columns illustrate the variety of prices according to the unity of measure. The column PN indicates how many times the price of a commodity was clearly specified in the contract, while the columns Pmin and Pmax indicate the minimum and maximum price per unit in *reales* in which the commodity was sold.

Long tree pieces were by far the most expensive commodities. But, contrary to what Nicolás de Melemburque's report suggested, they were not the most demanded imported naval provision. Sources do not specify the difference between *árboles* (trees) and *mástiles* (masts); it seems that both terms were used interchangeably to refer to any long piece of timber supporting the sails. If taken literally, masts would refer to a semi-manufactured product, while trees would refer to unprocessed trunks. Sources do not inform either about the tree species of these long timbers for the *arboladura*, although it can be assumed that they were north European pine.[50] *Palos*, which literally translates as "sticks," must have referred to yards of any size, while *berlinga*, for which an

---

50   A good introduction to the different types of timber imported to Seville, from a dendro-chronological perspective, is: Eduardo Rodríguez-Trobajo and Marta Domínguez-Delmás, "Swedish oak, planks and panels: dendroarchaeological investigations on the 16th century

TABLE 6.2   Provisions for ships of the *Carrera de Indias*

Category	Product	N	Unit	Qmin	Qmax	PN	Pmin	Pmax
Timber for masts	Árboles	14	Piece	1	6	14	88	1584
	Berlingas	2	Piece*	24	20	2	30	38
	Mástiles	6	Piece	3	5	5	123.75	800
	Palos	1	Piece	2	-	1	100	-
Timber planks and beams	Tablas de pinsapo	1	Dozen	4	-	1	60.5	-
	Tablas de pino de Flandes	17	Dozen	1	83.3	15	33	66
	Tablas de prusa	5	Piece*	12	60	5	12	26
	Tablas de roble	10	Piece*	2	50	7	22	75
	Vigas	4	Piece	1	135	4	16	32
Rigging	Cables	7	*Quintal*	11.3	101.13	7	60	154
	Calabrote	1	*Quintal*	8.25	-	1	143	-
	Cáñamo	7	*Quintal*	10.5	49	7	46	71.5
	Guindaleza	2	*Quintal*	8.5	-	1	66	-
	Jarcia	76	*Quintal*	4.18	3374.2	70	40	143
Tar and pitch	Alquitrán	13	*Barril*	40	9	5	18	70
	Brea	2	*Quintal*	38	-	1	33	-

Note: Products with * were sold per dozen, too

SOURCE: AHPSE, SP, 7764–7786 AND 9214–9308

English translation was not possible, were small yards attached to the mast for supporting the rigging; very probably, these were also made of north European pine. One single tree could cost up to 1594 *reales*, although some trees were sold for 88 *reales* only. Such a price variation must have been a consequence of the different size and quality of the pines rather than a change in the market. In any case, the purchase of this type of commodity represented a huge investment, especially because people normally bought more than one at a time, as the table indicates. Given that this was a considerable investment, ship owners probably avoided buying new ones if they could fix them by assembling different pieces, as De Melemburque explained in 1574.

Evangelistas altarpiece at Seville Cathedral (Spain)," *Journal of Archaeological Science* 54 (2015): 149.

According to the number of times appearing in promissory notes, rigging was the most purchased type of naval provision. Rigging normally appear in the promissory notes under the generic term of *jarcia*, mentioned in 76 deeds. The product was often described according to quality, such as *jarcia alquitranada* (tarry rigging), or provenance, such as *jarcia de Flandes* (rigging from Flanders). Some deeds specified the type of rigging: cables were mentioned in 7 promissory notes, *calabrotes* (a thick rope) in 1, *cañamo* (hemp) in 7, and *guindalezas* (a type of rope) in 2. A *quintal* (a unit of weight) of rigging could cost up to 143 *reales* or 154 *reales* in the case of cables. This was indeed a provision that suffered a continuous deterioration due to the stress of the sails, and new rigging must have been needed before every journey.

The same goes for caulking products, *alquitrán* (tar) and *brea* (pitch), used for making the hull of the ship watertight before the long journeys. These products were rarely traded by *Atarazanas* merchants; tar was supplied 13 times and pitch 2. This may indicate that tar and pitch were not imported from northern Europe and probably they were provided by suppliers other than the group of Flemish merchants. In fact, one of the two examples of tar indicate that the product came from the Biscay, in northern Spain ("*brea de Biscaya*").[51]

Sawn-timber commodities, generally in the form of planks (*tablas*), were the second most traded commodities. These products were normally described according to the tree species, their provenance, or both. The most demanded sort were the *tablas de pino de Flandes*. This description refers first to the tree species, pine (*pino*), and secondly to the provenance, from Flanders (*de Flandes*). For sure, the pines of these planks were not originally from the Low Countries, but from Scandinavian forests.[52] Thus, the term *Flandes* must have been used as a trademark to indicate a distinctive shape or quality of the commodity, evidencing the complexity reached by the Andalusian timber market and the important role of the Low Countries as a re-exportation region. Planks from Flanders were the cheapest of all types of planks. The ones from Prussian forests (*tablas de Prusa*) were significantly more expensive. While a dozen *Flemish* planks averaged 47.9 *reales*, a single *Prussian* plank could cost up to 26 *reales*. The higher price of planks from Prussia may imply a better quality or a larger size of this type. Oak planks (*tablas de roble*) were even more expensive than the pine planks from Flanders and the ones from Prussia. A single plank could be sold up to 75 *reales*.[53] Notarial sources do not elaborate on the

---

51   AHPSe, SP, 9304, 158r.
52   Jou, *Le commerce des Bois.*
53   AHPSe, SP, 9295, 733.

194

CHAPTER 6

provenance of the oak planks, and nothing indicates that they were imported from northern Europe. It is difficult to address its origin, because north Iberian forests was rich in quality oak, too. Finally, there is only one recognisable native product, which appears in only one document: the *pino de pinsapo*, Spanish fir, a regional variety of pine that was avoided in the oceanic shipbuilding industry, which may have been used in exceptional circumstances or for embellishment works.

When analysing a richer dataset of promissory notes involving any purchase of timber, not only the ones bought by ship captains or masters of the *Carrera*, the sample grows up to 455 deeds, in which planks become the type of product that these merchants sold the most. This larger dataset also evidences that the supplying activity of *Atarazanas* merchants was not only limited to the repair of ships, but to most naval-related industries in the region. A total of 268 promissory notes account for this diverse supply, such as barrel staves to coopers (*toneleros*), rigging to cable makers (*cordoneros*), and tar and pitch to ship caulkers (*careneros*).[54] They supplied other local industries too, especially artisans that worked with timber, such as carpenters (*carpinteros*), builders (*albañiles*) or sculptors (*entalladores*),[55] contributing not only to the maritime expansion of Seville but also to the urban expansion that the city experienced in the second half of the century.[56]

2   Supply to the Royal Navy

As tensions with the Ottoman Empire lessened in the Mediterranean after the Battle of Lepanto in 1571, England and the newly founded Dutch Republic began to contest the Habsburg hegemony in the Atlantic in the last third of the sixteenth century, interrupting the maritime connection between Spain and the Low Countries, threatening the American convoys and even attacking the Iberian coast. A combined offensive by the English and the Dutch against Cádiz in 1596 epitomised what Thompson defined as *Atlanticization of war*: the greater threats to the Spanish monarchy no longer came from the Mediterranean but from the Atlantic.[57] The *Atlanticization of war* brought the creation of

---

54   268 promissory notes reflect that supply. I.e. to a cooper (AHPSe, SP, 9224, 77r); to a cable maker (AHPSe, SP, 9243, 404v); to a ship caulker (AHPSe, SP, 9280, 1067r).
55   I.e. to a carpenter (AHPSe, SP, 9235, 14v); to a builder (AHPSe, SP, 9215, 908r); to a sculptor (AHPSe, SP, 7782, 63r).
56   Albardonedo Freire, *El urbanismo de Sevilla*.
57   Díaz Blanco, "Una armada de galeras;" Thompson, *War and Government*.

Spain's first permanent armadas in the Atlantic. The first was the *Armada de la Guarda de las Indias*, which escorted the convoys of the *Carrera de Indias* and was consolidated after the construction of twelve galleons in 1568.[58] The second was the *Armada del Mar Océano*, which turned into a permanent force protecting the Iberian Atlantic coast formed after the failure of the Great Armada, with the construction of other twelve galleons.[59] During this time, a permanent maritime defence for the American possessions was also organised with two fleers: the *Armada de Barlovento*, which patrolled the waters between the Caribbean Sea and the coast of Tierra Firme, and the *Armada del Mar del Sur*, which protected the Pacific coast of the southern American territories.[60]

The new maritime priorities required the construction of ships that were better suited than oared galleys for the needs and objectives of Atlantic navigation and war. After the losses of the Great Armada in 1588, Philip II made a notable effort to enlarge the number of warships under his direct control, as well as to promote the construction of private-owned mercantile ships that could be adapted for military purposes in case of necessity.[61] Given the incapacity of Andalusian shipyards to build large tonnage vessels and the autonomy of Portuguese shipyards regarding the Spain's maritime aspirations, the majority of the new Atlantic warships were constructed in northern Spain. The Cantabrian coast, which extended from the region of Galicia to the border with France, was a diverse territory where three main shipbuilding areas, with different jurisdictions and naval traditions, can be distinguished. The first is the Galician coast, with Ribadeo as the main shipyard, although only became important for the Habsburg's shipbuilding project in the next century. The second is the area of the *Cuatro Villas de la Costa de la Mar*, a confederation of the towns of San Vicente de la Barquera, Santander, Laredo and Castro Urdiales that broadly corresponds to the current region of Cantabria. The third, and most important in this period, was the Basque

---

58   Casado Soto, *Los barcos españoles,* 33.

59   In times of war, mercantile ships had to be seized for the formation of armadas. "To replace part of the losses of 1588," as Thompson noted, the monarchy commanded the construction of "twelve new 1,000-ton galleons, the famous Twelve Apostles." Thompson, *War and government,* 192.

60   Casado Soto, "Barcos para la Guerra," 32.

61   This included a system of loans and fiscal benefits to incentivise the construction of large-tonnage commercial vessels. that could, after some years of private use, be adapted to warfare and incorporated to the king's navy. Casado Soto, "La construcción naval atlántica española." Rodríguez Lorenzo, "Construcción naval cantábrica."

region, atomised in local communities with a long tradition of oceanic ship-building and shipping.[62]

Although Spain still relied on the confiscation of mercantile ships for military campaigns, the monarchy built 86 new warships in ten years to form the new established permanent armadas in times of peace and the core of its naval force in times of war. Table 6.3, taken from Thompson's work *War and Government*, contains the warships – ranging from 60 to 1300 tons –built between 1588 and 1598 through two different methods, by directly financing and supervising the construction (direct administration) or by outsourcing it to a contractor (*asiento*). Table 6.3 evidences that shipyards in the Basque provinces of Biscay and Gipuzkoa contributed the most to the construction of new royal warships, with the exception of the twelve galleons built in 1594 in Ragusa, Sicily. With the exception of the galleons of Ragusa, the construction of the new warships was financed and supervised directly by the monarchy instead of outsourced to private contractors (*asentistas*); a way of supply that became the norm in the following century.[63] Despite the growing financial difficulties of Philip II's reign, the royal treasury managed to sustain the increasing efforts to expand the royal navy.

The enlargement of the navy translated into an extraordinary development of Spain's naval bureaucracy that was reflected in Andalusia, despite the poor contribution of the region's shipyards to the monarchy's shipbuilding projects. When the conflict with the Ottoman Empire declined, Andalusia replaced Sicily as the region where the royal galleys operating in Mediterranean waters wintered and obtained provisions.[64] In the beginning, the officials of the House of Trade – originally established for American affairs – assumed the provision of the royal navy in the region until a general purveyor was finally established in Seville, who was independent of the bureaucratic structure of the House of Trade, in 1586. This appointment marks the culmination of Seville as the central node of the Spanish maritime empire.

---

62   Casado Soto, "Barcos para la Guerra." A situation that changed in the following century, when the monarchy of Philip III agreed with private contractors (*asentistas*) the construction of ships in Ribadeo, Cuatro Villas, Biscay and Guipuzcoa. Gasch-Tomás, Trápaga Monchet, Trindade, "Shipbuilding in times of war."

63   Thompson, *War and government*, 192 and 304. More recently, Torres Sánchez "Administración o asiento" and Valdez-Bubnov, "Shipbuilding Administration."

64   Thompson, "The Spanish Armada," 73. See also Manuel Lomas, *Governing the Galleys: Jurisdiction, Justice, and Trade in the Squadrons of the Hispanic Monarchy (Sixteenth–Seventeenth Centuries)* (Leiden: Brill, 2020), 107–118.

TABLE 6.3   Atlantic warships constructed for the service of Philip II

Year	Ship type	Method	Place of construction
1588	12 galleons of ca. 1000 tons each	Direct administration	Bilbao and Santander
1589	12 fragatas	Direct administration	Deusto (Biscay)
1590	2 zabras of 200 tons each	Direct administration	Unknown
1591	6 zabras of 200 tons each	Unknown	Gipuzkoa
1592	7 ships of 500 tons each	Unknown	Rentería (Gipuzkoa)
1594	6 light galleons of 250 tons each	Direct administration	Gipuzkoa
1594	12 galleons of 700 tons each	Asiento	Italy and Ragusa
1595	6 galleons of 1300 tons each	Direct administration	Rentería (Gipuzkoa)
1595	3 galizabras of 60 tons each	Direct administration	Rentería (Gipuzkoa)
1596	6 galleons	Direct administration	Gipuzkoa
1596	2 galizabras	Direct administration	Gipuzkoa
1597	12 galleons (2 of 1000 tons, 8 of 750)	Direct administration	Gipuzkoa and Biscay

The creation of a market for imported timber was a fundamental reason for the city's consolidation as an operative and logistical centre of both the *Carrera de Indias* and the royal navy. The warehouses of the *Atarazanas* offered royal officials sufficient stock to provide the armadas wintering in Andalusia as well as to supply materials for the construction of new warships in the Cantabrian shipyards. The purchase of naval provisions left ample evidence through the orders of payment issued by the royal administration, known as *libranzas*, which recognised the obligation of the monarchy to make a payment. Unfortunately, given the developing nature of the naval bureaucracy at the time, these sources are dispersed in different sections of Spain's main state archives, namely the *Archivo General de Indias* and the *Archivo General de*

Simancas, complicating a systematic analysis on how officials obtained imported naval provisions for the royal navy in Seville.[65]

Nonetheless, the relationship between *Atarazanas* merchants and royal officials was often documented in Seville's notarial registers, especially through receipt deeds, known as *cobros*, in which merchants formally recognised the liquidation of a *libranza* issued by a royal official.[66] There are 35 receipts recording the purchase of naval provisions by royal officials. Although the sample is limited, receipts usually described the concept of payment, which allows for a complete analysis of the types of commodities that royal officials usually bought and how they did it. Moreover, the sample of 35 receipts is complemented with 77 POAS in which *Atarazanas* merchants commissioned another individual to claim the payment of *libranzas* to the royal administration. This dataset provide a deep insight into the growing development of the naval bureaucracy in Seville and the relationship between naval officials and these foreign merchants.

2.1   *Demand of Imported Naval Provisions*

The sample of 35 receipts and 77 POAS offers an overview of the variety of timber and other provisions that royal officials purchased in the *Atarazanas*, shown in Table 6.4. The table follows the same organisation of Table 6.2 on the provisions supplied to the ships of the *Carrera de Indias*. It indicates the number of times a type of product appeared in deeds and the variations in quantity and prices. Receipts and POAS tended to be less detailed than promissory notes, especially regarding prices, which were normally presented as a total without specifying the value of each commodity. Because of this, this table is slightly less complete than the previous one; in any case, according to the available data, prices seemed to be generally lower when the provision was for the armada than those for the ships of the *Carrera de Indias*.

There are some important differences between Table 6.4 and Table 6.2. While rigging was the most supplied provision to ships of the *Carrera de Indias*, royal officials seldom purchased this type of provision in the *Atarazanas*. *Cáñamo* (hemp) and *jarcia* only appeared in five receipts. Similarly, royal officials rarely

---

65   Documents are organised in different archival sections concerning royal treasury as well as military affairs. As for the documents held in the *Archivo de la Marina* and the *Archivo del Museo Naval*, they only deal with a later period.

66   Although less frequent than POAS and promissory notes, receipts were also widely used notarial deeds in sixteenth-century Seville; *Atarazanas* merchants participated in 618 of such contracts in the notaries of Francisco Díaz (from 1570 to 1586) and Juan de Tordesillas (from 1587 to 1599).

TABLE 6.4   Naval provisions for the royal navy

Category	Product	N	Unit	Qmin	Qmax	PN	Pmin	Pmax
Timber for masts	Entenas	8	Piece	1	8	-	-	-
	Árboles	32	Piece	1	45	10	132	1760
	Mástiles	7	Piece	1	37	3	33	385
	Palos	7	Piece	1	6	6	33	154
	Pinos	1	Piece	12	-	-	-	-
Timber planks and beams	Barraganete	3	Piece	1	12	2	8	
	Bornes	4	Piece	3	238	-	-	-
	Medios bornes	1	Piece	532	-	-	-	-
	Espigón	2	Piece	1	14	-	-	-
	Remos	1	-	-	-	-	-	-
	Tablas de pino	16	Piece	20	960	9	22	55
	Tablas de roble	2	Piece	12	70	-	40	-
	Tablas de prusa	2	Piece	20	50	-	-	-
	Tripitrapes	2	Piece	120	1680	-	-	-
	Vigas	2	Piece	2	10	-	-	-
Rigging	Cáñamo	1	-	-	-	-	-	-
	Jarcia	4	*Quintal*	8.45	61	1	77	-
Tar and pitch	Alquitrán	7	*Barril*	2	134	4	18	25
	Brea	2	*Quintal*	14.4	18	-	-	-

SOURCE: PERSONAL DATABASE BASED ON AHPSE, SP, 7764–7786 AND 9214–9308

purchased caulking materials, like tar and pitch. Royal officials mostly resorted to the warehouses of the *Atarazanas* to buy timber. Pine planks from Flanders (*tablas de pino de Flandes*) were the second most sold commodity, appearing in sixteen deeds. They were always purchased in great numbers. For instance, Esteban Jansen sold 44 dozen pine planks for the preparation of the galleons commanded by general Juan de Urive in 1592.[67] The largest debt for the supply

---

67   AHPSe, SP, 9278P, 148r.

of pine planks concerns a Flemish merchant from Cádiz, Lorenzo Simay. In 1597, in the office of the notary Juan de Tordesillas, Simay granted a POA to the Flemish attorney Valerio Vandala to appear before the Royal Council in Madrid to collect a *libranza* for various commodities he had supplied, including 960 pine planks that officials had taken from his house for the service of the royal galleys.[68]

Tree trunks were the most demanded type of commodity, with a total of 55 references in the notarial deeds. Besides *palos*, which consisted of small yards for hanging the sails, there was probably no difference between the other types of provisions: *entenas*, trees, masts and pines. They were all large trunks that were meant to form the *arboladura* of ships, most likely imported from Scandinavian forests as the previous chapter demonstrated. They appear in at least 48 notarial deeds and were normally traded in great numbers. In 1592, Esteban Jansen commissioned Deifebo Roque, a Flemish resident in Madrid, to claim 25,268 *reales* for the value of more than 45 trees and three sails that the Duke of Medina Sidonia had taken from his house for the construction of twelve galleons that the king was building in Santander and Bilbao in 1588, the famous Twelve Apostles.[69]

The fact that royal officials preferred non-Iberian timber is not remarkable. Reports of royal officials and naval treaties of the time always highlighted the necessity of using pine from northern Europe for the construction of oceanic ships. In one of these treaties, Juan Escalante de Mendoza, a famous officer of Philip II's navy, noted: "masts and *entenas* must be very good if they are of the ones brought from Flanders, as it is demonstrated that there is not a more competent one than the pine that the Flemings call *prusa*."[70] What is indeed remarkable is that officials recommended obtaining those supplies in Andalusia. In a letter sent by Juan Martínez de Recalde, another important officer of the Spanish navy, to the Duke of Medina Sidonia about the construction of royal galleons in Cantabria, he stated that due to the shortage of masts there, they should be brought from Andalusia or Portugal.[71]

The words by Martínez de Recalde, in short, indicate that officials were aware that Seville's market was competitive enough to fulfil the demand of timber for the navy, and that they preferred this solution over enlisting an entrepreneur to import trees from northern Europe expressly for a particular shipbuilding

68   AHPSe, SP, 9298, 529v.
69   AHPSe, SP, 9269, 823r.
70   Gervasio de Artíñano y Galdácano, *La arquitectura naval*, 272.
71   Archivo Museo Naval, Colección Navarrete, t. 2, 76, 297 transcribed in Casado Soto, *Los barcos españoles*, 313.

project. The reputation of the commodities these merchants imported must have been high at Madrid's court. In 1578, some of the *flamencos* of the *Atarazanas* supplied imported oak for the construction of the organs of the palace-monastery of El Escorial.[72]

2.2 An Incipient Naval Bureaucracy in Andalusia

The 35 receipts and 77 POAs reveal the extension and complexity reached by Spain's naval bureaucracy in Andalusia during the reign of Philip II.[73] More than 50 officials can be identified in the sample, performing different functions for the royal navy, from the purchase of supplies to its payment. These officials depended on a variety of royal institutions that, despite being autonomous, were closely interrelated. The House of Trade, which ultimately depended on the Council of the Indies, ensured the provision of the armada escorting the American convoys. The Council of War was in charge of the operative organisation of the navy, setting Spain's military objectives and supervising the preparation of warships. Finally, the provision of the armadas and preparation of military campaigns ultimately depended on the Council of Treasury, which procured the financial means to pay for them.[74]

The factor of the House of Trade, Francisco Duarte, appears in many of the deeds during the 1570s and early 1580s, as the one responsible for taking provisions from the *Atarazanas* warehouses. He was the top official of the House of Trade, depending on the king and the Council of the Indies only.[75] He was the purveyor of the *Carrera de Indias*, supervising the logistical organisation of the American fleets and preparing the warships that escorted them, the *Armada de la Guarda de Indias*. In 1584, for instance, Duarte purchased thirteen trees from the houses of Esteban Jansen, Jaques Nicolás, Manas Enríquez and Francisco Roelant for the provision of "the galleons of the navy commanded by Juan Martínez de Recalde."[76]

As the military needs of the monarchy increased in the Atlantic, the royal navy developed its own institutional body in Andalusia. In 1586, the king

---

72 A carpenter appointed by the king bought 200 bornes (oak wainscots) from the houses of Gerónimo de Andrea, Esteban Jansen and Felipe Sarens. AHPSe, SP, 9219, 365r.

73 Irving A.A. Thompson, "The Armada and Administrative Reform: the Spanish Council of War in the reign of Philip II," *The English Historical Review* 82, no. 325 (Oct., 1967): 698–725.

74 Mena-García, "La Casa de la Contratación," 243.

75 Mena-García, "La Casa de la Contratación," 249. In the same collective publication, Rafael Donoso Anes, "El papel del tesorero en el desarrollo contable de la Casa de la Contratación," 89.

76 POA granted by Estaban Jansen, Jaques Nicolás, Manas Enriquez and Francisco Roelant to Juan de Bestoven in January 1585 (AHPSe, SP, 9242, 532r).

created two offices of general purveyor of the royal navy, one in Seville and one in Lisbon, which depended on the Council of War, anticipating the preparation of the Great Armada against England. Due to rising internal oppositions against Francisco Duarte within the House of Trade, the king named him general purveyor of the royal navy in Lisbon. Duarte nonetheless managed to delegate the office of factor to his son, also named Francisco Duarte. From Lisbon, Francisco Duarte Sr. continued resorting to the *Atarazanas* merchants. In October 1597, he ordered one of his officials to take timber and grain from the stores of Jaques Nicolás, Pedro Gisberto and Guillermo Corinse, to be transported to Lisbon, where the Great Armada was being prepared.[77]

The first general purveyor of the armadas in Seville was Antonio de Guevara, a member of the Council of Treasury who had formerly held the office of administrator of the *Almojarifazgo de Indias*, the tax on trade with the Americas.[78] The appointment of a member of the Council of Treasury as general purveyor of the armada, in close connection to the Council of War, reveals an important feature of Philip II's naval policy during that time: the necessity to conciliate the needs of the armada with the financial capacity of the royal treasury. Pedro de Ysunza held the office of general purveyor in 1591, when he took eleven trees for the galleys from the warehouse of Guillermo Corinse. He must have operated between Seville and the coast of Cádiz, where he signed some of the *libranzas*, like the one of Corinse.[79] Due to his frequent absences, he commissioned a representative in Seville, named Juan de Acuch, who took thirteen trees for the service of the galleys from the warehouse of Esteban Jansen.[80]

The responsibilities of the factor of the House of Trade were also lightened with the creation of a specific purveyor for the *Armada de la Guarda de las Indias*. This office was initially assumed by Cristóbal de Barros, a key figure in the expansion of Philip II's navy.[81] Before his arrival at the House of Trade, De Barros took a decisive role in the promotion of Cantabrian shipyards and of a sustainable exploitation of northern Iberian forest to meet the demands of the shipbuilding industry.[82] He moved to Seville in the early 1590s, when

---

77   POA to Pedro de Noayn in August 1587. AHPSe, SP, 9250, 693r.
78   Mena-García, "La Casa de la Contratación" 250. The full description of his office was *Provehedor general de sus armadas e fronteras*. AHPSe, SP, 9230,455r; 9250, 716v.
79   AHPSe, SP, 9268, 823v.
80   AHPSe, SP, 9276, 844r.
81   To the extent that Casado Soto even compared him to Colbert in France or Samuel Pepys in England. Casado Soto, "Barcos para la guerra" 35.
82   On the Barros, see Alfredo J. Martínez González, *Las Superintendencias de montes y plantíos (1574–1748): Derecho y política forestal para las Armadas en la Edad Moderna* (Valencia: Tirant lo Blanch, 2015).

his activity as purveyor of the *Armada de la Guardia de Indias* led him to deal-ing frequently with the merchants of the *Atarazanas*.[83]

The royal navy did not develop a bureaucracy of its own in the most impor-tant port on the Andalusian coast, Sanlúcar de Barrameda. To control this important maritime place, in the mouth of the Guadalquivir River, Philip II needed the collaboration of the lord of the town, the Duke of Medina Sidonia. This represented a decisive motivation for the Duke's appointment as general captain of the *Mar Océano y Costas de Andalucia* in 1588, which made him the top official for the protection of the Iberian coast and the Andalusian waters. Although the importance of the Duke's collaboration was already proven some years before, in the confiscations of 1574 and 1575, it was really after the death of the previous general captain of the *Mar Océano*, Álvaro de Bazán, in 1588, that his ascent in the navy began, substituting Bazán as commander the Great Armada against England.[84]

Since then, as general captain, the Duke of Medina Sidonia frequently resorted to Seville's market for imported timber. An evidence of this is the POA that Esteban Jansen granted Gaspar Loscarte in 1591, to inquire and make a report on how the Duke of Medina Sidonia had taken 26 large masts of Prussia and 37 masts of Andalusian pines (*pinsapo*) for the supply of the royal ships that were being built in Ferrol.[85] This report was to be presented before the Council of Treasury in Madrid to claim the debt. Similarly, some months later, Guillermo Corinse appointed the Flemish attorney Valerio Vandala to claim in Madrid 22,709 *reales*, which were still to be paid for the timber that the Duke had taken from his house, probably for the shipyards of Ferrol as well.[86] The active role he assumed in the preparation of the armadas and the construction of new warships resembled that of other general captains of armadas operat-ing in Andalusia. For instance, the *Adelantado Mayor de Castilla*, supplied the royal galleon that he was constructing in northern Spain with four trees from the house of Guillermo Corinse in 1593.[87]

---

83   AHPSe, SP, 9275, 969r, AHPSe, SP, 9284, 411r. He was later substituted by Rodríguez de
      Herrera AHPSe, SP, 9294, 249r.

84   Thompson, "The Appointment of the Duke of Medina Sidonia," Salas Almela, "Un cargo
      para el Duque de Medina Sidonia."

85   AHPSe, SP, 9266, 600v. (February 1592) Esteban Jansen claimed another debt to the
      Council of Treasury a year later with a similar case for the construction of the galleons in
      Bilbao and Santander, mentioned earlier AHPSe, SP, 9269, 823r.

86   AHPSe, SP, 9271, 902r. According to the testament, the sum was never paid (AHPSe, SP,
      9977, 742v).

87   AHPSe, SP, 9276, 639v.

Other regular captains of the navy did not usually get directly involved in the provision of the ships they commanded. They did not need to purchase provisions, because they were supplied by purveyors. In fact, only in exceptional occasions, like the ones described before, the mechanism of supply was a direct one, that is, one led by a top official of the navy from the *Atarazanas* warehouses straight to a shipyard or ship. Usually, officials commissioned by the general purveyors gathered supplies to be used in the near future, for the preparation of a military operation or for the construction of new ships. Storekeepers (*tenedores de bastimentos*) were in charge of storing and delivering those provisions when needed; notarial deeds often mentioned these officials as the receptors of the provisions that purveyors took from the *Atarazanas*.[88] A *cédula real* of 1578, in which Philip II ordered the officials of the House of Trade to take masts in Seville, shed some light on this supply mechanism:

> Our officials that reside in the city of Seville in the House of Trade of the Indies have informed us that to the river of this city has arrived a hulk from Flanders, filled with masts that could be appropriated for the two galleys that are being built in Biscay, as flagship and rear-flagship of the *Armada de la Guarda de las Nuestras Yndias,* and they are convenient for our service. And because it is convenient to rapidly take the said masts for us, we command you that after receiving this decree, you take them and pay the owners the *maravedís* that they seemed to be valued from our treasurer in this House [of Trade] and at your expense, as treasurer [of the House]. We command that they are properly stored in the *Atarazanas* of this city awaiting for further orders regarding what you should do with them.[89]

The polycentric nature of Spain's maritime empire is exemplified by this flow of communication between the officials in the Cantabrian shipyards that demanded a specific type of timber, the officials in Seville that knew the availability of stock and, finally, the court in Madrid that coordinated the construction of new warships. The text accurately describes how the purveyor of the House of Trade and his commissioners knew about the state of the market in Seville, reported about it and acquired the supplies if ordered by the king.[90] Then, the storekeeper received the products and stored them until they were

---

88   Mena-García, "La Casa de la Contratación," 253.

89   AGI, Indiferente, 1956, L.2, 60v (1578-1-29).

90   E.g. AHPSe, SP, 9276, 844r.

ready to be used; interestingly enough, as the quotation indicate, for this purpose they frequently rented some spaces in the *Atarazanas* to the *flamencos,* who had originally obtained the leasing from the king.[91] Finally, the treasurer of the House of Trade issued a *libranza* for the payment of the provision, for which the treasurer used the own revenues of the House.

The expenses of the armada for the protection of the *Carrera de Indias* fell under the responsibility of the treasurer of the House of Trade until 1591, when the *Consulado* assumed the financing of this naval force through the *avería.*[92] The Council of the Treasury was responsible for the expenses related to the rest of the navy, which was organised by the Council of War. Both the Council of Treasury and the House of Trade had an office especially for this task: the payers (*pagadores*).[93] These officials were at the service of the royal treasurers, another office present in each of the two councils, and their duty was to hand the money to the suppliers. Because of this, they normally appear as the granted party in receipts signed by the *Atarazanas* merchants, stating that payers had paid them a *libranza,* which had been issued by the purveyor and approved by a comptroller who worked for the royal treasurer.

As noticed in the decree, the king and his officials were aware that an effective payment was essential to ensure the supply in the future. Payments were never done immediately after the issuing of the *libranza* by the purveyor, yet the 35 receipts evidence that *libranzas* were often paid within a few months after they were issued. For instance, Justo de Bil notarised a receipt in March 1597, declaring that:

> I received and have received from Francisco de Agüero, general payer of his majesty and his Escort Armada of the Indies, citizen of this city, 475,013 *reales* that proceed from a *libranza,* [issued] by the gentleman purveyor don Pedro Rodríguez de Herrera, signed by his name, and Agustín de la Guerra, comptroller, issued on the 31st of January of this year, through which they order to pay me in return of a given quantity of cables, planks of oak and *pinsapo* and rigging that I gave for the service and preparation

---

91   AHPSe, SP, 9251, 76r.

92   Díaz Blanco, *Así trocaste tu gloria.*

93   The following *pagadores* are documented: Andrés Sanz del Portillo (1581–1587), Martín de Arriaga (1591), Bernardo de Castillo (1593–1596), Francisco de Agüero (1595–1596), Juan Pasqual (1597) and Martin de Urquiaga (1597). Unfortunately, the role has been very little studied, despite their importance for the navy Mena-García, "La Casa de la Contratación," 252.

of the galleons and frigates of the said Armadas, in different prices appearing in the said *libranza*.[94]

Given the precarious situation of the royal treasury, there are many and notable exceptions to the previous rule, as well. One of them was already analysed in the previous chapter, when several Flemish and Italian merchants that had imported grain to Andalusia insistently claimed such a large debt that the king eventually granted them the right to collect it from the *alcabalas* of several Castilian towns.[95] Esteban Jansen had a similar problem with Martín de Arriaga, "payer of the galleys of the king," who owed him 22,880 *reales* for unpaid timber provisions.[96] In August 1593, Jansen sent the notary Juan de Tordesillas to De Arriaga's house to notify him a claim for the payment of a *libranza*, which was annexed to the notification. Martín de Arriaga declared he was aware of the *libranza* but argued that he was incapable of completing the payment because he "has no order or money of His Majesty or any method to be able to pay it."[97] A year later, Jansen notarised a receipt of, at least, half of the *libranza* (11,3575 *reales*).[98]

Delays seemed to occur when the payment depended on the Council of Treasury in Madrid, and thus were not related to the House of Trade, whose bureaucratic apparatus proved to be more efficient according to the lack of notarised claims. The delays of the Council of Treasury accumulated and, by the 1590s, the monarchy had generated high debts with at least two *Atarazanas* merchants, Guillermo Corinse and Esteban Jansen, as revealed in their testaments. Guillermo Corinse stated that, at the time of notarizing his testament, he was creditor of 2508 *ducados* (27,588 *reales*) of timber that the Duke of Medina Sidonia had taken in 1591 from his house in Sanlúcar de Barrameda, to be sent to the shipyards of Ferrol, in Galicia.[99] The case of Esteban Jansen was even more problematic. By the time of his death in 1596, the king owed him 24,186 *ducados* (266,055 *reales*) for several unpaid *libranzas*, including the

---

94   AHPSe, SP, 9295, 732.

95   AHPSe, SP, 9282, 284r and 9282, 286r. The situation was not completely solved by
      1597: AHPSe, SP, 9295, 998 and AHPSe, SP, 9297, 585r.

96   "[P]agador general de las dichas galeras [de España]." AHPSe, SP, 9276, 844r.

97   "[E]l qual dijo quel no tiene horden ni dineros ningunos de su magestad de ningún género
      para poderla pagar." AHPSe, SP, 9276, 844r.

98   AHPSe, SP, 9282, 158r.

99   A debt that he had already claimed some months after the confiscation but was not paid
      after seven years later. AHPSe, SP, 9977, 739r-744v.

value of the trees taken by the Duke of Medina Sidonia in 1591 and several confiscations by Cristóbal de Barros.[100] These debts were mostly related to the provision of the shipbuilding projects of the monarchy in northern Spain, rather than to regular supplies for the preparation of warships wintering in Andalusia. These shipbuilding projects involved an extraordinary investment of the state, which royal officials could not always finance. The fact that these *Atarazanas* merchants assumed such a financial burden, in short, evidences the central position that the group reached in Spain's maritime organisation.

3   Conclusion

Coinciding with the Atlantic turn of Philip II's military priorities, Seville strengthened its position as logistical and operative centre of Spain's maritime affairs. The emergence of a competitive and diversified market of timber and other naval provisions, analysed in this chapter, was a fundamental part of this process. This market, dominated by the *flamencos* of the *Atarazanas*, was able to respond to the demand of the ships preparing to sail to America, as well as to the demand of the royal navy, which experienced an unprecedented expansion after 1588.

The expansion of the royal navy occurred far away from Andalusia. The new warships were mostly built in northern Iberian shipyards, where royal officials found a great deal of the skills, financial means and materials needed to implement the king's ambitious plans. But the construction of Atlantic vessels required the use of large pines for the *arboladura* that could not be obtained from Iberian forests and thus had to be imported from the Baltic and Scandinavian regions. Royal officials usually purchased these imported provisions in the thriving markets of Seville and Lisbon. This form of supplying differs from the assumption that the king outsourced this kind of activity to private entrepreneurs. The system of *asientos*, which became common in the seventeenth century for the construction of warships or the supply of strategic provisions, was not yet fully in place.[101]

Instead, a developing bureaucratic apparatus supervised and obtained supplies for the construction of the new warships and the preparation of

---

100   AHPSe, SP, 9289, 718r. This led to a claim by the executors and a legal process: AGI, Contratación, 252, N.1, R.24.

101   E.g. Supply of four trees bought for the construction of the *El Crucifijo* galleon, or eleven trees for the galleons that the general Juan de Urive was building for the service of the king. AHPSe, SP, 9276, 639v and AHPSe, SP, 9278, 64v.

the military campaigns. This bureaucratic apparatus found a central node in Seville, which benefited from the market of imported timber created in the *Atarazanas*. Thanks to the supply of imported naval provisions for the preparation of the *Carrera de Indias* biannual convoys, these merchants began to participate in the trade with the Americas, at least since 1590s, when captains and owners of *Carrera de Indias* ships notarised promissory notes to be paid in the Americas. Promissory notes allowed for a complex form of contracting, which permitted *Atarazanas* merchants to enforce the payment of the provisions in silver, while allowed buyers to make creditors – the *flamencos* in this case – bear the liability of the transaction until the ship arrived to America.

An overview of the products that the *flamencos* supplied to the private ships of the *Carrera* and to the warships of the royal navy demonstrates the existence of a developed market, which originated after the embargo of 1574. While their capacity to import masts and trees from northern Europe drove their specialisation in this trade, it was their capacity to enlarge and diversify their stock of imported provisions that ultimately strengthened their dominant position. Their control of the flourishing market of Baltic and Scandinavian provisions came at a cost for some of the merchants, like Esteban Jansen and Guillermo Corinse, to whom the monarchy still owed considerable debts at the time of their deaths. Yet this was probably a fair price to pay for being in control of a strategic market for Andalusia and the monarchy throughout the reign of Philip II.

Conclusion

Days before his death in 1596, the German merchant Esteban Jansen claimed in his testament that the monarchy owed him 25,000 *ducados* for unpaid timber he had supplied for the construction of new warships for the royal navy.[1] He certainly was the greatest trader of imported timber and rigging in Spain, but he was not the only north European merchant who, in the last third of the century, specialised in this trade in Seville. These northerners shared a similar migrant experience and business career: they came from the Low Countries and northern Germany, married the daughters of compatriots, and established their residences and stores in the *Reales Atarazanas*. Eventually, a second and a third generation of migrants born in Andalusia joined the trade in imported timber and naval provisions, which continued in the hands of *flamencos* well into the seventeenth century.

The reliance on private entrepreneurs, especially if they were foreign, to obtain strategic resources has traditionally fed a historiographical narrative of failure of the Spanish monarchy. This narrative, which was especially encouraged by Anglo-Saxon scholars in the past century, argued that, given the failure of centralist policies, Habsburg Spain came to lag behind other European maritime powers, like England and the Netherlands, whose parliamentary organisation was better suited for warfare and international trade. For this view, the growing reliance on foreign private hands epitomise the failure of the centralist policies of Spain's absolutist monarchy. This book does not fit this historical canon. The story of the *flamencos* who resided in the *Atarazanas* – their migration experiences, their relationship with local and royal authorities, and the central position they reached in Spanish maritime affairs in relatively few years – is a call for historians to rethink Spain's centralism and the state's policies regarding warfare and international trade. Instead, the Spanish monarchy should be regarded as a polycentric state, in which peripheral regions like western Andalusian and the Cantabrian coasts were intimately linked, and had a significant influence over the state's policies.

This book has reassessed the capacity of the Spanish monarchy to react to changing military and commercial conditions by highlighting its polycentric nature, showing how Seville's oligarchy lobbied the king's policy successfully. By attracting north European migrants and promoting their commercial activities, regardless of the opposition of some of Philip II's

---

1 AHPSe, SP, 9289, 718r.

© KONINKLIJKE BRILL NV, LEIDEN, 2022 | DOI:10.1163/9789004504110_009

most important counsellors, Seville consolidated a preeminent position in international trade and contributed greatly to the aspirations of the Spanish empire overseas. Only by overcoming the traditional narrative of the failure of Spain's absolutism can we cease to look at the reliance on this group of *flamencos* as a problem, instead of a solution for the increasing needs of Atlantic war.

The importation and supply of Baltic and Scandinavian timber in Seville remained a private affair dominated by few Flemish families throughout Philip II's reign. The basic unit of their business organisation was the household and the family firm, which were two faces of a same coin: the *casa*. This was formed by the merchant himself, his nuclear family, and the *servicio* – servants and slaves who took care of the domestic duties of the household and interns who helped with the running of the firm. Many *flamencos* that eventually made a name for themselves in Seville's mercantile community began their career working as interns for older north European migrants specialised in the trade of Baltic and Scandinavian timber. Young newcomers, even those who did not start working for someone else's firm, largely depended on the support of other compatriots that had migrated before to establish their own *casa* in town. Nowhere is this intergenerational cooperation more evident than in the marriages between young migrants and the daughters of older ones. Thanks to the dowries that fathers-in-law granted, which consisted of a capital income and often a space in the *Atarazanas*, newcomers obtained access to the material resources that allowed them to start their own enterprise and to the social capital the group of timber traders created.

Family ties and the residence in the same area of town, the *Atarazanas*, led to the creation of an intense social capital among the northerners trading in imported timber, prompting cohesion and collaboration. This translated into the coordination of strategies to strengthen their commercial position. By lobbying royal and local authorities, these foreigners were commissioned to transform the former shipyards of Castile into a complex of warehouses suitable for storing timber; the complex remained in their hands from the middle of the sixteenth century until well into the following century. The king also farmed them the *alcabala de madera*, a local tax on timber sales. To collect and administer the tax, *Atarzanas* merchants formed an *encabezamiento*, a guild-like organisation through which they controlled external and internal competition.

The social capital of the group also created a breeding ground for the establishment of partnerships between its members. They adapted different solutions for risk sharing, labour division and capital input, following two types of commercial associations prevalent throughout Europe at the time: the equity and

the commission partnerships. Despite the differences, these two partnerships shared similar aims: they sought to enlarge the scale of enterprises by
raising more capital and to curb the risks of long-distance trade by limiting
partners' liability. Partnerships, thus, enhanced their position in international trade.

Another cooperation solution that enhanced their position in international
trade was the transference of agency. Through the power of attorney, these
merchants delegated a variety of socioeconomic activities on local, regional
and global scales. Their wide resort to this notarial tool should serve as a call of
attention not to overlook this solution that proved essential for the organisation of international networks. The use of notarised agency should be regarded
in the same light than limited-liability partnerships, as a main breakthrough in
the development of long-distance trade in early modern Europe.

The study of their international business organisation does not suggest
that these merchants depended on commercial houses based abroad. The
second half of the sixteenth century saw a retreat of Spaniards in the navigation between Spain and northern Europe, while Dutch, English and German
networks began to dominate this activity. However, this did not necessarily
imply that merchants in southern Europe were mere factors of those based
in northern Europe, especially Antwerp and later Amsterdam. The experience
of *Atarazanas* merchants shows a more complete story. After migrating to
Seville, they developed their own business organisation and shipping strategies to obtain access to Baltic and Scandinavian markets, while investing in
Andalusian exports, such as salt. They reached a predominant position in the
trade between northern and southern Europe, by contracting directly with
Dutch and German shipmasters and gradually expanding abroad with their
own agents in the main ports of supply of timber.

Another reason that explains why *Atarazanas* merchants enjoyed a predominant position in this trade is their access to American silver and, hence,
liquidity. Their ease of access to silver is at odds with the way Spanish historians have normally looked at how foreigners participated in the *Carrera de
Indias*. For a long time, Spanish historiography neglected foreigners' activity in
the *Carrera*, assuming that they mostly participated through concealed ways
that were, by definition, almost impossible to study. Notarial deeds, nevertheless, shed light on the direct, legal ways in which foreigners, like the merchants
of the *Atarazanas*, engaged with American trade; in this case, the naval provisions supplied for the repair of the ships preparing to sail were paid once ships
arrived in the Americas. Since the decade of the 1590s, ship owners, captains
and masters of the *Carrera de Indias* issued their payments from American

ports, where these *flamencos* had expanded their presence with agents that operated on their behalf.

With silver, as well as Andalusian salt, Flemish and German merchants paid the shipments of timber and naval provisions to north European shipmasters. Only a few of these shipments arrived in Seville directly. Many were unloaded on the Andalusian coast, where these merchants developed a network of agents, too. In the sixteenth century, Andalusia grew into a hierarchical port system in which the commercial operations were concentrated in Seville, while Sanlúcar de Barrameda emerged as the head port for the international shipping circuits. The operations of *Atarazanas* merchants indicate the existence of two different shipping circuits between southern Spain and the north of Europe. One was dominated by Hanseatic shipmasters, which connected Andalusia with the Baltic markets via Lisbon and other Portuguese ports. Another was dominated by Dutch shipmasters that connected Andalusia with Norway via the Low Countries. Increasingly, *Atarazanas* merchants or their agents notarised in Amsterdam the transport of timber to Andalusia, evidencing the emergence of a commercial axis between Amsterdam and Seville by the 1590s.

Unfortunately, it is not possible to accurately measure how the volume of timber trade changed throughout the three decades covered by this study. The different types of notarial deeds are not consistent enough to conduct such an analysis. Yet, with the available deeds and complementary primary sources, we can draw some significant conclusions on the evolution of this trade in a qualitative way. Firstly, there was a shortage of timber in Andalusia before the early 1570s. This led to the first embargo in 1574, ultimately provoking the specialisation of the *Atarazanas* merchants in timber trade. Secondly, there are no complaints about the lack of masts and other imported timber products in the region after 1575, which indicates that this trade never stopped despite the embargoes. And thirdly, the increasing demand for timber for the *Carrera de Indias* and for the Spanish navy necessarily implied an increase in the volume of this trade in the last third of the century. This trade mostly occurred via Amsterdam, at least since the 1590s.

The fact that the emergence of an axis between Seville and Amsterdam coincided with the development of the Eighty Years' War is a paradox. To fight against the rebel territories, Philip II undertook a commercial war that sought to curtail their economic rise by prohibiting trade with them. The king ordered three embargoes against his enemies, which also included the English. Many authors have argued that this form of warfare turned out a failure. This is partially true; as this book shows, embargoes did not end the trade between the Iberian Peninsula and the Netherlands. However, the application of these embargoes in Andalusia reveals an aspect that historians have tended to overlook: there were arbitrary confiscations that targeted any north European shipmaster and the royal treasury usually compensated for the losses of those seizures. Embargoes did not just seek to undermine the economy of the enemies; they were primarily a tool of the monarchy to obtain resources for war at sea.

The predatory strategies proved very effective as an urgent solution for obtaining supplies for the navy, yet they soon became counterproductive. Compelled by the complaints raised from Andalusia, the monarchy stopped the arbitrary confiscations and allowed the *flamencos* in Seville to contract with north European shipmasters the importation of timber and the exportation of salt in return. As a consequence of the embargo of 1574, the monarchy changed its strategy for supplying timber to the royal navy in Andalusia: from indiscriminate confiscations to a collaboration with the *Atarazanas* merchants to ensure a sufficient stock of this strategic resource, which was demanded by the ships that joined the seasonal fleets of the *Carrera* as well as by the royal navy.

This challenges the traditional interpretation of how the Habsburg navy organised strategic activities, such as the supply of naval provisions, which assumes a dichotomy between direct administration by royal officials or the outsourcing to private contractors through *asientos*. This book evidences the existence of a more complex picture of supplying mechanisms. In this case, the king allowed the creation of a wholesale market of naval provisions in Seville, which was left in the hands of those best prepared for the trade: the Flemish and German merchants residing in the *Atarazanas*. Since the 1570s, the navy began to concentrate a good deal of its logistical operations in western Andalusia, regardless of the structural incapacity of the region's shipbuilding industry, and developed a bureaucratic apparatus there. The existence of enough stock of timber was surely a reason for the increasing logistical and administrative importance of Andalusia and Seville in Spain's naval organisation. In the *Atarazanas* warehouses, royal officials obtained Baltic and Scandinavian timber for the maintenance of the armadas wintering in the region and for the construction of new royal warships in Cantabrian shipyards.

The intermediation of Seville's oligarchy was fundamental for this change of the state's strategy. Eager to consolidate a commercial connection with northern Europe, any time the monarchy's predatory practices targeted Flemish and German migrants, the city council claimed their importance for the region's economy. Seville's protests often entailed a threat: if the trade with northern Europe was disrupted, then the city's annual contribution to the royal treasury would be reduced. The complaints raised from Seville did not put an end to

Spain's commercial war against the Dutch rebels. In fact, Philip II would call for new embargoes in 1585 and 1595. However, the king was well aware of the opposition to this measure and several times called for his officials in Andalusia to turn a blind eye regarding the commercial activities of northerners.

A generalised atmosphere of toleration towards north European trade was established in western Andalusia, leading to an unprecedented rise of the Flemish and German presence there. Seville's city council regularly protected this community from the suspicion of some of Philip II's most influential advisors, who accused Flemish and German migrants of collaborating with the king's enemies. In response, the city council often argued the loyalty of these migrants and their integration as *vecinos* (citizens) of Seville and *naturales* (natives) of Castile. Those claims evidence the easy integration of Flemish and German migrants as members of the local community; from the moment they owned a house and established their permanent residence there, they were recognised as citizens.

Another important factor for explaining the growth of the Flemish and German community in Seville is the existence of an advanced contracting system. This was based on two main open-access institutions, the notaries and the royal justice, which offered Spaniards and foreigners alike contract enforcement solutions. These merchants notarised almost all aspects of their lives – from family arrangements to their participation in international trade – which illustrate their high reliance on Spain's institutional framework and their easy assimilation into it. Given the extent and diversity of the notarised deeds, it would be wrong to assume that the formalisation of agreements merely sought to build trust between parties. On the contrary, most notarial deeds, including those involving international trade, seemed to have followed a more practical aim: to build reputation by providing information to third parties about an agreement and those who participated in it. As the scale of trade increased, and merchants became involved in more complex networks of relations, notarial deeds represented a useful means of sharing and disseminating information about economic operations, to enforce existing agreements and prompt new ones.

But was the market of Seville an open one? It would be wrong to assume that the existence of open-access institutions necessarily led to the emergence of an open market. The absence of such an open market is evident in both the trade with northern Europe and with the Americas. On the one hand, even if Seville managed to bypass the monarchy's prohibitions, trade with northern Europe was prohibited several times during the period. The king allowed this trade to occur, only in a dissimulated manner, by collaborating with a small group of merchants. As a result of this collaboration, the king and Seville's oligarchy favoured the merchants residing in the *Atarazanas* with advantages, such as the renting of the warehouses and of the taxes on timber sales. Thus, the group of *flamencos* residing in the *Atarazanas* had a privileged position in the market, which they used to their advantage trying to avoid external competition. On the other hand, commerce with the Americas remained restricted to Spanish natives. It is true that foreigners who successfully integrated into Seville's local society encountered little opposition, but problems could always arise with royal officials of the *Carrera de Indias,* as it occurred to Manas Enríquez.

The possibility of trading with the Americas, as historians have traditionally argued, surely attracted the migration of foreigners to Seville, but a developed institutional framework together with the support of the local oligarchy created an adequate environment for their integration. As such, this book emphasises the role of local authorities in attracting international merchants and creating a convenient context for long-distance trade. However, the question of how open the Andalusian market was is still to be researched. Early modern Andalusia would no doubt offer a fascinating case study for understanding to what extent the opening of global maritime routes reinforced connections among the main commercial centres in Europe, leading to the homogenization of contracting practices across the continent, and probably of open-access institutions, like the notary public.

The writing of this microhistory about the *Atarazanas* merchants was possible thanks to the extensive traces they left in Seville's notarial records. The many and diverse deeds studied in this research reflect personal stories and experiences that I have tried to encapsulate in this book in order to understand how merchants in the sixteenth century moved, traded and sometimes thrived. But, by writing the history of these *flamencos*, I have also attempted to write the history of a city and a region that, just like these individuals, went through profound transformations in the last third of the sixteenth century. This is, in short, a history of how individuals, cities and empires adapted to the challenges of war and the risks of trade in the Early Modern Period. Far from hindering the relations between southern and northern Europe, the war between Spain and the Dutch Republic boosted the commercial activity of Flemish and German migrants in Andalusia, turning the region into a bridge that brought northern Europe, the Mediterranean and America closer.

Annexes

A   List of *Atarazanas* Merchants

Merchant	Origin (nation)	Married to	Residence in Seville (period)	Death
Conrado Ledes	(Flemish)	Francisca Ysaac	Triana (1580s-1593)	1593
Cornieles Valdovinos	Vlissingen (Flemish)	Catalina Hedebaut	Atarazanas (1570s)	1580
Cornieles Jansen	Antwerp (Flemish)		San Telmo (1590s …)	17thCent
Cornieles Lamberto	(Flemish)		(1590s)	1600
Enrique Aparte	Antwerp (Flemish)	Vigna Sarens, Ana van Aca, Elvira Jacome, Bárbola Br.	Atarazanas (1560s-1581)	1581
Esteban Jansen	Danzig (German)	Catalina Aparte, Isabel de Lorenzana	Atarazanas (1575–1596)	1596
Federico Hinquel	(German)	Margarita Apart	(1590s …)	17thCent
Felipe Sarens	(Flemish)	Ana Jans de Breda	Atarazanas (1565–1585)	1585
Francisco Bernal	Bruges (Flemish)	Bárbola Gomar	Atarazanas (1550s-1587)	1587
Francisco Roelant	Cologne? (German)	Catalina Hedebout	Atarazanas (1570s-1590s …)	17thCent
Gertruds de Angelberto	Puerto de Sta. María	Widow of Manas Enríquez	Atarazanas (1590s …)	17thCent
Guillermo Corinse	Amsterdam (Flemish)	Margarita Sarens	Atarazanas (1577–1598)	1598
Jaques Nicolás	Utrecht (Flemish)	Ana Jacome, Bárbola Bernal	Atarazanas (1568–1590s …)	17thCent

© KONINKLIJKE BRILL NV, LEIDEN, 2022 | DOI:10.1163/9789004504110_010

Merchant	Origin (nation)	Married to	Residence in Seville (period)	Death
Jaques Sesbaut	(Flemish)		Corral de Jerez (1590s-1600)	1600
Juan Bernal	Bruges (Flemish)		Atarazanas (1590s …)	17thCent
Juan de Bestoven	Sanlúcar (Flemish)	María de Luna	Atarazanas (1580s-1599)	1599
Justo de Bil	Worcum (Flemish)		Corral de Jerez (1590s …)	1604
Juan Gras	Antwerp (Flemish)		Triana (1590s …)	17thCent
Juan Jacart	Lille (Flemish)	Bárbola Bambel, Beatriz Núñez	Atarazanas (1560s-1580)	1580
Juan Leclerque	(Flemish)	Francisca Seuste	San Vicente (1580s-1590s …)	17thCent
Juan Sarens	Seville (Flemish)	Isabel de Lorenzana	(1590s …)	17thCent
Juan Sesbaut	(Flemish)		Corral de Jerez (1580s-1593)	1593
Juan van Hooren	Amsterdam (Flemish)	Isabel Arbaut	(1580s-1590s …)	17thCent
Manas Enríquez	(Flemish)	Gertruds de Angelberto	Atarazanas (1580s-1592)	1592
Melchor de los Reyes	(Flemish)		Corral de Jerez (1590s …)	1600s
Miguel Arbauts	(Flemish)		Atarazanas (1550s-1594)	1594
Nicolás de Melemburque	Middelburg (Flemish)	Francisca de Bestoven	Atarazanas (1560s-1578)	1578
Pedro Gisberto	(Flemish)	Isabel Arbaut	Atarazanas (1584–1596)	1596
Simón Enríquez	(Flemish)	María Pantoja	Atarazanas (1580s-1600)	1600
Tobías Buc	Amsterdam (Flemish)	Ana Martínez	Atarazanas (1580s-1590s …)	17thCent

B   Glossary of Timber Products and Other Naval Provisions

Name of product in Spanish	Translation/type of product in English
Alquitrán	Pitch
Árbol(es)	Tree
Barraganete	Deck coaming
Berlinga(s)	Type of yard
Borne(s)	Oak tree
Brea	Tar
Cable(s)	Cable
Calabrote	Small cable
Cáñamo	Hemp
Espigón	?
Entena(s)	Type of yard
Guindalesa	Hawser
Jarcia	Cordage
Mástil(es)	Mast
Palo(s)	Spar
Pino(s)	Pine
Posavergas	Yard-holders
Remo(s)	Oar
Tabla(s) de pino	Pine planks
Tabla(s) de prusa	Planks from Prussia
Tabla(s) de roble	Oak planks
Tripitrape(s)	Pipe stave
Verga(s)	Yard
Viga(s)	Beam

C   Units

Quintal	Castilian weight measure used for rigging, tar and pitch; equivalent to 46 kilograms.
Barril	Castilian liquid measure used for tar and pitch; probably equivalent to about 35 litres.
Fanega	Castilian dry measure used for grain; equivalent to 55,5 litres.
Cahíz	Castilian dry measure used for salt. 1 cahiz = 12 fanegas (there are regional differences)
Last	Dutch unit of tonnage to measure capacity for ships.
Tonelada	Unit of tonnage, used in Andalusia and the Americas. In the text, it is translated as ton.
Rijksdaalder	Dutch silver coin.
Carolusgulden	Dutch golden or silver coin. 1 Carolusgulden = ca. 2.5 rijksdaalder.
Maravedí	Smallest unit of money of account in Castile.
Real	Silver coin. 1 real = 34 maravedís.
Ducado	Money of account in Spain. 1 ducado = 11 reales or 375 maravedís.

D   Archival References of Testaments

Cornieles Valdovinos	AHPSe, SP, 16712, 1288r
Felipe Sarens	AHPSe, SP, 19976, 501r
Nicolás de Melemburque	AHPSe, SP, 7771, 342r
Enrique Aparte	AHPSe, SP, 9227, 891r
Adriana Enríquez	AHPSe, SP, 9246, 1106r
Diego de Apontes	AHPSe, SP, 9250, 395r
Francisco Bernal	AHPSe, SP, 9251P, 73r
Jaques Enríquez	AHPSe, SP, 9265, 526r
Catalina Enríquez	AHPSe, SP, 9266, 523r
Pedro Gisberto	AHPSe, SP, 9272, 815r

Esteban Jansen and Catalina Aparte	AHPSe, SP, 9275, 213r
Esteban Jansen	AHPSe, SP, 9289P, 714
Miguel Arbauts	AHPSe, SP, 9276, 165r
Juan Sesbaut	AHPSe, SP, 9277, 942r
Federico Cornieles	AHPSe, SP, 9291, 488r; 9294, 558r
Justo de Bil	AHPSe, SP, 9301, 332r
Juan de Bestoven	AHPSe, SP, 9303, 122r
Jaques Sesbaut	AHPSe, SP, 9310, 163r
Cornieles Lamberto (Executors' activity)	AHPSe, SP, 9310P, 578v
Simón Enríquez	AHPSe, SP, 9312, 517r
Giles de Han	AHPSe, SP, 9526, 479v
Juan Hoben	AHPSe, SP, 9526, 607v
Guillermo Corinse	AHPSe, SP, 9977, 739r

E   Archival References of Dowry Promises

Germán de Frisia to Luis Jacart	AHPSe, SP, 7764, 234r
Bárbola Bernal to Carlos Malapert	AHPSe, SP, 7768, 173r
Enrique Aparte to Bautista Búcar	AHPSe, SP, 7770, 608r
Enrique Aparte to Esteban Jansen	AHPSe, SP, 7781, 947r
Margarita Aparte to Guillermo Estalengue	AHPSe, SP, 9215,558r
Francisco Bernal to Pedro Escolín	AHPSe, SP, 9216, 851r
Francisco Bernal to Jaques Nicolás	AHPSe, SP, 9224, 1143r
Miguel Arbauts to Pedro Monel	AHPSe, SP, 9228, 192r
Miguel Arbauts to Pedro Gisberto	AHPSe, SP, 9241, 801r
Guillermo de Lunia Juan de Bestoven	AHPSe, SP, 9245, 1165r
Miguel Arbauts to Silveetre de Gamarra	AHPSe, SP, 9252, 622r
Miguel Arbauts to Juan Bermero	AHPSe, SP, 9267, 789v
Elías Sirman to Juan van den Brug	AHPSe, SP, 9279, 1059r
Jaques Nicolas to Miguel Arbauts Jr	AHPSe, SP, 9298, 103r
Isabel Arbauts to Juan van Hooren	AHPSe, SP, 9298P, 590r
Margarita Sarens to Federico Hinquel	AHPSe, SP, 9306, 818r
Jaques Nicolás to Nicolás Antonio	AHPSe, SP, 9312, 520r

F   Archival References of Partnership Contracts

Geronimo Andrea & Cornieles Valdovinos	AHPSe, SP, 7775, 203r
Nicolás de Melemburque & Juan Jacart	AHPSe, SP, 7780, 281r
Jaques Enríquez & Simón Enríquez (POA)	AHPSe, SP, 9266, 910r
Esteban Jansen & Juan Esteban, Catalina Ruiz	AHPSe, SP, 9267, 225r
Simón Enríquez & Cornieles Jansen	AHPSe, SP, 9270, 722r
Miguel Arbauts & Francisco Ustarte	AHPSe, SP, 9279, 88r
Jaques Nicolás & Elias Sirman & Juan Gras	AHPSe, SP, 9282, 477r
Juan de Bestoven & Bernal Pérez	AHPSe, SP, 9298, 764v

G   Archival References of *Finiquitos*

Francisco Bernal & Nicolás de Melemburque	AHPSe, SP, 9217, 249r
Juan Jacart & Miguel Arbauts	AHPSe, SP, 9217, 919v
Cornieles Valdovinos & Juan de Bos	AHPSe, SP, 9219, 727r
Esteban Jansen & Sibol Wonderer	AHPSe, SP, 9237, 864r
Jaques Enríquez & Simón Enríquez	AHPSe, SP, 9266, 908r
Jaques Nicolas & Juan Bestoven	AHPSe, SP, 9269, 360v
Simón Enríquez & Jaques Giraldo	AHPSe, SP, 9272, 297v
Nicolás Estal & Justo de Bil	AHPSe, SP, 9290, 311r
Rodrigo Groenenberg & Justo de Bil	AHPSe, SP, 9293, 364r
Conrado Hinquel & Juan de Bestoven	AHPSe, SP, 9293, 404r
Conrado Hinquel & Francisco Roelant	AHPSe, SP, 9293, 885r
Jaques Sesbaut & Justo de Bil	AHPSe, , 9310, 63r
Juan Jacart & Francisco Bernal	AHPSe, SP, 7784, 1185v

H   Archival References of Slave Sales

Juan	AHPSe, SP, 7764, 500r
Francisco	AHPSe, SP, 7768, 782r
Luisa	AHPSe, SP, 7770, 130r
Catalina	AHPSe, SP, 7772, 868r
Ynés	AHPSe, SP, 7776, 743r
Miguel	AHPSe, SP, 7779, 907r
Pedro de Lasove and Felipa de Maricongo	AHPSe, SP, 9215, 870r
Juan	AHPSe, SP, 9218, 1129r
Pedro	AHPSe, SP, 9219, 563r
Juan	AHPSe, SP, 9226, 126r
Catalina and her daughter, Sebastiana	AHPSe, SP, 9232, 563r
Isabel	AHPSe, SP, 9242, 156r
Blanca	AHPSe, SP, 9248, 925r
Francisco	AHPSe, SP, 9256, 77r
Antón	AHPSe, SP, 9256, 778r
María and her baby, Francisco	AHPSe, SP, 9256, 780r
Esperança	AHPSe, SP, 9257, 321r
Antona	AHPSe, SP, 9257, 855v
Juan	AHPSe, SP, 9526, 165r
Ysabel	AHPSe, SP, 9272, 563r
Juan	AHPSe, SP, 9283, 663r
Francisco	AHPSe, SP, 9284, 669r
María	AHPSe, SP, 9286, 486r
Ana	AHPSe, SP, 9287, 51r
Ysabel	AHPSe, SP, 9287, 994r
Juana	AHPSe, SP, 9293, 453r
Juan	AHPSe, SP, 9291, 811r
Juan	AHPSe, SP, 9299, 376r
María Brama	AHPSe, SP, 9300, 381r

Digital Resources

All accessed on June 12, 2020:
Biblioteca Digital Hispánica, https://bdh.bne.es
Biblioteca Virtual del Patrimonio Bibliográfico https://bvpb.mcu.es/es/inicio/inicio.do
Diccionario de la Lengua Española, https://dle.rae.es
Museo del Prado, https://www.museodelprado.es/coleccion
Nuevo Tesoro Lexicográfico de la Lengua Española, Real Academia Española, http://ntlle.rae.es
Oxford English Dictionary, https://www.lexico.com
Wikimedia Commons, https://commons.wikimedia.org

Bibliography

Abadía Flores, Carolina. "La comunidad flamenca en Sevilla en el siglo XVI." *Archivo hispalense: Revista histórica, literaria y artística* 93, no. 282–284 (2010): 173–192.

Abreu, Pedro de, and Manuel Bustos Rodríguez. *Historia del saqueo de Cádiz por los ingleses en 1596*. Cádiz: Universidad de Cádiz, Servicio de Publicaciones, 2017.

Aglietti, Marcella. "El debate sobre la jurisdicción consular en la Monarquía hispánica (1759–1769)." In *Los cónsules de extranjeros en la Edad Moderna y principios de la Edad Contemporánea*, edited by Marcella Aglietti, Manuel Herrero Sánchez, and Francisco Zamora Rodríguez, 105–118. Madrid: Doce Calles, 2013.

Aguado de los Reyes, Jesús. *Fortuna y miseria en la Sevilla del siglo XVII*. Sevilla: Ayuntamiento de Sevilla, 1996.

Albardonedo Freire, Antonio José. *El urbanismo de Sevilla durante el reinado de Felipe II*. Sevilla: Guadalquivir Ediciones, 2002.

Alcalá-Zamora Queipo de Llano, José. *España, Flandes y el Mar del Norte (1618–1639): La última ofensiva europea de los Austrias madrileños*. Barcelona: Planeta, 1975.

Alloza Aparicio, Ángel. "Guerra económica y proteccionismo en la Europa del siglo XVII: El decreto de Gauna a la luz de los documentos contables." *Tiempos modernos: Revista Electrónica de Historia Moderna* 7, no. 24 (2012): 1–34.

Alvarez Nogal, Carlos. "Los bancos públicos de Castilla y el decreto de 1575." *Cuadernos de Historia Moderna* 42, no. 2 (2017): 527–551.

Alvarez Nogal, Carlos. *Los banqueros de Felipe IV y los metales preciosos americanos (1621–1665)*. Madrid: Banco de España, 1997.

Álvarez Nogal, Carlos, and Christopher Chamley. "Philip II against the Cortes and the Credit Freeze of 1575–1577." *Revista de Historia Económica - Journal of Iberian and Latin American Economic History* 34, no. 3 (2016): 351–382.

Amelang, James S. "The Peculiarities of the Spaniards Historical Approaches to the Early Modern State" In *Public power in Europe studies in historical transformations*, edited by James S. Amelang, 39–56. Pisa: Plus-Pisa University Press, 2006.

Amores Carredano, Fernando, and Agustina Quirós Esteban "Las Atarazanas: El tiempo y los usos." In *Recuperando las Atarazanas: Un monumento para la cultura* (Exposition: Seville, April 13-May 30 1999). Sevilla: Consejería de Cultura, 1999.

Antón Solé, Pablo. "El saqueo de Cádiz por los ingleses en 1596, y la Casa de la Contratación de las Indias de Sevilla." *Archivo hispalense: Revista histórica, literaria y artística* 54, no. 166 (1971): 219–232.

Antunes, Cátia. "Cross-Cultural Business Cooperation." In *Religion and Trade: Cross-Cultural Exchanges in World History, 1000–1900*, edited by Francesca Trivellato, Leor Halevi, and Cátia Antunes, 150–168. New York: Oxford University Press, 2014.

Antunes, Cátia, and Amélia Polónia. *Beyond Empires: Global, Self-Organizing, Cross-Imperial Networks, 1500–1800*. Leiden: Brill, 2016.

Appuhn, Karl Richard. *A Forest on the Sea: Environmental Expertise in Renaissance Venice*. Baltimore: Johns Hopkins University Press, 2009.

Aragón Ruano, Álvaro. "Transformaciones económicas en el sector costero guipuzco-ano central." *Manuscrits: Revista d'història moderna*, no. 26 (2008): 191–236.

Aragón Ruano, Álvaro, and Alberto Angulo Morales, eds. *Recuperando el Norte: empresas, capitales y proyectos atlánticos en la economía imperial hispánica*. Bilbao: Universidad del País Vasco, 2016.

Aram, Bethany. "La identificación y ocultación de extranjeros tras el ataque anglo-holandés de 1596." *Tiempos modernos: Revista Electrónica de Historia Moderna* 8, no. 31 (2015): 3–62.

Aranda y Antón, Gaspar de. *Los bosques flotantes: Historia de un roble del siglo XVIII*. Madrid: ICONA, 1990.

Arnade, Peter. *Beggars, Iconoclasts, and Civic Patriots: The Political Culture of the Dutch Revolt*. New York: Cornell University Press, 2008.

Artíñano y Galdácano, Gervasio de. *La arquitectura naval española (en madera): Bosquejo de sus condiciones y rasgos de su evolución*. Barcelona: Oliva de Vilanova, 1920.

Baetens, Roland. "The Organization and Effects of Flemish Privateering in the Seventeenth Century." *Acta Historiae Neerlandicae* 9 (1976), 48–75.

Baetens, Roland. "El desarrollo social y económico de Flandes durante los siglos XV, XVI y principios del XVII." In *Encuentros en Flandes: Relaciones e intercambios hispanoflamencos a inicios de la Edad Moderna*, edited by Werner Thomas, and Robert A. Verdonk, 75–88. Leuven: Leuven University Press, 2000.

Bang, Nina E. *Tabeller Over Skibsfart Og Varetransport Gennem Øresund, 1497–1660: Udarbejdede Efter De Bevarede Regnskaber Over Øresundstolden*. Copenhagen: Gyldendal, 1906.

Barkham, Michael M. *Report on 16th Century Spanish Basque Shipbuilding, c. 1550 to c. 1600*. Ottawa: Parks Canada, 1981.

Bello León, Juan Manuel. "El reino de Sevilla en el comercio exterior castellano (siglos XIV-XV)." In *Castilla y Europa: comercio y mercaderes en los siglos XIV, XV y XVI*, edited by Hilario Casado Alonso, 57–80. Diputación de Burgos: Burgos, 1995.

Bello León, Juan Manuel. "Comerciantes y artesanos de los Países Bajos en Castilla y Portugal (siglos XIII a XVI). Los precedentes de su paso a Canarias." In *Flandes y Canarias. Nuestros orígenes nórdicos*, edited by Manuel de Paz Sánchez, 111–152. Santa Cruz de Tenerife: Centro de la Cultura Popular Canaria, 2004.

Bernal Rodríguez, Antonio Miguel. *La Financiación de la Carrera de Indias (1492–1824): Dinero y crédito en el comercio colonial español con América*. Sevilla: Fundación El Monte, 1992.

Bonney, Richard, ed. *The rise of the fiscal state in Europe, c. 1200–1815*. Oxford: Oxford University Press, 1999.

Boyajian, James C. *Portuguese Bankers at the Court of Spain, 1626–1650*. New Brunswick: Rutgers University Press, 1983.

Brandon, Pepijn. *War, Capital, and the Dutch State (1588–1795)*. Leiden: Brill, 2015.

Braudel, Fernand. La *Méditerranée et le monde méditerranéen à l'époque de Philippe II*. Paris: A. Colin, 1982.

Braudel, Fernand. *Civilization and Capitalism, 15th-18th Century. Vol. II: The Wheels of Commerce*. London: W. Collins, 1982.

Brewer, John. *The Sinews of Power: War, Money and the English State, 1688–1783*. London: Hyman, 1989.

Brulez, Wilfrid. "De Diaspora der Antwerpse Kooplui op het Einde van de 16e eeuw." *Bijdragen voor de geschiedenis der Nederlanden* 15 (1960): 461–491.

Brulez, Wilfrid. *De firma della Faille en de internationale handel van vlaamse firma's in de 16e eeuw*. Brussels: Paleis Der Academiën, 1959.

Brulez, Wilfrid. "La navigation flamande vers la Méditerranée à la fin du XVIe siècle." *Revue belge de philologie et d'histoire* 36, no. 4 (1958): 1210–1242.

Bustos Rodríguez, Manuel. "La problemática acerca de los comerciantes de la Carrera de Indias," in *Comunicaciones transnacionales. Colonias de Mercaderes extranjeros en el Mundo Atlántico (1500–1830)*, edited by Ana Crespo Solana, 29–45. Madrid: Doce Calles, 2010.

Cachero Vinuesa, Montserrat. "Should we trust? Explaining trade expansion in early modern Spain: Seville, 1500–1600." PhD diss., European University Institute, Florence, 2010.

Carande, Ramón. *Carlos V y sus banqueros*. Barcelona: Crítica, 1977.

Cardim, Pedro, Tamar Herzog, José Javier Ruiz Ibáñez, and Gaetano Sabatini. *Polycentric Monarchies: How Did Early Modern Spain and Portugal Achieve and Maintain a Global Hegemony?* Brighton: Sussex Academic Press, 2012.

Casado Alonso, Hilario. "Los agentes castellanos en los puertos atlánticos: los ejemplos de Burdeos y de los Países Bajos (siglos XV y XVI)." In *Navegación y puertos en época medieval y moderna*, edited by Adela Fábregas García, 163–194. Granada: La Nao, 2012.

Casado Alonso, Hilario. *El triunfo de Mercurio: la presencia castellana en Europa : (siglos XV y XVI)*. Burgos: Cajacírculo, 2003.

Casado Alonso, Hilario. "Las colonias de mercaderes castellanos en Europa (siglos XV y XVI)." In *Castilla y Europa: comercio y mercaderes en los siglos XIV, XV y XVI*, edited by Casado Alonso, 15–56. Burgos: Diputación de Burgos, 1995.

Casado Alonso, Hilario. "El comercio internacional burgalés en los siglos XV y XVI." In *Actas del V Centenario del Consulado de Burgos (1494–1994)*, edited by Floriano Ballesteros Caballero, Hilario Casado Alonso, and Alberto C. Ibáñez Pérez, 175–248. Burgos: Diputación Provincial de Burgos, 1994.

Casado Soto, José Luis. "Barcos para la guerra: Soporte de la monarquía hispánica." *Cuadernos de Historia Moderna. Anejos*, no. 5 (2006): 15–53.

Casado Soto, José Luis. *Los barcos españoles del siglo XVI y la Gran Armada de 1588*. Madrid: San Martín, 1988.

Casado Soto, José Luis. "La construcción naval atlántica española y la Armada de 1588." *Cuadernos monográficos del Instituto de Historia y Cultura Naval* 3 (November 1988): 51–85.

Castillo Rubio, Juan Manuel, and Germán Jiménez Montes. "La construcción de un entrepôt: Organización urbana de los mercaderes extranjeros en Sevilla en la segunda mitad del siglo XVI." In *Monarquías en conflicto. Linajes y noblezas en la articulación de la Monarquía Hispánica*, edited by Fortea Pérez, J. I. et al, 325–335. Madrid, Fundación Historia Moderna, 2018.

Chaunu, Pierre. "Séville et la Belgique (1555–1648)." *Revue du Nord* 42 (1960): 259–292.

Chaunu, Huguette, Pierre Chaunu, and Guy Arbellot. *Séville et l'Atlantique, 1504–1650*. Paris: A. Colin, 1955–1959.

Chaunu, Huguette, and Pierre Chaunu. *Séville et l'Amérique aux XVIe et XVIIe Siècles*. Paris: Flammarion, 1977.

Christensen, Aksel Erhardt. *Dutch Trade to the Baltic About 1600: Studies in the Sound Toll Register and Dutch Shipping Records*. Copenhagen: Einar Munksgaard, 1941.

Concha Martínez, Ignacio de la. "El Almirantazgo de Sevilla. Notas para el estudio de las instituciones mercantiles en la Edad Moderna." *Anuario de Historia del Derecho Español* 19 (1948): 459–525.

Cózar Gutiérrez, Ramón. " 'De lo que yo el infrascripto escribano doy fe:' Los escribanos de la Villa de Albacete durante el siglo XVIII." *Revista de historia moderna: Anales de la Universidad de Alicante*, no. 28 (2010): 269–299.

Crailsheim, Eberhard. *The Spanish Connection: French and Flemish Merchant Networks in Seville (1570–1650)*. Cologne: Böhlau Verlag, 2016.

Crailsheim, Eberhard. "Extranjeros entre dos mundos: Una aproximación proporcional a las colonias de mercaderes extranjeros en Sevilla, 1570–1650." *Jahrbuch für Geschichte Lateinamerikas* 48 (2011): 179- 202.

Crailsheim, Eberhard. "Behind the Atlantic Expansion: Flemish Trade Connections of Seville in 1620." *Research in Maritime History* 43 (2010): 21–46.

Crespo Solana, Ana. "Wood Resources, shipbuilding and Social Environment: The Historical context of the ForSEAdiscovery Project." *SKYLLIS. Journal of the German Society for the Promotion of Underwater Archaeology* 15, no. 1 (2015): 52–61.

Crespo Solana, Ana. "El concepto de ciudadanía y la idea de nación según la comunidad flamenca de la Monarquía hispánica." In *Las corporaciones de nación en la Monarquía Hispánica (1580–1750)*, edited by Bernardo J. García García, and Óscar Recio Morales, 389–413. Madrid: Fundación Carlos de Amberes, 2014.

Crespo Solana, Ana. "El juez conservador ¿una alternativa al cónsul de la nación?" In *Los cónsules de extranjeros en la Edad Moderna y principios de la Edad Contemporánea*, edited by Marcella Aglietti, Manuel Herrero Sánchez, and Francisco Zamora Rodríguez, 23–34. Madrid: Doce Calles, 2013.

Crespo Solana, Ana. "Elementos de transnacionalidad en el comercio flamenco-holandés en Europa y la Monarquía Hispánica." *Cuadernos de Historia Moderna. Anejos* 10 (2011): 55–76.

Crespo Solana, Ana. "Merchants and Observers: The Dutch Republic's Commercial Interests in Spain and the Merchant Community in Cádiz in the Eighteenth Century." *Dieciocho: Hispanic enlightenment* 32, no. 2 (2009): 193–224.

Crespo Solana, Ana. "El comercio holandés y la integración de espacios económicos entre Cádiz y el Báltico en tiempos de guerra (1699–1723)." *Investigaciones de historia económica: Revista de la Asociación Española de Historia Económica*, no. 8 (2007) 45–76.

Crespo Solana, Ana. "Flandes y la expansión mercantil europea: Naturaleza de una red atlántica. Siglos XV-XVI." In *Flandes y Canarias, nuestros orígenes nórdicos*, edited by Manuel de Paz-Sánchez, 13–83. Santa Cruz de Tenerife: Centro de la Cultura Popular Canaria, 2004.

Crespo Solana, Ana. "Nación extranjera y cofradía de mercaderes: el rostro piadoso de la integración social." In *Los extranjeros en la España moderna: actas del I Coloquio Internacional, celebrado en Málaga del 28 al 30 de noviembre de 2002*, edited by María Begoña Villar García, and Pilar Pezzi Cristóbal, 175–187. Madrid: Ministerio de Ciencia e Innovación, 2003.

Crespo Solana, Ana. *Entre Cádiz y los Países Bajos: una comunidad mercantil en la ciudad de la ilustración*. Cádiz: Fundación Municipal de Cultura del Ayuntamiento de Cádiz, 2001.

Crespo Solana, Ana. "La acción de José Patiño en Cádiz y los proyectos navales de la Corona del siglo XVIII." *Trocadero: Revista de historia moderna y contemporanea* no. 6–7 (1994-1995): 35–50.

Crespo Solana, Ana, and Manuel Herrero Sánchez, eds. *España y las 17 provincias de los Países Bajos: una revisión historiográfica (XVI-XVIII)*. Córdoba: Universidad de Córdoba, 2002.

Degryse, Karel. *Pieter Seghers: Een Koopmansleven in Troebele Tijden*. Antwerpen: Hadewijch, 1990.

Díaz Blanco, José Manuel. "La construcción de una institución comercial: El consulado de las naciones flamenca y alemana en la Sevilla moderna." *Revista de historia moderna: Anales de la Universidad de Alicante*, no. 33 (2015): 123–145.

Díaz Blanco, José Manuel. "Una armada de galeras para la Carrera de Indias: El Mediterráneo y el comercio colonial en tiempos de Felipe II." *Revista de Indias* 74, no. 262 (2014): 661–692.

Díaz Blanco, José Manuel. *Así trocaste tu gloria: Guerra y comercio colonial en la España del siglo XVII*. Madrid: Marcial Pons, 2012.

Díaz Blanco, José Manuel, and Manuel F. Fernández Chaves, "Una élite en la sombra: Los comerciantes extranjeros en la Sevilla de Felipe III." In *Las élites en la época moderna, la Monarquía española. Volumen 3: Economía y poder*, edited by Enrique Soria Mesa et al, 35–50. Córdoba: Universidad de Córdoba, 2009.

Dijkman, Jessica, Jeroen Puttevils, and Wouter Ryckbosch. "Cities of Commerce: An Introduction to the Articles." *TSEG/Low Countries Journal of Social and Economic History* 11, no. 4 (2014): 55–59.

Domínguez Ortiz, Antonio. *Los extranjeros en la vida española durante el siglo XVII y otros artículos*. Seville: Diputación de Sevilla, 1996.

Domínguez Ortiz, Antonio. *Orto y ocaso de Sevilla*. Sevilla: Universidad de Sevilla, 1991.

Domínguez Ortiz, Antonio. "La concesión de naturalezas para comerciar en Indias durante el siglo XVIII." *Revista de Indias* 19, no. 76 (1959): 227–239.

Donoso Anes, Rafael "El papel del tesorero en el desarrollo contable de la Casa de la Contratación." In *La Casa de la Contratación y la navegación entre España y las Indias*, edited by Enriqueta Vila Vilar, Antonio Acosta Rodríguez, and Adolfo L. González Rodríguez, 67–100. Sevilla: CSIC and Universidad de Sevilla, 2004.

Drelichman, Mauricio and Hans-Joachim Voth. "The Sustainable Debts of Philip II: A Reconstruction of Castile's Fiscal Position, 1566–1596." *The Journal of Economic History* 70, no. 4 (2010): 813–42.

Dufournaud, Nicole, and Bernard Michon. "Les femmes et le commerce maritime a Nantes (1660–1740): un role largement meconnu." *Clio. Femmes, Genre, Histoire* no. 23 (2006): 311–330.

Dunthorne, Hugh. *Britain and the Dutch Revolt, 1560–1700*. Cambridge: Cambridge University Press, 2013.

Ebert, Christopher. *Between Empires: Brazilian Sugar in the Early Atlantic Economy, 1550–1630*. Leiden: Brill, 2008.

Ebert, Christopher. "Dutch Trade with Brazil before the Dutch West India Company, 1587–1621." In *Riches from Atlantic Commerce: Dutch Transatlantic Trade and Shipping, 1585–1817*, edited by Johannes Postma and Victor Enthoven, 49–75. Leiden: Brill, 2003.

Echevarría Bacigalupe, Miguel Ángel. "Presentación: Guerra y Economía en Flandes, siglos XVI y XVII." *Studia Historica, Historia moderna* no. 27 (2005): 17–23.

Echevarría Bacigalupe, Miguel Ángel. "Un episodio en la guerra económica hispano-holandesa: El Decreto Gauna (1603)", *Hispania: Revista española de historia* 46, no. 162 (1986): 57–98.

Echevarría Bacigalupe, Miguel Ángel. *Flandes y la Monarquía Hispánica, 1500–1713*. Madrid: Sílex, 1998.

Elliott, John H. "A Europe of Composite Monarchies." *Past & Present*, no. 137 (November, 1992): 48–71.

Elliott, John H. *Europe Divided 1559–1598*. London: Fontana, 1968.

Eloire, Fabien, Claire Lemercier, and Veronica A. Santarosa. "Beyond the Personal-Anonymous Divide: Agency Relations in Powers of Attorney in France in the Eighteenth and Nineteenth Centuries." *Economic History Review* 72, no. 4 (November 2019): 1229–1250.

Eltis, David. *The Military Revolution in Sixteenth-Century Europe*. London: Tauris Academic Studies, 1995.

Engels, Marie-Christine. *Merchants, Interlopers, Seamen and Corsairs: The 'flemish' Community in Livorno and Genoa (1615–1635)*. Verloren: Hilversum, 1997.

Espiau Eizaguirre, Mercedes. *La Casa de la Moneda de Sevilla y su entorno: Historia y morfología*. Sevilla: Universidad de Sevilla, 1991.

Esser, Raingard. "From Province to Nation: Immigration in the Dutch Republic in the Late 16th and Early 17th Centuries." In *Imagining Frontiers, Contesting Identities, vol. 2*, edited by Steven G. Ellis, and Ludá Klusáková, 263–276. Pisa: Pisa University Press, 2006.

Esser, Raingard. "Antwerpens "Altweibersommer." Wirtschaft und Kultur in der Scheldestadt zwischen "Fall" (1585) und "Frieden" (1648)." *Wolfenbuetteler Barock-Nachrichten* 43, no.1 (2016): 65–84.

Everaert, Janna. "A Trail of Trials. A 'Flemish' Merchant Community in Sixteenth-century Valladolid and Medina del Campo." *TSEG/ Low Countries Journal of Social and Economic History* 14 no. 1 (2017) 5–35.

Everaert, John G. "Infraction au monopole?: Cargadores-navegantes flamands sur la Carrera de Indias (XVIIe siècle)." In *La Casa de la Contratación y la navegación entre España y las Indias*, edited by Enriqueta Vila Vilar, Antonio Acosta Rodríguez, and Adolfo L. González Rodríguez, 761–777. Sevilla: CSIC and Universidad de Sevilla, 2004.

Extremera Extremera, Miguel Angel. "Los escribanos de Castilla en la Edad Moderna. Nuevas líneas de investigación." *Chronica nova: Revista de historia moderna de la Universidad de Granada*, no. 28 (2001): 159–184.

Fagel, Raymond. "La Nación de Andalucía en Flandes: Separatismo comercial en el siglo XVI." In *Comercio y cultura en la Edad Moderna: Actas de la XIII Reunión Científica de la Fundación Española de Historia Moderna, vol. 2*, edited by Juan José Iglesias Rodríguez, Rafael M. Pérez García, and Manuel F. Fernández Chaves 29–41. Sevilla: Universidad de Sevilla, 2015.

Fagel, Raymond. "En busca de fortuna. La presencia de flamencos en España 1480–1560." In *Los extranjeros en la España moderna: actas del I Coloquio Internacional, celebrado en Málaga del 28 al 30 de noviembre de 2002*, edited by María Begoña

Villar García, and Pilar Pezzi Cristóbal, 325–335. Madrid: Ministerio de Ciencia e Innovación, 2003.

Fagel, Raymond. "Cornelis Deque, un mercader flamenco en la Castilla del siglo XV: un debate sobre el concepto de 'vecindad' y 'naturaleza' entre mercaderes." In *Castilla y Europa: comercio y mercaderes en los siglos XIV, XV y XVI*, edited by Hilario Casado Alonso, 241–264. Burgos: Diputación Provincial de Burgos, 1995.

Fernández Chaves, Manuel F. and Rafael F. Pérez García. "Sevilla y la trata negrera atlántica: Envíos de esclavos desde Cabo Verde a la América Española, 1569–1579." In *Estudios de Historia Moderna en homenaje al Profesor Antonio García-Baquero*, edited by León Carlos Alvarez Santaló, 597–622. Sevilla: Universidad de Sevilla, 2009.

Fernández Duro, Cesáreo. *Armada española: Desde la unión de los Reinos de Castilla y de Aragón*. Madrid: Museo Naval, 1973. http://www.armada.mde.es/html/histori aarmada.

Fortea Pérez, José Ignacio. *Monarquía y Cortes en la Corona de Castilla: las ciudades ante la política fiscal de Felipe II*. Valladolid: Cortes de Castilla y León, 1990.

Fusaro, Maria, et al. "Entrepreneurs at Sea: Trading Practices, Legal Opportunities and Early Modern Globalization." *The International Journal of Maritime History* 28, no. 4 (2016): 774–786.

Fynn-Paul, Jeff, ed. *War, Entrepreneurs, and the State in Europe and the Mediterranean, 1300–1800*. Leiden: Brill, 2014.

Galbis Díez, María del Carmen. "Las Atarazanas de Sevilla." *Archivo hispalense: Revista histórica, literaria y artística* 35, no. 109 (1961): 155–184.

Gallagher, Nathan. "A methodology for estimating the volume of Baltic timber to Spain using the Sound Toll Registers: 1670–1806." *The International Journal of Maritime History* 28, no. 4 (2016): 752–773.

Gamero Rojas, Mercedes. "Flamencos en la Sevilla del siglo XVII: Actividades económicas entre Europa y América." In *Andalucía en el mundo Atlántico moderno: agentes y escenarios*, edited by Juan José Iglesias Rodríguez, and José Jaime García Bernal, 287–310. Madrid: Sílex, 2016.

Gamero Rojas, Mercedes. "Flamencos en la Sevilla del siglo XVII: La capilla de San Andrés." In *Comercio y cultura en la Edad Moderna: Actas de la XIII Reunión Científica de la Fundación Española de Historia Moderna, vol. 2,* edited by Juan José Iglesias Rodríguez, Rafael M. Pérez García, and Manuel F. Fernández Chaves, 715–730. Sevilla: Universidad de Sevilla, 2015.

Gamero Rojas, Mercedes, and José Jaime García Bernal, "Las corporaciones de nación en la Sevilla moderna." In *Las corporaciones de nación en la Monarquía Hispánica (1580–1750): Identidad, patronazgo y redes de sociabilidad*, edited Bernardo J. García García, and Óscar Recio Morales, 347–388. Madrid: Fundación Carlos de Amberes, 2014.

Gamero Rojas, Mercedes, and Manuel F. Fernández Chaves. "Nations? What Nations? Business in the Shaping of International Trade Networks." In *Merchants and trade networks between the Atlantic and the Mediterranean (1550–1800)*, edited by Manuel Herrero Sánchez, and Klemens Kaps, 145–168. New York: Routledge, 2016.

Gamero Rojas, Mercedes, and Manuel F. Fernández Chaves. "Flamencos en la Sevilla del siglo XVIII: Las estrategias familiares, redes clientelares y comportamientos económicos." In *Población y grupos sociales en el Antiguo Régimen, vol. 1*, edited by Juan Jesús Bravo Caro, and Luis Sanz Sampelayo, 571–586. Málaga: Universidad de Málaga, 2009.

Gamero Rojas, Mercedes, and Manuel F. Fernández Chaves. "Flamencos en la Sevilla del siglo XVIII: Entre el norte de Europa y América." In *Orbis incognitvs: avisos y legajos del Nuevo Mundo: homenaje al profesor Luis Navarro García, vol. 2*, edited by Fernando Navarro Antolín, 211–220. Huelva: Universidad de Huelva, 2007.

García Fuentes, Lutgardo. "Los vascos en la Carrera de Indias en la Edad Moderna: Una minoría predominante." *Temas americanistas*, no. 16 (2003): 29–49.

García-Baquero González, Antonio. "Los extranjeros en el tráfico con Indias: entre el rechazo legal y la tolerancia funcional." In *Los extranjeros en la España moderna: actas del I Coloquio Internacional, celebrado en Málaga del 28 al 30 de noviembre de 2002*, edited by María Begoña Villar García and Pilar Pezzi Cristóbal, 73–99. Málaga, Ministerio de Ciencia e Innovación, 2003.

García-Baquero González, Antonio. *La Carrera de Indias: Suma de la contratación y océano de negocios*. Sevilla: Algaida, 1992.

Gasch-Tomás, José L. *The Atlantic World and Manila Galleons: Circulation, Market, and Consumption of Asian Goods in the Spanish Empire 1565–1650*. Leiden: Brill, 2018.

Gasch-Tomás, José Luis, Koldo Trápaga Monchet, and Ana Rita Trindade. "Shipbuilding in Times of War: Contracts for the Construction of Ships and Provision of Supplies in the Spanish Empire in the Early Seventeenth Century." *International Journal of Maritime History* 29 no. 1 (2017): 187–192.

Gelabert González, Juan Eloy. "Guerra y coyuntura fiscal: El embargo general de 1598." In *IX Congreso de la Asociación española de Historia Económica, Murcia* (2008), 1–23.

Gelder, Maartje van. "Supplying the Serenissima: The Role of Flemish Merchants in the Venetian Grain Trade during the First Phase of the Straatvaart." *International Journal of Maritime History* 16, no. 2 (2004): 39–60.

Gelderblom, Oscar. *Cities of Commerce: The Institutional Foundations of International Trade in the Low Countries, 1250–1650*. Princeton: Princeton University Press, 2013.

Gelderblom, Oscar. "The Golden Age of the Dutch Republic." In *The Invention of Enterprise: Entrepreneurship from Ancient Mesopotamia to Modern Times*, edited by David S. Landes, Joel Mokyr, William J. Baumol, 156–181. Princeton: Princeton University Press, 2012.

Gelderblom, Oscar. "From Antwerp to Amsterdam: The Contribution of Merchants from the Southern Netherlands to the Commercial Expansion of Amsterdam (C. 1540–1609)." *Review (Fernand Braudel Center)* 26, no. 3 (2003): 247–82.

Gelderblom, Oscar. *Zuid-Nederlandse Kooplieden En De Opkomst Van De Amsterdamse Stapelmarkt (1578–1630)*. Hilversum: Verloren, 2000.

Gelderblom, Oscar. "Thinking about Cities of Commerce – A Rejoinder." *TSEG/ Low Countries Journal of Social and Economic History* 11, no. 4 (2014): 119–131.

Gelderblom, Oscar, and Regina Grafe. "The Rise and Fall of the Merchant Guilds: Rethinking the Comparative Study of Commercial Institutions in Premodern Europe." *Journal of Interdisciplinary History* 40, no. 4 (Spring 2010): 477–511.

Girard, Albert. *Le commerce français à Seville et Cadix au temps des Habsbourg: contribution a l'étude du commerce etranger en Espagne aux XVI et XVII siècles*. New York: Burt Franklin, 1967.

Girón Pascual, Rafael M. "La corte del mercader: la vivienda y el servicio doméstico de los genoveses de Granada (ss. XVI-XVII)." In *Vida cotidiana en la Monarquía Hispánica: Tiempos y espacios*, edited by Inmaculada Arias de Saavedra Alías and Miguel Luis López Guadalupe Muñoz, 293–306. Granada: Universidad de Granada, 2015.

Girón Pascual, Rafael M. "Los lavaderos de lana de Huéscar (Granada) y el comercio genovés en la edad moderna." In *Génova y la monarquía hispánica (1528–1713)*, vol. 2, edited by Manuel Herrero Sánchez, Yasmina Rocío Ben Yessef Garfia, Carlo Bitossi, and Dino Puncuh, 191–202. Genova: Società Ligure di Storia Patria, 2011.

Girón Pascual, Rafael M. *Las Indias de Génova: mercaderes genoveses en el Reino de Granada durante la Edad Moderna*. Granada: Universidad de Granada, 2013.

Girón Pascual, Rafael M. "Redes mercantiles en la Castilla del siglo XVI a través de las 'licencias de saca de lana con destino a Italia'." In *De la tierra al cielo. Líneas recientes de investigacion en historia moderna*, edited by Eliseo Serrano Martín, 757–771. Zaragoza: Fundación Española de Historia Moderna, 2013.

Glete, Jan. *War and the State in Early Modern Europe: Spain, the Dutch Republic and Sweden as Fiscal-Military States, 1500–1660*. London: Routledge, 2002.

Glete, Jan. *Warfare at Sea, 1500–1650: Maritime Conflicts and the Transformation of Europe*. London: Routledge, 2000.

Gómez-Centurión Jiménez, Carlos. *Felipe II, la empresa de Inglaterra y el comercio septentrional (1566–1609)*. Madrid: Editorial Naval, 1988.

Gómez-Centurión Jiménez, Carlos. "Las relaciones hispano-hanseáticas durante el reinado de Felipe II." *Revista de historia naval* no. 15 (1986): 65–84.

Góngora y Argote, Luis de. *Las firmezas de Isabela*. Málaga: Caja de Ahorros de Ronda, 1991. http://www.cervantesvirtual.com/obra-visor/las-firmezas-de-isabela--o/html.

González Cruz, David. "La red de salinas y el comercio de la sal en el estuario del Tinto durante la Edad Moderna: Huelva, San Juan del Puerto, Palos de la Frontera y Moguer." *Studia Historica. Historia Moderna* 42, no. 1 (2020).

González Enciso, Agustin. "Asentistas y fabricantes: El abastecimiento de armas y municiones al Estado en los siglos XVII y XVIII." *Studia historica. Historia moderna* no. 35 (2013): 269–303.

González Espinosa, Ignacio. "Andalucía como foco receptor de la población portuguesa (1580–1640). Distribución espacial y perfiles socioeconómicos." In *Movilidad, interacciones y espacios de oportunidad entre Castilla y Portugal en la Edad Moderna*, edited by Manuel Francisco Fernández Chaves and Rafael M. Pérez García, 21–40. Sevilla: Universidad de Sevilla, 2019.

González Espinosa, Ignacio. "Portugueses en Sevilla: sus oficios y profesiones durante el reinado de Felipe II." In *Comercio y cultura en la Edad Moderna: Actas de la XIII Reunión Científica de la Fundación Española de Historia Moderna, vol. 2*, edited by Juan José Iglesias Rodríguez, Rafael M. Pérez García, Manuel Francisco Fernández Chaves, 731–741. Sevilla, Universidad de Sevilla, 2015.

González Mariscal, Manuel "Inflación y niveles de vida en Sevilla durante la revolución de los precios." *Revista de Historia Económica / Journal of Iberian and Latin American Economic History* 33 n. 3 (2015): 353–386.

Goodman, David C. *Spanish Naval Power, 1589–1665: Reconstruction and Defeat.* Cambridge: Cambridge University Press, 2002.

Goris, J.A. *Étude sur les colonies marchandes méridionales (portugais, espagnols, italiens) à Anvers de 1488 à 1567: Contribution à l'histoire des débuts du capitalisme moderne.* Nueva York: Burt Franklin, 1971.

Grafe, Regina. "Was There a Market for Institutions in Early Modern European Trade?" In *Union in Separation: Diasporic Groups and Identities in the Eastern Mediterranean (1100–1800)*, edited by Georg Christ et al, 593–609. Rome: Viella, 2015.

Grafe, Regina. "On the Spatial Nature of Institutions and the Institutional Nature of Personal Networks in the Spanish Atlantic." Culture & History Digital Journal 3, no. 1 (2014): 1–11.

Grafe, Regina. "Polycentric States: The Spanish Reigns and the 'Failures' of Mercantilism." In *Mercantilism Reimagined: Political Economy in Early Modern Britain and its Empire*, edited by Philip J. Stern and Carl Wennerlind, 241–262. Oxford: Oxford University Press, 2013.

Grafe, Regina. *Distant Tyranny: Markets, Power, and Backwardness in Spain, 1650–1800.* Princeton: Princeton University Press, 2012.

Grafe, Regina. "The Strange Tale of the Decline of Spanish Shipping." In *Shipping and Economic Growth, 1350–1850*, edited by Richard W. Unger, 81–116. Leiden: Brill, 2011.

Greif, Avner. *Institutions and the Path to the Modern Economy: Lessons from Medieval Trade.* Cambridge: Cambridge University Press, 2006.

Greif, Avner. "Family Structure, Institutions, and Growth: The Origins and Implications of Western Corporations." *The American Economic Review* 96, no. 2 (2006): 308–312.

Grove Gordillo, María. "El papel de la comunidad mercantil inglesa en la industria del jabón en el Reino de Sevilla." In *Hacer historia moderna: Líneas actuales y futuras de investigación*, edited by Juan José Iglesias Rodríguez and Isabel María Melero Muñoz, 346–361. Sevilla: Universidad de Sevilla, 2020.

Hamilton, Earl J. "Revisions in Economic History: VIII-The Decline of Spain." *The Economic History Review* 8, no. 2 (1938): 168–179.

Haring, Clarence H. *Trade and Navigation between Spain and the Indies in the Time of the Hapsburgs*. Cambridge: Harvard University Press, 1918.

Herrero Sánchez, Manuel. "La Monarquía Hispánica y las repúblicas europeas: el modelo republicano en una monarquía de ciudades." In *Republicas y republicanismo en la Europa moderna (siglos XVI-XVIII)*, edited by Manuel Herrero Sánchez, Giovanni Levi, and Thomas Maissen, 273–327. Madrid: Fondo de Cultura Económica de España, 2017.

Herrero Sánchez, Manuel. "La red consular europea y la diplomacia mercantil en la Edad Moderna." In *Comercio y cultura en la Edad Moderna: Actas de la XIII Reunión Científica de la Fundación Española de Historia Moderna, Volume I*, edited by Juan José Iglesias Rodríguez, Rafael M. Pérez García, and Manuel F. Fernández Chaves, 121–150. Sevilla: Universidad de Sevilla, 2015.

Herzog, Tamar. "Maarten Prak's Citizens without Nations and the Legal History of Spain." *TSEG - The Low Countries Journal of Social and Economic History* 17, no. 3 (2020): 91–100. DOI: http://doi.org/10.18352/tseg.1169.

Herzog, Tamar. "Merchants and Citizens: On the making and Un -making of merchants in early-modern Spain and Spanish America." *Journal of european economic history* 42, no. 1 (2013): 137–164.

Herzog, Tamar. "Naturales y extranjeros: Sobre la construcción de categorías en el mundo hispánico." *Cuadernos de Historia Moderna Anejos* 10 (2011): 21–31.

Herzog, Tamar. *Defining Nations: Immigrants and Citizens in Early Modern Spain and Spanish America*. New Haven: Yale University Press, 2003.

Hofstraeten, Bram van. "The Organization of Mercantile Capitalism in the Low Countries: Private Partnerships in Early Modern Antwerp (1480–1620)." *TSEG/ Low Countries Journal of Social and Economic History* 13, no. 2 (2016): 1–24.

Hofstraeten, Bram van. "Private Partnerships in Seventeenth-Century Maastricht." In *Companies and Company Law in Late Medieval and Early Modern Europe*, edited by Bram van Hofstraeten, and Wim Decock, 115–148. Leuven: Peeters, 2016.

Houtte, Jan A. van. *Economische en sociale geschiedenis van de Lage Landen*. Zeist: De Haan, 1964.

Howell, Martha. *The Marriage Exchange: Property, Social Place, and Gender in Cities of the Low Countries, 1300–1550*. Chicago: University of Chicago Press, 1998.

Hye Hoys, M. *Fondations pieuses et charitables des marchands flamands en Espagne : souvenirs de voyages dans la Péninsule Ibérique en 1844 et 1845*. Madrid: Fundación Carlos de Amberes, 2000.

Iglesias Rodríguez, Juan José, and José Jaime García Bernal, eds. *Andalucía en el mundo Atlántico moderno: Agentes y escenarios*. Madrid: Sílex, 2016.

Iglesias Rodríguez, Juan José, José Jaime García Bernal, and José Manuel Díaz Blanco, eds. *Andalucía en el mundo Atlántico moderno: Ciudades y redes*. Madrid: Sílex, 2018.

Igual Luis, David, and Germán Navarro Espinach. "Los genoveses en España en el tránsito del siglo XV al XVI." *Historia. Instituciones. Documentos*, no. 24 (1997): 261–332.

IJzerman, J.W. *Amsterdamsche Bevrachtingscontracten 1591–1602*. The Hague: Martinus Nijhoff, 1931.

Irigoin, Alejandra, and Regina Grafe. "Bargaining for Absolutism: A Spanish Path to Nation-State and Empire Building." *Hispanic American Historical Review* 88, no. 2 (2008): 173–209.

Israel, Jonathan I. *The Dutch Republic: Its Rise, Greatness, and Fall, 1477–1806*. Oxford: Clarendon Press, 1998.

Israel, Jonathan I *Empires and Entrepots: The Dutch, the Spanish Monarchy, and the Jews, 1585–1713*. London: Hambledon Press, 1990.

Israel, Jonathan I *Dutch Primacy in World Trade, 1585–1740*. Oxford: Clarendon Press, 1989.

Israel, Jonathan I "España: Los embargos españoles y la lucha por el dominio del comercio mundial, 1585–1648." *Revista de Historia Naval* VI, no. 23 (1988): 89–106.

Israel, Jonathan I "The Decline of Spain: A Historical Myth?" *Past & Present* 91, no. 91 (1981): 170–180.

Israel, Jonathan I "Spanish Wool Exports and the European Economy 1610–40." *The Economic History Review* vol. 33, no. 2 (May, 1980): 193–211.

Janssen, Geert H. "The Republic of the Refugees: Early Modern Migrations and the Dutch Experience" *Historical Journal* 60, no. 1 (2017): 233–52.

Jeannin, Pierre. "Le commerce de Lubeck aux environs de 1580." *Annales. Économies, Sociétés, Civilisations* 16, no. 1 (1961): 36–65.

Jeannin, Pierre. "Le marché du sel marin dans l'Europe du Nord du XIVe au XVIIIe siècle." In *Le rôle du sel dans l'histoire*, edited by Michel Mollat, 73–96. Paris: Presses universitaires de France, 1968.

Jiménez Montes, Germán. "Sepan quantos esta carta vieren: poderes notariales y comercio transnacional en Sevilla, 1570–1600." *Studia Historica, Historia Moderna* 42, no. 1 (2020): 39–64.

Jiménez Montes, Germán. "Los inicios de una nación: Mercaderes flamencos en Sevilla durante el reinado de Felipe II." In *Andalucía en el mundo Atlántico moderno: agentes y escenarios*, edited by Juan José Iglesias Rodríguez, and José Jaime García Bernal, 215–241. Madrid: Sílex, 2016.

Jiménez Montes, Germán. "Sevilla, puerto y puerta de Europa: La actividad de una compañía comercial flamenca en la segunda mitad del siglo XVI." *Studia historica. Historia moderna* 38, no. 2 (2016): 353–386.

Jiménez Montes, Germán. "La comunidad flamenca en Sevilla durante el reinado de Felipe II y su papel en las redes mercantiles antuerpienses." *Comercio y cultura en la Edad Moderna: Actas de la XIII Reunión Científica de la Fundación Española de Historia Moderna*. Edited by Juan J. Iglesias Rodríguez, Rafael M. Pérez García, and Manuel Francisco Fernández Chaves, vol. 2, 43–56. Sevilla: Universidad de Sevilla, 2015.

Jou, Kyung-Chul. "Le Commerce des Bois entre Königsberg et Amsterdam, 1550–1650." PhD diss., École des hautes études en sciences sociales, Paris, 1992.

Kaiser, Wolfgang, and Guillaume Calafat. "The Economy of Ransoming in the Early Modern Mediterranean." In *Religion and Trade: Cross-Cultural Exchanges in World History, 1000–1900*, edited by Francesca Trivellato, Leor Halevi, and Cátia Antunes, 108–130. New York: Oxford University Press, 2014.

Kamen, Henry. *Spain, 1469–1714: A Society of Conflict*. London: Longman, 1983.

Kamen, Henry. "The Decline of Spain: A Historical Myth?" *Past and Present* 81, no. 1 (1978): 24–50.

Kellenbenz, Hermann. *Los Fugger en España y Portugal hasta 1560*. Valladolid: Junta de Castilla y León, 2000.

Kellenbenz, Hermann. "La factoría de los Fugger en Sevilla." In *Sevilla en el Imperio de Carlos V: encrucijada entre dos mundos y dos épocas: actas del Simposio Internacional celebrado en la Facultad de Filosofía y Letras de la Universidad de Colonia (23–25 de junio de 1988)*, edited Pedro M.Piñero Ramírez and Christian Wentzlaff Eggebert, 59–75. Sevilla: Universidad de Sevilla, 1991.

Kellenbenz, Hermann. *Unternehmerkräfte Im Hamburger, Portugal- Und Spanienhandel, 1590–1625*. Hamburg: Verlag Der Hamburgischen Bücherei, 1954.

Kooijmans, Luuc. "Risk and Reputation. On the Mentality of Merchants in the Early Modern Period." In *Entrepreneurs and Entrepreneurship in Early Modern Times: Merchants and Industrialists within the Orbit of the Dutch Staple Market*, edited by Clé Lesger and Leo Noordegraaf, 25–34. Den Haag: Stichting Hollandse Historische Reeks, 1995.

Labrador Arroyo, Félix, and Koldo Trápaga Monchet, eds. "Recursos naturales en la Península Ibérica: los aprovechamientos forestales e hídricos (siglo XV-XIX)." *Tiempos Modernos. Revista electrónica de Historia Moderna* 9, no. 40 (2019).

Lamikiz, Xabier. "¿Qué tipo de capital social generaron los gremios de comerciantes?: reflexiones a partir del ejemplo del Consulado de Bilbao, 1511–1829." In *Recuperando el Norte: empresas, capitales y proyectos atlánticos en la economía imperial hispánica*, edited by Alberto Angulo Morales and Álvaro Aragón Ruano, 103–112. Bilbao, Universidad del País Vasco, 2016.

Lamikiz, Xabier. *Trade and Trust in the Eighteenth-Century Atlantic World: Spanish Merchants and Their Overseas Networks*. Woodbridge: Boydell Press, 2010.

Lapeyre, Henri. *El comercio exterior de Castilla a través de las Aduanas de Felipe II*. Valladolid: Universidad de Valladolid, 1981.

Lapeyre, Henri. *Une famille de marchands les Ruiz: Contributions à l'étude du commerce entre la France et l'Espagne au temps de Philippe II*. Paris: A. Colin, 1955.

Lem, Anton van der. *Revolt in the Netherlands: The Eighty Years War, 1568–1648*. London, UK: Reaktion Books, 2018.

Lésger, Clé. *The Rise of the Amsterdam Market an Information Exchange: Merchants, Commercial Expansion and Change in the Spatial Economy of the Low Countries 1550–1630*. Aldershot: Ashgate, 2006.

Lomas, Manuel. *Governing the Galleys: Jurisdiction, Justice, and Trade in the Squadrons of the Hispanic Monarchy (Sixteenth– Seventeenth Centuries)*. Leiden: Brill, 2020.

Lopez, Robert S. "Proxy in Medieval Trade." In *Order and Innovation in the Middle Ages: Essays in Honor of Joseph R. Strayer*, edited by William Chester Jordan, Bruce McNab, and Teofilo F. Ruiz, 187–194. Princeton: Princeton University Press, 1976.

López Arandia, María Amparo. "Maderas para el real servicio y el bien común: Aprovechamientos forestales en la provincia marítima de Segura de la Sierra (ss. XVIII-XIX)." In *Árvores, barcos e homens na Península Ibérica (séculos XVI-XVIII)*, edited by Rosa Varela Gomes, and Koldo Trápaga Monchet, 25–40. Zaragoza: Pórtico Librerías, 2017.

López Martín, Ignacio. "Los 'unos' y los 'otros': Comercio, guerra e identidad." In *Banca, crédito y capital: La monarquía hispánica y los antiguos países bajos (1505-1700)*, edited by Carmen Sanz Ayán, and Bernardo José García, 425–458. Madrid: Fundación Carlos de Amberes, 2006.

López Martín, Ignacio. "Entre la guerra económica y la persuasión diplomática: el comercio mediterráneo como moneda de cambio en el conflicto hispano-neerlandés (1574–1609)." *Cahiers de la Méditerranée* 71 (2005).

López Martín, Ignacio. "Embargo and Protectionist Policies: Early Modern Hispano-Dutch Relations in the Western Mediterranean." *Mediterranean Studies* 7 (1998).

Lorenzo Sanz, Eufemio. *Comercio de España con América en la época de Felipe II*. Valladolid: Diputación Provincial de Valladolid, 1979.

Lucassen, Jan, and Leo Lucassen. *Migration, Migration History, History: Old Paradigms and New Perspectives*. Bern: Lang, 1997.

Martínez González, Alfredo José. *Las Superintendencias de montes y plantíos (1574–1748): Derecho y política forestal para las Armadas en la Edad Moderna*. València: Tirant lo Blanch, 2015.

Mathias, Peter. "Strategies for Reducing Risk by Entrepreneurs in the Early Modern Period." In *Entrepreneurs and Entrepreneurship in Early Modern Times: Merchants and Industrialists within the Orbit of the Dutch Staple Market*, edited by Clé Lesger, and Leo Noordegraaf, 5–23. Den Haag: Stichting Hollandse Historische Reeks, 1995.

Mauro, Frédéric. "Merchant communities, 1350–1750." In *The Rise of Merchant Empires: Long Distance Trade in the Early Modern World 1350–1750*, edited by James D. Tracy, 255–286. Cambridge: Cambridge University Press, 1993.

Mena García, Carmen. "La Casa de la Contratación de Sevilla y el abasto de las flotas de Indias." In *La Casa de la Contratación y la navegación entre España y las Indias*, edited by Enriqueta Vila Vilar, Antonio Acosta Rodríguez, and Adolfo L. González Rodríguez, 237–278. Sevilla: CSIC and Universidad de Sevilla, 2004.

Mena García, Carmen. "Nuevos datos sobre bastimentos y envases en armadas y flotas de la Carrera." *Revista de Indias* 64 no. 231 (2004): 447–484.

Milgrom, Paul R., Douglass C. North, and Barry R. Weingast. "The Role of Institutions in the Revival of Trade: The Law Merchant, Private Judges and the Champagne Fairs." *Economics and Politics* 2 no. 1 (1990): 1–23.

Mira Caballos, Esteban. "Pedro Menéndez de Avilés diseñó el modelo de flotas de la Carrera de Indias." *Revista de Historia Naval*, no. 94 (2006): 7–24.

Mollat, Michel, ed. *Le rôle du sel dans l'histoire*. Paris: Presses universitaires de France, 1968.

Morales Padrón, Francisco. *Historia de Sevilla. La ciudad del Quinientos*. Sevilla: Universidad de Sevilla, 1977.

Moret, Michèle. *Aspects de la société marchande de Séville: au début du XVIIe siècle*. París: Marcel Riviere, 1967.

North, Douglass C. "Institutions, Transaction Costs, and the Rise of Merchant Empires." In *The Political Economy of Merchant Empires: State Power and World Trade, 1350–1750*, edited by James D. Tracy, 22–40. Cambridge: Cambridge University Press, 1991.

North, Douglass C. *Institutions, Institutional Change, and Economic Performance*. Cambridge: Cambridge University Press, 1990.

Ogilvie, Sheilagh C. *Institutions and European Trade: Merchant Guilds, 1000–1800*. Cambridge: Cambridge University Press, 2011.

Oliveira Marques, António Henrique R. de. *Hansa e Portugal na Idade Média*. Lisbon: Presença, 1993.

Otte, Enrique. *Sevilla, siglo XVI: Materiales para su historia económica*. Sevilla: Centro de Estudios Andaluces, 2008.

Otte, Enrique. *Sevilla y sus mercaderes a fines de la Edad Media*. Sevilla: Universidad de Sevilla, 1996.

Otte, Enrique. "Sevilla y las ferias genovesas: Lyon y Besançon, 1503–1560." In *Genova-mediterraneo-atlantico nell'età moderna: Atti del III° Congresso internazionale di studi storici, (Genova 3–5 dicembre 1987)*, 249–276. Genova, 1983.

Otte, Enrique. "Sevilla, plaza bancaria europea en el siglo XVI." In *Actas del I Coloquio Internacional de Historia Económica. Dinero y Crédito (siglos XVI al XIX)*, 89–112. Madrid, 1978.

Parker, Geoffrey. *The Military Revolution: Military Innovation and the Rise of the West, 1500–1800*. Cambridge: Cambridge University Press, 1996.

Parker, Geoffrey. *The Army of Flanders and the Spanish Road, 1567–1659: The Logistics of Spanish Victory and Defeat in the Low Countries' Wars*. London: Cambridge University Press, 1972.

Perez, Béatrice. *Les marchands de Séville: Une société inquiète (XVe-XVIe siècles)*. París: Presses de l'Université Paris-Sorbonne, 2016.

Pérez García, Rafael M. "Mercaderes burgaleses en la Andalucía de los siglos XVI y XVII: procesos de enriquecimiento, ascenso social y ennoblecimiento." In *Monarquías en conflicto. Linajes y noblezas en la articulación de la Monarquía Hispánica*, edited by José Ignacio Fortea Pérez, Juan Eloy Gelabert González, Roberto López Vela, and Elena Postigo Castellanos, 617–627. Madrid: Fundación Española de Historia Moderna, 2018.

Pérez García, Rafael M. "La trayectoria histórica de la comunidad mercantil burgalesa en la Sevilla moderna: ascenso social y mutación económica. El caso del mercader Alonso de Nebreda." in *Andalucía en el mundo atlántico moderno. Ciudades y redes*, edited by Juan José Iglesias Rodríguez, José Jaime García Bernal, and José Manuel Díaz Blanco, 157–191. Madrid. Sílex, 2018.

Pérez García, Rafael M. "El gobierno de Castilla y la gestión de las crisis de subsistencia de mediados de siglo XVI en la ciudad y el reino de Sevilla." In *Do silêncio a ribalta: os resgatados das margens da História (sêculos XVI-XIX)*, edited by Maria Marta Lobo de Araújo and María José Pérez Álvarez, 205–226. Braga: Lab2PT - Laboratorio de Paisagens, Património e Território, 2015.

Pérez García, Rafael M., Manuel F. Fernández Chaves, and José Luis Belmonte Postigo, eds. *Los negocios de la esclavitud: Tratantes y mercados de esclavos en el Atlántico Ibérico, siglos XV-XVIII*. Sevilla: Universidad de Sevilla, 2018.

Pérez García, Rafael M. and Manuel F. Fernández Chaves. *Las élites moriscas entre Granada y el Reino de Sevilla. Rebelión, castigo y supervivencias* . Sevilla: Editorial Universidad de Sevilla, 2015.

Pérez-Mallaína, Pablo E. *Las Atarazanas de Sevilla. Ocho siglos de historia del arsenal del Guadalquivir*. Sevilla: Universidad de Sevilla, 2019.

Pérez-Mallaína, Pablo E. "Un edificio olvidado de la Sevilla americana: Las Reales Atarazanas." *Cahiers du monde hispanique et luso-brésilien*, no. 95 (2010): 7–33.

Pérez-Mallaína, Pablo E. "Auge y decadencia del puerto de Sevilla como cabecera de las rutas indianas." *Cahiers du monde hispanique et luso-brésilien*, no. 69 (1997): 15–39.

Phillips, Carla Rahn. *Six Galleons for the King of Spain: Imperial Defense in the Early Seventeenth Century*. Baltimore: Johns Hopkins University Press, 1986.

Phillips, Carla Rahn. "Spanish Merchants and the Wool Trade in the Sixteenth Century." *The Sixteenth Century Journal* 14, no. 3 (1983): 259–282.

Phillips, William D. "Spain's Northern Shipping Industry in the Sixteenth Century." *Journal of European Economic History* 17, no. 2 (1988): 267–301.

Phillips, William D., and Carla Rahn Phillips. "Spanish Wool and Dutch Rebels: The Middelburg Incident of 1574." *The American Historical Review* 82, no. 2 (1977): 312–30. doi:10.2307/1849951.

Pi Corrales, Magdalena. *'La Otra Invencible' 1574: España y las potencias nórdicas.* Madrid: San Martín, 1983.

Pike, Ruth. *Aristocrats and Traders. Sevillian Society in the Sixteenth Century.* Ithaca: Cornell University Press, 1972.

Prak, Maarten R. *Citizens without Nations: Urban Citizenship in Europe and the World, C.1000–1789.* Cambridge: Cambridge University Press, 2018.

Priotti, Jean-Philippe. *Bilbao y sus mercaderes en el siglo XVI: génesis de un crecimiento.* Bilbao: Diputación Foral de Bizkaia, 2005.

Priotti, Jean-Philippe. "El comercio de los puertos vascos peninsulares con el noroeste europeo durante el siglo XVI." *Itsas Memoria: Revista de estudios marítimos del País Vasco,* no. 4 (2003): 193–206.

Pulido Bueno, Ildefonso. *Almojarifazgos y comercio exterior en Andalucía durante la época mercantilista, 1526–1740: Contribución al estudio de la economía en la España Moderna.* Huelva: Artes Gráficas Andaluzas, 1993.

Puttevils, Jeroen. *Merchants and Trading in the Sixteenth Century: The Golden Age of Antwerp.* London: Pickering & Chatto, 2015.

Recio Morales, Óscar. "Los extranjeros y la historiografía modernista." *Cuadernos de Historia Moderna. Anejos,* no. 10 (2011): 33–51.

Rodger, N. A. M. "From the 'military revolution' to the 'fiscal-naval state.'" *Journal for Maritime Research* 13, no. 2 (2011): 119–128, doi: 10.1080/21533369.2011.622886.

Rodríguez Lorenzo, Sergio. "La financiación a riesgo marítimo en la carrera de Indias (c. 1560–1622)." Paper presented at the *Conference Iberians in the First Atlantic Economy, 1500–1650), University of Évora, February 7–8 2019* https://www.academia.edu/40041050/La_financiaci%C3%B3n_a_riesgo_mar%C3%ADtimo_en_la_carrera_de_Indias_c._1560-1622.

Rodríguez Lorenzo, Sergio "Construcción naval cantábrica y carrera de Indias (circa 1560–1622)." *Altamira: Revista del Centro de Estudios Montañeses,* no. 88 (2017): 37–74.

Rodríguez Lorenzo, Sergio "Sevilla y la carrera de Indias: las compraventas de naos (1560–1622)." Anuario de estudios americanos 73, no. 1 (2016): 65–97.

Rodríguez Lorenzo, Sergio "El fletamento de mercancías en la carrera de indias (1560–1622): introducción a su estudio." *Procesos de mercado: revista europea de economía política* 8, no. 1 (2011) 161–207.

Rodríguez-Trobajo, Eduardo, and Marta Domínguez-Delmás. "Swedish oak, planks and panels: dendroarchaeological investigations on the 16th century Evangelistas altarpiece at Seville Cathedral (Spain)." *Journal of Archaeological Science* 54 (2015): 148–161.

Rodríguez-Salgado, Mía J., and Simon Adams, eds. *England, Spain and the Gran Armada, 1585–1604: Essays from the Anglo-Spanish Conferences, London and Madrid 1988.* Edinburgh: Donald, 1991.

Rojas García, Reyes. "De la práctica diaria a la teoría de los formularios notariales: comercio y mercado en la Sevilla del siglo XVI." In *Les formulaires: compilations et circulation des modèles d' actes dans l'Europe médiévale et moderne. Actes du XIIIe Congrès de la Commission Internationale de Diplomatique, Paris, 3–4 septembre 2012* http://elec.enc.sorbonne.fr/cid2012/part12.

Rojas García, Reyes. *La práctica de los escribanos públicos de Sevilla: los manuales (1504–1550)*. Sevilla: Diputacion de Sevilla, 2015.

Rojas García, Reyes. "La memoria de lo privado en lo público: los escribanos públicos sevillanos" *Historia. Instituciones. Documentos* 31 (2004): 573–584.

Roover, Raymond de. *L'évolution de la lettre de change: XIVe-XVIIIe siècles. Affaires et gens d'affaires*. Paris: Armand Colin, 1953.

Royano Cabrera, Miguel. "Los mercaderes de la Corona de Aragón y su papel en el tráfico de letras de cambio entre la Baja Andalucía y el Levante peninsular durante el reinado de Carlos V." In *Nuevas perspectivas de investigación en Historia Moderna: economía, sociedad, política y cultura en el mundo hispánico*, edited by María Ángeles Pérez Samper and José Luis Betrán Moya, 130–141. Madrid: Fundación Española de Historia Moderna, 2018.

Royano Cabrera, Miguel "La comunidad mercantil catalano-valenciana afincada en la Sevilla de la primera mirad del siglo XVI." In *Familia, cultura material y formas de poder en la España moderna: III Encuentro de jóvenes investigadores en Historia Moderna, Valladolid 2 y 3 de julio de 2015*, edited by Máximo García Fernández, 121–130. Madrid: Fundación Española de Historia Moderna, 2016.

Ruiz Ibáñez, José Javier. "*Bellum omnium contra omnes*: Las posibilidades y contradicciones de la guerra económica por parte de la Monarquía Hispánica en la década de 1590." *Studia historica. Historia moderna*, no. 27 (2005): 85–109.

Ruiz Martín, Felipe. "La etapa marítima de las guerras de religión. Bloqueos y contrabloqueos." *Estudios de Historia Moderna* 3 (1953): 181–214.

Salas Almela, Luis. "Los antepuertos de Sevilla: señorío, comercio y fiscalidad en la Carrera de Indias (s.XVI)." In *Mirando las dos orillas: intercambios mercantiles, sociales y culturales entre Andalucía y América*, edited by Enriqueta Vila Vilar and Jaime J. Lacueva Muñoz, 105–127. Sevilla: Fundación Buenas Letras, 2012.

Salas Almela, Luis. "Un cargo para el Duque de Medina Sidonia: Portugal, el Estrecho de Gibraltar y el Comercio Indiano (1578–1584)." *Revista de Indias* 69, no. 247 (2009) 11–38.

Salas Almela, Luis. "Poder señorial, comercio y guerra: Sanlúcar de Barrameda y la política de embargos de la Monarquía Hispánica, 1585–1641." *Cuadernos de historia moderna*, no. 33, (2008): 35–59.

Salas Almela, Luis. *Colaboración y conflicto: la capitanía general del mar Océano y costas de Andalucía, 1588–1660*. Córdoba: Universidad de Córdoba, 2002.

Sánchez Durán, Álvaro. "El crédito portugués en la Monarquía Hispánica de Felipe IV: los asientos de la familia Núñez-Mercado (1640–1652)." *Cuadernos de historia moderna* 42, no. 1 (2017): 57–86.

Sanz Ayán, Carmen. "Negociadores y capitales holandeses en los sistemas de abastecimientos de pertrechos navales de la monarquía hispánica durante el siglo XVII." *Hispania: Revista española de historia* 52, no. 182 (1992): 915–945.

Scheltjens, Werner. *Dutch Deltas: Emergence, Functions and Structure of the Low Countries' Maritime Transport System, ca. 1300–1850.* Leiden: Brill, 2015.

Schreiner, Johan. *Nederland Og Norge, 1625–1650: Trelastutførsel Og Handelspolitikk.* Oslo: Dybwad, 1933.

Sentaurens, Jean. "Séville dans la seconde moitié du XVIe siècle: population et structures sociales. Le recensement de 1561." *Bulletin Hispanique* 77, no. 3–4 (1975): 321–390.

Steckley, George F. "Bottomry Bonds in the Seventeenth-Century Admiralty Court." *The American Journal of Legal History* 45, no. 3 (2001): 256–77.

Stols, Eddy. "Experiencias y ganancias flamencas en la Monarquía de Felipe II." In *Las sociedades ibéricas y el mar a finales del siglo XVI*, edited by Luis A. Ribot García, and Ernesto Belenguer Cebrià, 147–169. Lisbon: Sociedad Estatal Lisboa '98, 1998.

Stols, Eddy. *De Spaanse Brabanders, of De Handelsbetrekkingen Der Zuidelijke Nederlanden Met De Iberische Wereld, 1598–1648.* Brussel: Palais Der Academiën, 1971.

Stols, Eddy. "La colonia flamenca de Sevilla y el comercio de los Países Bajos españoles en la primera mitad del siglo XVII." *Anuario de historia económica y social*, no. 2 (1969): 356–374.

Stradling, Robert A. *The Armada of Flanders: Spanish Maritime Policy and European War, 1568–1668.* Cambridge: Cambridge University Press, 2004.

Sturtz, Linda L. "'As Though I My Self Was Pr[e]sent'. Virginia Women with Power of Attorney." In *The Many Legalities of Early America*, edited by Christopher L. Tomlins, and Bruce H. Mann, 250–271. Chapel Hill: University of North Carolina Press, 2001.

Thomas, Werner. "The Inquisition, trade, and tolerance in early modern Spain." In *Entrepreneurs, Institutions & Government Intervention in Europe [13th - 20th Centuries]: Essays in Honour of Erik Aerts*, edited by Brecht Dewilde and Johan Poukens, 279–291. Brussels: Academic & Scientific Publishers, 2018.

Thomas, Werner. Werner Thomas, "Los flamencos en la Península Ibérica a través de los documentos inquisitoriales (siglos XVI-XVII)." *Espacio, tiempo y forma. Serie IV, Historia moderna*, no. 3 (1990): 167–196.

Thomas, Werner, and Robert A. Verdonk, eds. *Encuentros en Flandes: Relaciones e intercambios hispanoflamencos a inicios de la Edad Moderna.* Leuven: Leuven University Press, 2000.

Thomas, Werner, and Eddy Stols. "La integración de Flandes en la Monarquía Hispánica." In *Encuentros en Flandes: Relaciones e intercambios hispanoflamencos a inicios de la Edad Moderna*, edited by Werner Thomas, and Robert A. Verdonk, 1–73. Leuven: Leuven University Press, 2000.

Thompson, Irving A. A. "The Spanish Armada: Naval Warfare between the Mediterranean and the Atlantic," in *England, Spain and the Gran Armada, 1585–1604*, edited by Mía Rodríguez-Salgado and Simon Adams, 70–94. Edinburgh: Donald, 1991.

Thompson, Irving A. A. *War and Government in Habsburg Spain, 1560–1620*. London: Athlone Press, 1976.

Thompson, Irving A. A. "The Appointment of the Duke of Medina Sidonia to the Command of the Spanish Armada." *The Historical Journal* 12, no. 2 (1969): 197–216.

Thompson, Irving A. A. "The Armada and Administrative Reform: the Spanish Council of War in the reign of Philip II." *The English Historical Review* 82, no. 325 (Oct., 1967): 698–725.

Tielhof, Milja van. *The 'Mother of All Trades': The Baltic Grain Trade in Amsterdam from the Late 16th to the Early 19th Century*. Leiden: Brill, 2002.

Tilly, Charles. *Coercion, Capital, and European States, Ad 990–1992*. Cambridge: Blackwell, 1992.

Torres Balbás, Leopoldo. "Atarazanas hispanomusulmanas." *Al-Andalus* 11 (1946): 175–209.

Torres Sánchez, Rafael. *El precio de la guerra: el Estado fiscal-militar de Carlos III (1779–1783)* Madrid: Marcial Pons Historia, 2013.

Torres Sánchez, Rafael. "Presentación. El negocio de la guerra: la movilización de recursos militares y la construcción de la monarquía española, XVII y XVIII." *Studia historica. Historia moderna*, no. 35 (2013): 23–32.

Torres Sánchez, Rafael. "Administración o asiento: la política estatal de suministros militares en la monarquía española del siglo XVIII." *Studia historica. Historia moderna*, no. 35 (2013): 159–199.

Trápaga Monchet, Koldo. " 'Traed madera': agentes y vías de provisión de madera para las flotas reales en Portugal (1598–1611)." In *Nuevas perspectivas de investigación en Historia Moderna: economía, sociedad, política y cultura en el mundo hispánico*, edited María Ángeles Pérez Samper, and José Luis Betrán Moya, 106–119. Madrid, Fundación Española de Historia Moderna, 2018.

Trápaga Monchet, Koldo. "Las armadas en el reino de Portugal en los reinados de los Felipes (1580–1640)." In *Familia, cultura material y formas de poder en la España moderna: III Encuentro de jóvenes investigadores en Historia Moderna, Valladolid 2 y 3 de julio de 2015*, edited by Máximo García Fernández, 843–854. Madrid: Fundación Española de Historia Moderna, 2016.

Trivellato, Francesca. *The Familiarity of Strangers: The Sephardic Diaspora, Livorno, and Cross-Cultural Trade in the Early Modern Period*. New Haven: Yale University Press, 2009.

Ulloa, Modesto. "Unas notas sobre el comercio y la navegación españoles en el siglo XVI." *Anuario de Historia económica y social*, no. 2 (1969): 191–237.

Ulloa, Modesto. *La hacienda real de Castilla en el reinado de Felipe II*. Roma: Sforzini, 1963.

Unger, Willem S. "Middelburg als handelsstad, XIIIe-XVIe eeuw)." *Archief, vroegere en latere mededeelingen voornamelijk in betrekking tot Zeeland, Middelburg, Zeeuwsch Genootschap der Wetenschappen* (1935): 1–177.

Valdez-Bubnov, Ivan. "Shipbuilding Administration under the Spanish Habsburg and Bourbon Regimes (1590–1834): A Comparative Perspective." *Business History* 60 no. 1 (2018): 105–125.

Valdez-Bubnov, Ivan. *Poder naval y modernización del Estado: política de construcción naval española (siglos XVI-XVIIII)*. Frankfurt am Main: Vervuert Verlagsgesellschaft, 2012.

Vandamme, Ludo, et al. "Bruges in the Sixteenth Century: A 'Return to Normalcy.'" In *Medieval Bruges: C. 850–1550*, edited by Andrew Brown and Jan Dumolyn, 445–484. Cambridge: Cambridge University Press, 2018.

Vandewalle, André. "De vreemde naties in Brugge." In *Hanzekooplui en Medicibankiers. Brugge, wisselmarkt van Europese culturen*, edited by André Vandewalle, 27–42. Oostkamp: Stichting Kunstboek, 2002.

Veluwenkamp, Jan Willem. *Archangel: Nederlandse Ondernemers in Rusland, 1550–1785*. Amsterdam: Balans, 2000.

Veluwenkamp, Jan Willem, and Werner Scheltjens, eds. *Early Modern Shipping and Trade: Novel Approaches Using Sound Toll Registers Online*. Leiden: Brill, 2018.

Vila Vilar, Enriqueta. "Sevilla, capital de Europa." *Boletín de la Real Academia Sevillana de Buenas Letras: Minervae Baeticae*, no. 37 (2009): 57–74.

Vila Vilar, Enriqueta. *Los Corzo y los Mañara: tipos y arquetipos del mercader con Indias*. Sevilla: Escuela de Estudios Hispano-Americanos, 1991.

Vila Vilar, Enriqueta, Antonio Acosta Rodríguez, and Adolfo L. González Rodríguez, eds. *La Casa de la Contratación y la navegación entre España y las Indias*. Sevilla: CSIC and Universidad de Sevilla, 2004.

Vries, Jan de, and Ad van der Woude. *The First Modern Economy: Success, Failure and Perseverance of the Dutch Economy, 1500–1815*. Cambridge: Cambridge University Press, 1997.

Warde, Paul. *Ecology, Economy and State Formation in Early Modern Germany*. Cambridge: Cambridge University Press, 2006.

Wee, Herman van der. *The Growth of the Antwerp Market and the European Economy (Fourteenth-Sixteenth Centuries)*. The Hague: Nijhoff, 1963.

Wijnroks, Eric. *Handel tussen Rusland en de Nederlanden, 1560–1640: Een netwerkanalyse van de Antwerpse en Amsterdamse kooplieden, handelend op Rusland*. Hilversum: Verloren, 2003.

Wing, John T. *Roots of Empire: Forests and State Power in Early Modern Spain, 1500–1750*. Leiden, Brill 2015.

Yun Casalilla, Bartolomé. "„Localism," Global History and Transnational History. A Reflection from the Historian of Early Modern Europe," *Historisk Tidskrift* 127, no. 4 (2007): 659–678.

Yun Casalilla, Bartolomé. *Marte contra Minerva: el precio del imperio español, c.1450–1600*. Barcelona: Crítica, 2004.

Yun Casalilla, Bartolomé, and Patrick O'Brien, eds. *The Rise of Fiscal States: A Global History, 1500–1914*. New York: Cambridge University Press, 2012.

Zabala Aguirre, Pilar. *Las alcabalas y la Hacienda Real en Castilla: Siglo XVI*. Santander: Universidad de Cantabria, 2000.

Index